Making the Compelling Business Case

Making the Compelling Business Case

Decision-Making Techniques for Successful Business Growth

Wolfgang Messner
Associate Professor, MYRA School of Business & Director, GloBus Research

First published 2013 by
PALGRAVE MACMILLAN

Palgrave Macmillan in the UK is an imprint of Macmillan Publishers Limited, registered in England, company number 785998, of Houndmills, Basingstoke, Hampshire RG21 6XS.

Palgrave Macmillan in the US is a division of St Martin's Press LLC, 175 Fifth Avenue, New York, NY 10010.

Palgrave Macmillan is the global academic imprint of the above companies and has companies and representatives throughout the world.

Palgrave® and Macmillan® are registered trademarks in the United States, the United Kingdom, Europe and other countries.

ISBN 978–1–137–34056–6

This book is printed on paper suitable for recycling and made from fully managed and sustained forest sources. Logging, pulping and manufacturing processes are expected to conform to the environmental regulations of the country of origin.

A catalogue record for this book is available from the British Library.

A catalog record for this book is available from the Library of Congress.

Typeset by MPS Limited, Chennai, India.

Reviews

CORPORATE LEADERS

"A useful, pragmatic, how-to-do-it book. The value proposition of a corporate investment has always been about reducing costs or increasing revenue. Messner shows companies how to ensure that projects are really doing that. It is this process of leveraging project expenditure which makes organizations successful."

– Heinz-Paul Bonn
Vice President
BITKOM (Germany)

"This superb text provides a powerful ensemble of formula, techniques, and guidelines for business case success. Comprehensive and complete, it is the long-thought link between financial business case mathematics and stakeholder management."

– Horst Ellermann
Editor in Chief
CIO Magazine (Germany)

"It is amazing how much the quality of business cases varies in both preparation and subsequent execution. Messner brings the voice of experience resulting in a clear, comprehensive, and up-to date guide on building solid business cases. You should have it on your bookshelf and consult it frequently."

– John Knowles
CIO
Allianz Insurance (UK)

"Today's information technology landscape is increasingly multifaceted and at the same time increasingly critical to business success. Its complex projects come with significant costs and are not easy to weigh up against each other. Funds are restricted and the company's financial management keeps on challenging project justifications.

A business case is the one and only instrument for the project originator to present all necessary facts: costs, benefits, risks, and strategic options. But it does not end here – even the best business case with the best net present value still needs to be presented to senior management for the ultimate go-decision.

Messner has created a thorough and systematic book; it gives you new inspiration and guidance to champion your projects professionally and successfully. I personally use these concepts and techniques in my position as CIO."

– Bernd Kuntze
CIO
Haas Food Equipment (Austria)

"This book very clearly brings out careful use of both quantitative analysis and several qualitative factors that are essential for key investment decisions. Drawing on a wealth of case studies and examples, Messner provides fresh ideas, profound advice, and useful structures that can be quickly applied in today's fast-moving business environment, where succinct and reliable information is the key to success."

– Som Mittal
President
NASSCOM (India)

"Messner took the concept of investments and the creation of business cases to a new level. His new book blends his deep hands-on project management and investment experience in emerging markets like India with an excellent understanding of modern investment theory. He emphasizes the need to consider risk and uncertainty in investment decisions; the frameworks and methods explained are most valuable for companies investing into business-growth areas and new markets. A must-read business book!"

– Clas Neumann
Senior Vice President & Head of Global SAP Labs Network
SAP (China)

"*Making the Compelling Business Case* belongs at the top of the reading list of account managers who want to turn selling around and become a trusted consultant. Customers do not buy from you because your product offers great features; they choose the offer with the best value proposition to their business as well as on a personal level. A business case in sales is a way of communicating this message and helping clients get what they need and want."

– Dirk Palder
Vice President
Capgemini Consulting &
Chairman of the Supervisory Board
Grieshaber Logistics Group (Germany)

"Leaders thrive on results. This excellent book should be of great interest to all executives who need to have continued success with their investment decisions. The approach described not only aligns organizations to take the right decisions, but to sustain delivered benefits over time."

– Dr Baru Rao
Principal Group Director
Capgemini (U.S.)

"Can we really end the litany of challenged projects? This wonderful book is full of fresh ideas and describes in simple terms how to analyze and evaluate investment propositions – decisions we have to face each day in running and growing our business."

– Enrico Rühle
Managing Director
TÜV Rheinland (India)

"*Making the Compelling Business Case* provides both essential advice and innovative ideas that can be directly applied by corporate managers when assessing an investment proposition and its alternatives. Using an inspiring wealth of case studies and examples, Messner's new book offers a compelling blueprint for decision making techniques."

– Dr Michael Schulte
Group Principal Director
Capgemini (Germany)

"Messner's new book *Making the Compelling Business Case* gives a very insightful look into the corporate decision making process in today's competitive business environment. Being comprehensive and complete, it helps to remove the doom and gloom of the business case process."

– Swaminathan K
Vice President & Head of IT and BPO Solutions
Robert Bosch Engineering and Business Solutions (India)

ACADEMIC THOUGHT LEADERS

"*Making the Compelling Business Case* is for both students of postgraduate business management and also practising managers who today cannot fail to be aware of how risk impacts on business and the manner in which decisions of all kinds are made. The book links topics from financial investment appraisal, decision making, and risk assessment that are not always considered in one source; it underpins them with case examples, illustrations, and statistical formula. When an organization targets growth, the benefits of risk taking by seeking innovation and comparative advantage are crucial – yet often overlooked in corporate practice. Scenario analysis could replace single point conclusions as these make increasingly little sense in the current choppy economic climate."

– Anthony Mitchell
Client & Programme Director
Ashridge Business School (UK)

"This is a great book that should be on the bookshelf of every senior executive. It is packed with real examples, concepts, frameworks, and techniques for preparing and evaluating business cases. The book is easy to read, and the figures and diagrams add to the flow of the text. Messner has distilled his academic and business experience into a fine contribution."

– Dr Avinash Mulky
Professor of Marketing
Indian Institute of Management Bangalore (India)

"Messner's comprehensive approach to investment decisions will help managers assess the financial aspects more carefully while preparing business cases. This step-by-step guide to comprehensively evaluate alternatives will help managers think through their plans before trying to persuade their CxOs who are always concerned about returns on their capital spending. In today's challenging business environment, persuasive business cases are even more relevant and Messner's book is an extremely useful guide for corporate managers."

– Dr G Shainesh
Professor of Marketing
Indian Institute of Management Bangalore (India)

"*Making the Compelling Business Case* tackles the most difficult part of a project, programme, or corporate investment – how to analyze the pros (benefits, strategic options) and cons (costs, risks), prepare the underlying business case, and advocate the idea to the CFO and other decision makers by using their financial language. Messner's new book is one of the most extensive works on business cases available; it is very inspiring, includes many interesting cases, and covers everything from fundamentals to hands-on techniques."

– Dr Yinshan Tang
Senior Lecturer of Business Informatics
Henley Business School, University of Reading (UK)

"*Making the Compelling Business Case* is not only relevant for any company hoping to unlock growth and remain competitive in a rapidly changing business environment, but offers serious students a deeper dive into key areas too. Thoughtful executives will find the ideas in this book insightful, the examples influencing, and the frameworks a good compass for building actionable business cases."

– Dr Shalini Urs
Chairperson
MYRA School of Business &
Executive Director
International School of Management,
University of Mysore (India)

Contents

List of Figures

List of Case Studies

About the Author

Wolfgang Messner is Associate Professor of International Management at MYRA School of Business (India) and Director of GloBus Research – Messner Consulting & Training Pvt. Ltd in Mysore, India; he is also an adjunct faculty at WHU – Otto Beisheim School of Management (Germany). Previously, he was an adjunct lecturer at Royal Docks Business School, University of East London (UK), and a visiting faculty at the Indian Institute of Management Bangalore (India).

He has written five books, most recently *Globalization of Professional Services* (2012; co-editors, Ulrich Bäumer and Peter Kreutter) and *Intelligent IT Offshoring to India* (2010). His many academic and practitioner publications have appeared in *Journal of Indian Business Research*, *Business Information Review*, *The Marketing Review*, and numerous other academic and practitioner outlets; they deal with business transformation, the business impact of information technology, and intercultural collaboration.

Having worked in senior management positions with leading corporates and consulting companies (BMW Group, Capgemini, Deutsche Bank, The Information Management Group (IMG)) in Europe and India, he now undertakes research, gives keynote presentations, runs workshops, and consults globally on strategic business transformation projects.

Wolfgang Messner holds a Ph.D. in Marketing from the University of Kassel (Germany), an M.B.A. in Financial

Management with distinction from the University of Wales (UK), and a first-class master's degree in Informatics after studies at the Technical University Munich (Germany) and the University of Newcastle upon Tyne (UK). He also studied at the Università per Stranieri di Perugia (Italy) and attended executive education on Strategic Marketing Management at Harvard Business School (US).

Preface

Nothing is more difficult, and therefore more precious, than to be able to decide.

Napoléon Bonaparte (1769–1821),
French military and political leader

Maximizing value for the enterprise, for its shareholders, and especially for its customers is the core of corporate business. And making business growth happen by extracting value from investments is what management is all about.

Yet managers continue to pour billions of dollars into projects with uncertain outcomes. Studies continue to show a scarily high number of project failures, missed delivery goals, and cost overruns. While the information technology sector seems to be leading the pack, many other investment areas are less openly scrutinized. Many of us feel we are playing roulette with our decisions – or could actually get better odds in our decision-making process by doing exactly that.

The common management response is to insist on business cases to select, justify, and manage investment decisions. Theoretically, this would be the right and effective approach – providing such business cases were appropriate, insightful, and correct. Corporate reality is different:

- "Go-decisions" for many investments are still passed without a business case justification. "We have to do it because the customer wants it," "the regulator asks us to do it," "analysts write about it," "the competition does it," etc. are frighteningly familiar phrases to all of us. Prestige projects to boost one's career, pet topics, and in-house politics add to the corporate investment portfolio – rarely a sign of professional decision management.

- Most business cases are at best defective, if not completely wrong. They provide neither a comprehensive and in-depth analysis, nor do they have the necessary buy-in from all affected stakeholders. They are neither mathematically correct, nor do they look at risks, uncertainties, and future strategic options. Decisions are taken based on an incorrect or incomplete information layer.

- Small expenditures (down to travel approvals) are examined in much more detail than the reasons behind large investments. Smaller investments are closer to home and a lot more intuitive to understand; managers are not comfortable building business cases, estimating larger expenditures, and forecasting future cash inflows.

In this context, and to explain the scope of this book, a *decision* is defined as the process of reaching a conclusion and the term *business case* is used both as a tool and as a process in financial planning. A business case supports the decision-making process on investment alternatives by building consensus among stakeholders and providing a top-down justification for a rational decision. The outcome of the business case process is a document that contains a recommendation backed by a robust cost–benefit analysis, together with an evaluation of risk and strategic future flexibility options. After the investment is commissioned, the business case changes its scope to a bottom-up tracking metric to ensure that the benefits are being reaped.

The book's central thesis is that most enterprises do not yet have the necessary organizational capability, know-how, and experience to put together compelling business cases that effectively support their decision management in selecting investments and justifying their decisions. Building capabilities in decision-making techniques would clearly help to:

- Increase the likelihood that projected investment benefits will actually be reaped leading to accelerated business growth.

- Decrease the time and effort in preparing investment decision papers.

- And last but not least, reduce politics and friction through stakeholder involvement, as well as increase senior management buy-in through objective reasoning.

Hence, investment justifications through business cases are multi-faceted. They are about careful mathematical calculations and percentages, as well as politics, psychology, and conversations with stakeholders. They need to focus obsessively on turning perceived intangible benefits into hard numbers that are bold, verifiable, and hold the commitment of the organization. This book provides the necessary background information and hands-on tools to do exactly this. If the choices between alternatives are not obvious, if funding decisions have a significant impact, and if investment decisions need to get the buy-in of senior management and many stakeholders, then this book is designed for you to help realize and maximize value. The principles and methods discussed can be applied to many kinds of investment decisions, such as strategic choices, capacity management, budget allocation alternatives, or choices related to information systems. They are just as applicable to decisions on smaller, tactical, and day-to-day investments, and they are relevant across all vertical sectors, for-profit and non-profit sectors, and geographies around the world.

It should be noted, however, that the theories of decision management and business cases are not in a general state of agreement, nor do they provide a complete toolbox solution for all investment decisions. In this book, I have made an attempt to highlight controversies, pitfalls, and inconsistencies in the theories and, if any, their implications for practical business cases.

The chapters of this book follow a red thread through the business case as a process, yet they are independent of each other. You are encouraged to browse through the book first reading the chapters that are most appropriate to your challenges, and then maybe turning back the pages to put things into a broader perspective.

The book embodies the three Rs. First, it is *relevant* because I have written it around company needs to increase value (or eradicate value destruction) by focusing on better investment alternatives for business growth. The discussions are grounded in business reality, with only one focus: helping companies to take better decisions. The frameworks and concepts for investment analysis provided can easily be customized by organizations of all kind. Second, the book is *real* in the sense of combining my own personal business experience of analyzing project proposals with a process-oriented framework and necessary mathematical concepts to get the financial analysis right. Third, I have made every attempt to write a *readable* book in plain language, with many real-life cases, examples, and illustrations. And because serious books on financial planning simply cannot make do without spreadsheet calculations and mathematical formulae, I have enriched (or spoilt) my otherwise non-technical and informal style with equations wherever it made sense. But I have still tried to keep the number of cryptic Greek letters to a minimum.

I have kept the book short and to the point – I know that your time is precious and that you just need to go out, analyze, decide, and implement the next project! Following the process for making a compelling business case as laid out in this book can improve your accuracy in decision management and get you business results faster than you may think after reading this preface alone.

Enjoy the book!

Wolfgang Messner

List of Abbreviations

AFC	Anticipated final cost
AMI	Advanced Metering Infrastructure
AU$	Australian dollar
B-2-B	Business to business
B-2-C	Business to consumer
BCR	Benefit–cost ratio
BPEO	Best practicable environmental option
CAD	Computer-aided engineering
CAPM	Capital-Asset Pricing Model
CBM	Component business model
CCA	Clinger–Cohen Act
CCD	Charged Coupled Devices
CRM	Customer relationship management
CRF	Crash reduction factor
CV	Customer value
CVB	Value of the customer base
CxO	Chief Executive/Financial/Information/Operation/... Officer
DNA	Deoxyribonucleic acid (containing genetic instructions)
DoD	Department of Defense
DoT	Department of Transportation
EBIT	Earnings before interest and taxes
ENPV	Expected net present value

EPA	Environmental Protection Agency
ERP	Enterprise resource planning system
EUR, €	Euro currency
FOC	Full Operational Capability
FY	Financial year
GBP, £	British pound currency
GDP	Gross domestic product
GLA	Greater London Authority
IOC	Initial operational capability
IRR	Internal rate of return
IS	Information systems
IS/IT	Information systems and technology
IT	Information technology
JIT	Just-in-time
LDA	London Development Authority
LRAC	Long-running average cost
LRUC	Long-running unit cost
MNCs	Multinational Corporations
MNS	Mission needs statement
MRQ	Most recent quarter
NDA	Nuclear Decommissioning Authority
NEOS	Near Earth Objects
NFV	Net future value
NPV	Net present value
ODA	Olympic Delivery Authority
OECD	Organisation for Economic Co-operation and Development
p.a.	per annum
PAT	Profit after tax
PI	Profitability index
PSFP	Public Sector Funding Project
PSIA	Poverty and social impact assessment
PV	Present value
P&G	Procter & Gamble
P&L	Profit and loss

RBV	Resource-based view
R&D	Research and development
ROI	Return on investment
R$	Real money $ (as opposed to nominal money)
TCO	Total cost of ownership
TTM	Trailing twelve months
TV	Terminal value
UC	Unified Communication
US	United States
USD, $	American dollar
VIP	Very important person
Y2K	Year 2000

Book Companion Website

www.thebusinesscase.info

This site contains information about the book and the author as well as downloads, teaching and learning materials.

1
Deciding on Corporate Investments

1.1 FINANCIAL GOALS VS. CORPORATE STRATEGY

The primary objective of a business in today's world is generating and maximizing wealth for its owners, shareholders, and stakeholders. These are the people who provide time, input, and funds to a business with the clear expectation of receiving the maximum possible increase in their wealth – given the level of risk they are facing by investing. Non-profit organizations, such as charities, museums, and schools, manage for maximum outcome and impact in order to make the most of their funding.

Several decades ago, being just a little more efficient than one's local competitor might have been sufficient to reach this primary objective of wealth generation. But today, in order to survive, firms compete on a global basis, where the customer has access to reliable information via the Internet. This shift is critical for corporate investment decisions because it short-circuits the business focus on wealth generation; if businesses do not delight their customers with value-for-money products, service which exceeds customers' expectations, and continuous innovation, customers will simply evaporate and the firms will ultimately die. Adding value to the customer and generating customer delight thus becomes a new strength that companies need to generate; it is the new corporate bottom line.[1]

What does "deciding on investments" mean?

One would think that business leaders would give serious thought to their business and how they delight their customers by managing and deciding on corporate investments. But many well-known case studies used in business schools and MBA teaching recount stories about visionaries who thought that they saw the future, made bold decisions, and either got it miraculously right – or got it completely wrong.

Case 1.1   Investment in innovation at Apple

How Steve Jobs (1955–2011) led *Apple* to renewed success is probably today's most over-cited example – and at the same time it was an extremely hard study because the subject never sat still for a case portrait, but kept creating and spinning out new innovations. Apple operates in a fast-cycle market in which its innovative capabilities are not shielded from imitation and where imitation can be very rapid and inexpensive; the company thus needs to be able to take the right decisions quickly. Constant innovation plays a dominant role if one is to succeed in such fast-cycle markets. Apple reported net revenues of $36.5 billion in 2009, $65.2 billion in 2010, $108.2 billion in 2011, and $156.5 billion in 2012.

Case 1.2   Investment in a product recall at Johnson & Johnson

Similarly, how *Johnson & Johnson* pulled all *Tylenol* capsules off the shelves in 1982 after the medicine had been deliberately contaminated with cyanide and introduced tamper-proof gelatin-enrobed capsules within ten weeks in order to ensure that it remained a trusted and top-selling painkiller in North America is another campfire story of corporate decision making.

In the space of a few days in September 1982, seven people died in the Chicago area after taking cyanide-laced capsules of Tylenol. Johnson & Johnson took the decision to invest $100 million in a recall of 31 million bottles of Tylenol and the subsequent re-launch of Tylenol. "Before 1982, nobody ever recalled anything. Companies often fiddle while Rome burns," said Albert Tortorella,[2] a managing director at Burson-Marsteller Inc., the public relations firm that advised Johnson & Johnson. But Johnson & Johnson's shareholders were hurt only briefly. Though the stock was trading near a 52-week high just before the contamination and witnessed panic selling, it recovered to its highs only two months later.[3]

Case 1.3   Ford Edsel – A wrong decision and a failed product

And how the *Edsel automobile* manufactured by Ford during 1958 to 1960 never gained popularity, because it was "the wrong car at the wrong time," is a pretty much outworn example of a famous corporate blunder.

In the early 1950s, the US economy was recovering from the effects of the Second World War; workers earned more money, moved into suburbs, and spent more money on bigger cars. But many of Ford's potential customers, wanting to upgrade, could not afford a Ford Mercury car and went to buy a new car from Chrysler or General Motors instead. Ford wanted to fill this gap with the Edsel automobile. A Special Products Division was founded, to be headed by a manager who had originally voted against the project, and generally staffed by employees who were just available (or as one says today, on the bench). Sales of the new car began in September 1957 and everyone wanted to see what the press had been speculating about: the showrooms were crowded. But few cars were actually sold, and the press turned to criticizing the design and the features. Quality issues and a problem with the availability of spares added to the woes. Two relaunches in 1959 and 1960 with significant changes did not help to drive up sales. Overall, Ford invested about $250 million on this attempt to increase market share in the medium price field; but in order to break even, something like 200–300 thousand units had to be sold each year. However, only some 110,000 cars were produced during the entire life of the Edsel experiment.[4]

What is the overarching lesson in business schools from the two success stories (Case 1.1 and Case 1.2) and the one corporate goof (Case 1.3)? Well, it probably is to go with your gut, except when it's the wrong gut feel.[5] Obviously, management vision and guru-like gut feel are not reliable techniques for making investment decisions in the corporate world.

Being serious about investments also means deciding between alternatives. Even Apple cannot develop all the product ideas that its leadership team is generating. Johnson & Johnson had to decide whether to recall the product and between several alternatives of how to do it. Ford had to make up its mind whether to pursue the medium price segment at all and how to go for it. *Deciding* on something therefore not only means to pass a judgment on a number of propositions and choose the right one, but also to cut off others. After all, the origin of "to decide" is the Latin word *decidere* and the phrase *decido caput* literally means to "cut off the head." In an interview, Judith C. Lewent, the former CFO at Merck & Co., explained that "our success or failure in R&D won't result from quality of our scientists alone; it will also come from the quality of our thinking about where to invest."[6]

The term *investment* refers to commitments of resources made now in the hope of realizing benefits in the future. The most basic idea of an *investment decision* is thus to derive future benefits from costs today – or, if one prefers, costs invested in the most promising opportunity. The standard way of taking investment decisions in the corporate world has expanded this simple idea into a rich discussion of potential benefits, so-called "advantages," "soft benefits," or "intangibles." But how on earth are uncertain benefits suddenly supposed to swing a corporate decision? Furthermore, in business lingo, there is a growing and most unfortunate tendency to equate financial goals with strategy.

A framework for good strategy

Generating and maximizing wealth, outcome, and impact are *financial goals*, and there is nothing wrong with them by any means: they are important for justifying the existence of any organization. But a coherent *corporate strategy* does not just set goals; it draws on existing strength and creates new strength through the coherence of its design. Even today, most organizations of any size do not (!) have such a strategy, but instead, they pursue multiple financial goals and unconnected objectives.

And worse, sometimes these goals and objectives are even in conflict with each other.[7]

Strategy involves focus and choice. *Focus* denotes the identification of promising areas in which to search for opportunities; *choice* means setting aside some goals in favor of others. Many business leaders hope to avoid tricky and painful decisions by not setting aside some goals in favor of others, pursuing all possible goals at the same time. However, by avoiding this hard and mostly unpleasant work, they gain nothing but a weak and amorphous company strategy. During any investment decision process, they will very soon notice that they are lacking a yardstick to justify their decision of selecting some investment propositions – and rejecting others.

Good strategy is a mixture of thought and action with a basic underlying structure. Referred to as the *kernel of strategy*, it contains the three elements shown in Figure 1.1: Diagnosis, guiding policy, and coherent actions.

The first of the three elements, the *diagnosis*, defines and explains the nature of the challenge that the company faces. In business, most deep strategic changes are initiated by a

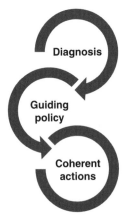

* Defines and explains the nature of the challenge
* Identifies critical aspects
* Simplifies the complexity of reality

* Overall approach for dealing with the challenge
* Channels actions in certain directions
* Does not yet define the exact measures

* Designed to carry out/accomplish the guiding policy
* Steps are coordinated with each other
* Accomplishes the guiding policy

Figure 1.1 *The Rumelt framework of good strategy*[8]

change in diagnosis, which is basically a change of the view of the company's situation. A good diagnosis should simplify the complexity of the business world, reduce it to certain critical aspects, and replace it with a simpler story, which allows business leaders to make sense of the situation and engage in solving the problem. The key to a successful business diagnosis is to make life simple and understandable for everyone.

The *guiding policy* is an overall approach that deals with the challenges identified in the diagnosis. It is only guiding in the sense that it is channeling actions in a certain direction by directing and constraining, but it does not yet fully define the exact form and content of these actions. Notwithstanding this, a good guiding policy is not a goal, a vision, or a description of a desired future state. Rather, it is the definition of a method of how to take care of the challenge defined in the diagnosis by drawing upon sources of advantage.

Finally, a *set of coherent actions* need to be planned to implement the guiding policy. The guiding policy alone is not yet a strategy, because it does not contain any concrete action. "Many people call the guiding policy 'the strategy' and stop there. This is a mistake. Strategy is about action, about doing something. The kernel of a strategy must contain action. [...] To have punch, actions should coordinate and build upon one another, focusing organizational energy" (Rumelt, 2011, p. 87). The main impediment to defining action remains the desperate hope that decisions about alternatives can be avoided. Interestingly, decisions on choices can best be sharpened and enforced by the sheer necessity to act.

This approach to strategy leaves out visions, missions, values, goals, and objectives and places them at the level of champions supporting the company's strategic way of thinking, stimulating the need for strategy creation, helping to identify sources of competitive advantage, communicating strategy to employees and shareholders, and finally stimulating its implementation in an energized company.

Case 1.4   From strategy to execution at Gucci

In 1991, with only $200 million in sales, a loss of $46 million, and just $10 million in cash, Gucci was a classic example of a family-owned firm that had not made a successful transition to professional management. Unbridled licensing had plastered Gucci's name and distinctive logo on 22,000 different products, from sneakers to playing cards and toilet paper. But within a period of only nine years, Gucci went to annual sales of $2 billion, projected profit of $350 million, and $3 billion in cash.

Domenico de Sole, a former tax attorney, was appointed CEO of Gucci in 1995. He wanted to tackle the turnaround challenge not by philosophy, but by data: by bringing strategy in line with experience rather than relying on intuition. The *diagnosis* was a true eye-opener; Gucci's greatest successes had not come from the traditional customer, the woman who cherished style, bought a classic item, kept it for a lifetime, and never went back to Gucci. Instead, it came from seasonal and trendier fashion items. Consequently, De Sole and his team decided to position Gucci in the upper middle of the designer market. The new *guiding policy* was luxury aimed at the masses. Lead designer Tom Ford created original, trendy, and exciting new clothing each year to draw customers into Gucci stores, where they would then also buy high-margin handbags. Advertising spending was doubled, stores modernized, and customer support upgraded. In the background, Gucci's supply chain was improved by providing suppliers with financial and technical support, helping to improve the efficiency and flexibility of logistics.

Everything De Sole and Ford implemented was coherent – from design, product line-up, manufacturing, distribution, pricing, and marketing all the way to organizational culture and management. This system of *coherent actions* was mutually reinforcing and aimed at producing high-quality products that were fashion forwarded and provided good value, as defined in the guiding policies of the new company strategy.

Decisions to build up such a system of coherent actions are binary investment choices: either they are identity-conferring commitments or they are not, and thus need to be discarded or modified. Nonetheless, it is rare to find such a well-honed system, extending seamlessly from strategy to execution.

> You and every leader of a company must ask yourself whether you have one – and if you don't, take the responsibility to build it. The only way a company will deliver on its promises, in short, is if its strategists can think like operators. (Montgomery, 2012)

Achieving and maintaining strategic momentum through the right investment decisions is a challenge involving choices – sometimes very difficult choices.[9]

Financial management

In order to decide, craft, and implement coherent actions, each and every business needs to take a number of financial decisions that ultimately lead to increased wealth for the company's owners and shareholders. These decisions can be broadly categorized into two areas:

- What should the business do? Where exactly should it invest in and spend money?

- How should it pay for the selected investments? How should it raise money?

A company's financial management juggles the above two questions. It stands between strategy and operations (what the business does) and the financial markets (where it gets the money from) and manages them in a cyclic way. The efficiency of financial management is judged by its success in achieving a corporation's goal.[10]

Figure 1.2 depicts how the financial manager raises cash either by selling securities or by borrowing money from the financial market (1) and uses this money to invest in the company's operations (2). As a return, these investments generate cash outflow, which should be bigger than the initially raised cash inflow (3). And this return is either reinvested (4) or returned to the financial markets in the form of dividends, interest payments, or a repaid loan (5). This cycle answers the first question "What should the business do?" on its left-hand side and the second question "How should it pay for it?" on its right-hand side. While both sides are relevant for a financial manager, the decisions are usually separated; the investment decisions are taken first and necessary funding questions are considered subsequently. However, all these decisions need to generate more returns than alternative investments. Otherwise, in the long term, the financial management would not be able to attract capital from the financial markets to fund them. Shareholders would then take their money back and invest it somewhere else.

This book focuses on the first part and left-hand side of the cycle; it helps the financial management to take investment

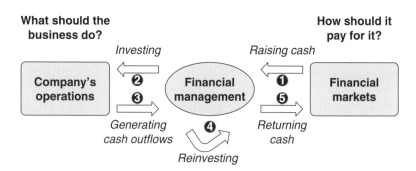

Figure 1.2 *Role of an organization's financial management*

decisions grounded in full-scope analysis and reality, which will ultimately achieve a greater return than other investments and thereby help to attract an investor's fund – this is the very first step of the cycle in Figure 1.2.

A business can be owned or managed by a single individual; these small ventures are called *sole proprietorships*. In other cases, several people may join forces and run a *partnership*. Most medium-sized and large businesses are organized as *corporations*, where the firm is owned by shareholders. Some corporations are *closely held* in private hands and their shares are not publicly traded. Others have expanded and raised fresh capital through issuing new shares to the general public, and thereby turned into *public companies*.

Corporations typically see a separation of ownership and management. While the shareholders jointly own the corporation, they do not manage it. Instead, they elect a board of directors, which represents the shareholders and appoints the company's top management. It also oversees that management acts in the interest of its shareholders. Shareholders are not personally responsible for the corporation's financial responsibilities; the limited liability of shareholders extends only to their individual investment, but no further.

Shareholders and other stakeholders, such as bankers, employees, and suppliers, have an interest in monitoring the firm's health to ensure that their own objectives are being met. To help them, companies produce three sorts of financial statements:

- Balance sheet,

- Profit and loss account (also referred to as P&L account or income statement), and

- Cash flow statement.

While the cash flow statement is mainly used for internal planning purposes, the balance sheet and the P&L account are required by law and appear in company reports as well.

Balance sheet

The balance sheet provides a snapshot of a company's assets and the sources of money used to procure those assets. Figure 1.3 shows the balance sheet of Procter & Gamble (P&G) for the financial year (FY) 2011/12.

A balance sheet does not show the market values of assets, but the original costs minus an amount for depreciation. Intangible assets, such as know-how, skills, and patents are generally not included in the balance sheet. The assets are sorted by how fast they can be turned into cash, i.e. current assets (such as cash and short-term investments, accounts receivables, raw material inventory, work in process, and finished goods) come before long-term fixed assets (such as land, buildings, plant, machinery, and investments).

- *Cash* (and equivalents to cash) represents short-term, highly liquid investments that are both readily convertible to known amounts of cash and so close to their maturity (three months or less) that they present insignificant risk of changes in interest rates. The category *short-term investments* consists of any investments in debt and equity securities with maturity of one year or less. The short-term nature refers to the actual maturity of one year from the balance sheet date rather than on the original maturity of a specific investment.

- *Accounts receivables* represents claims held against customers for goods sold or services rendered as part of normal business operations.

- *Inventories* encompasses assets held for sale in the ordinary course of business or goods that will be used and/or consumed in the production of goods to be sold. Inventories may include raw material, work in progress, and finished goods; depending on the company's business, other categories of asset items may also be classified as inventories.

Assets	$138,354.00	
Current assets	$21,970.00	
Cash and short-term investments		| $2,768.00
Accounts receivables		| $6,275.00
Inventories		| $7,379.00
Prepaid expenses		| $4,408.00
Deferred income tax		| $1,140.00
Net fixed assets	$21,293.00	
Gross fixed assets		|
Land & buildings (gross)		| $8,687.00
Machinery & equipment (gross)		| $32,820.00
./. less accumulated depreciation		| -$20,214.00
Goodwill (net)	$57,562.00	
Intangibles (net)	$32,620.00	
Intangibles (gross)		$36,832.00
./. less accumulated intangible amortization		-$4,212.00
Other long-term assets	$4,909.00	

Liabilities	$138,354.00	
Current liabilities	$27,293.00	
Accounts payable		| $8,022.00
Accrued expenses		| $5,817.00
Notes payable / short-term debt		| $6,987.00
Current portion of long-term debt / capital leases		| $2,994.00
Income taxes payable		| $786.00
Other current liabilities		| $2,687.00
Total debt	$22,033.00	
Deferred income tax	$11,070.00	
Minority interest	$361.00	
Other liabilities	$9,957.00	
Underfunded pension benefits		| $6,275.00
Other long-term liabilities		| $3,682.00
Shareholder's equity	$67,640.00	

(in millions of USD)

Figure 1.3 *Balance sheet*[11]

- *Prepaid expenses* represents goods or services that have already been purchased but are not yet fully consumed or used.

- *Deferred income tax* contains the deferred tax assets with a current maturity. It is an asset that may be used to reduce any subsequent period's income tax expense. Deferred tax assets can arise due to net loss carryovers, which are only recorded as assets if they are deemed to be used in future fiscal periods with a probability of at least 50 per cent.

- *Land* represents land and improvements on land at acquisition cost. Land is not depreciated, but land improvements are normally depreciated over time. The category *Buildings* represents the gross amount of buildings, and their attachments, before being reduced by accumulated depreciation of the buildings.

- *Machinery and equipment* encompasses the acquisition cost of machinery and other equipment (including office equipment, furniture and fixtures, factory equipment, tools, etc.) before being reduced by accumulated depreciation.

- *Accumulated depreciation* represents an aggregate of accumulated depreciation to each of the above fixed assets.

- *Goodwill* typically reflects the value of an intangible asset, such as a strong brand name, good customer relations, and good employee relations. Goodwill can often arise when one company is purchased by another company and the acquisition amount paid is over the company's book value, which would reflect on the bought company's intangible assets. Goodwill is always reported as a net figure, i.e. gross goodwill reduced by goodwill amortization. Goodwill may also include negative goodwill.

- *Intangibles* are in addition to goodwill and comprise other intangible assets, such as patents, copyrights, franchises, trademarks, trade names, and secret processes. The gross amount is reduced by *accumulated intangible amortization* leading to a net figure.

- *Other long-term assets* include advances to distributors, officers, and employees, cash surrendered, long-term customer deposits, long-term prepaid expenses, security deposits for renting, and unpaid capital/subscriptions receivable.

Similarly, the liabilities section first lists current liabilities that need to be paid off within one year (such as debt, accounts payable, and provisions). This is followed by the sources of cash used to purchase the net working capital, investments, and fixed assets. Some cash may have come from the issue of bonds to investors and from retained earnings that have been re-invested.

- *Accounts payable* represents balances owed to suppliers for materials and merchandise acquired on an open account.

- *Accrued expenses* embodies operational expenses accrued, but not yet paid. As current liabilities, such expenses are expected to be paid within one year or one operating cycle, whichever is longer.

- *Notes payable/short-term debt* denotes short-term bank borrowings and notes payable that are issued to suppliers.

- *Current portion of long-term debt/capital leases* represents the portion of a long-term debt instrument that is due within the following fiscal year.

- *Income taxes payable* are income taxes payable to the government, where such tax liability is already confirmed in terms of amount and payable date; this is different from deferred income tax, which is only an estimated liability.

- *Other current liabilities* are current liabilities which do not fall under the above categories.

- For industrial, utility, and insurance companies, *total debt* represents the total debt outstanding, which includes notes payable/short-term debt, and current portion of long-term debt/capital leases. For banks, total debt represents total deposits, interest bearing liabilities, short-term borrowings, and current portion of long-term debt/capital leases. Long-term debt with maturities beyond one year (e.g. long-term bank borrowings, bonds, convertible bonds) is also included regardless of industry vertical.[12]

- *Deferred income tax* is the estimated deferred income tax liabilities that are expected to come due beyond one year.

- *Minority interest* reflects the accumulated interest for minority shareholders in subsidiaries that are less than 100 per cent owned by the reporting parent company; the net worth of a subsidiary is assumed to be proportionally owned by parent company and other minority shareholders according to their respective ownership percentage.

- *Underfunded pension benefits* stands for the valuation of a pension fund where there are insufficient funds to support expected liabilities.

- *Other long-term liabilities* represents non-interest-bearing long-term liabilities other than the above listed items. They also include liabilities subject to compromise and negative goodwill.

Profit and loss (P&L) account

If the balance sheet is a snapshot, the P&L account is like a video,[13] as it is normally updated regularly; it measures a company's sales and expenses over a specified period of time and thus shows how much profit or loss a business is making. The function of a P&L statement is to total all sources of revenue and subtract all expenses and depreciations related to the revenue in order to show a company's financial progress during the time period being examined.

Figure 1.4 shows a P&L account building on data from P&G. *Net sales* represents sales receipts for products and services, less cash discounts, trade discounts, excise tax, and sales returns. The *operating income* (or earnings before interest and taxes, EBIT) is calculated as total revenues minus *cost of revenue* (i.e. all costs that can be directly attributed to the goods and services produced/purchased and sold), minus *cost of selling and general administrative expenses* (i.e. all costs of operating a business, marketing, and overhead other than the costs directly attributable to readying a specific product for sale), and minus *depreciation* (i.e. the representation of the account process that allocates the costs of tangible assets to expenses to those periods expected to benefit from the use of the assets). The *net income* (or profit after tax, PAT) is derived by subtracting *interest expenses* and a *provision for income taxes* from EBIT.

Net sales	$82,559.00
Other income	$0.00
Total revenue	**$82,559.00**
./. *less* cost of revenue	$40,768.00
Gross profit	**$41,791.00**
./. *less* cost of selling and general administrative expenses	$25,973.00
./. *less* depreciation	$2,292.00
Operating income (EBIT)	**$13,526.00**
./. *less* interest expenses	$629.00
Net income before taxes	**$12,897.00**
./. *less* provision for income taxes	$3,392.00
Net income after taxes (PAT)	**$9,505.00**
Dividends	$233.00
Retained earnings	$9,272.00

Figure 1.4 *P&L account*[14]

Cash flow statement

The cash flow statement is the third financial statement and is mainly used internally. It records the cash inflows and outflows of a business and helps to assess and maintain an adequate liquidity level. The main sources of cash inflows and outflows are depicted in Figure 1.5; the format used is a widely accepted one. Each column represents a period, and totals for cash inflows as well as outflows are shown. The difference between the totals of inflows and outflows in one period is the net cash flow for this period. Adding the net cash flow to the opening cash balance, which has been brought forward from the previous period, results in the closing cash balance, which then

	Jan	Feb	Mar	Apr	May	Jun	Jul
Cash inflows							
Cash from sales							
- Cash sales							
- Trade debtors							
Financing							
- Share capital issued							
- Loan capital issued							
Sale of fixed assets							
Other income							
Cash outflows							
Operating costs							
Cash purchases							
Overhead							
Purchases of fixed assets							
Trade creditors							
Taxation							
Dividends							
Loans redeemed							
Shares redeemed							
Net cash flow							
Opening balance							
Closing balance							

Figure 1.5 *General structure of a cash flow statement*

becomes the opening cash balance for the next period. Historic cash flow statements for external reporting purposes are usually prepared on an annual basis; projected cash flow statements for internal planning tend to be on a monthly basis. When preparing a projected cash flow statement, each piece of information needs to be examined to determine whether it involved a cash transaction (either cash inflow or outflow) and whether a cash transaction did take place. It is important to identify the month in which the cash movement actually occurred in contrast to when the transaction was agreed on.

When a cash flow statement is used externally, it sometimes only shows netted cash flows as opposed to detailing inflows and outflows separately. An example is P&G's cash flow statement, as shown in Figure 1.6.

Financial ratios

The three financial statements (balance sheet, P&L account, cash flow statement) together provide the basic information about a company's financial standing. But as they contain a huge amount of figures and data, they are usually condensed into key financial ratios, which help to answer questions like:

- What is the amount of debt the company has taken on? Can it lead to financial distress?

- How liquid is the company? Can it quickly raise cash if needed?

- Are the assets being used productively?

- What is the general profitability of the company?

- And, last but not least, how do investors see the company's performance?

Period ended	30.06.2011	30.06.2010	30.06.2009	30.06.2008	30.06.2007
Cash from operating activities	$13,231.00	$16,072.00	$14,919.00	$15,008.00	$13,410.00
Net income / starting line	$11,797.00	$12,736.00	$13,436.00	$12,075.00	$10,340.00
Depreciation / Depletion	$2,838.00	$3,108.00	$3,082.00	$3,166.00	$3,130.00
Deferred Taxes	$128.00	$36.00	$596.00	$1,214.00	$253.00
Non-Cash Items	$211.00	−$2,217.00	−$1,861.00	$271.00	$515.00
Changes in working capital	−$1,743.00	$2,409.00	−$334.00	−$1,718.00	−$828.00
Accounts receivable	−$426.00	−$14.00	$415.00	$432.00	−$729.00
Inventories	−$501.00	$86.00	$721.00	−$1,050.00	−$389.00
Payable / accrued	$358.00	$2,446.00	−$742.00	$297.00	−$278.00
Other assets % liabilities (net)	−$1,190.00	−$305.00	−$758.00	−$1,270.00	−$151.00
Other operating cash flow	$16.00	$196.00	$30.00	−$127.00	$719.00
Cash from investing activities	−$3,482.00	−$597.00	−$2,353.00	−$2,549.00	−$2,483.00
Capital expenditures	−$3,306.00	−$3,067.00	−$3,238.00	−$3,046.00	−$2,945.00
Purchases of fixed assets	−$3,306.00	−$3,067.00	−$3,238.00	−$3,046.00	−$2,945.00
Acquisition of intangibles					
Software development costs					
...					
Other investing cash flow items	−$176.00	$2,470.00	$885.00	$497.00	$462.00
Acquisition of business	−$474.00	−$425.00	−$368.00	−$381.00	−$492.00
Sale of fixed assets	$225.00	$3,068.00	$1,087.00	$928.00	$281.00
Investment (net)	$73.00	−$173.00	$166.00	−$50.00	$673.00
Cash from financing activities	−$10,023.00	−$17,255.00	−$10,814.00	−$14,844.00	−$12,453.00
Total cash dividends paid	−$5,767.00	−$5,458.00	−$5,044.00	−$4,655.00	−$4,209.00
Issuance (retirement) of stock (net)	−$5,737.00	−$5,283.00	−$5,689.00	−$8,180.00	−$4,079.00
Issuance (Retirement) of Debt, Net	$1,481.00	−$6,514.00	−$81.00	−$2,009.00	−$4,165.00
Short term debt (net)	$151.00	−$1,798.00	−$2,420.00	$2,650.00	$9,006.00
Long term debt issued	$1,536.00	$3,830.00	$4,926.00	$7,088.00	$4,758.00
Long term debt reduction	−$206.00	−$8,546.00	−$2,587.00	−$11,747.00	−$17,929.00
Net cash flow	−$111.00	−$1,902.00	$1,468.00	−$2,041.00	−$1,339.00
Opening balance	$2,879.00	$4,781.00	$3,313.00	$5,351.00	$6,693.00
Closing balance	$2,768.00	$2,879.00	$4,781.00	$3,313.00	$5,354.00
Foreign exchange effects	$163.00	−$122.00	−$284.00	$344.00	$187.00
Cash interest paid	$806.00	$1,184.00	$1,226.00	$1,373.00	$1,330.00
Cash taxes paid	$2,992.00	$4,175.00	$3,248.00	$3,499.00	$4,116.00

(in millions of USD)

Figure 1.6 *Annual netted cash flow statement*[15]

Figure 1.7 shows key financial ratios as reported by P&G.

There is no one right set of values with respect to the financial ratios that the financial management of a company like P&G should work towards. Different debt and liquidity levels come with their own advantages and disadvantages: one level may be appropriate for one company's business model but not suited to another. Hence financial managers not only compare financial ratios with the industry benchmark, but also tend to review their year-by-year development.

Position of the financial manager

So, who is the financial manager in a corporation? Only in the very smallest of businesses will there be a single person in charge of all the decisions. Much more often, the responsibility of financial management rests on the shoulders of many people, from top management to project managers, individual

Valuation

P/E	22.32	TTM	Calculated by dividing the current price of a share by the sum of the basic earnings per share from continuing operations *before* extraordinary items and accounting changes over the last four quarters.
Price to revenue	2.29	TTM	Current price of a share divided by the sales per share for the trailing twelve months.
Price to cash flow	15.64	TTM	Current price of a share divided by cash flow per share for the trailing twelve months. Cash flow is defined as income after taxes minus preferred dividends and general partner distributions plus depreciation, depletion and amortization.
Price to book	3.07	MRQ	Current price divided by the latest interim period book value per share.

Per share

Revenue / share	28.46	TTM	Trailing twelve month total revenue divided by the average diluted shares outstanding for the trailing twelve months.
EPS fully diluted	3.11	TTM	Adjusted income available to common stockholders for the trailing twelve months divided by the trailing twelve month diluted weighted average shares outstanding.
Dividend / share	2.14	TTM	Sum of the cash dividends per share paid to common stockholders during the last trailing twelve month period.
Book value / share	23.09	MRQ	Common shareholder's equity (total shareholder's equity minus preferred stock and redeemable preferred stock) divided by the shares outstanding at the end of the most recent intermin period.
Cash flow / share	4.17	TTM	Trailing twelve month cash flow (sum of income after taxes minus preferred dividends and general partner distributions plus depreciation, depletion, and amortization) divided by the trailing twelve month average shares outstanding.
Cash	1.61	MRQ	Total cash plus short term investments divided by the shares outstanding at the end of the most recent interim period.

Profitability

Operating margin [%]	15.80	TTM	Percentage of revenues remaining after paying all operating expenses; calculated as trailing twelve months operating income (total revenue minus total operating expenses) divided by the trailing twelve months total revenue.
Net profit margin [%]	11.13	TTM	Return on sales. Income after tax for the trailing twelve months divided by total revenue for the same period.
Gross margin [%]	49.34	TTM	Percentage of revenue left after paying all direct production expenses; calculated as trailing twelve months total revenue minus cost of goods sold divided by total revenue during the same period.

Growth

5-year annual growth [%]	5.95	Compound annual growth rate of sales per share over the last five years.
5-year annual revenue growth rate [%]	2.93	Compound annual growth rate of revenues of the last five years.
5-year annual dividend growth rate [%]	10.83	Compound annual growth rate of cash dividends per common share of stock over the last five years.
5-year EPS growth [%]	1.86	Compound annual growth rate of earnings per share (EPS) excluding extraordinary items and discountinued operations.

Figure 1.7 *Financial ratios*[16]

Financial strength

Quick ratio	0.61	MRQ	Acid test ratio. Total current assets minus total inventory for the most recent interim period divided by total current liabilities for the same period.
Current ratio	0.88	MRQ	Total current assets for the most recent interim period divided by total current liabilities for the same period.
LT debt to equity [%]	33.23	MRQ	Total long term devt for the most recent interim period divided by total shareholder equity for the same period.
Total debt to equity [%]	46.94	MRQ	Total debt for the most recent interim period divided by total shareholder equity for the same period.

Management effectiveness

Return on equity [%]	13.83	TTM	Income available to common stockholders for the trailing twelve months divided by the average common equity.
Return on assets [%]	6.89	TTM	Income after taxes for the trailing twelve months divided by the average total assets.
Return on investment [%]	8.57	TTM	Income after taxes for the trailing twelve months divided by the average total long term debt, other long term liabilities, and shareholders equity.

Efficiency

Asset turnover	0.62	TTM	Total revenues for the trailing twelve months divided by the average total assets.
Inventory turnover	6.01	TTM	Cost of goods sold for the trailing twelve months divided by average inventory. Measures how quickly the inventory is sold.

MRQ = most recent quarter; TTM = trailing twelve months

Figure 1.7 (*Continued*)

contributors, and marketing. For example, deciding on a marketing campaign and allocating marketing spend is an investment decision that needs to show its payback in terms of increased sales and revenue, and hence many functions in an organization will be involved in approving the business case for the marketing spend.

Investment cycle

The financial management of some corporations uses the expression *investment cycle* for the process of identifying an investment opportunity, developing a supporting business case, taking the investment decision, implementing the project, and reporting back on the success of the investment. Then the cycle may start again with add-on investments, adjustments to the original decision, or even a decommissioning of the project.

1.2   WHY INVESTMENT DECISIONS FAIL

Taking the right investment decisions is vital to the economic well-being, if not survival, of a business. Still, many investment decisions fail and studies continue to show us a bleak picture of this aspect of financial management.

Examples of failed investment decisions

A 2009 survey of information technology-related investment success by the Standish Group[17] (see Figure 1.8) shows that 44 per cent of all projects are somewhat challenged; while they may be completed and operational, they may be over budget, not on time, or providing fewer features and functions than originally specified. Twenty-four per cent of projects get cancelled somewhere during their lifecycle, leaving the corporation with no results but only costs. These percentages are certainly improved from 1995, where 53 per cent were challenged and 31 per cent cancelled, but it still only leaves a success rate of less than one third. Various other studies over the past 30 years

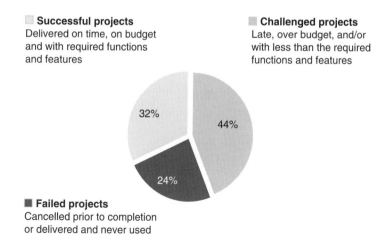

Successful projects
Delivered on time, on budget
and with required functions
and features

Challenged projects
Late, over budget, and/or
with less than the required
functions and features

32%

44%

24%

Failed projects
Cancelled prior to completion
or delivered and never used

Figure 1.8 *Information technology-related investment success*

have confirmed this picture.[18] Cases 1.5 to 1.8 show a variety of failed decisions about investments and projects from the world of information technology (IT).

Case 1.5   KIN phone by Microsoft

Microsoft's KIN phones were designed for the younger market to support their use of social networking sites (see Figure 1.9). After a two-year development project,[19] they were manufactured by Sharp and sold through Verizon Wireless in the USA. After just two months in the market in the first half of 2010, Microsoft pulled the plug. It is rumored that only 503 phones were actually sold. On the other side, the overall project costs of designing, producing, and marketing the KIN phone were reported to be around US$1 billion.[20] The failure can probably be attributed to tough competition, which made a new entry difficult. Many people never even heard about the KIN phone, showing a lack of marketing and suggesting also a lack of senior management support.[21] Reports also indicate that the phone lacked some basic functions required by users (such as a calendar or the ability to run games). The high cost of the data and texting plans may also have been a factor.

Case 1.6   Advanced Metering Infrastructure Project

In Victoria, Australia, the Advanced Metering Infrastructure (AMI) Project was set out in 2006 to replace accumulation meters in 2.4 million homes and small business by 2013. However, the costs to deploy smart

Figure 1.9 *Microsoft's KIN phone*[22]

electrical meters ballooned from the estimated and budgeted AU$800 million to AU$2.25 billion. A 2009 review by the Auditor-General even questioned its value to the residents of Victoria. The report noted that the "project has not used the checks and balances that would ordinarily apply to a major investment directly funded by the state. This highlights a gap in the project's accountability framework. There have been significant inadequacies in the advice and recommendations provided to government on the roll-out of the AMI project. The advice and supporting analysis lacked depth and presented an incomplete picture of the AMI project in relation to economic merits, consumer impact and project risks" (Pearson, 2009, p. viii). Additionally, the Auditor-General cast doubt on the business case behind the investment in smart meters: "The cost–benefit study behind the AMI decision was flawed and failed to offer a comprehensive view of the economic case for the project. There are significant unexplained discrepancies [...] These discrepancies suggest a high degree of uncertainty about the economic case for the project" (Pearson, 2009, p. ix). The AMI project and its audit report was also covered in the media[23] comparing it with more successful initiatives in the USA and Germany.

Case 1.7   Apple Services India

Apple, in April 2006, attempted to establish a captive customer support facility in India (*Apple Services India Pvt. Ltd.*) with 30 employees, but with plans to ramp up to a headcount of 600 within a year. However, the center was shut down only two months later and most of the work was handed over to an external Indian service provider. Apple told its employees in a staff meeting on 29 May 2006 that "the company is revaluating its operations and has thought of pulling back its Indian operations."[24] Employees were given a severance package of two months' salary and most of them re-joined their previous employer, but as of today, it remains unclear why exactly Apple decided to shut down the software development business in India immediately after starting it.[25]

Case 1.8   Google Wave

Google Wave was intended to be a web application that allowed users to communicate and collaborate in real-time via character-by-character live typing, drag-and-drop, and playback of the history of changes. According to an official company blog, people at Google were "jazzed about Google Wave internally, even though we weren't quite sure how users would respond to this radically different kind of communication. The use cases we have seen show the power of this technology [...] But [...] Wave has not seen the user adoption we would have liked [...] Wave has taught us a lot [...]" (Hölzle, 2010).

Investment decisions in other areas than IT fail as well; however, they are not so widely analyzed and discussed.

For example, marketing research shows that most new consumer product launches fail – thanks mainly to an overuse of promotional discounts.[26] Increased advertising spending lifts revenue for only 55 per cent of new products and 33 per cent of established products, so the necessity to carefully consider spending on advertising is clear – even more so because advertising spending typically consumes about 3 per cent of corporate revenue.[27] If advertising is not successful in the first year, it usually does not help to continue spending on the same advertising channel.[28]

Case 1.9 highlights an example of failed government decision making in the area of defense spending.

Case 1.9   Upgrade of the presidential helicopters

The US Government maintains a fleet of Sea King and Blackhawk helicopters for Presidential and very important person (VIP) transport (see Figure 1.10). In addition to providing the President and others with safe and timely transportation, presidential helicopters are equipped with specialized self-defense features and communication technology permitting the President to carry out critical command functions while aboard. They have to be big enough to carry a certain number of people and equipment, but still small enough to operate from the White House Lawn. Following the 9/11 attacks of 2001, the Department of Defense (DoD) decided to add urgency to the upgrade plan for the existing and ageing fleet of 19 presidential helicopters, which dated back to the 1970s and late 1980s,[29] in order to fully protect the President. The Navy conducted a competition for the so-called VH-71 program and intended to provide 23 new presidential helicopters in two increments with varying functionality. Lockheed Martin Corp. won the prestigious contract in January 2005 against Sikorsky, a leading US helicopter manufacturer and maker of the existing presidential helicopters. The proposed plan was to turn an existing helicopter design from the Anglo-Italian helicopter manufacturer Agusta Westland into an Air Force One-like war-ready machine and have it operational in the first quarter of the FY 2009. The Lockheed bid was chosen over the Sikorsky bid by the Navy in part because it was deemed more likely to be able to meet the program's operational requirements on time and at a lower cost. Some observers, however, criticized the Navy's award decision because it favored European companies over US ones. The program was treated with urgency by the White House and it repeatedly tried to prepone the initial operational capability (IOC) to 2007.

However, the VH-71 program proved to be far more complex than originally thought. The Government's requirements kept continuously evolving, and the costs of the program spiraled upward. For example, it was originally planned to retrofit the earlier increment with functionality from the second increment, but this idea was later dropped and it was planned to purchase the full requirement from the final version only. In January 2005, the total acquisition cost, comprising development plus procurement costs of the VH-71 helicopters, was estimated at about $6.5 billion; in January 2008, it was already projected at about $11.2 billion. Less than another year later, in December 2008, it was reckoned to be $13.0 billion – twice the original estimate. This growth in the estimated total acquisition cost crossed an established cost overrun threshold and triggered the Nunn–McCurdy provision, which required the DoD to notify Congress in January 2009. At the same time, the estimated IOC slipped by three and a half years for the first increment and a staggering eight years for the second increment. Full operational capability (FOC) was estimated to be reached more than six years later than originally planned.

In 2009, following a change in administration, the project was stopped after spending $2.9 billion with a decision to start afresh.[30] In a question-and-answer session at the Fiscal Responsibility Summit on 23 February 2009, the new President Barack Obama had an exchange on the topic with Senator John McCain:

President Obama: "[...] The idea here was to bring everybody together because it's been a long time since we had this conversation. And over the last eight years, I think we've seen a continued deterioration in the government's balance sheets. [...] and I want to see if, John, you've got some thoughts about where we need to go and some priority areas. I know you were in procurement, for example, which is an area I know we would like to work on together with you."

Senator McCain: "Just one area that I wanted to mention that I think consumed a lot of our conversation on procurement was the issue of cost overruns in the Defense Department. We all know how large the defense budget is. We all know that the cost overruns – your helicopter is now going to cost as much as Air Force One. I don't think that there's any more graphic demonstration of how good ideas have cost taxpayers an enormous amount of money. So we will – and I know that you've already made plans to try to curb some of the excesses in procurement. We really have to do that. We're going to have to pay for Afghanistan, as you well know, and we're not done in Iraq. But most importantly, we have to make some tough decisions – you, Mr. President, have to make some tough decisions about not only what we procure, but how we procure it. [...]"

President Obama: "Well, John, [...] this is going to be one of our highest priorities. By the way, I've already talked to Gates about a thorough review of the helicopter situation. The helicopter I have now seems perfectly adequate to me. (Laughter.) Of course, I've never had a helicopter before – (laughter) – maybe I've been deprived and I didn't know it. (Laughter.) But I think it is [...] an example of the procurement process gone amuck. And we're going to have to fix it. Our hope is, is that you, Senator Levin, and others, can really take some leadership on this. And one of the promising things is I think Secretary Gates shares our concern and he recognizes that simply adding more and more does not necessarily mean better and better, or safer and more secure. Those two things are not – they don't always move in parallel tracks, and we've got to think that through."[31]

Figure 1.10 *Presidential helicopter Marine One, a VH-3D Sea King*[33]

Remedies against wrong and bad decisions

With all the failed decisions, there is a big difference between a wrong decision and a bad decision. A *wrong decision* is to invest in A when the benefits would actually be reaped by exploiting B; the fault lies with the method of deciding to invest in A. A *bad decision* is investing in A when experts predict a near hundred per cent chance of finding the holy grail in B; the fault lies in having no decision-making method at all. This distinction is important as it separates method (bad decision) from process (wrong decision).[32]

A popular and typical remedy introduced in organizations to counter such investment decision disasters is top management involvement, and as the above case shows, sometimes even the President of the United States gets involved. Other common measures are tighter control, team-building measures, and possibly additional training. While these fixes can certainly reduce failure rates, they will not eliminate unfeasible projects right from the beginning. Often, investment or project issues are symptoms of deep rooted decision-making problems which can be traced back to the original business case. Historically, many organizations have frequently not bothered to put together a business case and if they have, it often contained erroneous logic and faulty calculations based on unrealistic assumptions. Some organizations have produced a so-called cost–benefit analysis or a technical feasibility study relying on simplified generalizations about paybacks and return on investments (ROIs), which have then all supported the investment go-ahead decision without looking at the business issues behind the investment. And because this link is often misunderstood, all the mathematical calculations in the business case are of little meaning, if not misleading and erroneous. Even worse, the countermeasures eventually introduced to save an investment will not and cannot address the original problem; they might even backfire.

For this very reason, and in order to improve corporate decision making, one needs to learn how to distinguish an upright and honest investment proposition from the one which is flawed with assumptions and gaps. Before the book can turn to this challenge in Section 1.5, a little more groundwork on investment decisions is required. The following paragraph compares the investment alternative of doing something with sitting still and waiting and Section 1.3 defines the term *business case*. Section 1.4 talks about business objectives and Section 1.4 lists relevant investment types.

Doing something vs. doing nothing: Changing the rules of the game

In some circumstances, it is better to do something rather than to do nothing. Deferring decisions and doing nothing basically means remaining paralyzed in the same position, but taking decisions and starting doing something at least means that the rules of the game are beginning to change.

For instance, both military and civilian air traffic controllers (see Figure 1.11) constantly take into account the speed of the airplane, its characteristics, the climb rate, and how fast the pilot is going to react to instructions. Paul Rinaldi, Air Traffic Controller at Washington Dulles International Airport IAD reports: "It's not so much analytical as it is making a decision quickly and sticking with it. You have to do that knowing that some of the decisions you're going to make are going to be wrong, but you're going to make that decision be right. You can't back out."[34]

In the world of investment banking, successful traders need to make decisions quickly; they cannot afford to spend much time regretting their earlier decisions or going back over them again and again. Some decisions will turn out to be wrong, but they need to move on. Simon Yates, Managing Director Equity Derivatives at Credit Suisse First Boston says: "In some ways it's like being a police officer: There's a lot of time when nothing

Figure 1.11 *US Navy air traffic controllers at work*[36]

is going on, and then suddenly you've got to be really fast. You can't wait until you have absolute confirmation. You're looking to get enough information to think that you probably have detected something, and based on that, you make your trades."[35] When a trader panics, basic emotional instincts take over the decision-making process and money will be lost – the scared trader will only take smaller positions and cut profits too quickly.

On a battlefield, soldiers do not have time to gather many opinions. They have to quickly assess their environment and make the best possible decision under uncertainty – based on their instinct, experience, and training. Soldiers are being given the responsibility to make decisions, for themselves and for their subordinates, with possible effects on the enemy, the civil population, the environment, and the budget. When a platoon moves in hostile territory, deferring decisions to turn left or right by deliberating too long can put it in a deadly situation – the enemy may just want to have it exactly there. A platoon leader (see Figure 1.12) therefore has the responsibility to take these decisions – and the leader needs to make these decisions to ensure the platoon's survival and success. By being collaborative whenever possible, the platoon leader builds trust, so that when a quick decision has to be made whether to turn right or left, soldiers are more likely to trust the leader's decision.[37]

The military does not only make operational battlefield decisions, it also takes strategic decisions. For instance, purchasing a weapon system is just like any other kind of business investment decision; being rushed with such a strategic matter would be completely out of place. Always going fast is obviously not a good decision-making strategy. Instead, recognizing a change or threat early, and then making full use of the available time window – whether short or long – to make the best possible and deliberate decision generally yields better outcomes than a non-coherent set of quick decisions. After all, coherent action is part of a good business strategy.[38] The key

Figure 1.12 *A platoon leader gives orders – A decision under uncertainty*[39]

question around decision-making speed and business outcome is thus not whether one should act quickly or slowly, but about the available time before the risk profile changes. What is more, the primary difficulty does not lie in answering this question, but in having the presence of mind to ask it in the first place.[40]

Business surprises

Business surprises are events that occur without warning – or with seemingly no warning. For virtually all events warning is available, although the information may not be in the right places until it is too late.

One well-known bolt from the blue was the terror attacks on the USA of September 11, 2001. This tragedy resulted in an investigation to determine how this horrible event, for which there had been no apparent warning, could have been avoided. The final report of the Joint Inquiry Staff of the Senate Select Committee stated:

> In short, for a variety of reasons, the Intelligence Community failed to capitalize on both the individual and collective significance of available information that appears relevant to the events of September 11. As a result, the Community missed opportunities to disrupt the September 11th plot by denying entry to or detaining would-be hijackers; to at least try to unravel the plot through surveillance and other investigative work within the United States; and, finally, to generate a heightened state of alert and thus harden the homeland against attack. No one will ever know what might have happened had more connections been drawn between these disparate pieces of information. We will never definitively know to what extent the Community would have been able and willing to exploit fully all the opportunities that may have emerged. The important point is that the Intelligence Community, for a variety of reasons, did not bring together and fully appreciate a range of information that could have greatly enhanced its chances of uncovering and preventing Osama Bin Laden's plan to attack these United States on September 11th, 2001. (US House of Representatives, 2002)

On an entirely different matter, namely the strength of the Chinese economy, Reuters, the news agency, reported in 2012 that

> China's economy stuttered unexpectedly in April with lower than expected output data, softening retail sales, and easing prices suggesting economic headwinds might be

stiffer than thought, requiring more robust policy responses to counter them. Industrial output expanded at its slowest annual pace in April in nearly three years, while fixed asset investment growth dipped to its lowest in almost a decade. The weak growth in fixed asset investment signaled that the impact of a prolonged credit crunch in China's real estate sector, and of flagging demand from export markets, was more severe than first thought. (Hornby & Chiang, 2012)

Meanwhile, in the business world, hundreds of companies announce business earnings different from what was expected; negative deviations are attributed to surprise events, unexpected weaknesses in the consumer sector, an unexpected fall of an economy into the double-dip recession, and so on. But do any of these announcements or profit warnings include a statement by the CEO that a task force was commissioned to unveil why early warning indicators were missed and why the change from target was unanticipated? What can be done to avoid such surprises in the future? Why do CEOs treat business surprises differently from terror attacks?

The problem is usually not bad managers, but it is far bigger and much more systemic: poor processes in the organization at hand and a troubled culture in the entire business world. Today, one often finds a corporate culture that has become satisfied and complacent in using outdated and irrelevant information when making decisions. Fixing this culture is, however, not a government or regulatory job. It requires business executives to change the culture in each of their respective corporations, one by one, through focusing their existing decision-making processes on relevant information and then getting this information to the business case team on time.[41] Only then can managers develop investment proposals to cope with what are today's unexpected events – and turn looming disasters into business opportunities.

1.3   DEFINITION OF A BUSINESS CASE

By and large, people in corporations, consulting companies, and other service providers use the term *business case* to describe a document delivering a cost–benefit justification for an investment proposition; it may also be called a *benefit analysis*, a *ROI study*, a *payback investigation*, or a *value finder*.

Business case as process and document

Much more importantly, a business case is not just a mandatory document following some pre-defined structure which is to be signed-off by senior management. It is much more something like a process, which sets up a lean project team to analyze the company's strategic objectives, suggest investments, work out alternatives, identify and align stakeholders in the decision-making process, and calculate respectively the ranks (the "worthiness") of these investment suggestions or alternatives. In short, the business case captures the reasoning for initiating a project, a task, or any other potential investment in the corporate world which is connected with spending money. It is a justification for how to pursue a course of action to meet an organization's goals. This justification helps management take rational decisions about the true business value of the monetary spending associated with a potential investment.

After commissioning the investment, the business case should not be shelved, but it should be used to track that value is generated through the chosen alternative. During this process, the business case evolves from a project in itself, to a decision document (the *top-down business case*), and finally into a tracking tool (the *bottom-up business case*) for the implementation of the agreed decision.

One-sentence business case

A good business case can be summarized in one sentence and provides input to all four of the place holders depicted in Figure

1.13: "In order to improve ___ we are doing ___, which is worth ___ and can be measured by ___."[42]

The first place holder addresses the business pain point: what do we need to improve in the organization? The second place holder describes the proposed investment and what will be done differently from today. This activity should be explained in non-technical plain English terms that a senior manager from the business line can easily understand. The third place holder details how much the investment is going to be worth after all costs have been taken care of. This will be the net present value (NPV) of the business case calculation, adjusted for risk with respect to uncertainty and future strategic options. In this book, the NPV calculation will be introduced in Section 2.2 and further explained in Chapter 5; Chapter 3 is dedicated to the topic of costs and Chapter 4 to identifying benefits. The topic of risk and uncertainty is covered in Chapter 6 and the role of future strategic options is explained in Chapter 7.

Last, but not least, once the plan is implemented the fourth place holder makes the investment proposition observable and measurable through metrics; it builds the link to the bottom-up business case, which will be discussed later in Chapter 9.

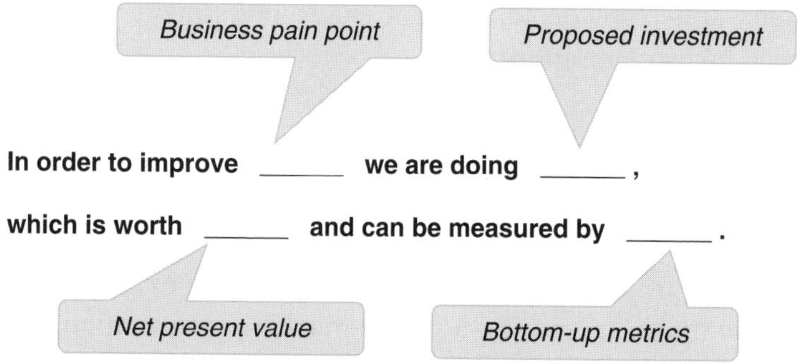

Figure 1.13 *The one-sentence business case*

To summarize, and to describe the stance that this book takes on the subject, a business case is defined as a process in corporate governance. It supports the decision-making process on investment alternatives by building consensus among stakeholders and providing a top-down justification for a rational decision. Its outcome is a document that contains a bullet-proof cost–benefit analysis, together with an evaluation of risk and strategic future flexibility options. After commissioning of the investment, the business case changes its scope from a decision document to a bottom-up tracking metric, which helps to ensure that in the real world the promised benefits are also being reaped.

1.4 CHARACTERIZING INVESTMENTS

As corporate decision making can be very complex, it is important to understand the characteristics of a proposed investment and how it is interrelated to other investments. Only then is it possible to choose the appropriate approach for designing and building the business case.

Investments can be categorized based on the types shown in Figure 1.14. All the investment types require slightly different approaches for the business case; for example, these differences can range from a relatively simple business case to detailed and complex ones, from delta investment investigations to a full scope analysis, and from deciding on a single investment to choosing between investment alternatives.

Large (strategic) and small (tactical) investments

Business cases are usually discussed in connection with *large investments* involving huge sums of funds, for example, entering a new market, running a major marketing campaign, implementing a new customer relationship management (CRM)

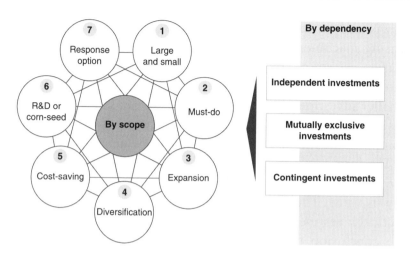

Figure 1.14 *Investment characteristics*

system, outsourcing customer service to a third party provider, or offshoring the maintenance of a software application system to a service provider in India. These are cases where taking the right decision has a big impact on the sustained success of the enterprise, where it affects the general course the company was running so far, and where it significantly changes the company's profits and risk profile. Such decisions on large *strategic investments* are directly linked to implementing the coherent actions as defined in the kernel of corporate strategy (see Section 1.1).

In contrast, *small* and/or *tactical investments* usually participate in a regular capital budgeting process, where, usually once a year, a budget for investments is agreed and distributed to investment projects which promise the greatest net benefit. The business case process helps to build the case and compare competing investments. Taking a tactical decision does not involve a major departure from what the enterprise was doing in the past.

Nonetheless, many techniques for managing strategic investment decisions, as discussed in this book, can easily be downsized to smaller investments as well, such as buying or leasing machinery, investing now or later, upgrading an information system or not, working with an internal team or hiring external consultants, or increasing advertising spending. Such smaller investments also involve decision making; the business case can often be a more informal process, which assesses and compares the merits of the suggested investments.

The larger and the more strategic an investment decision is, the more difficult it is usually to find reliable measures to quantify its value. The outcomes are more uncertain than for smaller tactical investments and this rather frustrating paradox leads to the conclusion that mathematical calculations cannot always entirely replace informed business judgment.

Must-do investments

There will be some investments where a business is not so very much concerned about measuring returns or where the exact return is not a major concern. Typical examples of such *must-do* or *non-discretionary investments* are often *legal investments* which are mandated by the regulator or by law. A financial services company may have to amend its core banking system to handle the introduction of a new tax in a certain country. Other must-do investments can be safety investments as simple as providing disinfectants in offices during the bird-flu scare; an enterprise IT system may need to be upgraded to meet security or other standards; or it may need to be migrated away from end-of-life platforms. Case 1.10 shows how companies in the late 1990s had to get ready for the introduction of the new euro currency (EUR, €).

To take such investment decisions, a business case will not be discussed in great detail. No panel will question the decision to invest, nor ask for a detailed evaluation along complex decision criteria – so why do a business case for "must-do" investments after all? There will be no incremental business benefit that can be put into the one-sentence business case shown in Figure 1.13, so a business case may appear to be not practical and a waste of corporate resources.

However, even in non-discretionary investment cases, the merit of a business case process can be found in evaluating alternatives and clarifying them by assigning costs. While the investment decision may be preordained, senior management may be better prepared to pick the right alternative with respect to advantages and disadvantages, cost and time differences, and resource requirements.[43] The goal of complying with a new tax or sufficiently protecting employees against the outbreak of an epidemic needs to be achieved at a good price.

Most legal or must-do investments have alternatives, from providing only the necessary functionality or solution to a more expensive, more comfortable, or more efficient option. The additional cost for the better alternative needs to be justified and can be considered as a discretionary optional investment for which the business case process should be started.

Each alternative is also likely to have a different risk profile. A seemingly less expensive in-house developed software solution may be more risky in terms of costs, delivery date, and functionality than a seemingly more expensive off-the-shelf established third-party solution. Documenting the risks will point the business case team to the optimal solution.

A tactical execution of the seemingly least expensive solution may meet existing legal requirements. Alternatively, the organization could think about implementing a more costly solution, which would enable it to meet its future needs at lower costs in the years to come. Such future needs may transcend the border of legally mandated must-do requirements. For example, in order to solve a reporting requirement, the company may choose between manually consolidating information or implementing a data warehouse, which enables it to meet future reporting needs at lower costs. Alternatives can create such strategic flexibility options (see Chapter 7); only a thorough business case analysis can unveil the best long-term decision.

Case 1.10   How Siemens got ready for the new euro currency

The euro as a new currency was established by the provisions of the 1992 Maastricht Treaty, and to participate in the new currency member states were meant to meet and keep strict criteria around budget deficit, debt ratio, low inflation, and convergence of interest rates around the EU average. The currency was introduced in non-physical form at midnight on 1 January 1999, when the national currencies of participating countries ceased to exist independently. The notes and coins of the old currencies continued to be used as legal tender until the new euro notes were introduced on 1 January 2002.

Financial institutions and companies alike had to tackle the challenges introduced by this cut-over to a new currency. It was a cut-over mandated by the EU and their governments. There was simply no choice: the introduction of the euro could not be avoided – clearly a must-do investment.

Companies had to prepare for the euro in a variety of business areas, including treasury and payments, taxes and legal, strategy, business transactions and procedures, purchasing, accounting and controlling, human resources, and data processing. Siemens, one of the largest electrical engineering and electronics companies, set up its euro project planning team as early as 1995 and was at the forefront of initiatives. The costs of its euro currency-related IT investment alone amounted to something in the range of €50 million.[44] Although Siemens was hoping to recoup this spend through savings from dealing with one currency instead of 11 eurozone currencies, a reduction in administration and hedging against the risk of currency fluctuations, and faster payment transactions, in principle it did not have a choice to vote against the investment; the company could only choose between alternative ways of getting ready for the euro.

Expansion investments

An *expansion investment* is an investment in existing or very similar product lines, services, or geographies in order to increase sales and gain more market share. Case 1.11 shows how a hospital decided to approve an expansion investment. Forecasts have to map operating costs to expected demand, competitor moves, and other changes, for instance in technology and regulations. All these forecasts are subject to the uncertainty of market conditions and they still need to be verified as accurately as possible by the business case team. The remaining uncertainty needs to be classified and dealt with mathematically as risk.

Case 1.11   Mayo Clinic expansion investment

The Mayo Clinic in Rochester, Minnesota, USA is part of an integrated medical center; its 33,500 staffs are dedicated to providing comprehensive diagnosis and treatment in virtually every medical and surgical specialty to 350,000 patients each year.[45]

After a three-year study, an expansion investment of $5 billion was proposed in January 2013 to make the Mayo Clinic a world destination for healthcare. And while the project requires $585 million in state money, it promises to create 35,000 to 45,000 new jobs over the next 20 years, generating more than $3 billion in new tax revenue.[46]

Diversification investments

A *diversification investment*, as opposed to an expansion investment, is an investment in new product lines, services, or hitherto not served markets. Case 1.12 exhibits why and how a food company diversified by establishing a new division. The challenge with diversification investments is that they are, when seen as standalone investments, unlikely to be lucrative. However, they can serve as a strategic entry point into new markets. They can set the path for other investments, which will build upon the initial ground work and then be profitable. Hence many diversification investments have an inherent strategic future option value and this has to be weighed alongside tangible cash inflows. Chapter 7 is dedicated to the art of valuing such future options in investment decisions. Case 1.13 is another example of how a an entire country diversified its national strategy away from only hydrocarbon and mining towards a more diversified production base by addressing structural challenges.

Case 1.12   Nestlé diversifies into the health business

Nestlé S.A. is a Swiss multinational company focusing on nutrition, health, and wellness. Measured by revenues, it is the world's largest food company and has some 8,000 brands with a wide range of products across a number of markets, including coffee, powdered milk, ice cream, baby food, chocolate, soups, and pet food.

In a change of strategic direction, Nestlé Health Science S.A. was founded and became operational on 1 January 2011 as a new wholly owned subsidiary. Its aim is to pioneer science-based nutritional solutions, together with the Nestlé Institute of Health Sciences, in order to deliver improved personalized healthcare for medical conditions, such as diabetes, obesity, cardiovascular disease, and Alzheimer's disease. Luis Cantarell, the first President and CEO of Nestlé Health Science S.A. says, "The largest drug you have in your repertoire is the food you eat."[47]

Nestlé bought three companies for the newly established division to support the effort to diversify into developing foods that can be used in the treatment of diseases:

- Vitaflo, a Liverpool-based firm making nutritional supplements for people with digestive disorder;

- The UK company CM&D, which has developed a chewing gum helping patients with kidney diseases; and

- San Diego-based company Prometheus Laboratories, which makes equipment used to diagnose and treat bowel complaints such as Crohn's disease.

It is thought to have paid about $1 billion for Prometheus Laboratories alone. The company aims to build the organization within two years, develop a product portfolio and pipeline within five years, and establish market leadership within a decade.

The reasons, simply stated, are to be found in growth and profit margins. Healthcare markets are expected to grow significantly faster than mature food product markets in the medium- and long-term. Especially in developing countries, which now have to handle an ageing population, consumers are increasingly prepared to spend more money on healthcare and nutrition. There is also sometimes a long lead time between new product development and product profitability, and profit margins in pharmaceuticals are generally much higher than those earned with food products.[48]

Case 1.13   Kazakhstan diversifies its national strategy

The Republic of Kazakhstan is the world's largest landlocked country (see Figure 1.15) and in the twenty years since its independence in December 1991, it has not only doubled its per capita income and halved its unemployment rate, but also emerged as a key economy in Central Asia, showing a strong economic performance with an average annual growth rate of over 9 per cent (real Gross domestic product (GDP)). However, the economy was narrowly concentrated in the hydrocarbon and mining sectors; oil and fuel products accounted for 65 per cent of Kazakhstan's exports. During the 2008–09 financial crises, it became obvious that there was a need to accelerate the diversification of the production base beyond these sectors.

The government adopted several measures to address structural challenges, for example the modernization of the banking sector, trade liberalization, adoption of an inflation target policy, and reduction of external debt. To support diversification into higher-value added industries, it invested in a number of development agencies and research centers, technology, and science parks. It approved a project in 2005 to design and develop clusters in tourism, textiles, agriculture and processed foods, minerals, and oil and gas. In the January 2010 annual message to the people of Kazakhstan, the president named the accelerated diversification of the economy as one of the five key directions and strategic targets for the next ten years.

Diversification investments in a country like Kazakhstan do not come without their very own challenges. The abundance of natural resources can lead to an appreciation of the country's real exchange rate, making the export of manufactured goods less competitive in comparison to other countries. This would increase imports and start a process of de facto de-industrialization. Such challenges can be tackled through the building of strong core capabilities, an appropriate use of energy revenues, improvement of institutional quality to fight corruption, creation of accountability through implementation of a free press, and an ongoing democratization process. Some resource-rich countries like Norway, Botswana, and Malaysia have successfully dealt with similar challenges in the past.[49]

Cost-saving investments

Cost-saving investments promise future cost savings through investing in something new, changing technology, or adapting

Figure 1.15 *Kazakhstan – The world's largest landlocked country*[50]

processes for example. Throughout the lifetime of the investment there will be a payback of the upfront investment through efficiency gains. Cases 1.14 and 1.15 show how two companies of different sizes have invested in new production facilities and innovation in order to bring in more efficiency, increase productivity, and save costs.

Cost-saving investment decisions are most often a question of choosing between the alternative of not doing anything and various options with different costs and different potential benefits. These benefits will often be intangible in nature, such as improved quality or improved speed, and the challenge of the business case is to convert such elusive arguments into quantifiable monetary metrics. Section 4.5 is dedicated to dealing with non-monetary benefits.

Case 1.14   Farmers Rice Milling invests in distribution facility

Farmers Rice Milling Company, a division of The Powell Group, operates the largest rice mill in Louisiana, USA, and employs more than 150 people in the rice mill and related facilities in and around Lake Charles and its headquarters in Baton Rouge. The company purchases rice from rice-growing regions throughout Louisiana, mills the rough rice, and then packages and distributes clean rice to customers in the USA and worldwide to more than 40 countries.

In January 2013, the mill announced a 55,000-square-foot expansion of the clean rice packaging and distribution facility. The project costs are estimated to be $13.4 million and the benefits are seen in increasing processing speed and volume. In addition to an increasing economic impact, the investment helps to retain jobs.[51]

Case 1.15   Procter & Gamble innovates to save costs

P&G is an American multinational corporation manufacturing a wide range of consumer goods; it recorded $82.6 billion in sales in 2011 and is focused on strategies that are right for the company's long-term health and delivering more than average total shareholder return. At P&G, restructuring work for cost savings and productivity improvement is managed as an ongoing business activity and deeply ingrained in the corporate culture. Productivity and savings projects cover all areas of the business and all elements of cost, for example[52]:

- Raw and packaging materials. The company's researchers continually search for new formulations and designs that lower cost, improve performance, and increase value for consumers. For instance, new formulations of laundry detergents significantly reduced the use of packaging material, leading not only to more consumer convenience and less waste for the environment, but probably most importantly to direct cost savings.

- Manufacturing expenses. The construction of more local and multi-category manufacturing plants closer to the consumer not only helps to build strong international relationships and deepen the understanding of local consumer needs, but above all, enables the sourcing of local materials, lowers distribution costs, and reduces the cost of import duties.

- Finished product logistics. By optimizing the finished-product supply chain and reducing the number of distribution centers, P&G not only improves its service levels to its customers, but also generates cost savings in shipping and warehousing.

- Marketing. Changing the mix of marketing tools results in targeting consumers more effectively. The television advertising budget for the feminine care products Always and Tampax was reduced in favor of magazine ads and building the website BeingGirl.com, which resulted in higher returns.

- Sales. Implementing faster decision-making processes, streamlining the organizational structure in developing markets, and implementing smaller local organizations reduces the go-to-market costs in Latin America, Central and Eastern Europe, and South-East Asia.

- Administration. Measuring overhead costs as a percentage of sales is implemented as a guideline for driving up organizational productivity. It is followed by measures aiming at reducing senior management positions, cutting the number of staff on international expatriate assignments, implementing a corporate shared services structure, and reducing staffing duplication among global, regional, and local organizations.

The savings achieved through productivity efforts and rigorous cost discipline in turn fund investments in innovation and marketing support. Alan G. Lafley, former Chairman of the Board and CEO, P&G, explains: "We see it as a virtuous circle. So, the more productive we become, the more we can invest or reinvest in innovation. The more innovation we create, the more growth we drive. And, we're very interested in the consistency and the sustainability of our growth. So we need to make sure that our productivity, strategies, and programs are consistent and sustained, and then we need to make sure that the investment that we make in innovation is consistent and sustained. And in the end, that our strategies and our processes of innovation consistently and sustainably turn out innovations that make consumers' lives better."[53]

R&D or seed corn investments

Just like expansion investments, *research and development (R&D) investments* are investments in the future of the business. Money spent today will help the organization to secure its place in the business arena of tomorrow. However, unlike with expansion investments, the company does not expect R&D investments to deliver direct future benefits, but aims to produce an economically viable investment proposal based on the outcome of the R&D investment. Hence R&D investments are sometimes also called *seed corn investments* and represent the management's belief that the company's future depends on researching and developing new cutting-edge products ahead of the competition. Therefore, companies should invest as much in a portfolio of seed corn investments as they can comfortably afford.

A business case is the right tool to evaluate and decide between many kinds of investments. However, given the special aim of R&D investments to produce new investment ideas, a business case is the wrong tool for managing seed corn investments. Nonetheless, from a review perspective, it may make sense to calculate an ex-post business case over the R&D outcome to see how well the company was doing with its seed corn investments.

Response options

Response options are investments or actions that may be taken to mitigate the negative effects of a *trigger event* before the *impact* is actually felt.[54] Likewise, they can help to leverage the positive aspects of an event. For instance, if the sales volume is falling (the trigger event), the company's revenue is likely to go

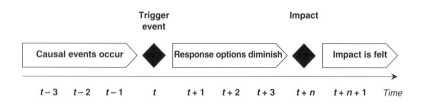

Figure 1.16 *Narrowing of responses to an event*

down (the impact). A possible response option could be to invest in more advertising in order to bring up the sales volume again.

However, as time passes after such a trigger event occurs, the company's leadership is left with fewer and fewer response options before the impact is noticeable, for example, in the next updated P&L account or later in the balance sheet. The narrowing of the possible responses is graphically shown in Figure 1.16; the somewhat spectacular Case 1.16 of charting response options for threatening Near Earth Objects (NEOs) expounds the idea once more.

It is thus crucial for the economic well-being (and survival) of an enterprise to understand its environment in *real time*, to be able to interpret the meaning and implication of information as it comes in, and use it for making sound decisions. As discussed in Section 1.2, there are no business surprises; instead, there is always a warning, and by monitoring the environment and the progress of the company in this environment on a daily basis, managers can not only avoid surprises, but turn them into opportunities by deciding on the right response options.

Case 1.16   Charting response options for Near Earth Objects

In March and June 2002, two asteroids passed close by the Earth, and even though they were each the size of a football field in width, their passing went by virtually unnoticed. Had either of them hit the Earth, an explosion about five thousand times larger than the Hiroshima nuclear bomb would have occurred. In its long history, the Earth has been hit by numerous asteroids and comets; such bodies are commonly referred to as NEOs. More than 160 impact sites are known the world over. It is estimated that the Earth will be struck by another 1 km wide NEO in the next hundred years with a probability of 0.1 per cent; a collision with an NEO wider than 2 km would mean a global catastrophe. The threat appears to be significant.

Is it possible to detect a threatening event like an NEO? What would be the impact of a collision? And what response options can be taken by mankind between the detection of an NEO and its collision with Earth to avoid the impact?

The direct and indirect impact of an NEO on Earth and the level of catastrophe caused depends largely on the characteristics of the body (size, speed, mass, material, composition, trajectory) as well as the characteristics of the impact site (land, ice, ocean, latitude) and the climatic conditions (season, stage of ice age). If the NEO were to hit an ocean, it would possibly generate a tsunami affecting coastlines globally. If it were to hit a land mass, shock waves would travel away from the impact. In addition, the dust thrown into the atmosphere would darken the sky up to a point that photosynthesis is reduced.

A major step in assessing this hazard is to identify causal events in the form of threatening objects, characterize them long before they come any close, and predict their path. Discovery techniques range from amateur telescopes to advanced methods using Charged Coupled Devices (CCD) with scanning techniques. Once a potentially threatening NEO event is detected, its orbit can be calculated using simple methods of astrometry and once it comes closer to Earth, radar can be used to follow up accurately.

One of the big problems after the event of detecting a NEO is the amount of real-time data to handle. Up to now, a great deal of data management has been done by astronomers themselves and of course, the speed at which this can be done is far from satisfactory.

Response options can be split into deflection, destruction, and protection. Unfortunately, deflection and destruction of NEOs in space is still in the realm of science fiction, although studies have shown the technical feasibility. This leaves impact mitigation as a possibility to protect the Earth. But as of today, there is neither funding nor an official program dedicated to the creation of an effective response system. Most studies and works are only theoretical proposals and suggestions. Does the threat of a NEO not warrant a business case?[55]

Investments by dependency

Investments can also be categorized according to their dependency on other investments into independent investments, mutually exclusive investments, and contingent investments (see Figure 1.14). The degree of mutual dependency between investments serves as a second category for distinguishing investments.

Independent investments can be considered independently of each other, and an investment decision depends upon whether they add value to the business. Provided there are sufficient resources to fund all of them, acceptance or rejection of any one of them does not directly eliminate or affect the likelihood of selecting the other investments.

When two or more investments cannot be pursued simultaneously, they are called *mutually exclusive investments*. They involve either-or decisions based on which will yield the highest value to the business; the acceptance of one prevents the acceptance of all others. For instance, a firm may either build an apartment building or a production plant on a plot of land; it may outsource fulfillment either to provider A or to provider B; and it may implement a CRM system by either vendor A or vendor B. Road safety can be increased by various measures; however, they are mostly mutually exclusive, as Case 1.17 shows. Such mutually exclusive investments should be identified early on in the investment decision process in order to avoid projects being started and cancelled again.

Case 1.17   Mutually exclusive highway safety alternatives

About 80,000 vehicles per day use the intersection of M-97 (Groesbeck Highway) and Metropolitan Parkway in Macomb County, Michigan, within the Detroit metropolitan area; both roads are multi-lane facilities and Metropolitan Parkway is divided by a median (use the coordinates 42.569302, −82.912244 to see the crossroads in a web mapping service application). No left turn is allowed on the intersection; near and far signal heads are in operation for M-97. Multiple driveway access points exist on M-97; a pedestrian over-bridge exists south of the intersection.

Based upon an analysis of three-year crash data, the location experienced an annual average of 23 human injury crashes and 47 property damage crashes, i.e. there is a crash almost every fifth day. A review of the site and of crash reports has resulted in the following probable reasons for the comparatively high number of crashes:

- No curbs on both streets

- Too many driveway activities

- Insufficient lane directions

- Heavy traffic on driveway around intersection

- Heavy right turn traffic from M-97 to Metropolitan Parkway

- Poor pavement condition

- Poor lighting at intersection

Countermeasures can be grouped into sets of six alternatives (see Figure 1.17). Each alternative consists of a number of improvements costing a certain amount of money to implement. Each improvement can be associated with a crash reduction factor (CRF); these are derived from other comparable post-project evaluations.

Obviously, the six alternatives are mutually exclusive and the Highway Authorities can only decide to implement one of them. The purpose of evaluating the alternatives is now to select the one with the highest benefit for implementation.

In a project investing in public infrastructure, the definition of highest benefit is probably governed by at least three policies:

- Constrained resource viewpoint. As resources available for funding public projects are generally short of demand, the least cost project should be selected (see Section 5.4 on capital rationing), where the benefits exceed the costs.

- Investment viewpoint. Of course, at the same time, the chosen alternative should fetch the highest return to the taxpayer. Marginal costs between alternatives should be examined and have to be justified. At the end, the alternative with the highest return to the taxpayer should be selected.

- Face value. Last but not least, there should be a measure of effectiveness, i.e. the chosen alternative should provide the highest amount of benefit per-unit cost.

The Highway Authorities now need to bring together a business case team (see Section 1.8) and evaluate each of the six alternatives under the three policy objectives. This case is continued as a worked example in Section 5.6.[56]

	List of countermeasures with individual CRFs included in alternative	Combined CRF	Initial investment required
Alternative 1	1. Install proper signs, CRF = 20% 2. Improve signal timings, CRF = 8%	26.4%	$110,000
Alternative 2	1. Close down multiple driveways and construct a new driveway with signalized operation to M-97, CRF = 10% 2. Improve pavement condition, CRF = 25% 3. Improve signal timings, CRF = 8%	37.9%	$214,000
Alternative 3	1. Prohibit on-street parking, CRF = 30% 2. Improve intersection lighting, CRF = 30% 3. Divide M-97 with raised median near intersection in order prohibit left turns, CRF = 30% 4. Improve signal timing, CRF = 8%	63.9%	$258,000
Alternative 4	1. Curbs on Metropolitan Parkway, CRF = 10% 2. Separate entry and exit gates by raised median at driveways, CRF = 10% 3. Divide M-97 with raised median near intersection in order to prohibit left turns, CRF = 30% 4. Install proper signs, CRF = 20% 5. Improve signal timings, CRF = 5%	64.2%	$444,000
Alternative 5	1. Curbs on Metropolitan Parkway (both directions), CRF = 10% 2. Install proper signs, CRF = 20% 3. Divide M-97 with raised median in order to prohibit left turns, CRF = 40% 4. Close down multiple driveways and construct a new driveway with signalized operation to the M-97, CRF = 10% 5. Improve pavement condition, CRF = 25% 6. Improve signal timings, CRF = 8%	73.1%	$694,000
Alternative 6	1. Install roundabout, CRF = 60% 2. Improve pavement condition, CRF = 25% 3. Close down multiple driveways and construct new opening away from roundabout, CRF = 10% 4. Install proper warning signs, CRF = 10%	81.7%	$916,000

Figure 1.17 *Countermeasures grouped into alternatives*

Contingent investments are complementary or substitute investments, i.e. the decision to accept or reject one is dependent on the acceptance or rejection of one or several other investments. For example, the opening of a health club and a restaurant complement each other in that they drive business from the health club to the restaurant and vice versa. Two different restaurants in the same shopping mall, however, may adversely affect each other's degree of success because there may not be sufficient customer footfall to generate enough demand.

1.5   INFRASTRUCTURE INVESTMENT FRAMEWORK

For many years corporations have struggled to achieve both short-term profitability and long-term growth through their infrastructure investments, for example, in IT, IS, office buildings, sales outlets, or manufacturing plants. Most corporations have expected profitability to come from expansion or diversification investments (see Section 1.4), i.e. from investments into new business areas. At the same time, they have regarded infrastructure investments as something that are at best a necessary evil for long-term survival.

Our increasingly networked business world, electronic integration of the supply chain, and ecommerce opportunities on the end-customer side, together with globalization, have changed these perceptions. Related infrastructure investments have now also become critical to short-term profitability.

Today, infrastructure investments differ along two dimensions[57]:

- Objectives, which highlight the trade-offs between short-term profitability and long-term growth; and

- Scope, which distinguishes between shared infrastructure and business solutions.

To address these two dimensions, four distinct types of infrastructure investments can be identified (see Figure 1.18):

- Transformation,

- Improvement,

- Renewal, and

- Experiment.

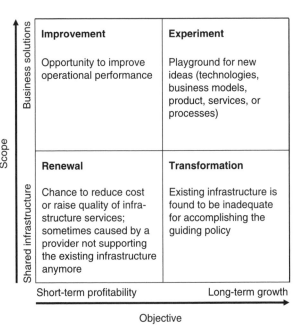

Figure 1.18 *Framework for infrastructure investments*[58]

Case 1.18   IT investment overhaul at Delta Air Lines

Back in 1997, when Leo Mullin became new CEO of Delta, the airline rated last on all three key customer metrics for the airline industry: on-time arrivals, customer complaints to the American DoT (Department of Transportation), and baggage handling statistics. Employees were demoralized and industry analysts regarded Delta as a laggard. In addition, the airline's outsourced IT infrastructure was seriously outdated and unlikely to cope with the millennium year change from 1999 to 2000, back then commonly known as the Year 2000 (Y2K) bug.

Seeking to avert a crisis, Delta Air Lines started investing $1 billion in its IT infrastructure in 1997 over a three-year period. It decommissioned dozens of functionally oriented applications which were each running on their own distinct platforms and replaced them with a shared-data environment supporting an entirely new suite of applications and services. The new infrastructure, referred to as the airline's Digital Nervous System, is built around the firm's core processes. Data is captured in nine central databases (location, schedule, flight, maintenance, equipment, employee, aircraft, customer, and ticket) and applications were able to access the databases through a middleware layer using Tibco technology. The key feature of this structure is a publish-and-subscribe environment,[59] which makes data on flights, customers, crews, equipment, and baggage simultaneously available in real time to everyone with a need to know. With this new infrastructure, Delta was able to develop applications serving customers accurately and efficiently, facilitating equipment and crew reassignments during operational irregularities, and supporting security measures.

Three years later, in 2000, Delta Airlines was ranked in the top three on all three customer metrics, and employee morale ranked in the top quartile among US companies. Delta's IT subsidiary, Delta Technology, won the Smithsonian Award for Technology Innovation and Leo Mullin was named a member of "The E-Gang" by *Forbes* magazine in July 2000, one of 12 executives who were forcing the web to grow up.[60]

Distinguishing between these four investment types is rather difficult, although they are conceptually well separated. Sometimes, investments of one type prompt a follow-up investment of a different type.

Transformation investments become necessary when an organization's existing infrastructure limits its ability to accomplish its guiding policy (see Section 1.1). Businesses whose outdated infrastructure has pushed them into a competitive crisis tend to invest heavily in infrastructure overhauls. Case 1.18 gives details of the three-year IT overhaul at Delta Air Lines. Transformation intentionally changes an organization's infrastructure; this change usually comes with improvements in the area of process change.

Improvement investments help to deliver short-term profitability; related investments are typically low-risk and focus on operational outcomes without fundamentally changing existing processes. They normally build on existing infrastructure and this makes their outcome very predictable.

Renewal investments provide a chance to reduce infrastructure-related costs or improve the quality of infrastructure services. Most technologies and other types of infrastructure equipment eventually need to be retired as they become outdated or providers withdraw their maintenance support as they introduce new releases. The potential benefits of renewal investments typically include improved maintainability, reduced training requirements, increased efficiency, and upgraded standards. Renewal may foster improvement, but this is not the primary objective of a renewal investment; the value of a renewal does not depend on achieving an improvement, for example, by making a change to a business process. Hence renewal investments are usually initiatives which are driven by the organization's infrastructure functions themselves.

Experimental investments are a playground for new ideas. Companies need a steady stream of such experiments in order to learn about new opportunities. Examples of experimental investments are gauging customer interest in different sales channels, new supermarket locations, and learning whether customers can self-serve themselves through an online platform. Building on what is learned by experimenting, business cases then help to justify additional and well-targeted investments. Section 6.11 picks up the idea of testing ideas on a small scale first before rolling investments out in a "big bang." In hindsight, an experiment and a subsequent investment of a different type may look like a single investment, but companies should always make a distinction between the two. An investment in an experiment is supposed to reveal potential profitability, whereas an investment in any of the other three types is expected to yield direct and immediate benefits.

1.6   TRUSTWORTHY BUSINESS CASES

Business case shortcomings

Many business cases, once presented, are immediately turned down with one of only two killer phrases:

- "I don't believe it," or

- "I don't understand it, it's too complicated."

Now the business case is dead, and the proposed investment will be delayed at best or not approved at all. But why do members of the top management either not believing or not understanding the business cases that their teams have created? The underlying causes are plentiful. Often terminologies are confused: no definitions for words which may have different meanings in different businesses or contexts are provided. Metrics are not trusted or believed by the decision makers. Formulae are used which are either not widely accepted or not accepted by the financial management in the organization. Calculations often hide in lengthy spreadsheet formulae and are neither openly shown in the document nor explained in plain language. Last, but not least, of the many shortcomings in business cases are arithmetic errors or wrong cell references in the spreadsheet used for the calculation; regardless of how few and how small their effect, such errors have a devastating effect on the quality image of the business case.

With so many challenges and requirements, putting structure into the business case project helps towards building a business case that its creators are comfortable with and that top management can rely on. Few organizations have mastered this skill and Case 1.19 shows a typical example.

Case 1.19   Evaluating joint ventures at Merck

Judith C. Lewent joined Merck in 1980 and made a career out of measuring risk and reward through scientific models while incorporating strategic financial principles into the challenging environment of a pharmaceutical company. She assumed the position of chief financial officer at Merck in 1990 and stayed in this position until 2007.

In 1983, her job was to evaluate capital expenditures and joint ventures. She built a business case using Monte Carlo simulation (see Section 6.8) as a way to evaluate the projects. Her boss at the time suggested that because "no one was going to be able to understand that [...] we aren't going to share it." Only later did Judith Lewent realize that her boss did not understand the business case himself and therefore immediately turned it down.[61]

Recognizing a trustworthy business case

Some business cases are believable, some are not. Fortunately, it is not too difficult to recognize which business cases offer quality and which not. The five characteristics that managers should look at when evaluating the trustworthiness of a business case are depicted in Figure 1.19:

- Scope fit for impact of investment? The level of detail provided in the business case, its boundary (i.e. what is included in the business case and what not), and the effort that has gone into its analysis need to match the scope of the proposed investment.

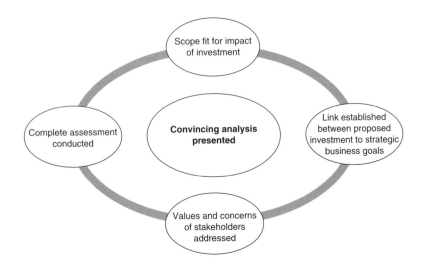

Figure 1.19 *Characteristics of a quality business case*

- Link established between proposed investments and strategic business goals? The investment's features and benefits need to link unambiguously to strategic business goals.

- Values and concerns of stakeholders addressed? All stakeholders participating in the decision need to be identified, along with their concerns and value systems. This increases the credibility of the assumptions in the analysis and ensures broad backing for the proposed investment.

- Complete assessment conducted? All tangible and intangible benefits, costs, uncertainties/risks, and future strategic options need to be assessed and combined into a NPV calculation; all assumptions have to be highlighted and explained.

- Convincing analysis presented? Last, but not least, and perhaps even most importantly, the analysis behind the business case should be to the point, proven, and convincing. The rationale of the calculation is explained and fully transparent.

The main body of the business case document should be between 5 and 10 pages long. Everything exceeding this should be banished to well-structured appendices. Business cases stretching over more pages are found tiresome; they diffuse their main message and will typically not be read in such great detail by the decision makers.

The document's format can either be a report (text document) or a presentation (slides). If one uses the presentation mode, it is recommended to work with a storyboard in the headline, sub-titles, and take-away boxes at the bottom of each page to facilitate understanding and coherency. The whole of Chapter 8 is dedicated to the fine art of presenting the business case.

Finally, a business case should not be outdated or timeworn. Once a business case has been written, it should not be left undecided and unimplemented for a long time. Business is typically in a flux of change, external factors will vary, costs may go up, the competition will act, and it might not be possible to reap the benefits according to the earlier estimation. Also, stakeholders may change their opinions or move to different positions in the organization, where they will have different responsibilities or interests – and where they may ultimately no longer support the original business case.

Required skills

It is not exactly difficult to build sound business cases. But the reality in today's corporate world is that selecting and deciding on investments is a breeding ground for politics, emotions, and resulting misunderstandings. Acting in this hotbed requires the business case creator to possess a certain skill-set, which can best be described by looking at the four distinct hats that the business case creator needs to wear in a business case project:

- *Project manager*. Intelligently organizes the process of putting together the business case, weighing the need for speed and keeping costs down against accuracy.

- *Politician*. Discovers the needs of stakeholders and differentiates their importance.

- *Investigative analyst*. Cleverly interviews stakeholders, extracts relevant data, and uncovers evidence. Appraises, weighs, and approximates information – and still manages to accurately calculate the financial rationale. Puts together a convincing report.

- *State attorney*. Constructs a rationale for the investment decision and presents it compellingly before top management.

Unfortunately, this skill-set can rarely be found in one person alone, so most business cases are built by a team rather than by an individual.

1.7   ENTERPRISE ANALYSIS

Well before an investment decision is put on the table, and certainly well before the business case team is assembled, *enterprise analysis* identifies areas of investment decision that make sense. It builds upon and refines the kernel of corporate strategy (see Section 1.1) and is composed of the three main activities shown in Figure 1.20:

- Creating the business architecture,

- Conducting feasibility studies, and

- Scoping the business opportunity.

Creating the business architecture

The creation of the *business architecture* is the first step of enterprise analysis. A business architecture helps to understand the current state of the organization and its plans for the future; it

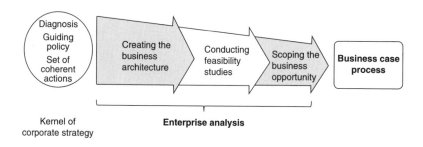

Figure 1.20 *Activities of enterprise analysis*

is essentially a summary of the strategy's coherent actions (see the Rumelt framework of good corporate strategy, Section 1.1) which help organize and make sense of all the changes a business has to manage. It is also somewhat paradoxical, in that it has to provide a solid structure and at the same time enough flexibility to accommodate changing requirements. In practical terms, creating the business architecture involves writing a set of documents which explain the company's business strategy and identify its main stakeholders.

Various techniques are used for business architecture modeling. For instance, a *component business model* (CBM) gives a complete view of the organization on a single page to show where changes need to be made and which changes will have the most impact, both internally as well as externally. Internally, components help firms rethink the leverage they can achieve with the assets and capabilities they own to achieve benefits of scale, flexibility, and efficiency. Externally, components help firms source specialized capabilities that they cannot feasibly create themselves, allowing them to redefine their competitive positions in the face of sweeping changes in the marketplace. CBMs are created by identifying the modular building blocks of a company and then assigning them to one of the three accountability levels: direct, control, and execute.[62] A *business process model* (BPM) describes the flow of activities with their inputs, outputs, and resources on an enterprise-wide perspective. It shows how business processes relate to each other so that redundancies can be eliminated. By focusing on outputs, it helps to determine what activities need to be completed to satisfy business needs.[63] *Class models* show relationships between static information in the form of hierarchical tree diagrams; they are useful in defining the design of applications where one wants to identify how different elements work together. *Use case models* describe complete business processes or information system functions. They are used to gain agreement among stakeholders on exactly what behavior or output is expected from a process or an application and to communicate these requirements throughout the entire implementation process to all professionals involved.[64] *Business scenarios* give a complete description of a business problem and help to establish what actions need to be taken when planned or unplanned events occur; they are used when an organization requires a complete picture of a challenge and its corresponding solution.[65] And finally, as employees in an organization need to make sense of information in order to use it effectively, *knowledge management* focuses on the relationship between people and information, thereby transforming intellectual property into a permanent asset.[66]

Frameworks help to maintain structure in creating the business architecture; some established frameworks are:

- Zachman framework,

- POLDAT framework, or

- Strategy Maps.

Most people treat these frameworks as mutually exclusive, but in reality they are complementary and one should pick and choose the elements which best contribute to solving the problem at hand.[67]

The *Zachman framework* is essentially a six by five matrix that allows collecting, organizing, and analyzing data. The rows represent the different perspectives of the enterprise: scope, business model, system model, technology model, and component configuration. The columns represent fundamental questions that have to be answered to design a business entity: what? (data), how? (function), where? (network), who? (people), when? (time), and why? (modification).[68]

The *POLDAT framework* is a somewhat simpler model in which tables, graphs, and other documentation are organized into six different categories from which the business situation is viewed:

- Business processes that generate and deliver value to the customer.

- Organizational elements that operate the business processes: management, staff, roles, competencies, knowledge, and skills.

- Physical location of the business units, for example, production sites, call centers.

- Data and information that pass through each process and are used to accomplish the business functions.

- Information systems (IS) applications enable business processes to function smoothly.

- Information technology (IT) and other infrastructure needed to support the functioning of the applications and processes.

If a change occurs in one category, changes must also take place in all the other five areas so that equilibrium in the organization can be maintained.[69]

A *Strategy Map* documents the primary strategic goals of an organization; as a framework, strategy maps have evolved from the four-perspective model of the balanced scorecard.[70] Just as one cannot manage what one cannot measure, one cannot measure what cannot be described. While the balanced scorecard focuses on the link between managing and measuring, strategy maps serve as a communication tool to describe and document strategic goals using four perspectives: financial perspective, customer perspective, internal process perspective, and learning and growth perspective.[71] Section 4.2 makes use of the concept of strategy maps to identify investment benefits.

Conducting feasibility studies

Once the business architecture has been developed and potential supporting investments, programs, and projects have been identified to plan for the future, the *feasibility study* as the second activity of enterprise analysis helps to determine which of the earlier ideas look most promising in terms of satisfying the business needs. The outcome of the feasibility study is a recommended solution, which will be shaped in the next phase and then further explored in the business case process. The study effort is usually broken down into five stages:

- Research and plan the study,

- Conduct an as-is assessment,

- Identify potential solutions,

- Determine their feasibility, and

- Communicate and document the results.

Market surveys, prototyping, and technology capability assessments are techniques commonly used to support the feasibility analysis. As a result, one might find that an investment idea is not sound and thereby save money and effort by killing the idea early on in the investment decision process.

Scoping the business opportunity

Now that the solution to the business problem is identified, the scoping of the business opportunity can take place. The outcome of this third activity of enterprise analysis is a document that describes the solution in enough detail to build a compelling business case. It involves a high-level description of the work that must be completed in order to implement the proposed investment project, breaking it down into smaller deliverables by means of a work breakdown structure, and putting together a high-level project milestone plan. Sometimes, first cost estimates are already included in this phase providing a first guideline to the business case team.

A clear definition of the investment project is a necessary input to the business case process. While the information collected during enterprise analysis will later need to be refined, it helps in building compelling business cases efficiently.

1.8 BUSINESS CASE PROJECT

The business case builds upon enterprise analysis (see Section 1.7); Figure 1.21 breaks down a typical *business case project* into six distinct phases with associated tasks. The first five phases belong to the *top-down business case*, after which the go-ahead for the investment is given. The sixth phase measures the investment's success through the *bottom-up business case*.

Phase 1: Understand

Many disappointments about business cases can be avoided by initially spending some time to determine the exact nature and challenge of the investment decision and the business case

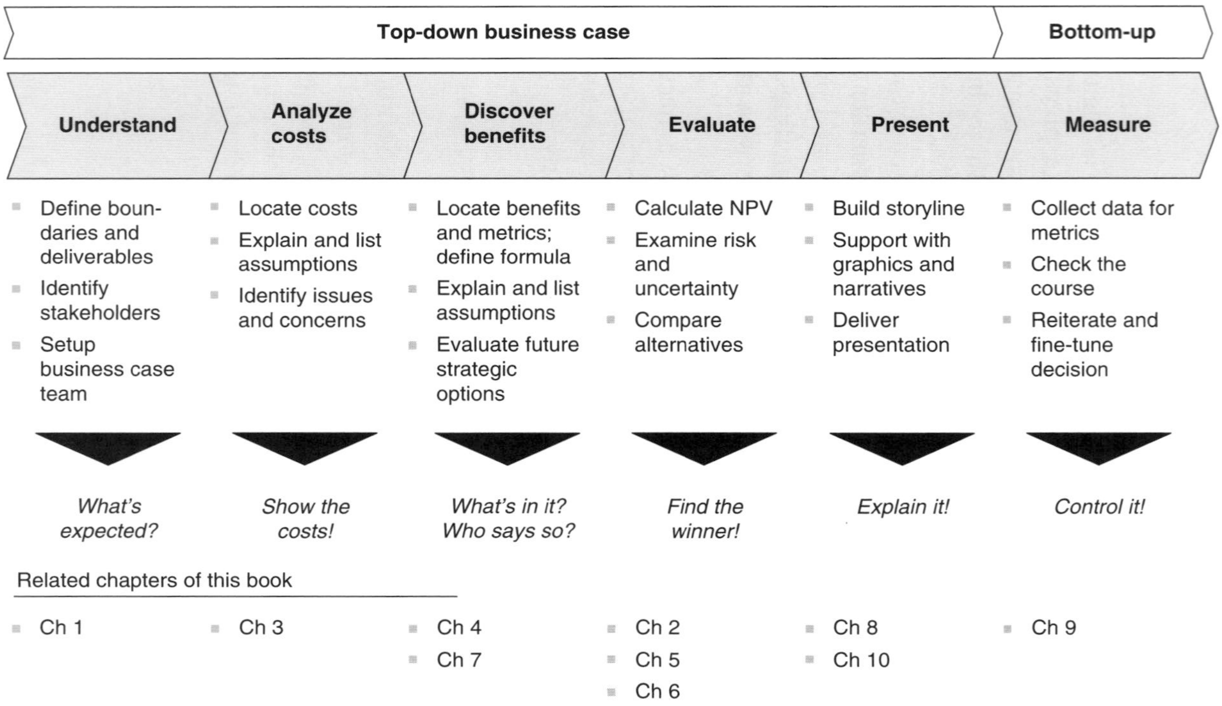

Top-down business case					Bottom-up
Understand	**Analyze costs**	**Discover benefits**	**Evaluate**	**Present**	**Measure**
▪ Define boundaries and deliverables ▪ Identify stakeholders ▪ Setup business case team	▪ Locate costs ▪ Explain and list assumptions ▪ Identify issues and concerns	▪ Locate benefits and metrics; define formula ▪ Explain and list assumptions ▪ Evaluate future strategic options	▪ Calculate NPV ▪ Examine risk and uncertainty ▪ Compare alternatives	▪ Build storyline ▪ Support with graphics and narratives ▪ Deliver presentation	▪ Collect data for metrics ▪ Check the course ▪ Reiterate and fine-tune decision
What's expected?	*Show the costs!*	*What's in it? Who says so?*	*Find the winner!*	*Explain it!*	*Control it!*

Related chapters of this book

▪ Ch 1	▪ Ch 3	▪ Ch 4 ▪ Ch 7	▪ Ch 2 ▪ Ch 5 ▪ Ch 6	▪ Ch 8 ▪ Ch 10	▪ Ch 9

Figure 1.21 *Business case project as a process*

to be constructed. During the first phase, *understand*, the focus should be on the following two points:

- Identify the parties holding a stake in this decision, determine what they care about, and understand the process by which the decision would be made.

- Assemble a small but powerful team who will work together throughout the entire business case process.

Part-time delegates from some stakeholder groups have no place in the core team. The task of constructing a business case is far too intensive (if not stressful), the results are far too important for the financial performance of the company, and the output politically far too important for the core team to be staffed with part-time employees. Experience shows that part-time members of the business case team cannot balance the requirements of their line job with the analytically challenging job of establishing a business case. If stakeholder groups try to press part-time delegates into the business case team, this request should be firmly denied. Instead, the same members of these stakeholder groups can later be interviewed and their opinions will be invaluable for estimating costs or establishing the benefit logic. However, they have no place in constructing the business case logic.

Phase 2: Analyze costs

The core task of the second phase, *analyze costs*, is to locate all business areas where the investment produces costs. Some of them may be immediately visible and linked to the investment; others may be transitive in nature and can only be discovered by thinking about cause and effect relationships. Estimates for costs need to be agreed with stakeholders, the reasoning and calculation behind the estimates documented, and all assumptions clearly listed, as they need to be revisited later when examining risk and uncertainty in the fourth phase. Implementation challenges and other issues need to be collected and documented, and the costs of their avoidance evaluated.

Phase 3: Discover benefits

New investments have to be aligned with the corporate strategy. Hence the task of the third phase, *discover benefits*, is to evaluate the logic of how positive outcomes of the investment can support the corporate strategy; this evaluation is called the benefit logic and it contains metrics to measure positive outcomes and formulae to aggregate them towards the corporate strategy. Needless to say, the benefit logic requires excellent documentation and an exhaustive list of assumptions for revisiting in the fourth phase. Some investments provide for flexibility, adaptability, and scalability, benefiting the business case of potential future add-on investments; the potential value of such strategic flexibility options needs to be examined and valued.

Phase 4: Evaluate

While the first three phases of the business case project are about collecting data and evidence, and establishing rationale, the fourth phase, *evaluate*, is where all the gathered information is put together, condensed, and processed to one final number. This number unveils the business reason for recommending or rejecting the proposed investment project(s). Of course, this involves financial calculations (most often using the NPV method), but also testing the outcome for risk and uncertainty, and finally comparing all the possible alternatives.

Phase 5: Present

A well-done story supported with graphics and narratives often makes or breaks the business case. It gives it the ability to communicate effectively with decision makers. The fifth phase, *present*, does exactly that: it puts together all the hard work and investigative results from the previous phases in an easy-to-understand format. The effort which goes into preparing the final presentation and passing it once more through the stakeholders for review and approval should never be underestimated. There might even be an iterative step back to one of the previous phases to collect further data or furnish assumptions with evidence.

Phase 6: Measure

Several events take place between the fifth and sixth phases after presenting the business case: the executive decision making, the commissioning of the investment, and the go-live into production.

And while nobody ever plans not to realize the benefits from an investment, Section 1.2 has shown many examples of failed investments in the international business arena. Benefits only come true when management continues to monitor the investment. Therefore, the sixth phase of the business case project, *measure*, has to be about ensuring that an ongoing management process exists, which in turn ensures ongoing project success.

First and foremost, data need to be collected to support measurement of the benefit logic as established in the third phase. These metrics then need to be monitored and analyzed, and the conclusions fed into an ongoing management decision process, which could mean a fine-tuning of the investment, add-on investments, or even the early decommissioning of a failed investment.

1.9 STRUCTURE OF A BUSINESS CASE

A business case can first and foremost be seen as a process, i.e. as a project with a start date, which takes information as input and produces a well-defined output (see Section 1.3). The real value of a business case project is in the learning that takes place while putting together the document. It may even stop an organization from embarking upon an unsound investment, and hence the benefits of the business case usually far exceed its costs – making a business case for the business case.

The structure of the output document is the second view of the business case; Section 8.2 goes into it in more detail and proposes a sample structure. But in its simplest form, a business case is assembled from the four main components shown in Figure 1.22:

- Costs,

- Benefits,

- Risk and uncertainty, and

- Strategic flexibility options.

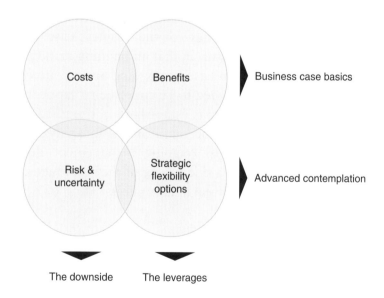

Figure 1.22 *Four main components of the business case*

While costs and benefits are the basics of every business case (see Chapters 3 and 4), studying risk and uncertainty associated with a suggested investment (see Chapter 6) and considering its strategic flexibility options (see Chapter 7) are the more advanced elements. Benefits and strategic flexibility options are in favor of the investment, costs and risk with respect to uncertainty weigh against the calculation.

Before any investment decision is made (in fact before a suggestion is even presented to the decision makers) it is beneficial to have all the facts organized according to these four components. However, organization alone does not yet build a compelling argument; one very much needs to understand the executive decision-making process in order to build a compelling decision package for senior management attention. Chapter 8 will discuss the art of presenting business cases.

1.10   CONSENSUS AND STAKEHOLDER MANAGEMENT

Importance of consensus and stakeholder management

Starting a new project to implement an investment decision is usually not a choice of business case rationality alone. Often it does not follow strict mathematical logic, but it affects and sometimes even threatens the interests of many groups in an organization. For an investment decision not to be a declaration of war, it is important to build consensus while the business case is being written, and certainly well before it is proposed to senior management. Such consensus building requires an understanding of important business issues.

A comprehensive business case involves looking beyond financial estimates and mathematical calculations and takes into account the central business issues, the firm's organizational structure, its processes and practices, and individual influencers. This certainly does not imply that a careful financial analysis is not central. Conversely, as any financial forecast is sensitive to uncertainty and change, it is important to understand that financial estimates and assumptions are always the opinions of individual contributors. Such individuals are *stakeholders* in the success of the investment decisions; they can either influence decisions or, vice versa, be affected by the same decisions themselves. As such, stakeholders want to be consulted and managed. The best possible financial estimate needs to rest on the shoulders of a broad majority of stakeholders.

How well the benefits of an investment can be achieved and how realistic the cost estimates were are always dependent on the commitment of the people involved in executing the investment project. And because the outcome of the investment is a function of the commitment of its stakeholders, a business case always contains a certain degree of subjectivity; therefore consensus building and stakeholder management is so important in the business case process.

Viewing this aspect from a slightly different angle, the aim to establish a business case can also serve as a vehicle to establish consensus among stakeholders by researching their differences in opinion and jointly resolving them. The final business case should then have resolved most of the differences and present a version to senior management, which is as objective as possible and has the buy-in of as many stakeholders as possible.

Although complete objectivity and complete buy-in of all stakeholders may not always be possible, it makes very much sense to set it as a target and work towards it. If consensus cannot be achieved among the stakeholders, then the investment's risk profile is very high and will ultimately endanger successful implementation.

Types of stakeholders

Although there can be many types of stakeholders, in an investment decision context it is useful to group them into the categories proposed in Figure 1.23.

As the execution of some investment decisions means changes at the very heart of the business, the firm's *top management* can

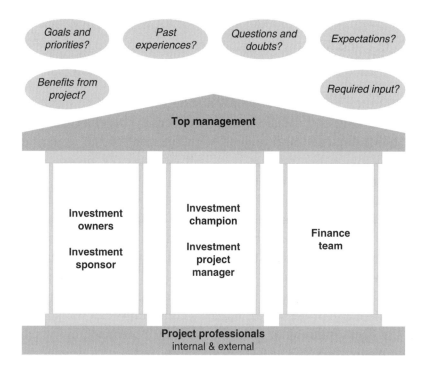

Figure 1.23 *Types of stakeholders and position analysis*

be a crucial overriding stakeholder and should therefore receive special attention in the stakeholder management process.

Then there is a group of employees in the company which is going to make intensive use of the investment once it has been commissioned. These *investment owners* are likely to have a high impact in making the investment successful. They can be found everywhere, from departmental managers to individuals processing business events or using an information system. One of the investment owners originally had the idea to initiate the investment or was senior enough to drive the investment suggestion through the approval process; this *investment sponsor* will take a personal interest in the business case and the investment's implementation.

Another person will assume the role of an *investment champion* and take ownership to ensure a successful implementation.

The *investment project manager* will assume a managerial perspective and take the investment from approval to go-live. Both the investment champion and the investment project manager usually only come on board after the investment decision has been taken and they have thus not been able to give input into the planning and decision-making process. Therefore they need to be on-boarded and aligned with the goal of the investment as quickly as possible, as they will become key people in the commissioning of the investment.

Last, but not least, *project professionals* execute the investment project in the commissioning phase by bringing in their subject matter or technical expertise. They can be either the company's own employees, external staff belonging to a consulting company or service provider, or a mix of the two. They can either work on-site in the company's premises or in a company's subsidiary anywhere else in the world. External consultants can work on-site in the firm's building or from the provider's premises, in the same country or abroad. The last option is referred to as a nearshore or offshore service delivery model.[72]

The job of the *finance team* is to make the necessary funds available, contract and pay for external services, and control the business case's cost forecast vs. actual spending. Hence they are important stakeholders in any investment decision for both the top-down as well as the subsequent bottom-up business case.

Stakeholder analysis

Each member of the above stakeholder groups will have different views of the investment. Stakeholder positions can best be analyzed by asking six powerful questions:

- What goals and priorities does the stakeholder have?

- What past experience does the stakeholder have with similar investments?

- How can the stakeholder benefit (or suffer) from the investment?

- What expectations about the project does the stakeholder have?

- What input is required from the stakeholder during the business case phase and during project implementation?

- What questions and doubts does the stakeholder have about the suggested investment?

At first glance these questions may not sound so powerful at all, maybe even simplistic, but finding answers to them can be challenging, and while it often involves a certain amount of guess work, it certainly requires time and a deep insight into the organization. Also, it is unlikely that one will get the answers right the first time; notwithstanding, the stakeholder analysis is an important instrument to analyze the possible thought structures, needs, and wants of people going to contribute information to the business case. Any approximation serves the purpose and it is a good idea to review the answers regularly to incorporate new insight information and also to see if stakeholders have changed their positions.

The first question on the goals and priorities of stakeholders is extremely important. It represents the stakeholder's decision criteria. Sometimes they are even hidden in the stakeholder's subconscious mind and this makes it even more central and challenging to fully identify them. Benefits generated through the proposed investment need to address these criteria to get the required stakeholder buy-in, but also, at the end of the chain, to support the firm's strategic objectives. Section 4.3 introduces the value panel as a powerful tool to support this difficult task.

Stakeholder mapping and management

With this information in mind, it is now possible to classify and segment stakeholders using three dimensions:

- *Supportiveness.* Are the stakeholders in favor of or against the investment? What do they gain or lose from the project?

- *Degree of activity.* Ideally, stakeholders should actively promote or oppose the investment as they are affected by the results. However, some may be more active (opinion formers) than others (influencers) and some may prefer to remain passive unless explicitly encouraged to voice their opinions (sleepers).

- *Importance.* How important is the stakeholder's opinion to the success of the investment project? How powerful is the stakeholder in supporting or hindering the project? Should one direct communication and influencing towards this person?

Figure 1.24 shows a possible stakeholder map showing all three dimensions. One could also differentiate between the stakeholder types by using different symbols; however, this usually overcomplicates the diagram and the type of stakeholder can best be captured in the naming itself. The relationship between different stakeholder groups can best be indicated by one-way or two-way arrows, showing who can influence whom. The absence of an arrow states that stakeholders are not connected and therefore do not influence each other.

Effort should be spent on managing stakeholders:

- *Sleeping partners* are supportive but with a low degree of activity; they should be incentivized to reach out to others and thereby moved up into the top right-quadrant of fans.

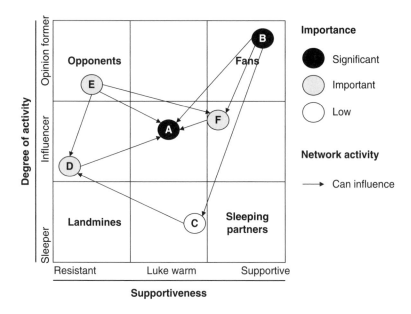

Figure 1.24 *Locating stakeholders*

- *Landmines* are resisting the investment but not actively fighting it; as a first step they should best be moved into the direction of sleeping partners.

- *Opponents* are actively opposing the investment and lobbying against it; every attempt should be made to control their ability to broadcast negative messages. Having them moved down to the bottom left-quadrant of landmines would be a first success in their management.

- *Fans* are actively supporting the investment. And while many of them will be self-directed, they still need to be fed with high-quality information around the investment, which they can further disseminate to others. Without this continuous stream of information input, their hands are bound and they are likely to descend to sleeping partners.

Decision participants

Decision participants are stakeholders who either directly influence or actually make the investment decision evaluated and presented by the business case team; they are often part of the top management team. They can be categorized into three groups:

- Decision makers,

- Decision recommenders, and

- Decision influencers.

These three groups together are the final audience for the business case, and this is the one which really counts for the go/no-go decision. Hence their members need to be identified by name and responsibility, and their values and goals need to be analyzed and understood. And again, the value panel which will be introduced in Section 4.3 is an appropriate framework for doing exactly this.

Case 1.20   Stakeholder analysis for the Zambia land reform project

The Republic of Zambia is a landlocked country in Southern Africa, bordering the Democratic Republic of Congo, Tanzania, Malawi, Mozambique, Zimbabwe, Botswana, and Namibia. The former British colony of Northern Rhodesia declared independence from the UK in 1964. The Zambian economy has historically been based on the copper mining industry, but the Government is pursuing an economic diversification program to promote tourism, gemstone mining, hydro-power, and agriculture. As part of a land reform program, the government proposed titling and converting some of the land under customary tenure (94 per cent of the land in Zambia) into state-owned land, thereby encouraging investment, development, and productivity through increased security and improved access to land. Due to a past history of reforms meeting resistance, the World Bank conducted a stakeholder analysis in 2002 and 2003 to provide a clear overview of the actors involved in the land reform as well as their positions and powers. The poverty and social impact assessment (PSIA) study was based on the premises that:

- Reform is a process,

- Implementation and policy design are equally important for a reform's impact,

- Unintended consequences are not always unpredictable, and

- In areas of uncertainty, an analysis of problems is most important.

The 33 identified stakeholder groups were categorized in four major categories:

- Government and state agencies,

- Private sector,

- Donors, and

- Civil society.

In order to place the stakeholders in a two-dimensional matrix similar to Figure 1.24, the stakeholder analysis needed to generate insights into the characteristics of the stakeholder groups with respect to the categories and how the reform would affect them; this insight would then relate to their anticipated support for or resistance to the reform. Information on the potential impact of the reform was derived from qualitative and quantitative analysis based on interviews, focus groups, and meetings. Interestingly, in the interviews, some stakeholders identified their positions themselves and their statements were then verified with data from the analysis.

Figure 1.25 reveals that the chiefs were to have a strong influence over the reform and at the same time also to be most harmed by the policy change. The Ministry of Agriculture also had a strong influence on the process, but was perceived to benefit from the reform and so was a potential driver of the reform process. The landless and minority ethnic groups had little influence over the process and were predicted to be harmed by the outcomes of the reform.

It was noticed, that there was a difference between interest and influence over decision making as compared to implementation of the reform. While some stakeholders, such as the Parliament or the President, have significant influence over decision making but not over implementation, others have a major influence over the implementation but relatively little over the reform design.

The PSIA study concluded that the benefits of the reform were questionable at best. Titling customary land would create conflict, and dispute-resolution mechanisms were not in place. It would also shift power to a centralized and not accountable bureaucracy, thereby undermining the traditional system which provides an important social safety net leading to social stability. In a nutshell, Zambia did not yet have the capacity to implement such a large-scale land reform without running great risks, and it therefore abandoned the idea.[73]

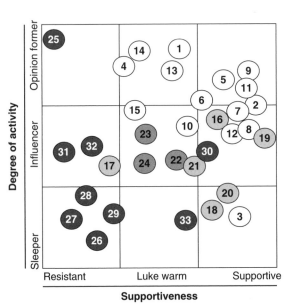

Degree of activity — Opinion former / Influencer / Sleeper

Supportiveness — Resistant / Luke warm / Supportive

⭘ **Government and state agencies**

1. The President
2. Ministry of Land
3. Lands Tribunal
4. Judiciary
5. Office of the Vice President
6. Ministry of Legal Affairs
7. Ministry of Local Government and Housing
8. City, municipal, and district councils
9. Ministry of Agriculture
10. Ministry of Works and Supply
11. Ministry of Commerce, Trade, and Industry
12. Ministry of Tourism, Environment, and Natural Resources
13. Ministry of Finance
14. Parliament
15. Police force, Ministry of the Interior

⭘ **Private sector**

16. Commercial farmers
17. Small-scale farmers
18. Surveyors
19. Lawyers
20. Foreign investors
21. Commercial banks

⬤ **Donors**

22. USAID
23. Word Bank/IMF
24. DFID, GTZ, EU

⬤ **Civil society**

25. Chiefs
26. Landless
27. Herders
28. FHHS, CHHs
29. Minority ethnic groups
30. Zambia National Farmers Union (ZNFU)
31. Local NGOs
32. International NGOs
33. Media

Figure 1.25 *Zambia land reform project*

2
Key Financial Concepts

When companies execute their corporate strategy, they search for assets, investments, or projects that are worth more to them than others. Unfortunately, in most cases they can only guess what the asset will be worth once they commission it and take it under their management. Therefore, financial managers and decision makers need to know how asset values are determined, today and in the future. They need to construct, understand, and apply a theory of value; in other words, they need to initiate a business case project.

This chapter provides an overview of key financial concepts. It first develops a theory of value and then moves on to outline selected financial models. These frameworks can be used first to capture investment ideas and scenarios and then to justify a decision using monetary terms and criteria.

2.1 TIME VALUE OF MONEY

The well-known and often quoted maxim

A dollar today is worth more than a dollar tomorrow

is probably the number one basic principle of finance. It is this simple because today's dollar can be invested to start earning interest immediately. And tomorrow's dollar can only be invested tomorrow: it is not available today and will thus lose out on immediate interest earnings.

Look at an example. If you were to invest $500,000 in government securities at an interest rate of, say, 5 per cent per annum (p.a.), a year from now you would receive:

$$\$500,000 \cdot (1+0.05) = \$525,000$$

Thus, the *future value* (FV) of $500,000 today is $525,000 a year from now. Two years from now the future value would be:

$$\$525,000 \cdot (1+0.05) = \$551,250$$

Substituting the first year equation into the second year equation enables us to calculate the future value of the second year directly:

$$\$500,000 \cdot (1+0.05) \cdot (1+0.05) = \$500,000 \cdot (1+0.05)^2$$
$$= \$525,000$$

In general, with x denoting the investment value, r the interest rate, and n the number of future periods, the future value function can be written as:

$$FV = x \cdot (1+r)^n$$

When interest is earned on interest, period after period, it is referred to as *compound interest*. The effect of compound interest is quite striking; Figure 2.1 illustrates how long it takes to double an initial investment making use of compound interest at different interest rates. At an interest rate of $r=1\%$ it takes almost 70 years to double the initial investment. At $r=3\%$ this comes down to 23 years, and at $r=15\%$ it takes only a short 5 years.

Let us turn the question around. Assuming that we already know the likely future payoff ($525,000), how do we uncover its present value (PV)? Obviously and in line with the previous

Interest rate r	Time until doubling $= \log_{1+r} 2$
0.50%	139.0 years
1.00%	69.7 years
1.50%	46.6 years
2.00%	35.0 years
3.00%	23.4 years
4.00%	17.7 years
5.00%	14.2 years
7.50%	9.6 years
10.00%	7.3 years
15.00%	5.0 years
20.00%	3.8 years

Figure 2.1 *Compound interest: Time until doubling*

discussion, one dollar next year must be worth less than a dollar today, because it cannot yet be invested today. Hence, as the time-value question is turned around, the future value formula can simply be reversed as well; the future payoff is now to be divided by $1 + r = 1.05$, resulting in the PV:

$$PV = \frac{\$525,000}{1.05} = \$525,000 \cdot \frac{1}{1.05} = \$500,000$$

Let C_1 now denote the expected payoff at one year from now (at date 1). The formula then reads:

$$PV = C_1 \cdot \frac{1}{1+r}$$

The multiplier $1/(1+r)$ is called the *discount factor* and r the *rate of return* which investors demand for accepting delayed payment. In financial management, the rate of return r is also referred to as the *discount rate, hurdle rate,* or *opportunity cost of capital*. All these terms are used interchangeably.

$t =$	$r =$ 1.00%	1.50%	2.00%	2.50%	3.00%	3.50%	4.00%	4.50%	5.00%	6.00%	7.00%	8.00%	9.00%	10.00%	11.00%	12.00%	13.00%	14.00%	15.00%
1	0.9901	0.9852	0.9804	0.9756	0.9709	0.9662	0.9615	0.9569	0.9524	0.9434	0.9346	0.9259	0.9174	0.9091	0.9009	0.8929	0.8850	0.8772	0.8696
2	0.9803	0.9707	0.9612	0.9518	0.9426	0.9335	0.9246	0.9157	0.9070	0.8900	0.8734	0.8573	0.8417	0.8264	0.8116	0.7972	0.7831	0.7695	0.7561
3	0.9706	0.9563	0.9423	0.9286	0.9151	0.9019	0.8890	0.8763	0.8638	0.8396	0.8163	0.7938	0.7722	0.7513	0.7312	0.7118	0.6931	0.6750	0.6575
4	0.9610	0.9422	0.9238	0.9060	0.8885	0.8714	0.8548	0.8386	0.8227	0.7921	0.7629	0.7350	0.7084	0.6830	0.6587	0.6355	0.6133	0.5921	0.5718
5	0.9515	0.9283	0.9057	0.8839	0.8626	0.8420	0.8219	0.8025	0.7835	0.7473	0.7130	0.6806	0.6499	0.6209	0.5935	0.5674	0.5428	0.5194	0.4972
6	0.9420	0.9145	0.8880	0.8623	0.8375	0.8135	0.7903	0.7679	0.7462	0.7050	0.6663	0.6302	0.5963	0.5645	0.5346	0.5066	0.4803	0.4556	0.4323
7	0.9327	0.9010	0.8706	0.8413	0.8131	0.7860	0.7599	0.7348	0.7107	0.6651	0.6227	0.5835	0.5470	0.5132	0.4817	0.4523	0.4251	0.3996	0.3759
8	0.9235	0.8877	0.8535	0.8207	0.7894	0.7594	0.7307	0.7032	0.6768	0.6274	0.5820	0.5403	0.5019	0.4665	0.4339	0.4039	0.3762	0.3506	0.3269
9	0.9143	0.8746	0.8368	0.8007	0.7664	0.7337	0.7026	0.6729	0.6446	0.5919	0.5439	0.5002	0.4604	0.4241	0.3909	0.3606	0.3329	0.3075	0.2843
10	0.9053	0.8617	0.8203	0.7812	0.7441	0.7089	0.6756	0.6439	0.6139	0.5584	0.5083	0.4632	0.4224	0.3855	0.3522	0.3220	0.2946	0.2697	0.2472
11	0.8963	0.8489	0.8043	0.7621	0.7224	0.6849	0.6496	0.6162	0.5847	0.5268	0.4751	0.4289	0.3875	0.3505	0.3173	0.2875	0.2607	0.2366	0.2149
12	0.8874	0.8364	0.7885	0.7436	0.7014	0.6618	0.6246	0.5897	0.5568	0.4970	0.4440	0.3971	0.3555	0.3186	0.2858	0.2567	0.2307	0.2076	0.1869
13	0.8787	0.8240	0.7730	0.7254	0.6810	0.6394	0.6006	0.5643	0.5303	0.4688	0.4150	0.3677	0.3262	0.2897	0.2575	0.2292	0.2042	0.1821	0.1625
14	0.8700	0.8118	0.7579	0.7077	0.6611	0.6178	0.5775	0.5400	0.5051	0.4423	0.3878	0.3405	0.2992	0.2633	0.2320	0.2046	0.1807	0.1597	0.1413
15	0.8613	0.7999	0.7430	0.6905	0.6419	0.5969	0.5553	0.5167	0.4810	0.4173	0.3624	0.3152	0.2745	0.2394	0.2090	0.1827	0.1599	0.1401	0.1229
16	0.8528	0.7880	0.7284	0.6736	0.6232	0.5767	0.5339	0.4945	0.4581	0.3936	0.3387	0.2919	0.2519	0.2176	0.1883	0.1631	0.1415	0.1229	0.1069
17	0.8444	0.7764	0.7142	0.6572	0.6050	0.5572	0.5134	0.4732	0.4363	0.3714	0.3166	0.2703	0.2311	0.1978	0.1696	0.1456	0.1252	0.1078	0.0929
18	0.8360	0.7649	0.7002	0.6412	0.5874	0.5384	0.4936	0.4528	0.4155	0.3503	0.2959	0.2502	0.2120	0.1799	0.1528	0.1300	0.1108	0.0946	0.0808
19	0.8277	0.7536	0.6864	0.6255	0.5703	0.5202	0.4746	0.4333	0.3957	0.3305	0.2765	0.2317	0.1945	0.1635	0.1377	0.1161	0.0981	0.0829	0.0703
20	0.8195	0.7425	0.6730	0.6103	0.5537	0.5026	0.4564	0.4146	0.3769	0.3118	0.2584	0.2145	0.1784	0.1486	0.1240	0.1037	0.0868	0.0728	0.0611
21	0.8114	0.7315	0.6598	0.5954	0.5375	0.4856	0.4388	0.3968	0.3589	0.2942	0.2415	0.1987	0.1637	0.1351	0.1117	0.0926	0.0768	0.0638	0.0531
22	0.8034	0.7207	0.6468	0.5809	0.5219	0.4692	0.4220	0.3797	0.3418	0.2775	0.2257	0.1839	0.1502	0.1228	0.1007	0.0826	0.0680	0.0560	0.0462
23	0.7954	0.7100	0.6342	0.5667	0.5067	0.4533	0.4057	0.3634	0.3256	0.2618	0.2109	0.1703	0.1378	0.1117	0.0907	0.0738	0.0601	0.0491	0.0402
24	0.7876	0.6995	0.6217	0.5529	0.4919	0.4380	0.3901	0.3477	0.3101	0.2470	0.1971	0.1577	0.1264	0.1015	0.0817	0.0659	0.0532	0.0431	0.0349
25	0.7798	0.6892	0.6095	0.5394	0.4776	0.4231	0.3751	0.3327	0.2953	0.2330	0.1842	0.1460	0.1160	0.0923	0.0736	0.0588	0.0471	0.0378	0.0304
26	0.7720	0.6790	0.5976	0.5262	0.4637	0.4088	0.3607	0.3184	0.2812	0.2198	0.1722	0.1352	0.1064	0.0839	0.0663	0.0525	0.0417	0.0331	0.0264
27	0.7644	0.6690	0.5859	0.5134	0.4502	0.3950	0.3468	0.3047	0.2678	0.2074	0.1609	0.1252	0.0976	0.0763	0.0597	0.0469	0.0369	0.0291	0.0230
28	0.7568	0.6591	0.5744	0.5009	0.4371	0.3817	0.3335	0.2916	0.2551	0.1956	0.1504	0.1159	0.0895	0.0693	0.0538	0.0419	0.0326	0.0255	0.0200
29	0.7493	0.6494	0.5631	0.4887	0.4243	0.3687	0.3207	0.2790	0.2429	0.1846	0.1406	0.1073	0.0822	0.0630	0.0485	0.0374	0.0289	0.0224	0.0174
30	0.7419	0.6398	0.5521	0.4767	0.4120	0.3563	0.3083	0.2670	0.2314	0.1741	0.1314	0.0994	0.0754	0.0573	0.0437	0.0334	0.0256	0.0196	0.0151

r: rate of return; t: number of time periods

Figure 2.2 *Present value of $1*

If a cash flow C_2 happens two years from now, its PV is:

$$PV = C_2 \cdot \frac{1}{(1+r)^2}$$

And if the cash flow C_t takes place t years from now, its PV is:

$$PV = C_t \cdot \frac{1}{(1+r)^t}$$

Figure 2.2 tabulates the PV of $1 depending on the number of time periods t and the rate of return r.

In a business case project, the time value of money principle is used to understand the additional return offered by an investment proposition as compared to putting the same money in government securities at, say, a 5 per cent interest rate. And if an investment proposition happens to offer a return of less than the prevalent interest rate of government securities, it is better to stay away from that investment and choose another proposition or put the money in government securities. But what if the investment proposition promises to increase customer satisfaction and the company's reputation in the market? Such benefits are called non-monetary benefits, and how to deal with them in a business case will be explained later in Chapter 4, especially Section 4.5.

Case 2.1   Planning retirement with the Latte Factor

The Latte Factor is a phrase coined by Bach (2005) and has become an internationally recognized metaphor for all of those unnecessary little expenditures with instant gratification that money is being wasted on every day – without realizing how much it all adds up (Case 2.1). The Latte Factor helps people realize how saving small amounts of money over a lifetime can make them "millionaires" at retirement.

Everybody spends money daily on small things. For example, an early morning espresso, cappuccino, or latte macchiato at a coffee shop on the way to work somewhere in New York may cost something like $5 every day.

This seemingly small amount of money adds up to a significant amount of cash in one year. Assuming 220 working days in a year, it sums to a total annual expenditure of $1,100.

If a 25-year old graduate, who is just starting a corporate career, were to let go of this latte macchiato habit and instead invest the money in a fixed deposit at 5 per cent interest rate, it would result in a nicely sized nest egg for retirement (at the age of 65) of $147,268, maybe paying for an apartment in Florida. Taking food from home every day instead of going to an overpriced eatery may add an additional $10 of saving every day, leading to a total retirement pool of $441.803.

If the interest rate were 10 per cent, which is about the average return offered by the US stock market, the retirement pool would already be either $585,322 or $1,755,967 for the $5 and the $15 daily saving options respectively (see Figure 2.3). However, since at least the 2008 financial crisis, everybody knows that the average return may not be the normal one.

These figures are obviously calculated using the time value of money concept and the formulas for future value together with the mathematical formula for commutation of pensions. Let us take the first example with an annual saving of $1,100:

$$
\begin{aligned}
FV &= \$1,100 \cdot (1+0.05)^{40} + \$1,100 \cdot (1+0.05)^{39} \\
&\quad + \$1,100 \cdot (1+0.05)^{38} + \$1,100 \cdot (1+0.05)^{37} + \cdots \\
&= \$1,100 \cdot [(1+0.05)^{40} + (1+0.05)^{39} + (1+0.05)^{38} + \cdots] \\
&= \$1,100 \cdot (1+0.05)^{40} + (1+0.05) \cdot \frac{(1+0.05)^{40} - 1}{0.05} \\
&= \$147,268
\end{aligned}
$$

The math is obvious and the result certainly eye-popping; seemingly small amounts add up over a working career and multiply with compound interest. But at the same time, the result is also completely misleading as life management advice. Many people just follow other people's intelligence without thinking for themselves – so if I avoid the coffee every morning or if I quit smoking, will I then have enough money for retirement? While there is certainly a degree of truth in this, many people would then just go and splurge on one good meal out, buy a few DVDs – and end up spending the same amount of money. The real key to wealth is not how much one can avoid spending, but how much one needs to set aside regularly to reach a long-term goal – basically the retirement fund. Once this goal is hit every month or year, buying a latte, going out for dinner, and buying these extra DVDs becomes possible again. Retiring comfortably means starting to accumulate wealth by directly thinking about how much one is keeping aside, but not necessarily by counting how many pennies one is spending.

The Latte Factor, as proposed by Bach (2005), looks at savings in raw numbers only. These savings are accumulated over a long period of time and ignore the very fact that instant gratification is more pleasurable and more certain than future consumption, i.e. while the Latte Factor uses compound interest, it strangely does not take into account the time value of money at the same time. Critics therefore sometimes call the Latte Factor fallacious: "David Bach's famous 'Latte Factor' ... is perhaps the most notable example of this fallacy. Bach ignored the time value of money" (Popick & Roth, 2001). The question of whether one would rather be a "millionaire" on retirement or enjoy life in the here and now, can be answered easily by discounting the saved retirement nest egg down to the present day, i.e. by calculating its PV:

$$PV = \$147,268 \cdot \frac{1}{(1 + 0.05)^{40}} = \$20,918$$

The PV of $147,268 reached by putting $5 a day, 210 days a year, for 40 years into a fixed-rate deposit of 5 per cent is about $20,918. So the right question to ask the 25-year old graduate is: "Would you rather have $20,918 today or $147,268 when you retire?" Nonetheless, the primary point of the Latte Factor – that cutting recurring costs can help to meet savings goals – remains completely valid.

2.2   NET PRESENT VALUE (NPV) CONCEPT

Let us assume someone has the opportunity to purchase real estate at the price of $470,000 and at the same time possesses market insight which clearly shows that it can be sold off again

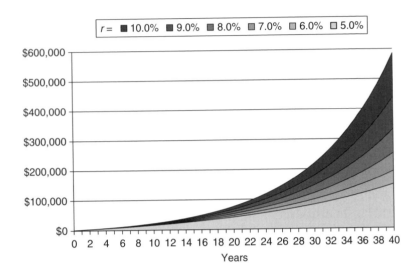

Figure 2.3 *The $5 Latte Factor*

at $525,000 a year from now. Would you advise this person to go for the investment – or rather stay away from it?

As shown in Section 2.1, the PV of $525,000 (the estimated sales price a year from now) at an opportunity cost of capital of 5 per cent is:

$$PV = \$525,000 \cdot \frac{1}{1.05} = \$500,000$$

Therefore, the PV of the estimated sales price is $30,000 more than the initially required investment of $470,000. This difference of $30,000 is called the *NPV* and can be found by subtracting the required investment from the PV:

$$NPV = PV - required\ investment$$
$$= \$500,000 - \$470,000 = \$30,000$$

In other words, this proposed real estate investment makes a net contribution to the investor's wealth; it delivers a better return than putting the same money into (relatively safe) government securities, and you should therefore recommend it.

Mathematically, the formula for calculating NPV can be written as:

$$NPV = C_0 + C_1 \cdot \frac{1}{1+r}$$

C_0 stands for the investment today at time 0. As an investment is usually a cash outflow, it will be a negative figure in most cases. C_0 is the net cash inflow (income minus expenses) generated in the year after commissioning of the investment. In this example:

$$NPV = -\$470,000 + \$525,000 \cdot \frac{1}{1+0.05} = \$30,000$$

Investment with risk

The $525,000 in the above example may represent the best forecast of real estate prices from today's perspective, but as this forecast is obviously not guaranteed, the NPV calculation and therefore the recommendation to buy the real estate becomes fuzzy, if not inaccurate. For sake of simplicity, the above introductory example did not consider any risks related to the investment. But in real life, how can one be certain about future values of real estate, especially when one considers the past experience of housing bubbles, financial crisis, fires, hurricanes, and earthquakes?

Let us assume that a different country offers 11.7 per cent interest on government securities, which come with much greater certainty than the real estate market (if one neglects the possibility of sovereign default). As investors now have an opportunity to achieve $525,000 by investing the same $470,000 in these government securities, the real estate seller will be forced to cut the price in order to lure potential investors away from government securities.

Investors apparently tend to avoid risk when they don't have to sacrifice return for it; this simple observation leads to the second most important principle in finance:

A safe dollar is worth more than a risky dollar.

Hence the proposed investment in the turbulent real estate market should ideally and realistically be compared with a similar risky investment, for example in the stock market, but certainly not with an investment in very safe government securities. Assuming that the stock market is forecast to give a 10 per cent return, then $r = 10\%$ becomes the opportunity cost of capital because the investor forgoes investing in the equally risky stock market. The new NPV computes at:

$$NPV = -\$470,000 + \$525,000 \cdot \frac{1}{1 + 0.10} = \$7,273$$

The proposed real estate investment continues to beat the stock market, but the increase in wealth is only a rather meager $7,273 as compared to $30,000 in the first calculation, which assumed a risk-free scenario.

This was a simple looking adjustment for risk, but unfortunately in real-life business cases it is much more complicated to adjust investment opportunities for both time and uncertainty and hence these two effects need to be dealt with separately. This chapter will continue to deal exclusively with time; the challenge of risk and uncertainty will be taken up later in Chapter 6. For now, all cash flows are assumed to happen with certainty.

Multi-period NPV

The above example assumed that the real estate would produce one cash inflow in the year following the cash outflow.

However, most assets and corporate investments do not produce value exactly and only one year from commissioning; there may be several cash inflow streams across many years, in varying amounts. Going back to the example, real estate usually generates rental income for many years and one last cash inflow when it is being sold off. Let us approach the multi-period NPV step by step.

The PV of a cash flow C_2 two years from now can be written as:

$$PV = C_2 \cdot \frac{1}{(1 + r_2)^2}$$

The discount rate r_2 is the annual rate of return for money invested in two-year securities. Future interest rates such as r_2 are unlikely to be constant; interest rates have historically varied quite a bit and will continue to be in a state of flux. Figure 2.4 shows the 12-year development of the 12-month Euribor (first rate of each year), which fluctuates between the extremes of 0.543% (2013) and 4.733% (2008). Because taking all this into consideration would make the PV formulas very messy, real-life

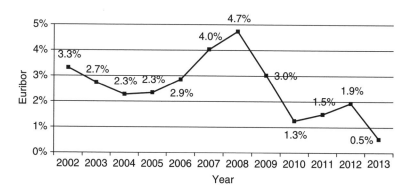

Figure 2.4 *12-month Euribor interest rate*[1]
Source: http://www.global-rates.com/interest-rates/euribor/euribor-interest-12-months.aspx.

business cases generally work with one standard rate of return r across the lifespan of an investment.

The main advantage of discounting future values of several periods to their PV equivalents is that they are being made comparable. As they are all expressed in current monetary terms, mathematical operations can be performed on them. An extended stream of cash flows across several periods can now be evaluated as a NPV by summing all the PV:

$$NPV = C_0 + \frac{C_1}{1+r} + \frac{C_2}{(1+r)^2} + \frac{C_3}{(1+r)^3} + \cdots$$

This is called the *discounted NPV formula* and a shorthand way to write it is:

$$NPV = C_0 + \sum_{t=1}^{n} \frac{C_t}{(1+r)^t}$$

In this formula, n denotes the number of years for which the cash flow stream is expected to come in.

The calculation process is once more graphically depicted in Figure 2.5; the future net cash flow are discounted to the current year and thus made comparable. Once the net cash flows are expressed in today's currency, they can be summed with the initial investment, leading to the NPV of an investment.

Let us revisit the real estate example and look at it from a different perspective. Our investor now changes plans and does not want to sell the real estate off immediately in the first year, but wants to keep it as an investment and reap the rental income. The purchase price remains at $470,000 and the rental income is estimated to be $12,000 p.a. for the first two years and thereafter $15,000 p.a. In the fifth year, the real estate will be sold off for a moderate $500,000, taking wear and tear into consideration. Should one advise the investor to go for this investment or would investing in government securities at 5 per cent yield a better income?

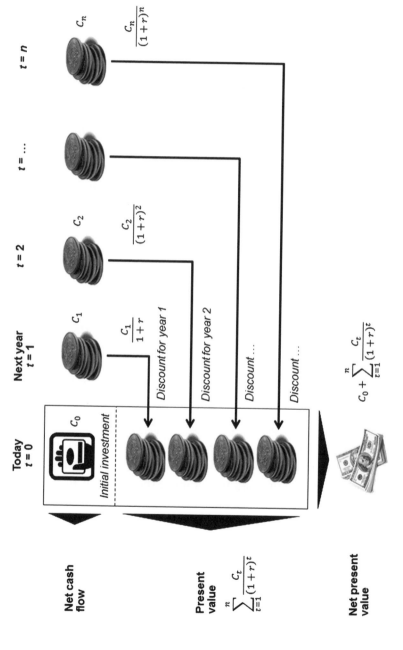

Figure 2.5 *Calculation of NPV*

The NPV calculation of the proposed real estate investment provides the answer; the formula is:

$$NPV = -\$470,000 + \frac{\$12,000}{1.05} + \frac{\$12,000}{1.05^2} + \frac{\$15,000}{1.05^3}$$

$$+ \frac{\$15,000}{1.05^4} + \frac{\$500,000}{1.05^5} = -\$30,628$$

Despite a continuous positive cash inflow through rents and a selling price higher than the original buying price, the NPV is negative. So what has happened? The suggested investment is not profitable when comparing it with investing the same amount in securities at a 5 per cent interest rate. It becomes obvious that either the rental income or the selling price is too low to make this real estate project a profitable one.

Calculating NPV with a spreadsheet

As an investment spans more than a handful of years, the NPV formula gets increasingly difficult to calculate by hand. Hence it is time to look at how a spreadsheet tool like Microsoft Excel can help to compute NPV.

Figure 2.6 shows the timeline of the investment in cells E5 to J5, the initial investment as a cash outflow (negative figure) in cell E7, the rental income (positive figures) in cells F8 to I8, and the disinvestment in the fifth year (positive figure) in cell J8. Cash outflow and inflow are now summed to compute the net cash flow in line 10. Line 12 calculates the discount factor for each year and line 14 discounts the net cash flow of each investment year to its PV by multiplying the net cash flow with the discount factor. The NPV of the investment is then simply calculated as the sum of the PVs, as shown before in Figure 2.5.

Excel also offers inbuilt functionality to calculate the NPV; this feature is supposed to offer a shortcut for people who do not understand the mathematics behind a problem and help

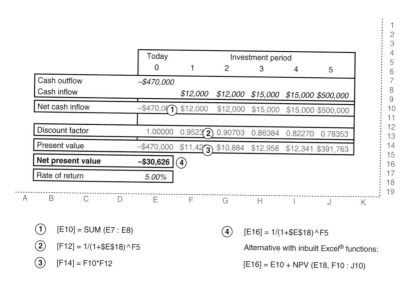

Figure 2.6 *Calculation of NPV in Excel*

condense otherwise complicated calculations. Not very surprisingly, the required function is called NPV:

$$NPV(rate, value1, value2, ...)$$

In this function, *rate* is the rate of return over one period; *value*1, *value*2, ... are 1 to 254 arguments representing the net cash inflow. In Excel logic, the investment begins one period before the date of the *value*1 net cash flow and ends with the last cash flow in the list. If the first cash flow occurs at the beginning of the first period (e.g. the initial investment of $470,000 in period 0) then the first value must be added to the NPV result; it must not (!) be included in the formula's value arguments. In the example, the NPV calculation would read as:

$$[E16] = E10 + NPV(E18, F10:J10)$$

This case in point shows an inherent danger of blindly applying inbuilt Excel functions without understanding the calculation formula in the background. Intuitively, and without reading the Excel help files, one would have computed the NPV as $[E16] = NPV(E18, E10:J10)$, resulting in $-\$29,168$ instead of $-\$30,626$. The lesson is to be very careful with black-box ready-made functionality.

Discussing and defending business case calculations with financial controllers and senior management is a challenging task; experience shows that it is always advisable to have a clear, explicit, and step-by-step calculation available, which can be used to walk discussion partners through the computation process. Transparency is probably the only successful way to remove doubt and ambiguity.

Analyzing the calculation dynamics

It is now time to revisit the result of the calculation: the NPV is negative and thus the calculation uncovers a non-profitable investment proposition. But what would happen if the rate of return drops from 5 per cent to 3.5 per cent? Changing the value in cell E18 to 3.5 per cent throws out a positive NPV in cell E16 and the investment proposition begins to make sense again. Alternatively, if the owner of the real estate manages to rent it out at higher rates, this could for example increase the cash inflow in the first two years to $20,000 and to $25,000 in the third and fourth year. Now the calculation shows a positive NPV of $1,115.

Spreadsheets like the one in Figure 2.6 help to experiment with the input data and thus facilitate a deeper understanding of an investment's otherwise hidden dynamics. This kind of experimenting is commonly referred to as *sensitivity analysis* and Section 6.6 examines its possibilities in greater detail.

Summary

The firm's wealth maximization goal (see Section 1.1) states that financial management should endeavor to maximize the NPV of the expected future cash flows by taking two basic parameters into account[2]:

- The longer it takes to receive a cash flow, the lower the value decision makers place on the cash flow today.

- The greater the risk associated with receiving a future cash flow, the lower the value decision makers place on that cash flow today.

The wealth maximization goal thus reflects the magnitude, timing, and risk associated with cash flows expected to be received in the future as a result of investment decisions. It tells financial management what investments are to be preferred and how to make decisions.

However, people often fail to understand the simple mathematical rationale of the time value of money, which is really the only principle behind calculating NPV. Instead, they perceive some other methods as methodically easier to understand, apply them instead, and in this process often mess up the correctness of the calculation. NPV is always (!) the most appropriate approach to calculating business cases; Sections 2.3–2.6 describe the most common alternative methods, highlight their weaknesses (and strengths, if at all), and explain why they are always (!) inferior to the NPV method when making decisions on investment propositions. Sometimes they are indeed appropriate to use, but the same decision can always (!) be reached with the much more straightforward NPV method. Chapter 5 is dedicated to the practical application of the NPV method.

2.3 PAYBACK AND DISCOUNTED PAYBACK METHOD

Some corporations require the initial investment on any of their projects (i.e. the cash outflow in year zero) to be recoverable within a specified period. Statements by executives like "The costs need to be recovered within the same financial year" or "The investment needs to show a leverage within the same quarter" are telling signs of this pre-set investment parameter. Other companies tend to compare and judge investment alternatives on how rapidly they can recover the cash outflow, obviously trying to impress shareholders and other stakeholders with quick results. And again, some business managers try to get their pet projects approved by promising "immediate returns" to their superiors.

Such requirements and approaches all refer to the *payback period*, which can be found by calculating the time it takes before the cumulative forecasted net cash flows from year one onwards equal the initial investment in year zero. In simple terms, the payback period is the time it takes to recover the initial spending on the investment.

Figure 2.7 looks at three different mutually exclusive project alternatives. All three projects initially invest $470,000, but differ in their cash flows in subsequent years. The first project reaps a positive cash flow of $25,000 in the first four years and then decommissions the investment with a positive cash flow of $470,000 in the fifth year. The second project offers twice as much positive cash flow in the first four years. The third project does not reap any annual cash flows, but decommissions the investment in the second year for $490,000.

The company's management wants to show business results quickly and examines how rapidly each of these alternatives pays back the initial investment of $470,000. And so the payback method is used. The clear favorite is the third project, which returns the investment in the second year with an additional $20,000 and thus has a payback period of only two years as compared to five years for the other two projects. In a spreadsheet, the *payback stream* is established via summing up of all cash flows period by period. The payback stream up to period 1 is the cash outflow (period 0) plus the net cash flow

	Today	Investment period					NPV	Payback period
	0	1	2	3	4	5		
Project 1: Net cash inflow	−$470,000	$25,000	$25,000	$25,000	$25,000	$470,000	−$13,094	5
Project 2: Net cash inflow	−$470,000	$50,000	$50,000	$50,000	$50,000	$470,000	$75,555	5
Project 3: Net cash inflow	−$470,000		$490,000				−$3,333	2
Rate of return	5.00%							

Project 1: Payback stream	−$470,000	−$445,000	−$420,000	−$395,000	−$370,000	**$100,000**
Project 2: Payback stream	−$470,000	−$420,000	−$370,000	−$320,000	−$270,000	**$200,000**
Project 3: Payback stream	−$470,000	−$470,000	**$20,000**	$20,000	$20,000	$20,000

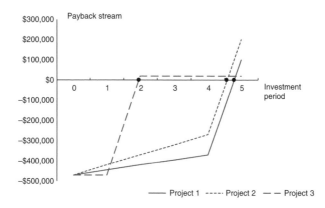

Figure 2.7 *Payback method: Three different projects*

in period 1; the payback stream up to period 2 is the payback stream of period 1 plus the net cash flow in period 2; and so on. The payback period is the time period in which the payback stream becomes positive for the first time. A graphical representation of the payback streams shows when the payback stream crosses the abscissa (see bottom diagram in Figure 2.7).

In order to determine the best project option, the business case team also conducts a NPV analysis, and the clear recommendation is now to go for the second alternative; only this project offers a positive NPV of $75,555. Both the first and the third project have a negative NPV. It looks like the payback method gives answers which contradict the NPV rule.

By using only the payback method, the company's management would be lured into making a loss-making investment decision! The NPV for the third project is not only lower than the NPV for the second project; what is more, it shows a negative value! The increase of $20,000 is not even good enough to outrun safe government bonds offering a rate of return of 5 per cent.

Why does the payback method give a different recommendation from the NPV rule? What are the underlying mathematical reasons?

- The payback method gives equal weight to all cash flows regardless of when they occur during the investment period; it basically ignores the time value of money principle. The NPV rule, on the other hand, attaches more value to earlier cash flows.

- The payback method generally favors short-lived projects and categorically rejects many good long-lived ones.

In an attempt to overcome these limitations, some companies first discount the cash flows by computing their PV before calculating the payback period. This approach is referred to as the *discounted payback method* and asks how many periods a project has to last in order to make sense in NPV terms. The approach is now obviously correct because it applies the time value of money principle, but it is extremely difficult to explain to senior management. Notwithstanding this corrected approach, as long as a company insists on fixed *cut-off dates* for investments the discounted payback method cannot take into account any cash flows after these cut-off dates.[3]

But why do companies introduce cut-off dates at all if this can lead to such bizarre decision-making mistakes? For one, senior management may not believe in the forecasting accuracy of later cash flows due to market uncertainty. Second, the method of discounting is often not understood and not applied. As a result of not applying the time value of money principle, distant cash flows invariably influence a business case considerably and a solution to this problem is attempted by introducing cut-off dates. Third, our fast-paced business world gets more and more pressured to report success on a yearly, if not already on a quarterly, basis. The lifespan of information systems (IS) gets shorter and shorter, innovation cycles become faster and faster, and a 180-degree turnaround of strategic decisions after a change of executive leadership is not a rare case any more. In such an environment, a fast payback is certainly desirable. Long-running investment decisions are likely to be abandoned and are not able to reap their forecasted but distant cash inflows.

To summarize, despite its simplicity, the payback method should never (!) be used to compare and judge investments. Instead, it should be applied as an appropriate device for *describing* the net cash flow of projects. In this respect, the payback method can add substantial value to the documentation of an investment proposition's business case. But it is not an appropriate decision-making tool in its own right.

2.4   RETURN ON INVESTMENT (ROI)

Return on investment (ROI) is a catchphrase broadly known among business managers. "What's the ROI of your project?" is a question frequently asked across the corridor. But herein lies the problem. ROI is an ambiguous phrase and it is interpreted differently by everyone. As a generic term, ROI means an investment analysis, i.e. a business case. As a specific method of calculation, it goes by different names: *average return on the book value*, *return on capital employed*, and *accounting rate of return* are just some examples. Here is just one paragraph from a case study by a management consulting company showing how ROI as a term can be overused: "To drive operational efficiencies and cost reduction, Accenture helped Meetic implement a new method for projecting cash and ROI of marketing campaigns that calculated a lifetime conversion value for each

subscriber to project accurate revenues over the next five years
[…]. Accenture also designed and implemented tools for automating daily ROI calculation for optimizing advertising campaigns […]. The analytics-led ROI calculation revolutionized
the way campaign operations were managed by the team across
the European market" (Accenture, 2013).

What is more, there is no commonly agreed formula to calculate the return of an investment, and thus different organizations
and different business managers within the same organization
have different ways of calculating ROI. Things could not be
more confusing.

In the broadest sense, ROI attempts to measure the profitability of an investment through dividing the benefit of an investment by its cost. The benefit is usually understood as a net
benefit and captured as the average net cash flow per year. The
cost of the investment is often defined as the average book value
of the investment over the investment period:

$$ROI = \frac{Average\ net\ profits\ of\ investment}{Average\ book\ value\ of\ investment}$$

Let us look at an example. By investing \$500,000 into a
production line in period 0, the firm expects running costs
of \$40,000 p.a. and revenues of \$100,000 in the first year,
\$150,000 in the second year and thereafter \$200,000 p.a.
It further assumes a five-year single-declining depreciation
period. Figure 2.8 shows the ROI calculation process in three
steps:

- First, the net book value in each investment period is calculated from the gross book value minus the accumulated
  depreciation. In the fifth period $(t = 5)$, the net book value is
  zero. The average book value is calculated as the average of
  the net book value between today $(t = 0)$ and the respective
  investment period t.

	Today			Investment period				
	t = 0	*t* = 1	*t* = 2	*t* = 3	*t* = 4	*t* = 5	*t* = 6	*t* = 7
Investment	*$500,000*							
Gross book value	$500,000	$500,000	$500,000	$500,000	$500,000	$500,000	$500,000	$500,000
Depreciation		*$100,000*	*$100,000*	*$100,000*	*$100,000*	*$100,000*		
Accumulated depreciation		$100,000	$200,000	$300,000	$400,000	$500,000	$500,000	$500,000
Net book value	$500,000	$400,000	$300,000	$200,000	$100,000	$0	$0	$0
Average book value [0..*t*]		$450,000	$400,000	$350,000	$300,000	$250,000	$214,286	$187,500
Revenue		*$100,000*	*$150,000*	*$200,000*	*$200,000*	*$200,000*	*$200,000*	*$200,000*
Costs		*$40,000*	*$40,000*	*$40,000*	*$40,000*	*$40,000*	*$40,000*	*$40,000*
Net cashflow (= revenue – costs)		$60,000	$110,000	$160,000	$160,000	$160,000	$160,000	$160,000
Net profit (= net cashflow – depreciation)		–$40,000	$10,000	$60,000	$60,000	$60,000	$160,000	$160,000
Average net profit [0..*t*]		–$40,000	–$15,000	$10,000	$22,500	$30,000	$51,667	$67,143
ROI [0..*t*]		**–8.89%**	**–3.75%**	**2.86%**	**7.50%**	**12.00%**	**24.11%**	**35.81%**

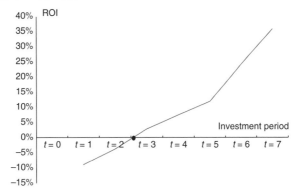

Figure 2.8 *ROI calculation*

- Second, the net profit in each investment period is derived from the projected revenue in each period minus the costs and the depreciation. And again, the average net profit is calculated as the average of the net profit between today $(t=0)$ and the respective investment period t.

- Third, the ROI achieved in each investment period t is the average net profit divided by the average book value, always regarding the respective investment period.

The curve in the bottom of Figure 2.8 nicely shows how the ROI goes up with the lifetime of the investment. In the third investment period, the ROI graph crosses the abscissa and this is where, as many managers put it, the "investment achieves the ROI." After the fifth investment period, the ROI shoots up because the investment is fully depreciated in the company's books.

While the ROI method is a familiar concept, it has many flaws. First, and most importantly, it does not take into account the time value of money. In the above example, revenue increased in the second and third year, after which it stayed constant. If these revenue flows were to be discounted to present time, the average profits shown would be lower. However, when using the above ROI formula, discounting is not possible. One must not put the average forecasted profits in relation to the average book value, as book values cannot be discounted. Second, the forecasted profits in the numerator of the equation depend not only on the generated net cash flow, but also on the accounting system used in the company; finance knows many depreciation models and methods to account for inventories. By cleverly reducing the book value of an investment through an accelerated rather than a linear depreciation, the perceived return on the investment would be increased even though nothing has changed in the underlying investment. This is obviously a statistical illusion and it certainly does not indicate a better or worse investment. Third, the cost of capital r does not appear anywhere in the calculation as it is not captured in accounting profit. Hence it is not possible to know whether an investment judged by the ROI formula generates value for the company in comparison to a safe investment alternative in government bonds; using the ROI formula nobody can say for sure whether the proposed investment is acceptable to a firm's management or not.

So, when is a ROI calculation useful? One can really only use the ROI method in business cases to compare the ROI of investment projects to other previous (successful) investments or with an industry average. But this is not only difficult, because as we all know from the stock market, the success rate of past investments is not a good indicator for future performance and should therefore not influence today's decisions. And what is even more important is, as the ROI calculation formula is not uniformly defined, the business case team could run the danger of comparing apples with pears.

2.5 INTERNAL RATE OF RETURN (IRR)

The internal rate of return (IRR) is a handy measure which is frequently used in finance departments. However, as the examples in this chapter will show, it can also be a very misleading metric.

IRR is defined as the rate of return that makes the NPV zero. In order to find the IRR for a proposed investment, the following equation needs to be solved:

$$NPV = C_0 + \frac{C_1}{1+IRR} + \frac{C_2}{(1+IRR)^2} + \frac{C_3}{(1+IRR)^3} + \cdots = 0$$

There is no ambiguity in calculating the IRR for an investment that only generates one single cash flow after one period. In fact, the calculation is pretty simple:

$$NPV = C_0 + \frac{C_1}{1+IRR} = 0$$

$$IRR = \frac{C_1}{-C_0} - 1$$

The expression for longer investment periods is much more difficult, if not impossible, to solve arithmetically and usually requires a trial-and-error linear interpolation approach, for which a spreadsheet such as the one in Figure 2.6 comes very handy.

Let us revert to the previous real estate example and modify it a little: After an initial investment of $470,000 into real estate, the investor now expects a rental income of $30,000 p.a. There is a plan to sell the real estate in the fifth year for $500,000. A trial-and-error interpolation, as shown in Figure 2.9 using the NPV formula results in an $IRR \approx 6.38\%$, which is the rate of discount at which the investment's NPV becomes zero ($NPV = 0$). If the cost of capital is 5 per cent, as

	Today	Investment period				
	0	1	2	3	4	5
Cash outflow	−$470,000					
Cash inflow		$30,000	$30,000	$30,000	$30,000	$500,000
Net cash inflow	−$470,000	$30,000	$30,000	$30,000	$30,000	$500,000

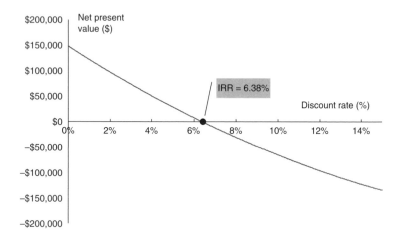

Figure 2.9 *IRR calculation through interpolation*

assumed in the examples before, then this investment with an IRR of 6.38 per cent is therefore to be accepted, because then the investment will have a positive NPV when discounted at 5 per cent.

Of course, Excel offers inbuilt functionality to calculate the IRR and this is what most financial managers use. The function is called IRR:

$$IRR(value1, value2, … [, guess])$$

where *value1*, *value2*, … are 1 to 254 arguments representing the net cash inflow. Excel calculates IRR through an iterative search procedure starting with an estimate for IRR – specified as a *guess* – and then repeatedly varies that value until a correct IRR is reached. Specifying a *guess* argument is optional; Excel uses 10 per cent as the default value.

The IRR is not to be confused with the opportunity cost of capital r just because it appears as a rate of return in the same NPV formula. While the IRR is a proper financial profitability measure depending on the amount and timing of the net cash flows, the opportunity cost of capital is an input value for the NPV formula helping to calculate how much a project could be potentially worth. The opportunity cost of capital is only a financial threshold for profitability giving details about what return other projects, investments, or assets with the same risk index as the proposed venture can usually offer.

Hence the IRR rule calls for the acceptance of business cases if their IRR is greater than the opportunity cost of capital. Many finance departments prefer the IRR rule to the NPV method. While mathematically both formulas are equivalent, the IRR method can be outright dangerous if not presented properly. In order to understand why one should always (!) use the much safer NPV method in business cases instead of the IRR rule, the following looks at four investment scenarios which are pitfalls in a sense that they directly lead to the wrong investment decision if their IRRs are blindly compared.

Trap 1: Borrowing instead of investing

Not all projects necessarily have NPVs that decline as the opportunity cost of capital goes up. For instance, if one hurriedly compares the two projects A and B in Figure 2.10, one might be tempted to think that they are equally attractive investments, as each one of them has an IRR of 6.38 per cent.

So, where is the difference? Project A is the typical investment project discussed many times in this book; there is a cash outflow

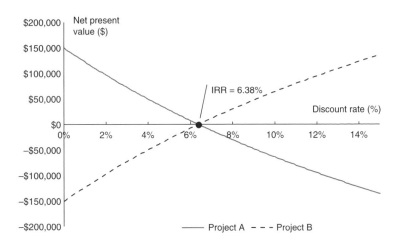

Project A	Today		Investment period			
	0	1	2	3	4	5
Cash outflow	$470,000					
Cash inflow		$30,000	$30,000	$30,000	$30,000	$500,000
Net cash inflow	–$470,000	$30,000	$30,000	$30,000	$30,000	$500,000

Project B	Today		Investment period			
	0	1	2	3	4	5
Cash outflow		$30,000	$30,000	$30,000	$30,000	$500,000
Cash inflow	$470,000					
Net cash inflow	$470,000	–$30,000	–$30,000	–$30,000	–$30,000	–$500,000

Figure 2.10 *IRR Trap 1: Borrowing in period 0*

in period 0 followed by cash inflows in the subsequent periods. The NPV of project A therefore decreases as the discount rate is being raised. Project B, on the contrary, has an NPV which goes up as the discount rate is brought down. The company borrows money (cash inflow in period 0) and returns it over subsequent periods as cash outflows; it thus looks for a low rate of return. But when one invests (or lends) money, one looks for a high rate of return.

When using the IRR method, one first needs to establish whether the investment project under scrutiny is about investing or borrowing as this determines whether a higher IRR or a lower IRR is desirable. While this is easy to make out from the simple cash flows in Figure 2.10, it may not be as easy as this in real life investment scenarios.

The NPV method, however, gives the right answer right away when comparing both projects at an IRR, for example of 5 per cent: Project A offers an $NPV \approx \$28,142$ and project B automatically turns any investor away with a negative $NPV \approx -\$28,142$.

Trap 2: Sign changes in net cash flow

Net cash flows can go from positive to negative in different periods due to later expenditures. Such a change can be caused by decommissioning costs at the end of the investment period, such as clean-up costs or a decontamination of the project site. Other expenditures, such as part replacements of the investment or renovation costs of buildings can also turn the net cash flow into negatives during the investment period.

Let us take up the real estate example once more (see Figure 2.11). After an initial investment of \$470,000, the project is now estimated to return an annual \$170,000 for four periods. In the fifth year, clean-up costs of \$120,000 are required. A trial-and-error interpolation coupled with plotting the NPV curve makes the project's NPV zero for two discount rates, namely at $IRR_1 \approx -56.21\%$ and $IRR_2 \approx 9.33\%$. Unfortunately, the inbuilt Excel function IRR returns only the first one it finds, which is closest to the guess value provided.

The graph in Figure 2.11 shows that the project's NPV initially rises and then declines again; this is caused by the change in the sign of the net cash flow stream. Mathematically, there can be as many different solutions to a polynomial equation as it has changes of sign, i.e. there can be as many internal rates of return for a project as there are changes in the sign of the net cash flows. For example, if a hotel needs a renovation every

	Today	Investment period			
	0	1	2	3	4	5
Cash outflow	$470,000					$120,000
Cash inflow		$170,000	$170,000	$170,000	$170,000	
Net cash inflow	−$470,000	$170,000	$170,000	$170,000	$170,000	−$120,000

Figure 2.11 *IRR Trap 2: Sign changes in net cash flow*

five years, resulting in a negative cash flow every fifth year, this can be very confusing for the financial manager who is using the IRR rule. And if this were not enough, there are also cases which do not have any IRR at all.

A popular remedy in such oscillating cases is to discount later cash flows back at the cost of capital to remove the change in the sign of the cash flows and to calculate the IRR on the new series.[4] However, this overcomplicates the process to such a level that a non-financial person is no longer able to follow the calculations. As discussed in Section 1.5, many business cases are turned down with the comment "I don't understand it," and this is what the business case team should try to avoid at the start. And, of course, such artificial modifications are unnecessary, as there is a much simpler solution at hand – the NPV method.

Trap 3: Add-on projects

Businesses sometimes have to choose between two different investments or between two different ways of doing things, which both cater to the same strategic business objectives, but which can't both be implemented – only one can be chosen. In other words, they are mutually exclusive investment options. Examples are manual vs. automatized processes or low-cost vs. high-cost solutions. Manual processes or other low-cost solutions may require less initial setup costs than automated processes or high-cost solutions, but might return lesser benefits later on.

Figure 2.12 revisits the real estate example once more. Project A invests $470,000 into real estate and expects a rental income of $30,000 p.a.; in the fifth year, the building will be sold off for $500,000. At 5 per cent opportunity cost of capital, Project A has an $NPV_A = \$28,142$ and an $IRR_A \approx 6.38\%$. Project B, on the other side, invests $900,000 in the same real estate building but includes a full-scope remodeling of the building to better meet the tenant's needs. As a result, the rental income goes up to $58,000 p.a.; in the fifth year, the firm expects to sell the building for $930,000. At the same opportunity cost of capital, project B has an $NPV_B = \$34,344$ and an $IRR_B \approx 5.89\%$.

If a financial manager looks only at the IRR as an investment decision criterion, project A would be selected as it offers a higher IRR than project B. However, when comparing the NPV of both investments, project B suddenly looks better, and by choosing project B the company would be $6,203 richer. Is this a contradiction?

The reason that the IRR method is misleading is that project B is in fact an incremental investment to project A; IRR as a measure for investment decisions tends to be unreliable in ranking investments of different scale as well as investments which offer different patterns of early or late cash outflows.

Project A	Today		Investment period			
	0	1	2	3	4	5
Cash outflow	$470,000					
Cash inflow		$30,000	$30,000	$30,000	$30,000	$500,000
Net cash inflow	−$470,000	$30,000	$30,000	$30,000	$30,000	$500,000

Project B	Today		Investment period			
	0	1	2	3	4	5
Cash outflow	$900,000					
Cash inflow		$58,000	$58,000	$58,000	$58,000	$930,000
Net cash inflow	−$900,000	$58,000	$58,000	$58,000	$58,000	$930,000

Additional project B - A	Today		Investment period			
	0	1	2	3	4	5
Additional cash outflow	$430,000	$0	$0	$0	$0	$0
Additional cash inflow	$0	$28,000	$28,000	$28,000	$28,000	$430,000
Additional net cash inflow	−$430,000	$28,000	$28,000	$28,000	$28,000	$430,000

Project A			Project B			Add. project B - A	
IRR	NPV at 5%		IRR	NPV at 5%		IRR	NPV at 5%
6.38%	$28,142		5.89%	$34,344		5.34%	$6,203

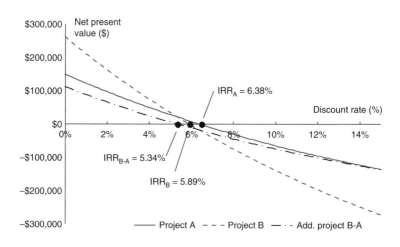

Figure 2.12 *IRR Trap 3: Add-on projects*

In the above example, the IRR method should be first applied on project A and then on the incremental investment that project B proposes; a new incremental project B–A needs to be created. Based on the calculation in Figure 2.11, one would accept project A as an investment proposal and for the incremental project calculate $NPV_{B-A} = \$6{,}203$ and an $IRR_{B-A} \approx 5.34\%$. As $IRR_{B-A} > r = 5\%$, one would accept the incremental project proposal as well. Now the decision is in line with what the NPV method suggested right from the beginning.

Working with incremental investments is extremely difficult as it will in many cases introduce changes of sign in the incremental net cash flow, leading back to the problems described before as the IRR's second trap. We are entering a vicious circle trying to find a remedy to one of IRR's traps and at the same time maneuvering ourselves into another trap.

Trap 4: Different short- and long-term rates of interest

All the above considerations have only assumed one opportunity cost of capital r pretending that there is no difference between short-term and long-term interest rates. Of course this is an assumption of simplicity, which is frequently used in business case calculations. The general NPV formula (Section 2.2), however, allows discounting the net cash flows at different interest rates:

$$NPV = C_0 + \sum_{t=1}^{n} \frac{C_t}{(1+r_t)^t} = C_0 + \frac{C_1}{1+r_1} + \frac{C_2}{(1+r_2)^2} + \frac{C_3}{(1+r_3)^3} + \cdots$$

C_1 is discounted at the opportunity cost of capital r_1 for one year, C_2 at the opportunity cost of capital r_2 for two years, C_3 at r_3 for three years, and so on. Even though this makes the NPV calculation more complex, it is not entirely impossible to map this rare case.

Using the IRR method, this special case becomes a real challenge. The IRR rule accepts an investment proposal when the IRR is greater than the opportunity cost of capital. If there are different opportunity costs of capital for different years, this would call for computing a weighted average r first and comparing this to the IRR. However, this gets messy very quickly and one runs into the trap of producing business cases that are rejected because nobody understands and trusts them any more.

2.6   PROFITABILITY INDEX (PI) AND BENEFIT–COST RATIO (BCR)

Some firms use the PI or BCR for selecting projects. The PI is defined as a ratio between an investment's NPV and the upfront investment, the initial cash outflow C_0:

$$PI = \frac{NPV}{C_0}$$

The BCR is defined as the ratio between PV and the upfront investment C_0:

$$Benefit\ cost\ ratio\ (BCR) = \frac{PV}{C_0}$$

With $PV = NPV + C_0$ (Section 2.1), the PI and BCR are interlinked concepts:

$$BCR = PI + 1$$

If a project has a positive PI or BCR, it also has a positive NPV, and vice versa. Therefore all three ratios are equivalent decision-making tools.

The PI is mostly used by finance managers to rank projects when there are limitations on the investment program that prevent the company from undertaking all projects with a positive NPV. Under circumstances of capital rationing, companies need to concentrate on picking the projects that offer the highest NPV of initial expenditure. However, the simple PI is really only suitable in very simplistic circumstances; Section 5.4 deals with the many more intricate challenges of making investment decisions when resources are limited.

3
Fundamentals I: Costs

The first two chapters of this book have focused on the importance of investment decisions for the economic well-being of companies, appropriate mathematical methods of modeling the cash inflows and outflows associated with an investment, and how to identify investment opportunities, select the best alternative, and finally take decisions for business growth. However, the best processes and theoretically correct methods are of not much value if the information fed into them is of insufficient quality; the well-known principle of "garbage in, garbage out" applies to business cases as well. Hence this and the next chapter concentrate exclusively on the two basic types of input into a compelling business case and the investment justification process: costs in this Chapter and benefits in Chapter 4.

3.1 COST STAGES

During the deliberation, realization, and utilization of an investment, *costs* are incurred at five stages: pre-business case, pre-commissioning, commissioning, operation, and decommissioning (see Figure 3.1).

Pre-business case costs

Well before an investment idea comes to the table and its merits are analyzed with a business case, a company has typically

Pre-business case	Pre-commissioning	Commissioning	Operating	De-commissioning
Definition of phase				
Before the idea for the investment comes up and before the business case is commissioned	From initiation of the business case process to the go/no-go decision	From decision on the investment to its commissioning (hand-over to operations)	Entire lifetime of the investment after its commissioning	Ramping down the investment at the end of its lifetime
Examples				
All costs spent before the business case, e.g. research	Costs of writing the business case	Purchasing of infrastructure, IT hardware, licenses	Human resources	De-installation
Re-used infrastructure	Planning	Installation	Infrastructure maintenance & servicing	Re-training
...	Management, accounting, auditing, lobbying	Provider selection & contract initiation	Licensing, hiring, leasing	Compensation
	Selection of providers	Recruitment, training	Business continuity management	Terminal value as inflow, if applicable
	...	Transition costs	Communication costs	...
		...	Consumables	
			...	
Sunk costs	Partly sunk costs, partly included in business case	Fully included in business case		

Figure 3.1 Cost stages

already spent some money on research, preliminary feasibility checks, meetings, and discussions. Also, some investment ideas suggest using pre-existing infrastructure, such as manufacturing lines or computer networks, that can be re-used, but which are not yet completely written off. All of these costs are pre-business case costs and they are treated as *sunk costs*, i.e. they are not taken into account when preparing the business case for the new investment. Whether there will be a go or no-go decision for the investment, these costs will neither change nor miraculously go away again; they have already been spent and thus should never influence the decision at hand. A business case only considers new and additional costs, which are strictly related to the investment under consideration; the business case never goes into the past to justify previous spending.

Pre-commissioning costs

Pre-commissioning costs occur between initiation of the business case and before the organization decides to go ahead (or not go ahead) with the investment. Typical cost categories during this period are mainly:

- Compensation payments to various stakeholders, especially lobbying expenses (see note 1)

- Legal support and regulatory approvals

- Management, accounting, and auditing

- Market studies and surveys

- Planning bureau

- Selection of providers and contract initiation (RfI, RfP)

- Writing the business case

Compensation payments to stakeholders during the pre-commissioning phase are typically in the form of *lobbying*, which is generally considered to be the act of trying to influence legislation. An organization will be regarded as attempting to influence legislation if it contacts, or urges the public to contact, members or employees of a legislative body for the purpose of proposing, supporting, or opposing legislation, or if the organization advocates the adoption or rejection of legislation.[1]

For many routine investments, pre-commissioning costs may be insignificant or may be part of the company's general overhead management costs and may therefore be chosen to be ignored. For other investments, they may be limited to the costs of putting together the business case and they may be treated as sunk costs. On the other hand, for some major investments, like introducing a new product, entering a new market, or building an airport, substantial amounts of money need to be spent before it can be decided whether the investment can be initiated. There are no hard and fast rules around pre-commissioning costs. It is usually up to the business case team to decide which of these costs to be included in the calculation and which ones to be treated as sunk costs.

Commissioning costs

Commissioning costs span all costs incurred from the time the investment is decided until it is handed over to operations. While it can be a matter of only a few days or weeks to order equipment, wait for the delivery, and install it, on the other hand, it can take several years to build a new airplane or construct a new airport. These costs can be substantial; however, they are usually "closed" when the investment is handed over to operations.

Typical cost categories are:

- Compensation to various stakeholders

- Installation

- IT hardware and software licenses

- Legal support and regulatory approvals

- Payments to employees to encourage transition

- Project management, accounting, and auditing

- Purchasing of land and construction of buildings

- Purchasing of machines and other infrastructure

- Recruitment and/or training of specialist staff

- Redundancy payments to staff

- Selection of providers and contract initiation

- Transition costs from status-quo to the new investment

Bribery can be a form of stakeholder compensation prevalent in the commissioning phase of an investment. Bribery is the act of offering, giving, receiving, or soliciting money or any other object or promise of value with the aim of altering the behavior of the recipient. While in many countries, giving and receiving bribes is a criminal offense, for many years, many governments (and sometimes the same ones) considered bribes to foreign government officials as tax-deductible payments. Starting in 1996, the OECD (Organisation for Economic Co-operation and Development) Council[2] started discouraging bribery, and most OECD countries have now revised their tax policies. In Germany, for example, paying bribes abroad was legal until 1999 and German companies could deduct bribes from taxable income.[3] Notwithstanding government regulations, if "soft expenses" are required to commission an investment somewhere in this world, the same need to be put into the business case for a complete picture of all costs.

Operating costs

Operating costs are incurred after the investment is handed over to production and is up and running. This phase focuses attention on the fact that some investments have a lifetime of many years and therefore need maintenance effort to keep them going. Maintenance generally generates operating costs. Typical categories for these kinds of running costs are:

- Communication costs (telephone, leased lines, network infrastructure)

- Consumables

- Ensuring business continuity, including provisions for disaster recovery and insurance costs

- Human resources (own employees and external providers)

- Licensing costs, hiring, and leasing costs

- Maintenance and servicing of infrastructure

- Management time

Sometimes the total sum of the operating costs over the lifetime of an investment can drastically exceed the costs incurred in the previous phases; Case 3.1 is a classic example of how the relatively inexpensive one-time installation of trash cans is followed by operating costs on an annual basis.

Case 3.1   The operating costs of trash collection in Philadelphia

Philadelphia is the sixth most populous city in the USA and the largest city in Pennsylvania, with about 1.5 million inhabitants. With its many historical sites relating to the founding of the USA, the city attracts millions of tourists and also business travelers each year.

The volume of pedestrians in downtown Philadelphia poses a major waste collection challenge. In order to keep the streets clean, 700 trash receptacles are put up in the center city district and each is collected 17 times per week via four distinct collection routes. Every route takes on average 5.25 hours. The city administration employs 33 people who are working three full-time shifts and are clocking a total of 18,564 hours annually to operate the trash collection. Every hour of trash collection comes at a cost of $124, which includes:

- Human resources

- Vehicle costs (leasing, maintenance)

- Vehicle operating costs (fuel)

The annual cost of this trash collection operation in downtown Philadelphia is thus $2,302,000. The one-time commissioning costs of installing the dustbins are small compared to the ongoing annual operating costs.[4]

Decommissioning costs

Some investments do not run for ever, some have a definite expiry day, and some need to be upgraded to new technology after a few years. Decommissioning costs capture every activity and spend that is required to ramp down the investment at the end of its planned life cycle. As Case 3.2 on the decommissioning of nuclear power plants shows, these costs can be substantial. Typical cost categories are:

- Clean-up effort and de-installation

- Compensation to various stakeholders

- Re-training

Some investments have a terminal value after their economic lifetime is over; however, this is always subject to a purchaser being found who takes over the investment and is willing to pay a price for it. The handling of the terminal value in the business case calculation is dealt with in Section 5.2. However, if there is no secondary market for the investment, then the terminal value is hypothetical and a realistic business case needs to include decommissioning costs instead.

Case 3.2   Planning framework for nuclear decommissioning

The Nuclear Decommissioning Authority (NDA) in the UK is a non-departmental public body set up by the government in April 2005; its purpose is to create a UK-wide plan to clean up existing public sector nuclear sites with a focus on environmental restoration.

To understand the business of nuclear decommissioning, it is helpful to look at a nuclear reactor's typical life cycle in Figure 3.2; it includes all clean-up of radioactive and other material as well as a progressive dismantling of the site. For example, at the Chapelcross Nuclear Power Station in Scotland, building activities (the commissioning phase) began in 1955 and the power station began generating electricity four years later in 1959 (the operating phase). Power generation ceased in 2004 after 45 years of operation and the cooling towers were demolished in 2007 (the decommissioning phase; see Figure 3.3). In 2009, the first flask with radioactive elements left for reprocessing at Sellafield. The timeline for total decommissioning of Chapelcross will be in the range of 120 years and it is estimated that more jobs will be created in the decommissioning than in the operating phase.

In order to clean up the UK's first generation of nuclear power plants, a cash outflow of £73 billion is needed; this estimate from 2008 is up by 18 per cent from the initial estimates in 2005 when the NDA was established. New nuclear plants are now planned with decommissioning in mind. EDF Energy, the energy company which is part of the European EDF Group, says: "EDF has considered the cost of decommissioning to be part of the business case for new nuclear [plants] from the very beginning of our projects [...] We are confident new plants can be built and run safely and economically in the UK without subsidy. That includes all costs associated with construction, operation, decommissioning, and waste disposal."[5] EDF Energy further explains: "The company decommissioning [...] plans have evolved over a number of years and have been developed using multi-attribute decision analysis to ensure that the Best Practicable Environmental Option (BPEO) is being pursued. The strategy and plans [are] taking due consideration of the nuclear, industrial and environmental safety implications. The company policy and strategy objective of decommissioning is to return the power station sites to a state suitable for unrestricted alternative use."[6,7]

3.2 FINANCIAL ISSUES WITH COSTS

While the concept of costs and cost stages as outlined in Section 3.1 is generally well understood, certain types of costs come with financial issues relevant for building the business case. Figure 3.4 shows a summary of cost types and whether they are to be included in the business case or to be left out.

Hidden costs

Any costs which come up after the investment is approved and have not been thought about during the initial business case are referred to as hidden costs. The following categories are some

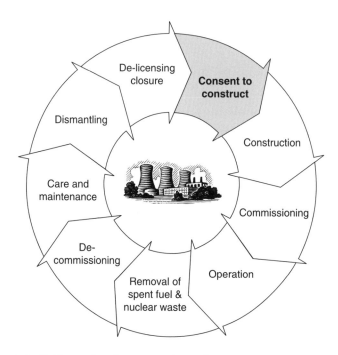

Figure 3.2 *Life cycle of a typical nuclear reactor site*

Figure 3.3 *Decommissioning of the Chapelcross nuclear power station*[8]

classic examples of hidden costs which are often neglected in the business case:

- In order to lay off employees who are no longer required, compensation needs to be paid.

- Government officials ask for compensation to get (legal) things done. While bribery is a criminal offense in most countries and while most companies have strict anti-bribery rules in place, corporate reality is unfortunately still different. In some countries government approval processes do not appear to work without "speed money." In order to show a clean face to the regulator, shareholders, and the public, such bribes are usually built into subcontractor fees. A realistic business case needs to account for these "soft expenses" as well (see Section 3.1, commissioning costs).

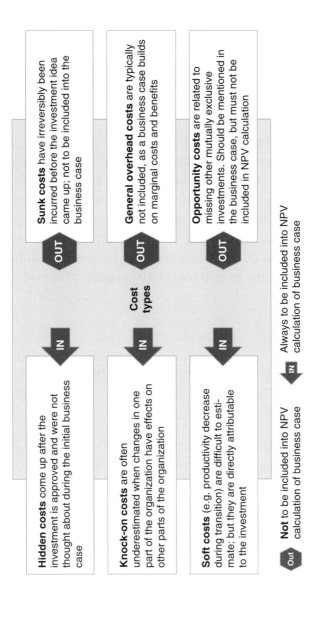

Figure 3.4 *Cost types and financial implications for the business case*

- Possible unforeseen changes in legislation, regulation, and other requirements imposed by law can make costs spiral upwards; this chance needs to be addressed and factored in under risk and uncertainty (see also Chapter 6).

- Climatic events or unfortunate accidents can delay the implementation process; this should also be budgeted for under risk and uncertainty.

While hidden costs by their very nature are not easy to identify and usually come as a surprise, a good business case should always strive to reduce the number and size of surprises. Some hidden costs will not be caught in the initial business case. Should they surface later (i.e. once the process of commissioning the investment has been started), the impact of these newly identified costs on the business case needs to be analyzed. It has to be decided whether the investment remains profitable and whether the implementation of the investment can be continued.

Knock-on costs

Changes in one part of the organization, be it a process, an IS/IT system, or machinery, can have effects on other parts of the organization. For example:

- A new computer program produces data in a different format and this new format cannot be picked up by a second computer program used in another department. Manual intervention and data conversion are therefore required – or programmers need to spend effort to fix the second computer program.

- The output produced by new and more efficient machinery now has more tolerance than before. This requires replacement of other machinery in the production process which can handle the less accurate input.

These are examples of knock-on effects leading to costs arising somewhere else in the organization; they need to be correctly estimated and built into the business case.

Soft costs

The costs listed under the cost stages in Section 3.1 include both hard and soft costs. While *hard costs* can be easily extracted from accounting systems as cash-out payments and are therefore readily agreed by all stakeholders as being attributable to the investment, *soft costs* are about productivity decreases during switch-over to a new system and potential mistakes during the learning curve. It is much more difficult to arrive at an agreement on soft costs with the stakeholders. Nonetheless, as they are directly attributable to the investment suggestion, they form an important part of the business case calculation.

Sunk costs

Sunk costs are costs that have irreversibly already incurred (i.e. before the business case was started or as part of the pre-commissioning phase; see Section 3.1). Any such sunk costs are *not* to be taken into account for the business case.

In real life, sunk costs often affect management decisions due to a typical human tendency to try to avoid losses and not appear wasteful. The costs already incurred become a benchmark for value, whereas they should actually be ignored for any further decision-making; this leads to irrational behavior in decision-making. Daniel Kahneman and Amos Tversky developed the Nobel-prize winning *prospect theory* of behavioral economics, saying that people in real life do not necessarily take optimal decisions, but use other heuristics for making decisions on the potential value of losses and gains.[9] Other studies show that the sunk cost effect is so deeply manifested in human psychology that even taking prior courses in economics (or reading books like this one) does not lessen its influence on decision-making.[10]

General overhead costs

Business cases are generally built on marginal costs and benefits, i.e. investment decisions are taken based on the direct changes that an investment brings into the organization. However, general overhead costs are typically *not* included in a business case in order to avoid double counting of costs or improvements. Examples of such general overhead costs are:

• Computer network infrastructure

• Human resources department

• Real estate maintenance

Opportunity costs

Opportunity costs are related to missing other mutually exclusive investment options; the true cost of something also includes what one gives up in order to get something else. This specifically also includes the missed economic benefits of one alternative because a decision was made to go for another alternative. The notion of opportunity costs is a basic concept in the study of economics and describes the basic relationship between scarcity and choice. For instance, by deciding to build a hospital on a plot of land, one foregoes the chance to build a factory or to simply make money by selling the land to a real estate developer.

However, a business case does *not* include opportunity costs, and this is where the main difference can be found between economic and accounting cost concepts. In a business case, opportunity costs are only documented in the appendix (see Section 8.2) and may be discussed as a part of the final business case presentation, but they must not make their way into the financials and the NPV calculation.

3.3 ESTIMATING COSTS

Obtaining consistent and dependable cost estimates has always been a challenge, and the failure to do so has contributed its fair share to many overruns in project budgets across industry verticals and countries. The very recent example of the London 2012 Olympic Games (Case 3.3) illustrates how difficult it is to obtain reliable and robust cost estimates.

Case 3.3   Estimating costs for the London 2012 Olympic and Paralympic Games

The Olympic Park has become so familiar on the East London Skyline that it is easy to forget the contaminated industrial land that was there before. In just six years a new park, complemented with new transport links and shopping facilities, was built by the Olympic Delivery Authority (ODA). The ODA was established by the London Olympic and Paralympic Games Act 2006 as a non-departmental public body and made responsible for building the permanent venues and infrastructure needed for the Games. But was the ODA on course to deliver the program within budget?

Comparing summer and winter Olympic Games over the past fifty years, we can see that the eventual cost of the Olympic Games is always over budget, by 179 per cent on average. While staging Olympic Games is probably one of the riskiest major projects, estimations have been improved. Whereas the average overrun between 1968 and 2000 was a staggering 258 per cent, since Sydney in 2000, the Games have become closer to achieving their bid budget with average overruns of "only" 47 per cent.[11] Bent Flyvbjerg of the Saïd Business School, University of Oxford says: "While all major programmes are prone to cost overruns, due largely both to optimism and conscious strategic misrepresentation, overruns of the Games are in a league of their own. When compared with typical overruns on other major programmes, such as transport and IT programmes, budget overruns for the Olympic Games are extreme, both for their size and frequency."[12] So where does London 2012 stand?

The total London 2012 budget was planned to be £4.2 billion in 2005[13] when London bid for and won the Olympics 2012. In 2010, the spending review baseline was set at £9.298 billion which remained stable until the start of the Games 2012, but with shifts in spending from construction to operational delivery. Figure 3.5 shows the cost breakdown as per the March 2012 forecast, i.e. the last one before the start of the Games. The ODA's anticipated final cost (AFC) stands at £6.761 million, including costs of site preparation and infrastructure, venues, venues operations, transport, park-wide projects, media center and village, and program delivery. An amount of £88 million was kept aside to cover assessed risk program contingencies. Further costs to gear up for London 2012 and spent outside the ODA included costs for park transformation, policing and wider security, elite and community sports, venue security, the Paralympic Games, the park operations, other operations projects, "look" of London and wider UK projects, city operations, tourism campaigns, Greater London Authority (GLA) programs, and further contingencies.

It is to be assumed that the cost figures as available in the public domain, and as shown in Figure 3.5 are not quite the real and the final costs of the Games; rather they can be assumed to be politically acceptable costs. The real costs are probably not reported in any one single place – unless a significant auditing and investigation is conducted after the Games.[14]

But what is the underlying reason for the AFCs (£9.298 billion) being so much higher than what was originally presented in 2005 (£4.2 billion) and based on which the decision to bring the Olympics to London was made?

The reason is most likely not the absence of political good-will or incapability of planning investment decisions, but it may lie in the nature of the investment, the Olympic Games, itself. Only a few of the people involved in budgeting and planning for the Olympic Games would have had prior experience with Olympic Games – and this is very much unlike any other major program, such as building an airport or implementing an IT system. The most significant problem is a lack of information transferred from other host cities, and this experience gap means that the committee always needs to start from scratch in many areas – making the same estimation mistakes all over again.

The overall public sector funding for London 2012 is sourced from central government (£6.248 billion), the GLA and London Development Authority (LDA) (£0.875 billion) and the National Lottery (£2.175 billion), which includes contributions of £750 million from dedicated Olympic Lottery games, £340 million spending by Sports Lottery distributors of their existing funds, and £1.085 billion which is transferred from general Lottery proceeds held in the National Lottery Distribution Fund.

Site preparation and infrastructure		£1,822
Powerlines	£287	
Utilities	£235	
Enabling works	£386	
F10 bridge	£55	
Other structures, bridges, and highways	£565	
South park site preparation	£82	
Prescott lock	£5	
Other infrastructure (landscaping)	£207	
Venues		**£1,051**
Stadium	£428	
Aquatics	£251	
Velopark	£87	
Handball	£41	
Basketball	£40	
Other Olympic park venues	£101	
Non-Olympic park venues	£103	
Venues operations		**£55**
Transport		**£894**
Stratford Regional Station	£120	
DLR (Docklands Light Railway)	£80	
Thorntons field	£23	
North London Line	£107	
Other transport capital projects	£99	
Other transport operating expenditure	£465	
Parkwide projects		**£896**
Logistics for site construction	£239	
Security for park construction	£228	
Section 106 and masterplanning	£94	
Insurance	£50	
Parkwide operations	£209	
Security screening and operational areas	£49	
Other parkwide projects	£27	
Media centre and village		**£1,230**
Stratford City land and infrastructure	£618	
Stratford City development plots	-£71	
Village construction - public sector funding	£712	
Village receipt	-£324	
International Broadcast Centre/Main Press Centre (IBC/MPC)	£295	
Programme delivery (ODA)		**£729**
Taxation and interest (ODA)		**-£4**

Park transformation by London Legacy Development Corporation		£296
Policing and wider security		**£475**
Elite and community sports		**£290**
Venue security		**£553**
Paralympic Games		**£95**
LOCOG park operations		**£68**
Funding available to LOCOG		**£183**
Ceremonies	£41	
Contribution to Village	£25	
Venue changes	£11	
Pre-Games perimeter security	£16	
Stadium works	£12	
Capital works	£12	
Paralympic conversion	£6	
Cultural Olympiad	£3	
Finalisation of Olympic Park venues and infrastructure	£9	
Stadium concession pods	£8	
Games-time training venues	£5	
Structural resilience of venues	£5	
Pre-Games operational security	£4	
Other funding set aside	£26	
Operational provisions		**£102**
Last Mile, road events, and Central London Zone	£61	
Operational transport	£20	
Utilities resilience	£13	
Games-wide testing	£3	
Transport	£5	
'Look' of London and wider UK		**£33**
City operations		**£23**
Domestic and international tourism campaigns		**£4**
Greater London Authority (GLA) Olympic and Paralympic programmes		**£13**
Risk and contingency		**£491**
Assessed risk programme contingency for ODA	£88	
Public sector funding package (PSFP)	£403	
contingency and other savings remaining		
Total Anticipated Final Cost (AFC)		**£6,673**

Figure 3.5 *Total AFCs for London 2012*[15]

Obtaining cost estimates

Cost estimates can be obtained through a variety of ways and sources:

- *External contributors.* Costs invoiced from suppliers, service providers, contractors, etc. can be obtained by issuing a request for information/proposal (RfI, RfP). Negotiating a fixed price or an outcome-based pricing model instead of a time and material offering leads to a more reliable input for the business case.

- *In-house contributors.* In addition to external effort, some implementation and commissioning work needs to be carried out by in-house staff. Effort spent in training programs and change-over activities needs to be considered. In-house contributions are usually billed internally from one cost center to the next on a time-and-material basis rather than using a fixed price model. Hence such internal estimates are always prone to error and underestimation.

In order to reduce inaccuracies in cost estimates, it is a good idea to *benchmark* the estimated costs of internal as well as external contributors against previous comparable projects. Unfortunately, internal benchmarks are rarely officially recorded and thus information is mostly only available through personal contacts with other departments. Many firms therefore revert to market research companies and consultancies for external benchmark data. However, even they have difficulties getting access to accurate comparable projects. They usually do not have full access to a client's cost structure and clients rarely provide full and transparent internal information to them. As a result, most available external benchmarks are industry averages which do not provide enough information about the concrete investment circumstances. The business case team runs the danger of comparing apples with pears.

Some companies believe in pressing their providers into *fixed price contracts* assuming they get a guaranteed delivery at predictable costs. They put together a team fairly familiar with the job to be provided by the third party; but in many cases, this team handles a provider selection and RfP process for the very first time. It simply does not know how to put together stringent RfP documents that the provider is forced to – and also willing and able to – respond to without adding plenty of assumptions. Assumptions are softeners for any third-party contracts and allow the provider to gradually increase the price during the delivery in order to meet the target.[16]

Another technique used to arrive at reliable cost estimates is *activity-based costing*. This method helps to measure the development and performance cost of resources, activities, and items. Using this technique, the true cost of a product or service can be determined. It allows total costs to be related to the work accomplished and is thereby more accurate than traditional cost accounting.

Sources of cost advantages

Some firms choose *cost leadership* as a business strategy and attempt to gain competitive advantage by lowering their economic costs below those of their competitors. There are many sources of cost advantage, which can in turn be used as estimating techniques in the business case calculation for decreasing operating costs over the lifespan of an investment.

When there are significant *economies of scale* in manufacturing, distribution, and even other functions like services or marketing, bigger volumes can up to a certain extent lead to per unit cost advantages. As the volume increases, the average cost per-unit decreases until some optimal volume is reached, after which the diseconomies of scale kick in and the per-unit costs begin to increase again (see Figure 3.6). Several functional forms have been widely used in the estimation of such cost functions, including translog, hybrid translog, and generalized quadratic functions.[17] Case 3.4 looks at economies of scale in the financial services industry and derives a generalized quadratic function for long-run average operating expenses in relation to total assets under management in a bank.

Case 3.4   Economies of scale in financial services

An early study in the US savings and loan industry collected data from 86 institutions in a region comprising Idaho, Montana, Oregon, Utah, Washington, and Wyoming. As it is very difficult to measure the volume of production x directly in this kind of services industry, the total assets under management in each institution were used as a measure and it was hypothesized that the larger the asset base of an institution, the higher its profitability. Long-running average cost (LRAC) is measured by average operating expenses. For the year 1975, a quadratic long-run average cost function was estimated:

$$LRAC = 2.38 - 0.6153x + 0.0536x^2$$

where x is the total assets of each savings and loan association measured in million dollars and $LRAC$ is the bank's average operating expenses. The U-shaped quadratic curve in Figure 3.6 reaches its point of minimum average cost when the total assets of a savings and loan association reach \$574 million.[19] At this point, the average operating expenses of the savings and loan industry are 0.61 per cent of its total assets.[18]

There are various reasons why larger volumes often lead to lower average per-unit costs:

- *Specialized machines and automated processes*. When a firm handles high volumes, it is typically able to use specialized

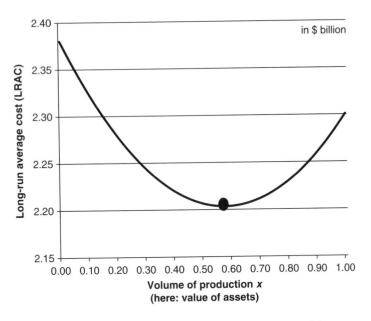

Figure 3.6 *Economies of scale LRAC for savings and loan industry*

manufacturing tools or invest in setting up automated processes.

- *Building and other infrastructure costs.* High volumes may require larger operations, for instance in terms of the size of its buildings, plants, or information technology infrastructure. Increases in the size of buildings come at a less-than-proportionate rise than the cost to build them because of their physical cube-like geometry.

- *Industrialization effects.* High volumes are associated with narrow employee specialization, division of labor, and industrialized delivery. Industrialization effects happen both in the manufacturing as well as in the services industry.[20]

- *Overhead costs.* Unavoidable management and other overhead costs[21] can be spread over more units when the volumes are high and thereby reducing the attributable overhead costs per unit.

Just as economies of scale can generate cost advantages for larger investment proposals, if the investment grows too big beyond an optimal point, diseconomies of scale can lead to an increase in costs. Sometimes there are real physical limits in the underlying engineering of manufacturing, but more often, as an endeavor increases in size or geographical market coverage, it can become increasingly complex to manage and control. This leads to the need of introducing additional management levels and reporting lines, which can bring down efficiencies.

In some circumstances, increasing cumulative volume levels can lead to cost advantages as projects move up the learning curve. The concept of the *learning curve* is very closely linked to the economies of scale, but provides a more dynamic view. It is also commonly referred to as the experience curve or the progress curve. While economies of scale focuses on the discrete relationship between volume and average unit cost at a given point of time, the learning curve is a continuous approach focusing on the relationship between cumulative volume over the investment period and average unit costs. It is to be noted that the learning curve concept does not know a concept of diseconomies of scale when projects grow too big to handle. Rather, costs continue to fall until they reach the technologically possible lowest cost. The driving forces behind the learning curve are improvements of work methods, fine-tuning of processes, and in general a detailed learning about how to make an operation as efficient as possible. The shape of the learning curve has been derived from empirical observations and can mathematically best be represented as a geometric progression that forecasts the cost reduction from one unit of production to its succeeding unit:

$$LRUC = ax^{-\beta}$$

where a is the cost associated with producing the first unit, x is the total number of units produced, and β is a coefficient describing the rate of learning in producing the output; LRUC is the long-running unit cost when all x units are produced.

Suppose, it takes an employee 60 minutes for the first time to complete a data-entry process in a BPO environment and it takes her or him 48 minutes the second time. With these two observations, it is now possible to predict the rate of learning for data entry. With $a = 60$ min for the first data entry and a 20 per cent improvement for the second data entry, unit cost of production for the succeeding unit $x = 2$ becomes $LRUC = 48$ min. With this information, the learning rate β can be calculated by transforming the above equation:

$$\beta = log_x \frac{a}{LRUC} = log_2 \frac{60\,\text{min}}{48\,\text{min}} = 0.321928$$

Now

$$LRUC = 60 \ \text{min} \cdot x^{-0.321928}$$

can be used to anticipate the time of data entry in future periods for a business case. Figure 3.7 illustrates the learning curve for this example.

A learning curve is usually named in percentages representing the slope. An 80 per cent learning curve means that, for every doubling of volume, the cost of new volume is only 80 per cent, i.e. the improvement rate is 20 per cent. The slope can be used to express the ratio of the cost of any unit value to the cost of twice the unit value. As volume doubles from one unit to two units to four units, etc., the learning curve descends quite sharply as costs decrease dramatically. As volume increases, it takes longer to double previous volume, and the learning curve flattens out. Thus, costs decrease at a slower pace when volume is higher.

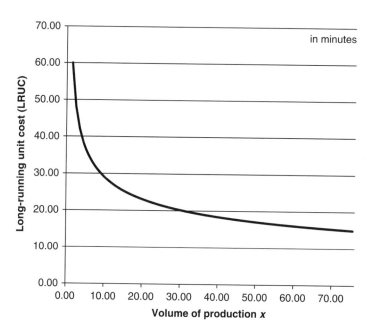

Figure 3.7 *Learning curve LRUC for data entry (80 per cent)*

There is a mathematical relationship between the name of a learning curve (*slope*) in percentage and its β in the learning curve equation:

$$Slope\ (\%) = 100 \cdot 2^{-\beta}$$

$$\beta = log_2 \frac{100}{Slope\ (\%)}$$

The following guidelines can be used for estimating the slope of the learning curve in different production environments with a combination of hand assembly and machine manufacturing[22]:

- 75 per cent hand assembly and 25 per cent machining: 80 per cent

- 50 per cent hand assembly and 50 per cent machining: 85 per cent

- 25 per cent hand assembly and 75 per cent machining: 90 per cent

Or per industry:

• Aerospace	85 per cent
• Shipbuilding	80 to 85 per cent
• Complex machine tools for new models	75 to 85 per cent
• Repetitive electronics manufacturing	90 to 95 per cent
• Repetitive machining or punch-press operations	90 to 95 per cent
• Repetitive electrical operations	75 to 85 per cent
• Repetitive welding operations	90 per cent
• Raw materials	93 to 96 per cent
• Purchased parts	85 to 88 per cent

If learning curves are plotted from actual cost data or observations, the business case team has to be very careful on its application. First and foremost, the first unit of production has to be defined. Rarely will the cost of producing the first sample unit be anywhere comparable to producing the first unit in a production sequence. A sample unit has a different purpose, namely of working out design and production problems. Hence it cannot be assumed to represent the start of a production sequence. It does, however, provide input for estimating the time needed for the first production unit, which should become the starting point of the learning curve. Both the costs spent on the first production unit as well as the slope of the improvement curve hence become guesstimates. Errors in one can be compounded by the effects of the other.

A suggested practical approach is to estimate the costs for a later production unit a few weeks or months after production starts and then to construct the improvement curve through this point. The theoretical costs of the first unit can then be derived by going back up the learning curve to unit one. Another good idea is to go by comparison and derive the costs of the first unit as well as the slope from historical data in similar environments. However, this requires a detailed analysis of the differences between the two environments.

Whatever approach is taken towards costs, estimates must be as accurate as possible. They should not be too aggressive, because this will inevitably lead to cost overruns in the implementation phase; nor should they contain too much buffer for risk and uncertainty, as this will blow up the cost estimates to a level where a company may let go of an otherwise profitable investment.

The business case methodology has approaches in place to investigate the investment dynamics caused by risk and uncertainty; these will be discussed in more detail in Chapter 6.

3.4 TAXES

Taxes impact the business case calculation of investments in two ways. First, a successful investment produces net profits and these will attract corporate taxes, which are a cost to the company. Second, expenditure linked to the investment may provide the possibility to claim capital allowances as tax deductions.

The business case for any investment project needs to look at how to calculate the tax burden and when exactly the taxes have to be paid, i.e. when the cash outflow happens. As a rule of thumb, business cases are always to be calculated on cash leaving or coming into the organization, i.e. they are to be constructed as an after-tax study. The taxes and their impact on cash flows must not be ignored in the business case study.

Taxable profit

When the business case forecasts cash inflows based on profit generated by the investment, the corresponding tax payments should also be captured as cash outflows leading to a reduced net cash flow. Getting the timing of tax payments right may be a little tricky as corporate taxes are not paid immediately when profit is generated; in most countries, the actual payment of corporate taxes is delayed and usually does not occur until the following tax year.

Tax deductions

Depreciation expenses find their way into P&L statements and the annual reports. However, depreciation expenses are added back to operating profits in the tax accounts; whether a straight-line or an accelerated depreciation is chosen does not influence the tax burden. Hence depreciation expenses are generally not to be captured in the business case.

Notwithstanding this general guideline, some governments offer provisions for companies to deduct *capital allowances* according to prescribed rates and durations for different investment types, such as investments in plant or machinery, converting building space above commercial premises to flats for renting, and R&D equipment. Capital allowances take the place of the depreciation shown in the financial statements, which is not allowable for corporation tax purposes. Capital allowances are usually only available in the financial year (FY) following the expenditure linked to a purchase. Depending on when exactly the purchase was made and whether the country's FY follows the calendar year or not, capital allowances can lag behind up to one year and a half. As a rule of thumb, it is recommended for the purpose of the business case to delay cash inflows through capital allowances to the second year after the related cash outflow.

If an asset is resold before all the capital allowances are recovered, the difference between its net book value (the purchase value adjusted for the redeemed capital allowances) and its selling price needs to be settled with the tax authorities. If the selling price is higher than the net book value, the excess capital allowances are claimed back through a *balancing charge*. If the selling price is lower than the net book value, a further capital allowance is usually offered.

Sometimes governments offer special tax allowances as incentives to drive investments in certain fields or geographical areas. Such *tax shields* can be substantial and should be included in the business case. Nonetheless, tax shields should never be used to turn a bad investment into a profitable one; regardless of government incentives, every corporate investment should be able to stand on its own legs.

Lastly, capital allowances only have an impact on the benefits of the business case if the investment has started to make a profit and the capital allowances can be offset against the profit, or the company as a whole can offset the capital allowances from this investment against profits from other investments.

3.5   LEASING

Through *leasing* a company can obtain the use of fixed assets for a pre-defined period of time for which it has to make a series of contractually agreed period payments; the *lessee* is the receiver of the assets under the lease contract and the *lessor* is the owner of the assets.

Leasing vs. buying

No book on decision management and investment decisions would be complete without considering the option of leasing versus buying. In general, leasing is an expensive way of acquiring assets for an investment project; an outright purchase of the same assets is usually less expensive even if the company needs to borrow funds on a credit line basis. What is more, leases are usually for multiple years, typically three to ten years, and difficult to terminate before the agreed end date, taking away some of the organization's flexibility. So, why would a company still go for leasing instead of buying?

Leases on machinery, computers and vehicles typically include some of the servicing and other running costs, providing a worry-free full-service package. The company also does not have to worry about upgrading or disposing the items after they are no longer required. While a cyclic upgrade does make sense for computer equipment in an office building, the requirement of the leasing company to change computer equipment at predetermined dates can be detrimental for computer equipment installed onsite at worldwide construction sites. In extreme cases, the equipment would have to be de-installed somewhere in Siberia (for example), brought back to the home country, and replaced with new equipment, having to go through all export/import procedures all over again. When owning the equipment, the company is free to use it at the construction site for as long as it is required and thereafter can dispose of it locally instead of bringing it home in order to meet the lessor's requirement of returning the leased assets.

The main advantage of leasing, however, is its off-balance sheet financing capability, i.e. leasing is not taken into account when calculating a company's debt capacity (see Section 1.1 on financial statements and ratios).

As a general rule, and as financial management is made up of the two independent cycles of investing and raising cash, the justification for the investment decision in a business case should also be dealt with independently of the financing decision. A company should always have direct access to the necessary funds for paying the investment-related costs. The question of whether to lease, finance, or purchase should never affect the investment decision.

Net present value of leasing

A NPV calculation of leasing vs. buying/financing highlights the following key differences between the two main options:

- The value of the option to abandon,

- Implication of taxes, and

- Timing of payments.

Consider the following example: Company CAD Ltd is into computer-aided engineering (CAD) and decides to invest into a new high-end plotter. While it has already decided to go ahead with the investment, it still needs to find the best way of procuring the plotter; alternative one is to buy it outright with a cash payment and alternative two is to lease the plotter from the manufacturer for a set period. The list price of the plotter is $50,000 and the company would be eligible for capital allowances of 25 per cent; the lifetime of the plotter is estimated to be five years, after which it loses its print accuracy and would need to be replaced with a new plotter. A service and maintenance contract costs $2,000 p.a. The leasing alternative amounts to $17,000 p.a., which includes the service and maintenance contract. The leasing contract runs for three years with an option to renew thereafter on an annual basis at a reduced rate of $10,000. The after-tax nominal opportunity cost of capital is set at 6 per cent by the company's financial management; the corporate taxes are 30 per cent. Should CAD Ltd buy or lease the plotter?

As this is a financing decision (and not an investment decision any more!), the alternative with the lowest net present cost value needs to be determined. The net present cost values are calculated in Figure 3.8 and amount to −$44,981 for buying the plotter and −$46,234 for the leasing option; as the buying option has a smaller net present cost value, buying would be more favorable.

This calculation, however, does not yet consider the value of flexibility which comes along with the leasing contract; the contract

Net Present Value of <u>Buying</u> the Plotter

	Today			Investment period			
	0	1	2	3	4	5	6
Purchasing costs	−$50,000						
Service contract	−$2,000	−$2,000	−$2,000	−$2,000	−$2,000		
Capital allowance		$12,500	$12,500	$12,500	$12,500		
Tax saved			$600	$4,350	$4,350	$4,350	$4,350
Net cash inflow	$52,000	−$2,000	−$1,400	$2,350	$2,350	$4,350	$4,350
Discount factor	1.00000	0.94340	0.89000	0.83962	0.79209	0.74726	0.70496
Present value	−$52,000	−$1,887	−$1,246	$1,973	$1,861	$3,251	$3,067
Net present value	−$44,981						
Rate of return	6.00%						
Corporate tax rate	30.00%						

Net Present Value of <u>Leasing</u> the Plotter

	Today			Investment period			
	0	1	2	3	4	5	6
Leasing contract	−$17,000	−$17,000	−$17,000	−$10,000	−$10,000		
Tax saved		$5,100	$5,100	$5,100	$3,000	$3,000	$0
Net cash inflow	−$17,000	−$11,900	−$11,900	−$4,900	−$7,000	$3,000	$0
Discount factor	1.00000	0.94340	0.89000	0.83962	0.79209	0.74726	0.70496
Present value	−$17,000	−$11,226	−$10,591	−$4,114	−$5,545	$2,242	$0
Net present value	−$46,234						
Rate of return	6.00%						
Corporate tax rate	30.00%						

Figure 3.8 *NPV of buying vs. leasing (example)*

Net Present Value of <u>Buying</u> the Plotter

	Today		Investment period				
	0	1	2	3	4	5	6
Purchasing costs	-$50,000						
Service contract	-$2,000	-$2,000	-$2,000	-$2,000			
Capital allowance		$12,500	$12,500	$12,500	$12,500		
Tax saved			$600	$4,350	$4,350	$4,350	$3,750
Net cash inflow	-$52,000	-$2,000	-$1,400	$2,350	$4,350	$4,350	$3,750
Discount factor	1.00000	0.94340	0.89000	0.83962	0.79209	0.74726	0.70496
Present value	-$52,000	-$1,887	-$1,246	$1,973	$3,446	$3,251	$2,644
Net present value	**-$43,820**						
Rate of return	6.00%						
Corporate tax rate	30.00%						

Net Present Value of <u>Leasing</u> the Plotter

	Today		Investment period				
	0	1	2	3	4	5	6
Leasing contract	-$17,000	-$17,000	-$17,000	-$10,000			
Tax saved		$5,100	$5,100	$5,100	$3,000	$0	$0
Net cash inflow	-$17,000	-$11,900	-$11,900	-$4,900	$3,000	$0	$0
Discount factor	1.00000	0.94340	0.89000	0.83962	0.79209	0.74726	0.70496
Present value	-$17,000	-$11,226	-$10,591	-$4,114	$2,376	$0	$0
Net present value	**-$40,555**						
Rate of return	6.00%						
Corporate tax rate	30.00%						

Figure 3.9 *Flexibility option in leasing (example continued)*

locks in CAD Ltd for only three years and afterwards offers an annual prolongation option. Assuming that CAD Ltd notices after four years that the plotter's technology is now outdated, does not provide the company with a competitive edge, and that it therefore needs to replace the plotter earlier than originally estimated (and assuming further that there is no market to sell used and outdated plotters), the new NPV calculation as performed in Figure 3.9 gives a different vote. The revised NPV amounts to -$43,820 for buying the plotter and -$40,555 for the leasing option. Given this additional information and flexibility requirement, the tide has turned in favor of the leasing option.

4
Fundamentals II: Benefits

Next to estimating costs, looking at potential benefits is the second fundamental aspect of any investment decision-making process. While costs bring down the business case, benefits support the suggested investments. As simple as this may sound, identifying, evaluating, and estimating business benefits are three challenging tasks. In the business case process, they are perceived by many as akin to predicting the future by looking into a crystal ball. Getting only one of these tasks wrong can lead to financial disaster. Not knowing what benefits to expect is a sure-fire way for the investment not to deliver any benefits at all. And what is worse, this disaster will not be immediately visible; instead, it will hide beneath the surface. It is only long after the investment has been commissioned and when management suddenly begins to notice that benefits are not being reaped according to the forecast that people begin to question the original business case again.

Not so long ago, during the dot-com boom in the late 1990s, companies rushed to implement some innovative IT system in order to block competition, increase market share, and secure their space in the e-commerce economy. It was all about business integration and a networked economy.[1] Benefits were deemed to be certain to be enjoyed somewhere down the road. Needless to say, some of these benefits were elusive at best and not quite as low-hanging as initially suggested. Today, companies are more serious about using investments for competitive advantage and they are most serious about determining the business impact of an investment.

To find an appropriate measure of the business impact that an investment can deliver, it is first and foremost important to understand the different types of benefits to look out for and second to have credible methods at hand which help to identify, evaluate, and estimate their business impact.

4.1 BENEFIT TAXONOMY

Feature vs. benefit

In the heat of the benefit identification process, many business managers tend to confuse features with benefits. This mix-up is even more pronounced with sales people, who are trying to "help" their clients with their purchase decisions by highlighting a product's (or service's) benefits in a flamboyant way. More often than not, they fall short of describing business impact and produce nothing but an endless list of features. Chapter 10 is all about how a business case can be used in sales and can help to speed up buying decisions.

There is a clear distinction between features and benefits. While a *feature* only represents an element of functionality within the context of a change, a *benefit* is a much bigger thing and relates to the business outcome of the change.

For example, the introduction of cross-selling propositions "frequently bought together" and "other customers who have bought this item also bought" to e-commerce websites such as Amazon, *per se*, is a feature; however, if one of the business goals of Amazon is to drive up sales and thereby increase revenue, and if this e-commerce feature on the website actually generates cross-sales which would not have taken place otherwise, then the features become a benefit with a business outcome. On the other hand, if customers do not click on the other books or if such clicks do not result in sales, the cross-selling suggestions remain little more than a programmer's artwork. Something which does not have commercial value cannot be treated as a benefit and remains – at best – a feature.

When seen in isolation, features are only solution components and therefore they have no place in a business case. Nonetheless, features can very much be the cause for benefits in a cause-and-effect relationship; they have the power to kick-start a benefit generation process. Section 4.4 introduces the technique of benefit discovery charts in order to identify how features enable business benefits.

Monetary vs. non-monetary benefits

The benefit taxonomy makes an important distinction between benefits with a monetary outcome and benefits with a non-monetary outcome (see Figure 4.1).

Monetary benefits are advantages which either reduce costs or increase revenue. Costs can be reduced in relation to

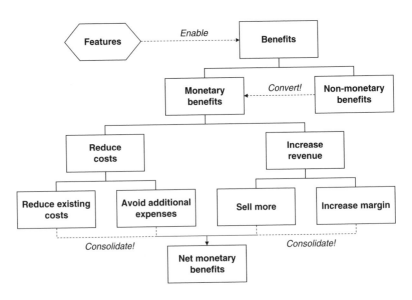

Figure 4.1 *Benefit taxonomy*

already existing costs or by avoiding additional expenditure. Cost-cutting programs or investments into programs aiming to increase efficiency are examples of the first category. Failing to upgrade computer hardware, reducing the amount of external training, or not complying with regulatory requirements (and thereby maybe even risking penalty payments) are examples of avoiding expenditure. Revenue can be increased by selling more or by increasing the profit margin of every item sold.

Ultimately, consolidating the two dimensions of costs and revenue again leads to *net monetary benefits*. For instance, replacing the sales force with an online e-commerce platform may reduce headcount and the human resource costs of the sales force. At the same time, IT administration costs will go up. And if the lack of customer intimacy makes the sales revenue decrease by a large amount, the net result will be declining profitability. This simple example reinforces the need for a holistic view of an investment or change-related business case.

Non-monetary benefits are of an intangible nature, i.e. they cannot be directly captured in financial terms. Examples are improvement of customer perception, increased publicity due to reporting about the company in trade journals, installing exhaust filters to improve the air quality in the surrounding neighborhood, or giving the company's management access to industry insight information. Such benefits are difficult to comprehend fully and therefore the attaching of a financial value to them is perceived to be difficult. Because of their intangible nature, they are elusive and risk not being adequately represented in the decision-making process. Often they are also elusive with respect to not being operationalized at all during the lifespan of an investment; their realization is difficult to measure and control. Section 4.5 focuses exclusively on non-monetary benefits and what to do with them in a business case context. The good news is that despite their seemingly intangible nature, quite a number of non-monetary benefits can nonetheless be turned into financial benefits.

4.2 STRATEGIC BENEFIT MAPS

Looking at and applying generic benefit criteria can help to jump-start the benefit identification process for a selected investment proposition. The reason is that most corporate investment projects share a common underlying structure of benefits, and to tell the story of how value is created for an organization, *strategic benefit maps* are an excellent communication tool.

Strategic benefit maps as a tool are based on the concept of *strategy maps*,[2] which have evolved from the four-perspective model of the *balanced scorecard* and was originally proposed by Kaplan and Norton in the early 1990s as a performance measurement framework that added strategic non-financial performance measures to traditional financial metrics to give managers and executives a more "balanced" view of organizational performance. *Strategic benefit maps* show a logical, step-by-step connection between value drivers and strategic benefits in the form of a cause-and-effect chain. Understanding these cause-and-effect chains can be extremely helpful in pinpointing benefits for building a business case. Generally speaking, improving performance in the intangible objectives found in the *learning & growth perspective* enables the organization to improve its *internal process perspective* objectives, which in turn enables the organization to create desirable results in the *customer perspective* leading to monetary results in the *financial perspective*.

Ultimately, a company's financial perspective is fuelled from the revenue it generates from its customers. Therefore any investment that strengthens a bond with customers has a shorter *revenue distance* to the financial perspective than an investment that improves, for example, internal processes. As the revenue distance increases, the benefits of an investment become less clear and the benefit justification in a business case more nebulous.[3]

Organizations in a high-growth phase in a nascent industry or market tend to focus more on value creation for their customers than established organizations in mature markets, whose primary focus is usually on revenue capture. Creative and innovative investments will therefore have a bigger impact on companies in their growth phase; cost savings investments will have a bigger impact on revenue capture in mature industries. Case 4.1 highlights how Bharti Airtel in India's high-growth telecommunication market concentrates on creating value at the customer interface and sheds non-core activities by outsourcing them to third parties.

Case 4.1 Bharti Airtel

Bharti Airtel is a leading integrated telecommunications company headquartered in New Delhi, India, with operations in 20 countries across Asia and Africa. It has over 246 million customers (February 2012) across its operations and ranks among the top five mobile service providers globally in terms of subscribers.[4] The Indian telecommunications industry is one of the fastest growing in the world, driven by wireless revolution adding more than 18 million new subscribers every month to an installed base of 903 million (January 2012); the sector contributes to nearly 2 per cent of Indian GDP and has emerged as the prime engine of economic growth.[5]

Owing to this growth, multinational telecommunication companies are expressing their interest in investing in India's telecommunication industry. Bharti Airtel therefore focuses its activities and investments on creating customer value (CV) through responsive sales, service, and new product development. At this rapid growth stage of the industry's lifecycle it is more important for Bharti Airtel to create CV than to capture revenue from activities like IT, customer service centers, network management, and tower infrastructure ownership. Consequently, it has outsourced many of these activities and even created a separate company, Bharti Infratel, to handle the erection and maintenance of telecommunication towers.[6]

Financial perspective

The strategic benefit map's financial perspective describes the tangible monetary outcomes of the strategy in financial terms. Companies can either make more money (increased cash flow leading to long-term shareholder value) by selling more (increased revenue) or spending less (reduced costs resulting in increased productivity); everything else is secondary. For any investment to create value for the company, it needs to enable the company either to sell more or to spend less.

Companies can increase revenue by deepening relationships with existing customers. This allows them to sell more products or services thereby improving the value and profitability of existing customers. In a strategic marketing context, this is referred to as *cross-* or *up-selling*. In addition, companies can generate revenue by leveraging new sources of revenue in new markets, introducing new products, or cooperating with new partners.

The reduction of costs through productivity improvements can occur either through an improved cost structure or through increased asset utilization. First, by lowering direct cash expenses, the same quantity of output is produced while spending less on input factors such as materials, supplies, energy, and people. Indirect expenses can be reduced by eliminating defects and waste. Second, by utilizing financial or physical assets more effectively, the working and fixed capital to support a company's operations are reduced. For instance, just-in-time (JIT) approaches enable production or sales with fewer inventories; a reduction of machine downtime allows producing the same amount of output with a decreased equipment park; even smaller incremental investments may help to eliminate bottlenecks and speed up the production process.

Investments to improve revenue growth generally take longer to create measurable benefits than investments to improve productivity. The tendency in today's business world with quarterly reporting to shareholders is to favor the short term over the long term. Nonetheless, a firm's overarching objective must be sustained growth in shareholder value, which can only be achieved by balancing both short-term productivity and long-term growth perspectives. Long-term growth cannot be achieved through cost cutting, but realistically only through increased revenue.

Customer perspective

The customer perspective defines an organization's value proposition for targeted customers. Thus it also provides the context for how an organization's internal processes, intangible assets, and investments can ultimately create value. In short, an investment proposition will be successful when aligned with the CV proposition. Common measures for a successful outcome of a new investment initiative are increases in:

- *Customer acquisition.* The identification and qualification of new customers should finally lead to securing new business.

- *Customer satisfaction.* How products and services supplied by a company meet or surpass customer expectation is a key performance indicator within a business, indicating consumer purchase intentions and loyalty. Customer satisfaction is driven by the product, the service associated with the product, the price (and hence the perceived value for money), and the image related with consuming the product.

- *Customer retention.* Most businesses have the objective of keeping their customers and thereby retaining their revenue contribution. The aim is to prevent customers from defecting to alternative brands or the competition.

- *Market and account share.* While market share measures the percentage of a company's sales to total industry sales, account share refers to the company's proportion of a given customer's (or group of customer's) purchases. Market share as a metric is mostly used in business-to-consumer (B-2-C) markets and account share mostly in business-to-business (B-2-B) markets.

- *Customer profitability.* The difference between the revenues earned and the costs associated with a customer relationship should yield a profit stream in a specified period. The biggest challenge is the direct assignment of costs to an individual customer relationship.

These measures themselves are cause-and-effect relationships, i.e. an increase in customer satisfaction usually leads to increased retention and further to increased profitability, as acquiring new customers is usually more expensive than retaining customers.

Having satisfied and loyal customers is not a benefit in its own right, but it is merely a value driver, which (hopefully) leads to a tangible monetary benefit in the financial perspective. Once the business case team understands which the targeted customer segments are that will benefit from the investment project, it can draw up the objectives and benefit measures for the *investment value proposition.* The investment value proposition defines the investment's strategy for the customers by describing what the company expects to do better or differently once the investment is commissioned. Such value propositions for customers typically fall under one of four categories. First, *low cost/best buy* propositions emphasize attractive prices, good quality, good selection, immediate gratification through short lead/cycle times, ease of purchase, etc. Second, *product innovation and leadership* propositions promise superior functionality, allowing the company to ask for above-average prices. Third, a *complete solution* proposition tailors customized products and services to the customer, thereby making the buyer believe to be understood with all needs and wants.

And fourth, *lock-in* cases arise when businesses create high switching costs for their customers through, for instance, proprietary technology, big training effort to start using the product, or being a dominant supplier.

Customers value different things. Every CV the same thing differently, and at different times in different ways. The creation of CV has long been recognized as a central concept in marketing and even as the purpose of an organization.[7] There is no one true and contingent value; there is also no commonly accepted conceptualization, framework, or typology of CV.[8] Value is extremely personal and both the economic context at the objective level and the subjective meaning are inextricably connected. From a business case perspective it is important to realize where an investment proposition can generate additional value for the customer and how, through cause-and-effect relationships, this value can lead to tangible monetary benefits for the company.

From a customer's perspective, CV is what they get (benefits) relative to what they have to give up (costs and other sacrifices). Four distinct interpretations of object- and subject-based value with respect to products and services can be identified[9]:

- *Exchange value.* This interpretation is object-based and primarily influenced by the nature of the products or services and the market in which they are offered. The customer can influence the process of ascribing value through accepting, rejecting, or negotiating the offered value.

- *Intrinsic value.* This interpretation is object-based and is perceived before or during consumption of the products or services.

- *Use value.* This interpretation is subject-based and is perceived during or after consumption.

- *Utilitarian value.* This interpretation is subject-based and can be identified through a comparison of intrinsic value and use value on the one hand, with the sacrifices the customer has to make in order to receive the products or services on the other hand.

The longitudinal perspective of value for the customer as depicted in Figure 4.2 offers another interpretation[10]:

- *Ex-ante value.* Before the purchase, customers tend to have ex-ante ideas about the value they are going to experience later.

- *Point-of-purchase value.* In some cases, a sense of value is experienced at the point of sales. For example, customers buying an expensive car might feel valued through good treatment in the showroom.

- *Experience value.* After making and completing the purchase decision, the product is used and/or the services are experienced. In this post-purchase phase, subject-based use value is experienced.

- *Disposition value.* Even when the product is decommissioned or the service no longer used, experience value may continue to last.

To identify the contribution of an investment proposition towards generating value for the customer, it is a good idea to

Figure 4.2 *Longitudinal perspective of value*

review the above value perspectives always asking "Where does the investment generate value from a customer point of view?" This leads to the second perspective of value: value for the firm, which in the marketing literature is often referred to as customer lifetime value.[11] This second perspective helps to close the circle to customer profitability of the strategy benefit map.

Internal process perspective

The internal process perspective describes how the CV proposition as defined in the customer perspective is accomplished in a company. Internal processes accomplish two goals for the benefit calculation of an investment: They deliver the value proposition for customers and they reduce costs through increasing productivity for the cost components of the financial perspective.

Internal processes can be grouped into four clusters: operations management, customer management, innovation, and regulatory/social processes.

Operations management processes are the basic processes by which a business produces and delivers its existing products and/or services to its customers. This includes supply, production, distribution, and risk management. Value drivers are found in the area of efficiency increase, avoidance of bottlenecks, reduction of wastage, etc.

Customer management processes work on the value of the relationship with customers by selecting targeted customers, acquiring customers, growing their business, and retaining clients. Value drivers to look for are better segmentation and targeting, needs-based selling and target pricing based on customer intelligence, faster closing cycles, improving service and responsiveness to customer requests and complaints, loyalty improvements, cross-selling, and establishing a trusted relationship with clients.

Innovation processes develop new products and services; they allow the company to enter new areas for reaping monetary revenue and growth benefits. Value drivers are influenced by the quality of the opportunity, length of the product development cycle, and how quickly production and sales can be ramped up.

Regulatory and social processes help to continually grant companies the legal right to operate in their respective countries through managing regulatory and social performance along dimensions of environment, health and safety, employment practices, and community investment. Good performance in these areas lowers operating costs by avoiding penalties imposed by the regulator, attracting and retaining employees, and reducing environment- and human resource-related accidents. It also positively influences the company's image, which is not only a value driver of the customer perspective, but can also improve the company's refinancing capabilities with socially conscious investors.

Learning and growth perspective

The learning and growth perspective identifies which jobs (the human capital), which information capital based on the information systems and technology (IS/IT) infrastructure, and what kind of organizational climate are bundled together with internal processes to leverage them as value drivers. Whereas most companies endeavor to develop their employees, systems, and culture, most do not fully align these efforts with their corporate strategy.

Human capital is the availability of required skills, talent, and know-how; it is put to maximum leverage by motivating employees to deliver high performance. In order to identify how human capital investments can lead to monetary benefits, organizations first need to identify their human capital requirements, estimate the gap between the requirements and the current situation, and then see how the proposed investment can help to close the gap. The strategy map identifies the critical few internal processes that create differentiation and these processes are enabled with strategic job families. Human capital investments will be most useful in exactly these areas.

Information capital consists of two components; information systems (IS) build on information technology (IT). Together, information systems and technology (IS/IT) summarize all the information capital available to an organization required to support its strategy. Information systems (IS) can be categorized into three areas. A transaction processing application automates the basic repetitive transactions of an enterprise; analytic applications promote the analysis, interpretation, and sharing of information respectively knowledge within the company; and transformational applications change the prevailing business model of the enterprise. Together they rest on the organization's technology infrastructure (IT). A benefit value driver identification approach needs to shift from the traditional evaluation by cost and reliability statistics to measuring how IS/IT systems can contribute to fulfilling the organization's strategic mission through supporting the critical internal processes as value drivers. Thereby, investments in IS/IT systems can generate additional cash benefits.

Organization capital is the ability of the organization to mobilize and sustain the process of change through its culture, leadership, alignment, and working together towards executing the strategy as a team. Strategic investment projects operate at the core of a firm's DNA (Deoxyribonucleic acid (containing genetic instructions)) and this requires changes in the behaviors and values of the employee workforce. Benefits can be achieved through the value drivers when investments pounce on one or more of the following areas:

- Creating accountability,

- Driving results,

- Encouraging creativity and innovative behavior,

- Establishing an open communication culture,

- Focusing on the customer,

- Understanding the company's mission, strategy, and corporate values, and

- Working as a team.

4.3 VALUE PANEL

Building on the strategic benefit map, the *value panel* combines the strategic view with the perspective of individual decision-makers. Decision participants are important stakeholders who make, recommend, or influence the final decision about an investment proposition (see Section 1.10). In this process, they consciously or unconsciously rely on certain tangible and intangible factors to judge the investment attractiveness from their point of view. The business case presentation should therefore make sure to address these decision criteria. However, these criteria are not plainly obvious and need to be carefully identified. Having erroneous criteria can lead to an incomplete benefit calculation, misleading the decision participants into making the wrong decision. If such defects are found during the decision-making process, the business case loses its entire credibility.

Powerful yet simple tools are required to support the benefit criteria identification process. While the strategic benefit map (see Section 4.2) is more of a conceptual framework, this section introduces the value panel and the Section 4.4 describes the benefit discovery chart, which are both tools for visually mapping decision criteria. The value panel and the benefit discovery chart are best deployed in a workshop-style environment on a brown paper[12] with sticky notes.

For the value panel, consider an organizational pyramid from *strategic interests* to *tactical objectives* down to *operational concerns*. The top two layers of the pyramid – strategy and tactics – are especially important for every business. However, many business cases still provide too many arguments for the

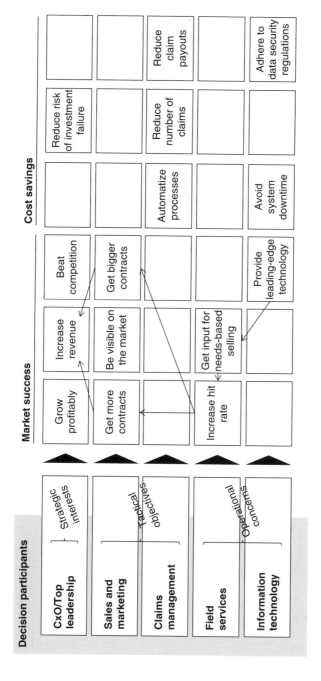

Figure 4.3 *Value panel*

operational layer and the departmental managers, but completely fail to address the needs of the company's top leadership at CxO (Chief Executive/Financial/Information/Operation/... Officer) level, directors, and vice presidents.

Figure 4.3 shows a value panel for an insurance company and the personal health division with the organizational pyramid and its decision participants listed on the vertical axis. The idea of a value panel workshop is to build upon the strategic benefit map and as a first step come up with possible decision criteria, align them to decision participants, classify them as having either a revenue increasing or cost saving intention, and stick them on the panel. The rows of the value panel show who of the decision participants care about what.

As a second step, arrows between the decision criteria can highlight a cause-and-effect link between the interests of different stakeholders. For example, the information technology manager may get excited about introducing leading-edge technology, which can help the field service agents through analytical applications to introduce needs-based selling, which in turn increases the hit rate, gets more and larger contracts, and enables the company to increase its revenue and grow profitably.

As a third step, it is now relatively straightforward to achieve an alignment between the value panel and the strategic benefit map. Instead of sorting the decision criteria by decision participants, the criteria are now being linked to the four different categories of the strategic benefit map. Most likely this will require a few iterations as the strategic benefit map presents a top-down strategy-driven benefit identification process and the value panel introduces a more bottom-up people-driven process; the iteration helps in achieving completeness of the benefit criteria.

4.4 BENEFIT DISCOVERY CHART

The value panel helps the business case team to understand the objectives of the stakeholders and therefore also provides a glimpse into their underlying decision-making criteria. But one has to be very critical before making a stakeholder's objective a key strategic goal for the company. For example, while increased employee satisfaction may be an objective of the HR department, it does not *per se* generate value taken as a standalone objective. Nonetheless, employee satisfaction leads to lower attrition rates and to lower hiring costs. It also leads to increased employee productivity, to more contracts with clients being signed, and thus to increased revenue. Reduced hiring costs as well as increased revenues directly contribute to a company's financial bottom line. Hence increased employee satisfaction should not be considered as a strategic goal, but only as a derived goal supporting the strategic goal of increased cash flow.

Such relationships can be uncovered with a benefit discovery chart; it is a cause-and-effect diagram that shows how a suggested investment generates value and contributes to cash flow generation. It establishes the logical links between costs respectively revenue, benefit areas, and components of the proposed solution.[13]

Figure 4.4 shows a very simple example of a benefit discovery chart for an insurance company that plans to introduce a customer relationship management (CRM) system consisting of two components: workflow management and analytical customer intelligence. One starts the discovery chart by plotting the functional components of the investment (workflow system and analytical CRM) on the left-hand side and the general monetary benefits on the right-hand side: increased revenue and reduced costs lead to an increase in the company's cash flow. By moving from right to left, from the resulting monetary benefits to the *value drivers* and back to the components of the investment, and always considering how the goals can be achieved, the benefit chart with its value drivers gets developed. From the right, starting with the goal of increasing revenues, sample questions to ask would be:

- How can the company increase its revenues? For example, by contracting more deals and larger deals with customers, increasing the price if targeting a premium market segment.

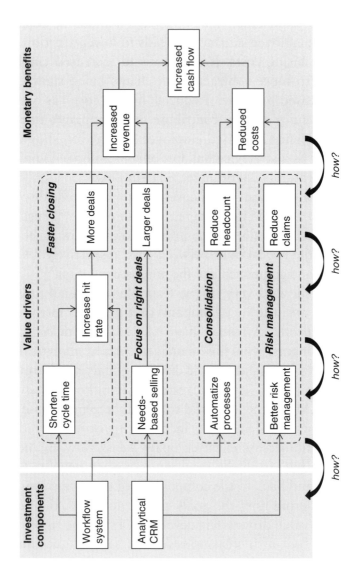

Figure 4.4 *Benefit discovery chart*

- How can the company seal more deals? For example, by increasing the hit rate.

- How can the company increase the hit rate? For example, by needs-based selling and shortening the cycle for closing a deal.

- How can the company reduce the time to close a deal? For example, by introducing a workflow-based computer system, which is a solution component of the proposed investment.

- How can the company introduce needs-based selling? For example, by implementing an analytical CRM system, which is another solution component of the proposed investment.

And similarly for the goal of reducing costs:

- How can the company reduce its costs? For example, by reducing headcount at the back office or by reducing customer claims.

- How can the company reduce headcount in the back office? For example, by automating processes.

- How can the company automate processes? For example, by introducing a workflow-based computer system.

- How can the company reduce customer claims? For example, by introducing a better risk management system.

- How can the company improve the risk management system? For example, by introducing an analytical CRM system, which again justifies the proposed solution component of analytical customer intelligence.

Once the benefit chart has been completed, the value drivers can be grouped into *value areas*. In the above example, the following four value areas can be identified:

- Faster closing,

- Focus on right deals,

- Consolidation, and

- Risk management.

Other groupings are possible. The key principle is to look for relative independency between these groupings, meaning that they can be implemented without much interference from each other. Later on these groupings will form the basis for benefit quantification because of their substantial financial impact. Ultimately, as discussed in Section 1.3 (see Figure 1.13), the business case should be phrased in one sentence only: "In order to improve ___ we are doing ___, which is worth ___ and can be measured by ___." Now is the right time to start thinking about the first placeholder, namely the business pain point, and identifying the primary business case value message; the value areas give us just about the perfect input.

The benefit chart also helps to identify missing solution components, which should be added to the investment proposition. It also draws attention to non-value-adding solution components, which produce unnecessary implementation costs; they can be cut out as they do not contribute to the value generation process.

Case 4.2 reveals how a supplier of specialty gas mixtures used the essence of the benefit discovery chart tool to understand how a new online ordering system generates CV.

Case 4.2   Scott Specialty Gases

Beginning with work in atmospheric monitoring in the early 1960s, Scott Specialty Gases with headquarters in Philadelphia, USA and about 500 employees went on to become a supplier of specialty gas mixtures needed to accurately monitor air quality and EPA (Environmental Protection Agency) protocol gases.[14]

At the beginning of the dot-com era in the early 1990s, Scott Specialty Gases did not blindly introduce an e-commerce platform, even though the benefits were clear. There were savings in data entry costs, as customers would enter the orders themselves, fewer mistakes, and data-entry staff could be moved to revenue-generating areas of the firm.

However, Scott Specialty Gases did not simply assume that customers would just love this new platform and therefore change their ordering habits automatically. Instead, the company looked into ways of becoming more customer-oriented, helping its customers to save costs, and ultimately make their customers more competitive in their respective markets. Customers could now go online, place orders, or check the order status online at any time; many of them had 24×7 operations and Scott Specialty Gases, being a smaller company, could only offer normal office hours. Further analysis showed that making customers capture orders online themselves would actually reduce order capture costs at the customer location by 90 per cent, from $100–$250 to $10–$25. In addition, Scott Specialty Gases was able to spot redundant inventory or unused gas containers that the customer was renting and paying money for. It also monitored expiry dates for their customers and made sure that EPA-compliancy was achieved.

This benefit analysis helped to shape the features of the supply chain management product eScott, which was finally launched in 1998. It also helped the privately held relatively small company Scott Specialty Gases to hold its field against much larger competitors.[15]

4.5   MANAGING NON-MONETARY BENEFITS

Even when applying the benefit identification techniques suggested in the previous chapters, it remains difficult to understand how to express non-monetary benefits in financial terms; they are of an intangible and often evasive nature (see Section 4.1 for the benefit taxonomy). But obviously non-monetary benefits do exist and risk not being adequately represented in the business case.

Opinions in the business world differ widely on what to do with *intangible* benefits, right from "ignore them – they are wishful thinking" to "important to every selection process – they are true decision factors." As all decisions, in both the private sphere as well as the business world, have intangible components, it is well worth trying to understand the nature of non-monetary benefits a little better. After all, decision-making is also about instincts and unconscious factors of reasoning.

Definition of intangibility and tangibility

In financial analysis, an asset is called intangible when there is no generally accepted standard of quantification and accounting. In law, intangibles are incorporeal properties such as bank deposits. Intangible ideas refer to something imprecise or unclear to the mind. In general, the word *intangible* refers to something being incapable of being realized, defined, or perceived by the senses.

Tangible monetary benefits, as discussed so far in the business case calculations, can be distinguished from their intangible sisters and brothers by six questions[16]:

- Is there a *hypothesis* as an underlying fundamental belief of the benefit?

- Is there a *cause-and-effect relationship* that leads to this benefit?

- Are there any *mathematical calculations* to capture the extent of the benefit?

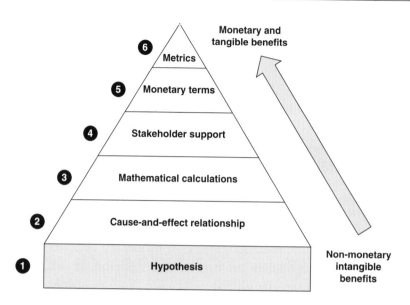

Figure 4.5 *The pyramid of tangibility*

- Do relevant *stakeholders support* this calculation logic?

- Can this calculation logic be expressed in *monetary terms*?

- And finally, can *metrics* be assigned to measure how the benefit is reaped in post-implementation of the investment?

Together these questions build the pyramid of tangibility, as shown in Figure 4.5. Questions should be answered in the order provided and the more questions can be answered with a "yes," the less intangible and the more tangible the benefit is.

Alternatives for handling non-monetary benefits

Investment decisions sometimes need intangible input to filter decisions between alternative courses of action. For instance, one project alternative may rely on a known provider with a good reputation in the industry and the other alternative proposes engaging someone else without a proven track record. Which way does the decision go? Does it really only depend on the NPV of the two alternatives? The decision obviously has an intangible element as well. The question is thus not whether non-monetary criteria should be included as an integral part into the business case, but how to do it.

Typically, non-monetary intangible benefits are handled in one of the following ways:

- *Banning from business case.* This is a very rare way of handling intangible benefits. By order of either the company's top or financial management, non-monetary benefits are not allowed to influence an investment decision at all. It may also be a counterproductive decision, as intangibles always have a place in the subconscious mind of every decision-maker.

- *Allowing selected non-monetary benefits.* Selected non-monetary benefits are considered in parallel with the NPV calculation of the business case. However, such permitted non-monetary benefits are strict exceptions and should only be used to decide between two alternatives that are very close to each other based on their NPV calculation. This scenario is very common in the industry and basically brings non-monetary benefits into the decision-making process through the back door. While it makes sense for selected non-monetary benefits, such as provider reputation, bringing in most other intangible criteria will deviate from a strict business case process and make the entire investment justification exercise worthless.

- *Converting non-monetary benefits into financial ones.* As monetary benefits are perceived to be of more value to decision-makers than non-monetary benefits, some intangible benefits can be turned around and assigned a financial value. The business case methodology knows a few helpful techniques to help achieve this turnaround (see below for a discussion of such techniques).

- *Scoring of non-monetary benefits.* If converting does not work and if intangible benefits are really of a non-monetary nature and do not directly affect the firm's cash flow, but are still somehow quantifiable, they can be used as scoring criteria together with their NPV to evaluate alternative investment proposals (see below for further details).

Converting non-monetary benefits into financial ones

Some intangible benefits may still be quantifiable in monetary terms if conversion strategies are applied. Running intangible benefits through a conversion should always be attempted first; it is needless to say that monetary benefits always and undoubtedly count more than their non-monetary brothers and sisters.

First, one can look at *grouping intangibles* together and then performing a monetary calculation on the grouped benefits. For example, efficiency savings can be more easily estimated at a higher aggregated level. However, this technique undoubtedly leads to aggregated numbers relying heavily on assumptions. This uncertainty should partly be taken out by cutting the savings again by at least fifty per cent to reflect the aggregation risk.

Second, *analogies* from different business areas, geographies, or even disciplines can be a great help in making an intangible benefit measurable.

Third, *avoid subjective measures* such as customer satisfaction or employee morale. These are fuzzy and difficult to quantify, but at the end of the day translate to reduced turnover costs. Instead, replace them with harder measures such as up- and cross-selling success or employee attrition rate.

Fourth, cause-and-effect relationships should be considered to go *beyond departmental boundaries*. Sometimes, benefits can positively affect stakeholders beyond the primary interest group of the investment proposition, and this can make non-monetary benefits more measurable.

Fifth, *advanced business case techniques* can help to analyze the value of some intangible advantages. Investment projects that can be easily modified, expanded, cut back, or abandoned are more valuable than others that do not offer such flexibility. In general it can be said that the more uncertain a business environment is, the more valuable "easy-to-modify" investments are. Chapter 7 introduces real options to describe such opportunities in monetary terms.

Scoring of non-monetary benefits

If conversion of non-monetary intangible benefits into financial ones fails and the intangible benefits are nonetheless perceived to be important by the decision-makers, then a carefully crafted scoring technique can help to bring both needs together. As a necessary precondition for a scoring technique to work, the weight of non-monetary benefits needs to be understood. By embedding them into a cause-and-effect benefits relationship, they may still be scoreable if not measurable, even though their impact may not necessarily directly affect the firm's cash flow.

A popular way is to integrate such benefits into the investment decision-making process through a score sheet. A score sheet lists all the important decision criteria, right from the NPV calculation to the intangibles, and assigns weights of importance to each criterion. Intangible criteria are best structured using the balanced scorecard perspectives of financial, customer, internal process, and learning and growth (see Section 4.2) as a guideline. Investment alternatives can now be graded according to how closely they match each of the criteria. Subsequently, the total weighted scores are calculated and compared.

As a guideline for this approach, there should be a balance between monetary criteria (the NPV calculation) and all the other non-monetary criteria. This could be anywhere between 90–10 and 50–50, and while the relative importance of the non-monetary criteria is the team's decision, the monetary criteria should never be weighted less than fifty per cent. Arriving at these weights is an interesting team-building exercise for the decision team, as all the underlying assumptions are uncovered and the subconscious targets of stakeholders come into the open.

4.6 CUSTOMER VALUE FOR THE COMPANY

From product to customer profitability

It is somewhat surprising that today most companies still focus on identifying the profitability of their products or product lines rather than the profitability of their customers. After all, it is the customers who generate profits, not the products. Products create only costs, but customers ultimately create profits[17] – or, in the language of financial management, benefits to the company.

> "It is the customer who determines what a business is. For it is the customer, and he alone, who through being willing to pay for a good or for a service, converts economic resources into wealth, things into goods. What the business thinks it produces is not of first importance – especially not to the future of the business and to its success. What the customer thinks he is buying, what he considers 'value,' is decisive – it determines what a business is, what it produces and whether it will prosper. The customer is the foundation of a business and keeps it in existence" (Drucker, 1954, p. 37).

Product costs are mostly relevant to evaluating internal processes. Product costs do not depend on customers as long as there are no individual customer requirements on the products which need to be taken into consideration and which cannot be directly allocated to the customer's purchase of the product.

The difference between a profitable and a loss-making product is mostly determined after the product is manufactured. The costs of storing, delivering, and providing after-sales support for products are significant factors and often underestimated. Customers differ very much in the way they order products and, ask for certain types of delivery, and also in the kind of products they purchase. Putting all these factors together leads to widely differing customer servicing costs. Notwithstanding, many companies wrongly assume that there is an average cost of serving a customer. They thus forgo the opportunity to target the customer segments that have a real potential for transforming the company's financial bottom line. A cost-by-cause allocation of revenues and costs determines a meaningful monetary CV: the customer profit contribution.[18]

Customer profit contribution – focusing on the right customers

In marketing management, the so-called *Pareto law* – sometimes also called the *80/20 rule*,[19] states that 80 per cent of the total profit of a business is generated by just 20 per cent of its customers and that 80 per cent of all the customer servicing costs are incurred by only 20 per cent of its customers. However, in most cases these will not be the same 20 per cent.

This uneven spread of profit leads to a cumulative profit distribution shape, as illustrated in Figure 4.6. On the left-hand part of the curve, a few important customers make a disproportionate contribution to the company's profit. This first segment is followed by smaller customers who still contribute to growing profitability. The top part of the curve shows customers who are not very profitable, yet add to the overall profit. The right-hand end of the curve contains customers who are actually producing a loss for the company and eating up the profits generated by the other customers.

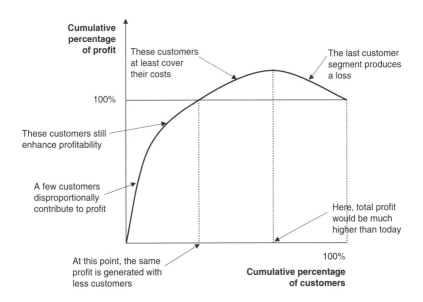

Figure 4.6 *The Pareto law*

Ideally, the company should only seek intense relationships with customers and invest in segments which are profitable or which are likely to turn profitable through an additional investment. This is one more example of how a business case can be used to support business growth. In order to calculate the business case, it is essential to understand which customers fall into which segment. A marketing investment spread over the entire customer base on a sprinkler principle will probably not deliver very effective benefits; however, if the same marketing spend is concentrated on a narrower but more promising customer segment, the benefits delivered can be much higher. For calculating a business case it is therefore important to predict in which customer segment the investment proposition is going to deliver the most benefits. And in order to do so, "we must shift the focus of companies back to the customer and away from shareholder value. In other words, we must turn our attention back to the real market and away from the expectations market" (Martin, 2011, p. 37).

Value of the customer base

Summation of the value of all of a company's current and future customers results in the value of its customer base CVB and similarly a summation across one customer segment results in the value of the customers in this particular segment.[20] If investment projects target improving customer satisfaction and retention rates, this directly influences the growth and profitability of the customer base. The calculations below suggest a way to model the value of a company's customer base depending on adjustments in the following parameters:

- Profit contribution (margin) per customer (m),

- Retention rate (ret),

- Acquisition costs per new customer (c), and

- Number of new customers acquired per year (n).

These variables should be seen as averages either across the customer base or across a sub-segment of the customer base.

The CVB can be calculated as the sum of the lifetime value of today's customers and all future potential customers. During a period t, an individual customer generates a profit contribution m_t. Empirical marketing research shows that the customer's profit contribution m_t continues to grow during the customer lifecycle. However, it has not so far been possible to prove this development for contractually bound customers.

A customer's future profit contributions have less value than more PV contributions, thus they receive a lower weighting. The time concept of money, as introduced in Sections 2.1 and 2.2, uses an interest rate r (the opportunity costs of capital) in order to discount future cash flows to PV. The same concept is applied here, and thus the CV of each individual customer is:

$$Customer\ value\ (CV) = \sum_{t=0}^{\infty} \frac{m_t}{(1+r)^t}$$

One hundred per cent customer loyalty is a prerequisite for this formula. In reality, every customer relationship has a potential risk attached to it. The retention rate ret describes the probability of an existing customer still remaining a customer at the end of a period. The retention rate can be influenced with (marketing) investment decisions, but is also subject to variations in other environmental factors, such as new competitors entering the market, a changing regulatory environment, or different customer behavior.

During the initial review period $t = 0$, the customer is an existing customer, i.e. the probability of retention is:

$$ret_{t=0} = ret_0 = 1$$

In the first period it is:

$$ret_{t=1} = ret_0 \cdot ret_1 = ret_1$$

And in general in period t:

$$ret_t = \prod_{l=0}^{t} ret_l$$

The value of the customer at risk of attrition can thus be described as follows:

$$CV = \sum_{t=0}^{\infty} \left(\frac{m_t}{(1+r)^t} \cdot \prod_{l=0}^{t} ret_l \right)$$

The company usually balances the loss of existing customers by acquiring new customers. From period $t = 1$ onwards, the company acquires n_t new customers per period at c_t acquisition costs. The customers acquired in one period form a cohort, which in turn follows the retention cycle described above.

Looking at the columns of Figure 4.7, the CV of the entire first cohort CVB_1 can therefore be calculated as:

$$CVB_1 = n_1 \sum_{t=0}^{\infty} \left(\frac{m_t}{(1+r)^t} \cdot \prod_{l=0}^{t} ret_l \right) - \frac{n_1 c_1}{1+r}$$

And generally for cohort k:

$$CVB_k = n_k \sum_{t=k}^{\infty} \left(\frac{m_{t-k}}{(1+r)^t} \cdot \prod_{l=k}^{t-k} ret_l \right) - \frac{n_k c_k}{(1+r)^k}$$

Consequently, the CVB is the sum of the CV of all cohorts:

$$CVB = \sum_{k=0}^{\infty} n_k \left(\sum_{t=k}^{\infty} \left(\frac{m_{t-k}}{(1+r)^t} \cdot \prod_{l=k}^{t-k} ret_l \right) - \frac{n_k c_k}{(1+r)^k} \right)$$

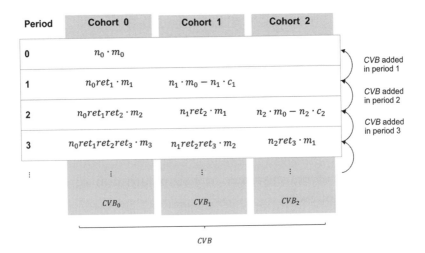

Figure 4.7 *Cohort-based CV calculation*

Looking at the rows, one can derive the incremental incr-ease of the company's CV base in each period based on changes in the above-mentioned variables, profit contribu-tion per customer, retention rate, acquisition costs per new customer, and number of new customers per period. This is great input for the monetary benefit calculation of a business case.

In order to implement this formula in a practical spreadsheet, a few simplifications should be made; more sophisticated cal-culations are better implemented with higher programming languages.

- The company has an initial existing customer base of n_0 and then acquires from period $t=1$ onwards n new customers for every cohort.

- The retention rate r is constant from period $t=1$ onwards, i.e. $r_0=1$ and the investment project changes r afterwards: $r_1=r_2=\cdots=r$; the same for the acquisition costs per customer: $c_1=c_2=\cdots=c$. The achieved customer profit contribution does not depend on the duration of the customer relation-ship: $m_1=m_2=\cdots m$; only cohort zero has an initial profit contribution of $m_{k=0}$.

Figure 4.8 shows such a calculation for a company with a customer base of 10,000, a retention rate of 95 per cent, a customer profit of $25 p.a., acquisition costs of $5 per new customer and a projected addition of 1,000 new custom-ers per year. The rightmost column shows the dynamic of the delta changes of the CV base, which can be fed directly into the business case's NPV calculation at the respective period. The diagrams at the bottom of Figure 4.8 illustrate the acquisition of new customers in each period and how each of these cohorts loses its customers again due to attrition of 5 per cent.

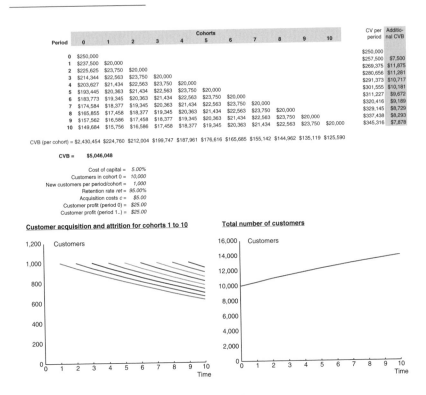

Figure 4.8 *Cohort-based CV calculation*

4.7 ENSURING BENEFIT CRITERIA COMPLETENESS

Sometimes the business case calculation depends on the discovery of one crucial benefit criterion. The methods described above certainly help to discover this one important criterion. However, all brainstorming and charting techniques can still fail and this is why it is important to get industry experts on board who have calculated similar business cases before and know "where to look" and "what to look for" in order to identify important criteria and ensure benefit completeness. Industry experts typically look for such crucial benefits in a few areas:

- Effectiveness,

- Avoidance of unnecessary activities,

- Time-sensitive processes,

- Error avoidance, and

- Avoiding the do-nothing alternative.

Effectiveness

Effectiveness is not the same as efficiency. While *efficiency* describes the extent to which time or effort is well used for the intended task or purpose ("doing the thing right"), *effectiveness* is the degree to which the objectives are achieved ("doing the right thing"). Reducing the manufacturing costs of a product is about efficiency, but adapting the product so that it is right for the targeted market segment is about effectiveness. Streamlining the process for inter-company invoices is good and about efficiency, but eliminating them altogether is even better and is what effectiveness is all about. After all, a company should be invoicing customers but not parts of the same organization.

Effectiveness benefits are less obvious than efficiency benefits and hence are frequently missed. However, effectiveness benefits can be much larger than efficiency benefits. The following three questions can help to identify effectiveness benefits:

- Does this activity or investment help the company to do the right thing?

- Is the output produced by a process or by an investment really needed by the company?

- If there are efficiency improvements, can the time freed be re-invested into effectiveness benefits?

Avoidance of unnecessary activities

Unnecessary activities are not related to the core business function of a company, but they keep reappearing in one organization after another. Their avoidance can lead to increased efficiency and tangible monetary benefits in the business case. Common examples where unnecessary activities can be avoided are:

- *Eliminate information-searching activities.* Having employees spend unnecessary time searching for information is a highly ineffective use of their time. They are not working on their core responsibility, i.e. they are not doing the right thing. Investments in knowledge management platforms can reduce this effort.

- *Eliminate unofficial systems.* Many process owners build their own IS/IT shadow landscape, duplicating and/or extending functionality of the officially provided IS/IT systems. This shadow landscape exists because many process owners do not have confidence in the official systems or they are disappointed by their functionality. A discontinuation of this redundancy can not only lead to process cost savings through elimination of double data entry, but also to elimination of the costs associated with maintaining and upgrading such shadow infrastructure.

- *Empower the employee.* Finding a way of giving end users direct access to the data they need can not only save time in the back office but also improve the productivity of the end users, since they can access the data they need whenever they want it. Empowering employees to take routine decisions (e.g. travel bookings) without approval from their managers can free management time, which can be more effectively used somewhere else.

Time-sensitive processes

Speeding up the cycle time of time-sensitive processes has a direct effect on revenue generation, for instance through closing deals faster, coming back to customers more quickly and thereby improving the likelihood of not losing the customer to the competition, or by faster filling of job vacancies with direct and measurable revenue impact.

Error avoidance

Correcting errors can be costly and reduce the profit generated from transactions. Avoiding errors altogether can have measurable benefits not only on process costs, but also on customer satisfaction and motivation of employees.

Avoiding the do-nothing alternative

Last, but not least, the do-nothing alternative deserves a closer look. What are the costs, losses, and missed benefits associated with continuing the status quo? When companies decide not to invest and do nothing, they will still have costs. Sometimes these costs can be avoided by implementing an alternative investment suggestion; such cost savings are measurable benefits for the business case. Similarly, an investment may stop losses from occurring or leverage benefits. All this will count as benefits for the business case.

5
Making Investment Decisions with NPV

The previous chapters have set out the basic model of a business case using the net present value (NPV) technique. While the model is simple and straightforward, it can very well manage to cope with all kinds of complexity that real-life investment decisions throw at the business case team. Yet NPV and the need for formal investment decision methods are frequently discussed in organizations. Approving new investments often means a change in the way an organization does business and runs its processes; change of any sort is always a challenge in an organization. But most managers who argue against formal investment decision methods are only criticizing the way in which these methods are applied, and rarely the underlying processes or methods themselves. In order to overcome such concerns, this chapter takes the introduction to NPV as provided in Section 2.2 a step further and highlights a few areas which require attention and consideration in practical business cases:

- What if cash flows do not occur once a year, but come in and leave the company continuously? (Section 5.1)

- What method to use for estimating the terminal value of an investment at the end of the investment's lifespan? (Section 5.2)

- How to compare investments with different time horizons, i.e. which do not necessarily start and end at the same time or where the start time is an option? (Section 5.3)

- How to deal with resource constraints? (Section 5.4)

- If there is a risk of inflation, how does the NPV calculation need to be adjusted? (Section 5.5)

Theoretical considerations of NPV often make the method look more complex and complicated than necessary. This is not necessary, and Sections 5.6 and 5.7 introduce two worked examples of business cases to give some ideas about how NPV can be a simple and straightforward analysis.

5.1 CONTINUOUS CASH FLOWS

Most business case calculations – including all the ones in this book – assume that cash flows occur annually and instantaneously at the end of each period and that interest is therefore being compounded annually as well. This assumption makes the business case easier to read and understand. However, in real life cash flows usually occur monthly, weekly, daily, or even continuously. While the simplification of annual cash flows in business cases is a very practicable and acceptable one, it is of course possible to model more frequent cash flows mathematically as well.

In order to convert a nominal interest rate j, which is compounded m times during the year to an equivalent annual ($n = 1$) interest rate r, the following formula can be used:

$$(1+r)^n = \left(1 + \frac{j}{m}\right)^{m \cdot n}$$

For example, if cash flows happen every quarter, then the nominal interest rate needs to be compounded every quarter, i.e. $m = 4$. For a nominal interest rate of $j = 5\%$, this results in an equivalent slightly higher annual equivalent interest rate of:

$$r = \left(1 + \frac{0.05}{4}\right)^4 - 1 = 5.0945\%$$

If cash flow is generated and re-invested on a daily basis, i.e. if $m = 365$, the equivalent annual equivalent interest rate is:

$$r = \left(1 + \frac{0.05}{365}\right)^{365} - 1 = 5.1267\%$$

Now if m is allowed to approach infinity, this results in an annual equivalent interest rate of:

$$r = \lim_{m \to \infty} \left(1 + \frac{j}{m}\right)^m - 1 = e^j - 1$$

Or in the specific example with $j = 5\%$:

$$r = e^{0.05} - 1 = 5.1271\%$$

If a business case considers more than one annual cash stream, continuous (or quarterly, monthly) compounding leads to a higher annual equivalent interest rate. As a result, the NPV of the investment will be smaller compared with the use of discrete annual compounding.

5.2   TERMINAL VALUE

Every investment project has a life span. The *technological life span* depicts how long an asset will be technologically viable before it becomes outdated and needs to be upgraded by a new technology. The *physical life span* conveys how long an investment will function properly or be physically available. The *economic life* of an investment is the period in which it will serve the corporation to reap benefits. The technological life of an investment is usually longer than the physical life, which is again usually longer than the economic horizon.

Therefore investments have a *terminal value* at the end of their economic life, which can be understood as the project's residual value after the initial economic horizon. Depending on the investment type, this terminal value can be large, small, or even negative for cases in which the organization needs to tidy up the environment or make redundancy payments.

Estimating the terminal value in the NPV process accounts for value provided extending beyond the investment period considered for the business case. Calculating the terminal value is not without complexities and the correct method depends on what is going to happen with the investment after the period considered for the business case. Will it be a dead-end and will it be wound up? Or is it an ongoing project even after the business case's investment period? Another factor is how conservative the estimation should be and whether the NPV of the business case depends a lot on what will be done with the asset after the investment period.

Terminal value for dead-end investments (liquidation and book value method)

The most conservative method for estimating the terminal value of investments coming to a definite end is the *liquidation value method*. It assumes that the company has no more use for any of the assets and therefore the assets need to be liquidated by offering and selling them on the market.

As estimating the future sales price of an asset on the market is prone to uncertainty, the terminal value needs to be calculated conservatively. A general approximation formula for the liquidation value method is:

- 100 per cent of cash,

- Plus 90 per cent of accounts receivable,

- Plus 70 per cent of non-perishable stocks, minus costs for disposing perishable stocks,

- Plus 50 per cent net value of property, plant, and other equipment,

- Minus current liabilities, and

- Minus present value of non-cancelable leases and other contracts.

Another, slightly less conservative, method is the *book value method*. It seeks to estimate the balance sheet value of all tangible assets at the end of the investment period. All intangible assets (brand equity, know-how, etc.) are removed from the investment's book value because they are difficult to estimate subjectively. Hence the book value method is often applied for investments in the area of manufacturing, plants, and infrastructure equipment, which are winding down either abruptly at the end of the investment period or within the following one or two years. The book value method should definitely not be applied for investment projects with a substantial service component, as the hardware may not be separable from the intangible service component.

Terminal value for ongoing investments (perpetuity method)

The *perpetuity method* views an investment's terminal value as a perpetuity,[1] i.e. as an ongoing investment, where the net cash flows C have settled down to a regular pattern in the last years of the investment period and where the further cash flow growth g is constant and significantly less than the discount rate r.[2] The terminal value (TV) calculated according to the perpetuity method is the NPV of the indefinite cash flow after the end of the initial investment period:

$$TV = \frac{C_n \cdot (1+g)}{1+r} + \frac{C_n \cdot (1+g)^2}{(1+r)^2} + \frac{C_n \cdot (1+g)^3}{(1+r)^3} + \cdots$$

$$= (1+g) \cdot \left[\frac{C_n}{1+r} + \frac{C_n \cdot (1+g)}{(1+r)^2} + \frac{C_n \cdot (1+g)^2}{(1+r)^3} + \cdots \right]$$

As this rather heavy-handed formula is an infinite geometric series, it simplifies after a few substitutions to[3]:

$$TV = \frac{C_n \cdot (1+g)}{r - g}$$

Consider the following example: Company Optics Ltd purchases a precision tool instrument for making glasses at $100,000, leading to a cash flow of $20,000 in the first year, which they are able to grow by $2,500 every year up to the fifth investment period, where the cash flow will be $30,000 = $20,000 + 4·$2,500 (see also the cash inflow calculation in Figure 5.1). Then this machine would have lost its high-precision capabilities and Optics Ltd would need to buy a new machine, but would continue to use the old machine at a capacity of 20 per cent for cheaper products with lower precision requirements. They estimate growing these cheaper products at 2 per cent annually. The company's opportunity cost of capital is 6 per cent. What is the terminal value of the investment at the end of the fifth year?

$$TV = \frac{20\% \cdot \$30,000 \cdot (1+2\%)}{6\% - 2\%} = \$153,000$$

The NPV of this investment project is calculated in Figure 5.1 using the standard NPV spreadsheet and amounts to $118,414; without considering the future use of the high-precision machine

	Today	Investment period				
	0	1	2	3	4	5
Cash outflow	-$100,000					
Cash inflow		$20,000	$22,500	$25,000	$27,500	$30,000
Terminal value						$153,000
Net cash inflow	-$100,000	$20,000	$22,500	$25,000	$27,500	$183,000
Discount factor	1.00000	0.94340	0.89000	0.83962	0.79209	0.74726
Present value	-$100,000	$18,868	$20,025	$20,990	$21,783	$136,748
Net present value	$118,414					
Rate of return	6.00%					

Figure 5.1 *Case: NPV with TV and perpetuity method*

and its terminal value, the NPV would still be positive, but only offer a tiny amount of $4,084.

Terminal value for ongoing investments (annuity method)

If the investment only goes on for another couple of years (rather than indefinitely), the NPV of the future cash flows needs to be calculated as an *annuity*[4] rather than as a perpetuity.

Building on the same example above, Optics Ltd now assumes that the machine is only good enough for another five years to produce less precise products. Again, the company is able to grow this side business at 2 per cent annually. However, after another ten years the machine is no longer good enough even for the less precise products and has no further residual market value.

The IRR for the present value calculation is to be calculated at $r-g=6\% - 2\%=4\%$. However, one cannot take the cumulative present value factor at 4 per cent for ten years as this would indicate the cash flow to have begun in period 1 and lasted till period 10. Instead, the cash flow will begin only in period 6 and last till period 15. There are two possible approaches for overcoming this challenge and calculating the annuity.

For the first approach,[5] the cumulative present value factor for 5 years needs to be subtracted from the cumulative present value factor for 15 years. For the calculation, one can build upon the present value formula introduced for the discount factor (Excel formula number 2 in Figure 2.6) and then do the summation as in Figure 5.2; the cash flow growth of 2 per cent is calculated in the right-most column.

The terminal value can now be calculated as:

$$TV = 20\% \cdot \$30,000 \cdot (PV_{15} - PV_5)$$
$$= 20\% \cdot \$30,000 \cdot (12.11839 - 5.45182)$$
$$= \$6,000 \cdot 6.66657 = \$39,999$$

Rate of return (r)	6.00%
Rate of growth (g)	2.00%
Rate for PV (r–g)	4.00%

Period	PV factor	Cumulative PV factor			Cash flow growth
0	1.00000	1.00000			
1	0.96154	1.96154			
2	0.92456	2.88609			
3	0.88900	3.77509			
4	0.85480	4.62990			
5	0.82193	5.45182			
6	0.79031	6.24214			$6,000
7	0.75992	7.00205			$6,120
8	0.73069	7.73274			$6,242
9	0.70259	8.43533		Delta PV	$6,367
10	0.67556	9.11090		6.66657	$6,495
11	0.64958	9.76048			$6,624
12	0.62460	10.38507			$6,757
13	0.60057	10.98565			$6,892
14	0.57748	11.56312			$7,030
15	0.55526	12.11839			$7,171

Figure 5.2 *Case: Cumulative PV calculation for the annuity method*

The terminal value is now already discounted to the present date. Of course, the terminal value calculated as an annuity limited to a few years is substantially lower than when calculated as a never-ending perpetuity.

For the second approach,[6] a little trick is applied to the annuity streams. The first stream represents a perpetuity that produces a cash flow in each year beginning in the first year; it has a present value of:

$$PV = \frac{C}{r - g}$$

A second stream represents a perpetuity producing a cash flow in each year beginning with $t+1$. In year t, it has a present value of $PV_t = \dfrac{C}{r-g}$ and therefore its present value in today's perspective is:

$$PV = \frac{C}{(r - g) \cdot (1 + r - g)^t}$$

The difference between these two streams represents an annuity for t years:

$$PV = C \cdot \left(\frac{1}{r - g} - \frac{1}{(r - g)(1 + r - g)^t} \right)$$

The present value now needs to be shifted to the time when Optics Ltd is going to start using the machine for manufacturing low-precision products, i.e. to the sixth period. This can be achieved by discounting the above present value with another factor $\dfrac{1}{(1 + r - g)^l}$ with $l = 5$. Filling in all the values of the Optics Ltd example, this leads to the same terminal value discounted to present day as calculated in the first method above:

$$TV = \frac{1}{(1+r-g)^l} \cdot C \cdot \left(\frac{1}{r-g} - \frac{1}{(r-g)(1+r-g)^t} \right)$$

$$= \frac{1}{(1+0.04)^5} \cdot 20\% \cdot \$30,000 \cdot \left(\frac{1}{0.04} - \frac{1}{0.04 \cdot (1+0.04)^{10}} \right)$$

$$= 0.82193 \cdot \$6,000 \cdot (25 - 16.88910) = \$39,999$$

Terminal value with price/earnings ratio method

Yet another way of appraising the terminal value of an investment is by asking how much the investment would fetch in the market place at the end of the investment period. This line is taken when it is not realistic to forecast cash flows and their growth rate beyond the investment period or when the cash flows are not expected to follow a steady pattern, which allows using the perpetuity or annuity method. Following this approach, the terminal value equals the market value of the investment at the end of the investment period and the *price/earnings ratio method* can be used to estimate the same. At least theoretically, in order to appraise a part of the investment with the price/earnings ratio method, it should be in a sellable state, i.e. separable from the rest of the investment.

The terminal value is then defined as the earnings after tax in the last year of the investment period multiplied with an appropriate future price/earnings (P/E) ratio. The future P/E value is a guesstimate for the industry that has an interest in buying the investment, but not for the industry that is selling it.

5.3 TIME HORIZONS

Time horizons can affect the collecting of information for the NPV calculation and also the investment decision. A number of questions in a business case project are related to time horizons:

- When there are two investment alternatives with differing time horizons, which is the better one?

- Shall the investment be commissioned now or later?

- When is the best time to upgrade or replace an existing investment?

- Does collecting additional information reduce the risk and what happens with the NPV in this process?

- How can interdependencies in the project portfolio be handled?

Investments of different time horizons

Sometimes an investment decision has to be taken between two alternatives with differing time horizons. For example, cheaper equipment (lower upfront investment costs) may need to be replaced more often (short lifetime) than more expensive equipment (higher upfront investment costs but longer lifetime). Running a production facility at maximum output can result in higher wear and tear; the equipment needs to be replaced more frequently (shorter lifetime). If the same production facility could be run at 80 per cent capacity only, the load on the equipment would be less, possibly resulting in a longer trouble-free operation (longer lifetime).

In order to find the better investment alternative in NPV terms, a business case needs to be able to compare different time horizons. There are two ways in business case methodology to accomplish this task.

One way is to look at all alternatives and establish the lowest common time denominator and make this common denominator (or a multiplier of it) the new time horizon for the business case. Assume machinery costing $40,000 with a two-year life span has to be compared with machinery costing $50,000, but featuring a three-year life span. The lowest common time denominator of two and three years is six years. In these six years, the first machine has to be replaced two more times and the second machine only once. This method is fine if the investment period of six years makes sense, but it becomes difficult to justify and calculate a common denominator of for example, 15 years for investments with three-year and five-year life spans. It is highly unlikely that over the next 15 years no technical upgrades will happen and that machinery will always be replaced with the same type of machinery.

A second and more flexible method is utilizing the concept of *life cycle costing*, which aims to assess investment costs over the whole of its economic or intended life. It builds on the concept of equivalent annuities (see Section 5.2):

$$PV = C \cdot \left(\frac{1}{r} - \frac{1}{r(1+r)^t} \right)$$

This formula simply needs to be turned around to compute the equivalent annual cost (EAC):

$$EAC = \frac{Investment\ Cost}{\left(\frac{1}{r} - \frac{1}{r(1+r)^t} \right)}$$

Given a rate of return of 5 per cent, the equivalent annual cost of the $40,000 and $50,000 investments into the two-year and three-year machinery, respectively, would be:

$$EAC_{2\text{-}year} = \frac{\$40,000}{\left(\frac{1}{0.05} - \frac{1}{0.05(1+0.05)^2} \right)} = \$21,512$$

$$EAC_{3\text{-}year} = \frac{\$50{,}000}{\left(\dfrac{1}{0.05} - \dfrac{1}{0.05(1+0.05)^3}\right)} = \$18{,}000$$

The three-year option carries a lower annual cost burden and is to be favored over the two-year variant given that both machines have the same servicing expenses and produce the same output. Should there be any difference in running costs or benefits generated, then the equivalent annual costs have to be distributed across the investment periods in the NPV calculation.

Initiation of the investment

For every proposed investment, management is always faced with two mutually exclusive alternatives:

- Go for it now; or

- Postpone the decision, wait, and decide later.

This sounds simplistic, but the implications are real. A project with a negative NPV may turn into a valuable opportunity later if circumstances change. Even a project with a positive NPV is not necessarily best undertaken immediately – the NPV could even increase if the project is delayed. Think about harvesting crops, timber, or farming cattle where the value of the crops, the timber, or the cattle may grow if one waits just a little longer. Likewise, the best timing option may be now (or may already lie in the past) and from now on the project's NPV will only decrease. Once the crop is ready to be harvested, waiting will not add any value and will probably just destroy the harvest. Likewise, an old cow cannot be turned into expensive beef steak, but maybe into less expensive minced meat.

Under conditions of certainty, the optimal timing of an investment is not very difficult to uncover and follows four simple steps. First, study the potential alternative start dates t for commissioning a project. Second, calculate the project's net future value NFV_t as of each alternative start date t. Third, discount the NFV_t for each alternative start down to present day in order to calculate NPV_t:

$$NPV_t = \frac{NFV_t}{(1+r)^t}$$

Fourth, choose the start date that has the highest NPV_t.

As long as the NPV_t increases between every alternative start date t by more than the discount rate r, then the gain in value is greater than the cost of capital that is withheld by not initiating the project. If the gain in NPV to the next possible start date is less than r but still positive, waiting will no longer maximize the NPV of the investment.

Unfortunately, this simple approach misses an important practical point. The sooner the first harvest is brought in, the sooner the second crop can be seeded on the same plot of land. The NFV of the second crop thus depends on when the first crop is brought in. Such investments are called *rollover investments*. A rollover is a move of assets and profits from one maturing investment and making other investments with them.[7] Of course, there are ways of solving this problem and building business cases for rollover investments as well.

One possibility is to construct several series of feasible rollover or harvest dates and to find the series with the best NPV. This series than features the optimal rollover dates.

A second possibility is to estimate the future value of bare harvested land as part of the payoff to the first harvest; this future value mathematically includes the value of all subsequent harvests. While the second method is simpler to calculate, it largely depends on the payoff estimate of harvested land and thus the first method will give a more accurate result.

Take another example (Case 5.1). In a production process, it can make sense to delay the final configuration of a unit until a very late stage when all the information is available – even if this brings up the per-unit production costs. What is a sure curse to the average production engineer can in fact turn out to be a neat solution for a production optimization problem.

Case 5.1   Localization of inkjet printers at Hewlett Packard

Inkjet printers need to be localized for different regions before selling them to customers. Localizing them in the main factory is cheaper than setting up satellite localization factories in the different regions. In the 1980s, Hewlett Packard localized its inkjet printers at the main factory and then shipped the fully finished and localized product to warehouses across the world. However, Hewlett Packard kept getting the demand forecast wrong and ended up with too many printers for one region and too few for another. The company then decided it would be smarter to only partially assemble the printers in the main factory and once it had received firm orders from the regions, dispatch them and localize them at the region's warehouses. As a consequence, production costs rose because economies of scale could not be achieved at the local warehouses; local customization was more expensive than centralized customization. However, supply could be more effectively matched with demand through delaying the configuration choice until concrete orders were on the table, and Hewlett Packard managed to save about $3 million a month. Subsequently Hewlett

Packard introduced this thinking in other areas as well. For example, it calculated the value of introducing flexible inkjet mechanisms which work across a number of products from different divisions. This was initially against the interest of the individual divisions, who were only looking at optimizing production costs and margin for their own products. But as a whole Hewlett Packard benefited from the value of flexibility and created incentives for its divisions to look beyond their own boundaries and act in the best interests of the entire company.[8]

Time value of additional information

Collecting more information about a proposed investment can help to establish its feasibility and reduce the likelihood of failure. But collecting evidence through market research or technical feasibility studies requires time, which delays the commissioning of the investment and therefore also its benefits. Hence, before deciding to collect additional information, the following three factors need to be weighed against each other in a NPV model:

- There are the costs for conducting additional research, for example, the market survey or the technical feasibility study.

- Second, all projected cash inflows are delayed to a later period, because through all the additional information-collecting activities, the investment's date of commissioning is delayed to a later period.

- Third, and on the other side of the scales, the likelihood of investment success goes up and lower risk provisions are required as the business case team has more clarity about the investment's feasibility.

These factors can provide a real dilemma for decision-makers, as Case 5.2 shows with the example of an intelligence gathering system.

Case 5.2   SCOPE system

In the UK, the SCOPE system was a multimillion-pound computer project designed to share intelligence between separate groups in the intelligence-gathering community in a matter of minutes rather than hours. It was intended to replace paper intelligence briefing documents with a more sophisticated electronic method. SCOPE was already partly up and running, albeit after a two-year delay and tens of millions of pounds invested, when it was scrapped in 2009. The annual report of the Intelligence and Security Committee reported "We remain very concerned, however, by the numerous delays to this important programme, including: delays to the delivery of Phase I and Phase II; a general lack of preparedness for full implementation amongst SCOPE partners; and difficulties in providing a secure environment for the deployment of SCOPE overseas" (Murphy, 2008). As the alternative of using a wiki platform for collecting and sharing such highly sensitive intelligence information[9] is obviously not desirable, the question is whether an in-depth feasibility study may have helped to clear the path. Considering that such secure technology has not yet been tested in many places before and that information is not freely be available from other governments, the costs of such an in-depth study would have had to be weighed against the time delay in implementing Phase I, which turned out to be at least somewhat successful, and thereby putting the country at risk through this time delay and a potential terrorist attack.

Replacement and upgrade decisions

Finding the right time to upgrade or replace machinery (or another type of investment) is another variation of the time problem.

In such a scenario it is important to compare the right cash flows. One cash flow will be the net cash flows of the existing machinery and the salvage value (or costs). The second cash flow is the initial investment of the replacement machinery and the net cash flows generated by the replacement machinery. The option with the better NPV should be pursued.

A slightly different approach also leads to a valid result. Depending on the business situation, the business case can be a very intuitive one:

• Through decommissioning of the old machinery, cash outflow is avoided and this counts as cash inflow for the business case of upgrading/replacing the old machinery.

• The decommissioning costs of the old machinery, the initial investment costs of the replacement machinery, and its ongoing maintenance count as cash outflows.

• Should there be a productivity increase through the new machinery, this increase counts as cash inflow for the business case.

As long as the NPV of this calculation is positive, an upgrade/replacement of the old machinery makes commercial sense.

Let us look at a concrete example. The previous year a company installed a client–server based office application. It purchased hardware for $100,000 and now spends $10,000 p.a. on related hardware maintenance. The software license fees amount to $90,000 p.a. For deploying the software in the company, the roll-out costs were $55,000, and operation of the software package now costs another $45,000 annually. The vendor of the office application package now offers an upgrade to a cloud-based solution, which comes with no hardware costs at all and only ongoing annual costs of $20,000 for the software license and $14,000 for operations. The data conversion and deployment of the new package are estimated to cost the company some $11,000.

For calculating the business case, all costs incurred last year for installing the earlier client–server based version (hardware costs of $100,000 and deployment costs of $55,000) are considered to be sunk costs and are therefore not to be considered for the business case. To build the NPV calculation in Figure 5.3, the initial deployment costs of the cloud application as well as ongoing operations and software licensing costs are considered to be the cash outflow. The savings on operations, hardware, and software maintenance are taken as cash inflow, carefully estimated to kick in only in the second year from now, due to a handover process from the client–server system to the cloud application.

The NPV of this replacement suggestion is a stunning $297,477 based on a 5 per cent rate of return. Assuming that

	Today	Investment period				
	0	1	2	3	4	5
Coud deployment	−$11,000					
Cloud operations	−$14,000	−$14,000	−$14,000	−$14,000	−$14,000	−$14,000
Cloud software licence	−$20,000	−$20,000	−$20,000	−$20,000	−$20,000	−$20,000
Saved hardware maintenance			$10,000	$10,000	$10,000	$10,000
Saved software licences			$90,000	$90,000	$90,000	$90,000
Saved operations			$45,000	$45,000	$45,000	$45,000
Net cash inflow	−$45,000	−$34,000	$111,000	$111,000	$111,000	$111,000
Discount factor	1.00000	0.95238	0.90703	0.86384	0.82270	0.78353
Present value	−$45,000	−$32,381	$100,680	$95,886	$91,320	$86,971
Net present value	$297,477					
Rate of return	5.00%					

Figure 5.3 *Example: Upgrading from client–server to cloud application*

the software provider has correctly estimated the data conversion and deployment costs of the cloud application, the company should immediately change to the cloud version. And even if the provider's estimate was too optimistic, the company still has up to $297,477 to spend on internal retraining measures and so on; the investment suggestion will still be positive.

Project portfolio interdependencies

The business case and NPV calculations generally assume that investments are standalone and mutually exclusive. However, the timing of investments can be further complicated when investments are viewed in a portfolio of projects.

There can be logical interdependencies in the project portfolio; one project requires input from another and therefore cannot be started before the other one is completed.

Also, while two investment projects may have similar NPVs, one may generate cash flows in the early years and the alternative may release its cash flows only much later. If the first project is chosen, it may be impossible to take on a third investment project because the available funds are tied up in the first project. This leads us to the issue of decision-making under capital restrictions.

5.4   CAPITAL RATIONING AND CAPITAL RESTRICTIONS

The rationale of the NPV method is based on the assumption that companies accept all investment proposals with a positive NPV. As such, it assumes that companies have unlimited access to funds to commission all positive proposals. The NPV method, however, does not consider any capital restrictions on the investment program. In the real life of business, companies can face two variants of capital rationing: soft and hard rationing.

Soft capital rationing is a constraint set by top management on their divisions to guide them in the process of prioritization and selecting the most powerful investments. This helps over-enthusiastic divisional managers to focus on their top priori-ties and to reduce the strain on employees by not taking up too many opportunities at a time. Of course, a budget limit is only an imperfect proxy to implement law and order in the investment process, but it is a powerful one considering that there are not any real alternatives. Soft capital rationing is a provisional con-straint which can be easily removed should it become necessary to approve a really powerful investment opportunity with more capital needs.

Hard capital rationing, on the other hand, implies imper-fections in the capital market where a firm cannot raise any more money. A company's access to capital may be restricted if it has already fully utilized its agreed credit lines with the banks, its majority shareholders veto issuing more stock, or if angel investors turn a blind eye to the company's future and investment ideas.

In Section 2.6, the PI and cost–benefit ratio were introduced as a way of ranking projects when there are limitations on the investment program. This ranking method is based on the NPV method and the initial investment. Unfortunately, it only works for very simple and rather unrealistic cases when:

- Capital is only rationed in the first year. But sometimes firms are restricted in their access to fresh capital over a number of years.

- There are no other constraints than capital rationing. However, investments can be mutually exclusive or depen-dent on each other (see Section 1.4).

- No money is left over in the firm's budgeting process. There are combinations of investments and opportunity costs of capital when it is more beneficial to spend all available funds rather than only accepting the investment projects with the highest NPVs.

One way to tackle investment decisions with multiple constraints is to examine all possible combinations for feasibility, calculate their NPV, and then compare them. Depending on the number of proposed investments on the table this can be quite a cumbersome and enormous task. Let us look at the mathematics of combinatorics.

If P is an investment portfolio with n investment propositions, the number $C_n^{(j)}$ of *distinct subsets* with j investment propositions that can be chosen from the investment portfolio P is denoted by the binomial coefficient $\binom{n}{j}$ – pronounced as "n choose j" and calculated as:

$$C_n^{(j)} = \binom{n}{j} = \frac{n!}{j! \cdot (n-j)!}$$

$n!$ is the number of permutations of n distinct objects, denoted as "n factorial," and calculated as $n! = n \cdot (n-1) \cdot (n-2) \cdot \ldots \cdot 2 \cdot 1$; the Excel function to calculate a factorial is called FACT(n). Figure 5.4 provides a table for the binomial coefficients with up to $n = 15$ investment propositions.

If the individual investment propositions can be implemented more than once, i.e. if the subsets are not to be distinct but allow for a repetition (*subsets with repetition*), the number $C_{n,repeat}^{(j)}$ of combinations calculates as:

$$C_{n,repeat}^{(j)} = \binom{n+j-1}{j} = \frac{(n+j-1)!}{j! \cdot (n-1)!}$$

Let us take an example of $P = \{a, b, c\}$. The subsets of P are:

$$\{\varnothing\}, \{a\}, \{b\}, \{c\}, \{a,b\}, \{a,c\}, \{b,c\}, \{a,b,c\}$$

	n = 1	2	3	4	5	6	7	8	9	10	11	12	13	14	15
j = 1	1	2	3	4	5	6	7	8	9	10	11	12	13	14	15
2		1	3	6	10	15	21	28	36	45	55	66	78	91	105
3			1	4	10	20	35	56	84	120	165	220	286	364	455
4				1	5	15	35	70	126	210	330	495	715	1001	1365
5					1	6	21	56	126	252	462	792	1287	2002	3003
6						1	7	28	84	210	462	924	1716	3003	5005
7							1	8	36	120	330	792	1716	3432	6435
8								1	9	45	165	495	1287	3003	6435
9									1	10	55	220	715	2002	5005
10										1	11	66	286	1001	3003
11											1	12	78	364	1365
12												1	13	91	455
13													1	14	105
14														1	15
15															1

n: number of investment propositions; j: number of investment propositions that can be chosen from n

Figure 5.4 *Table for the binomial coefficient*

There is one subset with no elements ({ø}), three subsets {a}, {b}, {c} with exactly one element, three subsets {a, b}, {a, c}, {b, c} with two elements, and one subset {a, b, c} with three elements. Thus, $\binom{3}{0} = 1$, $\binom{3}{1} = 3$, $\binom{3}{2} = 3$, and $\binom{3}{3} = 1$. In all, there are $2^3 = 8$ subsets. In general, an investment portfolio with n investment propositions has 2^n subsets. For $n = 5$ investment propositions, the number of possible combinations already becomes $2^5 = 32$ and for $n = 10$ investment propositions the number of possible combinations is an absolutely unmanageable $2^{10} = 1024$.

A mathematical technique known as *linear programming* can be used to maximize the combined benefits of an investment project portfolio, given that not all projects can be undertaken. It maximizes the NPV per scarce monetary unit of the available investment budget, and software programs are available to undertake this analysis.

5.5 INFLATION

In dynamic economies, price changes take place constantly as a result of shifts between supply and demand. However, such specific price changes do not necessarily imply a change at the general level. Only if there is a strong tendency for many prices to move up or down does the average price level increase or decrease. A rise in the average price level is called *inflation*, a problem with which most economies and modern businesses have to cope. *Deflation* is a decline in the average price level.

When making investment decisions, it is important to recognize the phenomenon of inflation – it will impact both cash flows and the discount rate over the life of the project. The good news is that the basic principles of NPV business case analysis are also applicable when there is a risk of inflation. However, the analysis needs to be done in a consistent manner and most real-life business cases attempting to consider the effects of inflation are confused at best, if not entirely wrong.

Nominal and real moneys

Why is it so difficult to get the effects of inflation right in a business case? Economists differentiate between *nominal* and *real* money.

Let us look at an example. Going forward, nominal money will be denoted with $ and real money with R$.[10] A one-year security of $10,000 with a 5 per cent interest rate promises to pay back $10,500 after one year. However, it does not give any indication of how much this nominal cash flow of $10,500 will buy after one year in real money. The purchasing power of $10,500 will depend on the rate of inflation. If the general price level increases by more than 5 per cent, the investor will have lost ground in terms of buying power in real money. Hence, inflation relates to the change in the value of the money itself.

Let us now assume an inflation rate of 3.5 per cent p.a. At the end of one year, the nominal cash flow of $10,500 is going to buy goods worth $\dfrac{\$10,500}{1+0.035} = R\$10,145$

today, which is the real payoff of the investment in the one-year security.

The general formula for converting nominal cash flows at a future period t to real cash flows is:

$$Real\ cash\ flow\ [\text{R\$}] = \frac{nominal\ cash\ flow\ [\$]}{(1 + r_{inflation})^t}$$

The disadvantage of considering inflation in a business case is that it makes the business case and thereby the task of analyzing different investment propositions more difficult and complex.

The business case can be both calculated in real as well as in nominal cash flows – but mixing the two is detrimental. There is a rule of thumb that helps to decide which cash flow to take as a basis[11]:

- If costs and benefits are determined to a large extent by the market forces of inflation or deflation during the investment period, estimates in real cash flows are generally more accurate.

- If there are long-term fixed-price contractual relationships which determine the costs and benefits of the proposed investment, then estimates in nominal cash flows are more truthful.

Most corporate business cases are about long-term investments and can thus be safely calculated on nominal cash flows only.

Nominal and real interest rates

Interest rates – and thus also the opportunity cost of capital – are usually quoted in nominal rather than in real terms. A *nominal interest rate* tells you how quickly your investment will grow; the *real interest rate*, on the other hand, gives you information on how much better off you are after taking inflation into account. The nominal interest rate is certain; the real rate is only a guesstimate based on anticipated inflation; the actual real rate can only be calculated at the end of the year when the actual inflation rate has been established.

It is imperative that with nominal cash flows only a nominal interest rate is used and that with real cash flows only a real interest rate is used. Not obeying this basic rule of consistency is a frequent source of errors in the practice of business cases.

The formula for converting nominal interest rates into real interest rates is:

$$1 + r_{real} = \frac{1 + r_{nominal}}{1 + r_{inflation}}$$

In the above example with $r_{nominal} = 5\%$ and $r_{inflation} = 3.5\%$, the real interest rate would be:

$$r_{real} = \frac{1 + r_{nominal}}{1 + r_{inflation}} - 1 = \frac{1 + 0.05}{1 + 0.035} - 1 \approx 1.449\%$$

It should be noted that the result $r_{real} \approx 1.449\%$ is slightly less than the typical lay calculation of $5\% - 3.5\% = 1.5\%$.

Conversely, suppose management requires an investment to return at least 5 per cent p.a., i.e. there is a requirement for the real rate of return to be $r_{real} \geq 5\%$. Assuming that inflation is estimated to be at $r_{inflation} = 3.5\%$, then the nominal interest rate should be at least:

$$\begin{aligned} r_{nominal} &\geq (1 + r_{real}) \cdot (1 + r_{inflation}) - 1 \\ &= r_{real} + r_{inflation} + r_{real} \cdot r_{inflation} \\ &= 5\% + 3.5\% + 5\% \cdot 3.5\% = 8.68\% \end{aligned}$$

Again, this is slightly higher than the approximate calculation of $5\% + 3.5\% = 8.5\%$.

Considerations for the business case

The worth of an investment should not (and does not) depend on whether it is analyzed in nominal or real terms as long as the corresponding interest rates are used. It is only logical that real cash flows can never sensibly be discounted using a nominal discount rate.

In addition, the following points need to be watched for:

- During good economic times, salaries and labor costs per hour increase faster than the selling prices of consumer goods, because real wages go up in an expanding economy driven by productivity improvements. In a recession, however, selling prices of consumer goods can increase faster than salaries.

- In countries with very high and unpredictable inflation, it can be assumed that all the relevant cash flows increase more or less directly in line with inflation at the same time. It is therefore advisable to calculate the business case based on real cash flows and at a real discount rate.

- Tax laws in most countries allow only the original costs of assets to be depreciated; hence tax savings from depreciation do not increase with inflation.

In general, companies that are being taxed (see Section 3.4) experience lower after-tax returns than companies that are exempt from taxes. How much lower the *after-tax returns* are depends on the tax bracket the company falls into. In addition, there are interdependencies between inflation and tax effects. A taxable company realizes a nominal after-tax return of

$$(1 - T) \cdot r_{nominal}$$

with T being the marginal tax rate corresponding to the relevant tax bracket. Building on the formula of converting nominal interest rates into real interest rates as introduced before, the after-tax real return depending on the tax bracket $r_{real}(T)$ can be stated as:

$$r_{real}(T) = \frac{1 + (1 - T) \cdot r_{nominal}}{1 + r_{inflation}} - 1 = \frac{r_{nominal} \cdot (1 - T) - r_{inflation}}{1 + r_{inflation}}$$

Assume inflation is at $r_{inflation} = 3.5\%$ and that a corporation ONE Ltd achieves a nominal (taxable) return of an investment of $r_{nominal} = 10\%$. Assume further that ONE Ltd is liable for tax at $T = 20\%$. Then the after-tax real return will be:

$$r_{real}(T = 20\%) = \frac{0.1 \cdot (1 - 0.2) - 0.035}{1 + 0.035} = 4.34\%$$

Assume now that TWO Ltd operates the same investment, but is liable for tax at $T = 10\%$. Two Ltd has a higher after-tax return of:

$$r_{real}(T = 10\%) = \frac{0.1 \cdot (1 - 0.1) - 0.035}{1 + 0.035} = 5.31\%$$

Company THREE Ltd is exempted from taxes ($T = 0\%$) and can therefore show an even higher return of:

$$r_{real}(T = 0\%) = \frac{0.1 - 0.035}{1 + 0.035} = 6.28\%$$

These equations are useful for estimating the effective real return for a company, given a certain tax rate, a nominal rate of interest, and an expected rate of inflation. Depending on the tax bracket, an investment's merit will vary among companies.

5.6 WORKED EXAMPLE: HIGHWAY SAFETY ALTERNATIVES

This chapter introduces a worked example of a business case illustrating the following:

- Estimation of costs and benefits.

- Calculation of the NPV using a spreadsheet approach.

- Making a decision under capital restrictions.

The example builds on the information presented in the earlier Case 1.17 on the alternatives for improving highway safety. The Highway Authorities now need to make a decision on which safety improvement alternative to implement; they are commissioning a business case team with the task of scrutinizing each of the six alternatives.

Costs

The initial investments required for implementing the six different safety improvement alternatives have already been outlined in Figure 1.17. Annual operating and maintenance costs are assumed to be 10 per cent of the initial investment. The expected lifespan is 10 years and the terminal value is assumed to be zero for all alternatives, i.e. any improvement made to the intersection in terms of pavement conditions, signal operation, or warning signs cannot be dismantled and put up somewhere else again. On the other hand, it can also be assumed that there is no need to decommission any equipment and that the installed equipment will just as well continue to serve its purpose beyond the 10 years. So the business case team decides to set the investment period at 10 years with no decommissioning costs.

Benefits

The benefits of improving highway safety lie in reducing the number of crashes. While this can be seen as an intangible benefit, the business case team nonetheless attempts to put a monetary figure to them.

The average costs caused by accidents with fatal outcome, injury, and property damage only are estimated as $1,200,000, $55,000, and $8,200, respectively, following data from the National Safety Council. Data from the highway intersection shows an annual average of 23 injuries and 47 property only damages for this intersection; there have not been any accidents leading to a loss of human life to date. The total annual average damages caused by accidents at this crossroads can therefore be calculated as:

Annual damages = 23 · $55,000 + 47 · $8,200 ≈ $1,650,000

The annual savings measured in monetary terms from the reduction in number of crashes are termed "worth of crash saved." These are the monetary benefits the business case team is looking for. The percentage of crashes which can be saved by implementing one of the safety improvements is estimated by experts through the crash reduction factor (CRF), which is listed in Figure 1.17.

Estimates also suggest that traffic volume will increase by 4 per cent annually, so the number of accidents avoided should also increase by 4 per cent every year, if not more, because denser traffic usually leads to more accidents. Hence the business case team sets the annual increase of benefits at a conservative 4 per cent.

NPV calculation and investment decision

Figure 5.5 shows the NPV calculation for all six alternatives, plus two more variants which will be discussed later. The result is pretty astonishing as all six alternatives have a positive NPV ranging from $3.7 million to $10.5 million. In a corporate environment the alternative with the highest NPV (alternative 6) should be chosen.

Decision management under capital rationing

Going back to the policies for public investing outlined in Case 1.17, both the criteria of "investment view point" as well as "face value" are covered by the NPV analysis (see the whole of Chapter 2 for the reasoning). However, public funds are never unlimited and borrowing on the financial markets is usually constrained as well. So things can be slightly different in the case of the Highway Authorities.

The Highway Authorities currently have an annual budget of $645,000 for road improvements across the state. Future year budgets are assumed to increase by 6 per cent every alternate year over a five year planning horizon.

This constraint immediately eradicates the possibility of implementing alternatives 5 and 6 and the menu of options to choose from is reduced to alternatives 1 to 4. A smart financial manager may now propose to save the money by waiting for one year, carrying the budget over to the next period, and then go for the best possible alternative. The business case for this approach is modeled in Figure 5.5 as alternatives 5a and 6a. Nothing happens in the current period 0, but the investment takes place in period 1. In order to make the costs comparable to the previous idea[12] of investing immediately, the missed benefits in terms of crash reduction in period 1 need to be added to the costs of period 1. This reduces the NPV of alternatives 5a and 6a to $7.0 and $7.6 million, respectively, making postponement of the investment not so very attractive as compared to alternatives 3 and 4, which invest immediately.

Of course, the smart financial manager may come up with other modified courses of action. For instance, the Highway Authorities may consider implementing alternative 1 with the least cash outflow as an interim solution, save the rest of the annual budget and carry it over to period 1 or 2, then decommission alternative 1 and only implement one of the more sophisticated alternatives. Another run of the NPV calculation would have to show the worth of this idea.

The Highway Authorities would also have to consider the bigger picture of highway safety across the state. They are obviously responsible not only for the intersection of the M-97 with the Metropolitan Parkway, but will have many more hotspots to

Cost estimates

	Today 0	1	2	3	4	5	6	7	8	9	10	CRF
Alternative 1	-$110,000	-$11,000	-$11,000	-$11,000	-$11,000	-$11,000	-$11,000	-$11,000	-$11,000	-$11,000	-$11,000	26.40%
Alternative 2	-$214,000	-$21,400	-$21,400	-$21,400	-$21,400	-$21,400	-$21,400	-$21,400	-$21,400	-$21,400	-$21,400	37.90%
Alternative 3	-$258,000	-$25,800	-$25,800	-$25,800	-$25,800	-$25,800	-$25,800	-$25,800	-$25,800	-$25,800	-$25,800	63.90%
Alternative 4	-$444,000	-$44,400	-$44,400	-$44,400	-$44,400	-$44,400	-$44,400	-$44,400	-$44,400	-$44,400	-$44,400	64.20%
Alternative 5	-$694,000	-$69,400	-$69,400	-$69,400	-$69,400	-$69,400	-$69,400	-$69,400	-$69,400	-$69,400	-$69,400	73.10%
Alternative 6	-$916,000	-$91,600	-$91,600	-$91,600	-$91,600	-$91,600	-$91,600	-$91,600	-$91,600	-$91,600	-$91,600	81.70%
Alternative 5a	-$1,948,396	-$69,400	-$69,400	-$69,400	-$69,400	-$69,400	-$69,400	-$69,400	-$69,400	-$69,400	-$69,400	73.10%
Alternative 6a	-$2,317,972	-$91,600	-$91,600	-$91,600	-$91,600	-$91,600	-$91,600	-$91,600	-$91,600	-$91,600	-$91,600	81.70%

Benefit estimates

	Today 0	1	2	3	4	5	6	7	8	9	10
Alternative 1		$453,024	$471,145	$489,991	$509,590	$529,974	$551,173	$573,220	$596,149	$619,995	$644,794
Alternative 2		$650,364	$676,379	$703,434	$731,571	$760,834	$791,267	$822,918	$855,835	$890,068	$925,671
Alternative 3		$1,096,524	$1,140,385	$1,186,000	$1,233,440	$1,282,778	$1,334,089	$1,387,453	$1,442,951	$1,500,669	$1,560,696
Alternative 4		$1,101,672	$1,145,739	$1,191,568	$1,239,231	$1,288,800	$1,340,352	$1,393,967	$1,449,725	$1,507,714	$1,568,023
Alternative 5		$1,254,356	$1,304,572	$1,356,755	$1,411,025	$1,467,466	$1,526,165	$1,587,211	$1,650,700	$1,716,728	$1,785,397
Alternative 6		$1,401,972	$1,458,051	$1,516,373	$1,577,028	$1,640,109	$1,705,713	$1,773,942	$1,844,900	$1,918,695	$1,995,443
Alternative 5a		$1,254,396	$1,304,572	$1,356,755	$1,411,025	$1,467,466	$1,526,165	$1,587,211	$1,650,700	$1,716,728	$1,785,397
Alternative 6a		$1,401,972	$1,458,051	$1,516,373	$1,577,028	$1,640,109	$1,705,713	$1,773,942	$1,844,900	$1,918,695	$1,918,695

Net cash flow

	Today 0	1	2	3	4	5	6	7	8	9	10
Alternative 1	-$110,000	$442,024	$460,145	$478,991	$498,590	$518,974	$540,173	$562,220	$585,149	$608,995	$633,794
Alternative 2	-$214,000	$628,964	$654,979	$682,034	$710,171	$739,434	$769,867	$801,518	$834,435	$868,668	$904,271
Alternative 3	-$258,000	$1,070,724	$1,114,585	$1,160,200	$1,207,640	$1,256,978	$1,308,289	$1,361,653	$1,417,151	$1,474,869	$1,534,896
Alternative 4	-$444,000	$1,057,272	$1,101,339	$1,147,168	$1,194,831	$1,244,400	$1,295,952	$1,349,567	$1,405,325	$1,463,314	$1,523,623
Alternative 5	-$694,000	$1,184,996	$1,235,172	$1,287,355	$1,341,625	$1,398,066	$1,456,765	$1,517,811	$1,581,300	$1,647,328	$1,715,997
Alternative 6	-$916,000	$1,310,372	$1,366,451	$1,424,773	$1,485,428	$1,548,509	$1,614,113	$1,682,342	$1,753,300	$1,827,095	$1,903,843
Alternative 5a	-$1,948,396	$1,184,996	$1,235,172	$1,287,355	$1,341,625	$1,398,066	$1,456,765	$1,517,811	$1,581,300	$1,647,328	$1,647,328
Alternative 6a	-$2,317,972	$1,310,372	$1,366,451	$1,424,773	$1,485,428	$1,548,509	$1,614,113	$1,682,342	$1,753,300	$1,827,095	$1,827,095
Discount factor	1.0000	0.9434	0.8900	0.8396	0.7921	0.7473	0.7050	0.6651	0.6274	0.5919	0.5584

Present value

	Today 0	1	2	3	4	5	6	7	8	9	10
Alternative 1	-$110,000	$417,004	$409,527	$402,170	$394,930	$387,808	$380,801	$373,908	$367,130	$360,463	$353,907
Alternative 2	-$214,000	$593,362	$582,929	$572,649	$562,522	$552,548	$542,726	$533,055	$523,535	$514,163	$504,940
Alternative 3	-$258,000	$1,010,117	$991,977	$974,127	$956,564	$939,287	$922,292	$905,577	$889,138	$872,973	$857,078
Alternative 4	-$444,000	$997,426	$980,188	$963,185	$946,418	$929,888	$913,595	$897,539	$881,718	$866,314	$850,763
Alternative 5	-$694,000	$1,117,921	$1,099,299	$1,080,888	$1,062,693	$1,044,716	$1,026,962	$1,009,431	$992,127	$975,051	$958,204
Alternative 6	-$916,000	$1,236,200	$1,216,136	$1,196,267	$1,176,598	$1,157,136	$1,137,886	$1,118,853	$1,100,042	$1,081,455	$1,063,096
Alternative 5a	-$1,838,109	$1,054,642	$1,037,074	$1,019,706	$1,002,540	$985,581	$968,832	$952,293	$935,969	$919,859	$919,859
Alternative 6a	-$2,186,766	$1,166,226	$1,147,299	$1,128,554	$1,109,998	$1,091,638	$1,073,478	$1,055,522	$1,037,775	$1,020,241	$1,020,241

Net present value

Alternative 1	$3,737,648
Alternative 2	$5,268,429
Alternative 3	$9,061,129
Alternative 4	$8,702,874
Alternative 5	$9,673,290
Alternative 6	$10,567,670
Alternative 5a	$7,038,887
Alternative 6a	$7,643,964

Rate of return   6.00%

Figure 5.5 *NPV business case for highway safety alternatives*

fix. The challenge is therefore not only to decide on the best possible alternative for the M-97/Metropolitan intersection, but to find the best possible allocation of resources and alternatives for all hotspots. Most public authorities and businesses today are not capable of doing such kinds of sophisticated resource allocation planning and therefore go for the shortcut of selecting the least cost project, where the benefits exceed the costs in order to be able to "fix" as many hotspots as possible – even though these fixes may turn out to be "quick-fixes" and are suboptimal solutions from an overall perspective.

5.7   WORKED EXAMPLE: UC REPLACES TELEPHONY SYSTEM

Here is another example of a business case illustrating the following:

- Identification of costs and benefits.

- Analyzing benefits for credibility.

- Calculation of the NPV using a spreadsheet approach.

The case is about unified communication (UC) and collaboration capabilities in a software-based environment, which allows companies to integrate real-time and non-real-time communication services and offer communication solutions to their employees from within their familiar desktop environments. There is no need to go to a videoconferencing room to do a videoconference and there is no need for desk-based or even mobile telephones any more – everything can be accomplished on the employee's desktop or laptop.

For the worked business case, let us assume a management consulting company with 5,000 employees in 40 locations around the world. The consultancy uses strategic insight, tailored solutions, and a collaborative working style to help clients achieve sustainable results. A range of experts across the world is engaged in a variety of industries and services, which requires the consulting company to have collaborative tools to bring together these experts in order to serve their clients. This consulting company evaluates the implementation of a UC server to provide instant messaging, conferencing, desktop sharing, and voice capabilities.[13]

Costs

The following cost categories are associated with the deployment and management of a UC server:

- Server software licenses. A number of software licenses for the communication servers and corresponding maintenance packages for the following years need to be purchased.

- User software licenses. In addition to server software licenses, user software licenses for 5,000 employees plus related maintenance packages are required.

- Hardware costs for servers and user devices. Additional server hardware, database servers, communication gateways, etc. are to be bought; this investment is loaded with annual maintenance fees as well. In addition, a number of IP phones and headsets for the users are required.

- Professional services. An external provider is engaged to configure and roll-out the system.

- IT administration costs for ongoing management and support. The business case team estimates that any additional IT administration can be covered by the existing team and thus no additional expenses will be occurred.

- End-user training. About half a day of training and ramp-up time is required for each employee, partly through online tutorials, lunchtime events, and experiential activities. Note that the end user training expenses will not stop after the initial roll-out, but a certain percentage needs to be accounted for in the following years. First, there is attrition in the workforce and new employees need to be trained. It can be argued that this training will happen as part of the onboarding days and that these costs are already there and need not be considered in the business case. Second, maintenance packages will deliver updates with new functionality, which may require additional end-user training; this should be accounted for in the business case.

• Decommissioning costs. The old hardware-based telephone system needs to be removed from the offices and either sold (if there is a buyer) or recycled (which will come with recycling fees).

Gathering input for estimating these costs follows the techniques described in Chapter 3; Figure 5.6 shows the results of the cost estimation and sums the costs per investment period.

Benefits

The monetary benefits of UC software are mainly realized by *reducing existing costs*; see the benefit taxonomy as introduced in Section 4.1. The business case team identifies five benefit categories in interviews with the provider and with various departments and end users of the management consultancy. Four of them make it to the NPV calculation sheet in Figure 5.6:

• Replacing telephone hardware with software. Maintenance labor costs of the old telephone system can be avoided.

• Reduction in teleconferencing services. A certain percentage of pay-per-minute web and teleconferencing can be

Cost estimates	Today	Investment period				
	0	1	2	3	4	5
Server software licences	−$80,000	−$10,000	−$10,000	−$10,000	−$10,000	−$10,000
User software licences	−$620,000	−$160,000	−$160,000	−$160,000	−$160,000	−$160,000
Hardware	−$400,000	−$1,000	−$1,000	−$1,000	−$1,000	−$1,000
Professional services	−$90,000					
IT administration						
End-user training	−$1,300,000	$65,000	$65,000	$65,000	$65,000	$65,000
Decommissioning	−$50,000					
Total costs	**−$2,540,000**	**−$106,000**	**−$106,000**	**−$106,000**	**−$106,000**	**−$106,000**

Benefit estimates	Today	Investment period				
	0	1	2	3	4	5
Replacing hard- with software		$3,500	$7,000	$7,000	$7,000	$7,000
Reduction in teleconferencing		$100,000	$120,000	$150,000	$135,000	$122,000
Freeing of support labour		$135,000	$270,000	$540,000	$540,000	$540,000
Fewer help desk calls			$75,000	$75,000	$75,000	$75,000
Total benefits	**$0**	**$238,500**	**$472,000**	**$772,000**	**$757,000**	**$744,000**

NPV Calculation	Today	Investment period				
	0	1	2	3	4	5
Cash outflow	−$2,540,000	−$106,000	−$106,000	−$106,000	−$106,000	−$106,000
Cash inflow	$0	$238,500	$472,000	$772,000	$757,000	$744,000
Net cash inflow	−$2,540,000	$132,500	$366,000	$666,000	$651,000	$638,000
Discount factor	1.00000	0.95238	0.90703	0.86384	0.82270	0.78353
Present value	−$2,540,000	$126,190	$331,973	$575,316	$535,579	$499,890
Net present value	**−$471,052**					
Rate of return	5.00%					

Figure 5.6 *NPV business case for UC*

substituted with UC technology. To estimate the associated savings, a phase-out of pay-per-minute services over maybe two or three years is considered together with an estimated drop in the costs of such services due to increased competition, for example, caused by a proliferation of free UC services.

• Freeing of support labor. Gradually, UC frees IT support staff for other activities. In order to include these savings in the business case, it needs to be ensured that today's support staff can easily be utilized elsewhere or is migrated to a third-party outsourcing provider. Otherwise this benefit turns into a cost component entailing severance pay or retraining effort.

- Fewer help desk calls. After an initial rise in help desk calls (which should be dealt with as part of the costs and covered under end-user training, for example), it can be assumed that the ease of the system's interface will lead to a net reduction in help desk calls. The same consideration holds true as for the freeing of support labor.

- Travel cost savings. It is to be assumed that most of the possible travel cost reductions have already been leveraged through web and teleconferencing technologies and that any further travel cost reductions are not possible. Of course, even if 50 per cent of the consulting company's employees could save only one business trip (estimated at $2,000) per year, this would amount to a whopping $5 million per year and would be a great benefit leverage for the business case. However, the business team decides to classify such savings as speculation and leaves the topic of travel cost savings entirely out of the business case calculation.

Another type of benefit can potentially be found in *avoiding additional expenses*. For instance, if the company has an age-old telephone system in place which would need to be upgraded during the next one or two years, such saved additional expenses would positively influence the business case as benefits. However, the business case team is not able to identify any such expenditure avoidance.

As shown in Section 4.1, the second leg of monetary benefits is *increased revenue*. This affects the consulting company's bottom-line financials and is much more important than cost savings. Providers of UC solutions usually claim increased employee productivity, such as in the following statements taken from real-life marketing material: The customer "sees an advantage in the unified [...] client interface. Employees no longer need to switch applications for different types of conference calls; with a single click, they can start an audio or video conference [...], which gives them quicker access to clients than ever before and means they can resolve issues more quickly when they arise. [...] [With the UC solution, the company] continues to provide the technology that helps its mobile consultants be more productive at their jobs and more effective at keeping the lines of communication open with partners and clients."[14]

If only an hour at an average employee's cost rate of $50.00 is saved every week and if only 50 per cent of this can be captured as real productivity benefit,[15] this would mean a grandiose saving of $6 million[16] every year! Even if this were to be further discounted with a slow adoption of maybe 25 per cent and 50 per cent during the first one or two years, the productivity saving figures would remain enormous.

While these savings may certainly be realistic and can be argued with many functions and features available in UC technology, when presented in a business case they will typically be laughed away by the decision-makers. Why is this so?

The answer lies in the management consulting company's business model, which is based on knowledge management and providing expertise to clients, who typically pay a fixed daily rate for a consultant. Management consultants anyhow work overtime and whether they are marginally more productive really only benefits their work–life balance, but not their charge-out rates. If the business case team were to draw up a value panel as proposed in Section 4.3, it would become clear that none of the senior decision-makers in the management consulting company has employee productivity as one of their goals. Hence, in order to avoid the feedback of "I don't believe the business case," a productivity increase should be dropped as a monetary benefit and only listed as a non-monetary benefit. While this may torpedo the overall attractiveness calculation of UC technology as an investment for the consulting company, it certainly saves the credibility of the business case.

Similarly, the same marketing material as quoted before, promises: "The company enabled federation to help employees communicate with clients. 'With federation, our project work happens more in real time,' [the consulting company is quoted]. 'If clients have questions, they can see immediately if someone is available and send an instant message or click to call instead of sending an email or making a phone call. It speeds up the process and helps us build better relationships.'" These soft factors of better client relationships and better responsiveness are certainly true and will certainly lead to contract extensions and better success in cross-selling opportunities, and maybe even justify higher charge-out rates for the consultants. However, unless the business case team can find proper proof of a revenue increase, the business case calculation should refrain from speculations and it would be better to drop such benefits before a senior decision-maker comes up with the statement like "I don't believe the estimates."

NPV calculation and investment decision

Unfortunately, as the completed NPV calculation in Figure 5.6 shows, the costs of implementing a UC solution outweigh the monetary benefits that were included in the business case calculation. The investment's NPV is negative: –$470,000. From a strict financial perspective, this is a loss-making investment and it should not be pursued.

However, one might still want to push through with this investment based on non-monetary benefits. The competition may already have it, clients may already use it, and five years from now, it may be the standard way of communicating, just like today's cell phones. At least the company's financial management team has an honest business case on the table, which classifies the investment proposition as an investment in the company's future and does not over-promise returns which may not be directly attributable to UC technology.

Now it is up to the senior management to decide whether to take up the investment proposition as a strategic investment and go ahead or whether to postpone it. As Section 5.3 on time horizons discussed, the NPV may look better two years from now: The technology may have matured even further, hardware costs may fall further, and licenses may have become less expensive as UC technology moves into the mainstream.

6
Factoring Risk and Uncertainty

Risk is a part of every business activity, in fact of every human endeavor. It is something virtually all human beings dislike and would want to wish away, if only they could. The old Romans dealt with it by worshiping *Fortuna*, the goddess of randomness and the personification of luck in the Roman religion (see Figure 6.1). Fortuna was not always positive; she was also doubtful (*Fortuna Dubia*), could be "fickle fortune" (*Fortuna Brevis*), or could mean downright evil luck (*Fortuna Mala, Atrox Fortuna*). As such she claimed the young lives of Emperor Augustus' two hopeful grandsons Gaius and Lucius, educated to take up princely roles in the Roman Empire.[1]

Business is all made up of decisions and the quality of decisions makes the decision takers valuable. The old Persians discussed and made important decisions while they were drunk, only to repeat the same discussion the next day in a sober state. And if they still approved it in a sober state, they adopted it; if they didn't like it the next day, they abandoned it.[2] In today's business world, the hardest decisions are being rolled up the corporate hierarchy. The CEO's job is to take the decisions that cannot be delegated any more.[3]

Most humans will do anything to avoid risk; some of us even defer decisions, thereby giving away power to control the outcome. Making a call on a decision takes courage, so passion matters in real-life decision making.[4] And while some of our exposure to risk may not be completely voluntary, humans as

Figure 6.1 *Fortuna, the Roman goddess of randomness*

well as businesses seek out some risks on their very own. And yet there is little consensus among academics and practitioners alike about how to define risk.

6.1 DEFINITION OF RISK

In business and investing, risk has traditionally been viewed negatively. Every investment has the potential for risk and because investments deal with relatively long timescales and involve a lot of money, a lot of things can go wrong between taking the investment decision and reaping the benefits.

Hazards are things that can go wrong and cause harm to the investment project. For example, the unit cost of production could be more than the forecast, competitors could enter the market with a superior product, bringing down your company's own sales figures, or currency fluctuations in global markets could reduce your margins. For each hazard, the business case needs to be clear about what part of the investment and also what part of the business case calculation might be harmed; this will help to identify the best way of managing risk.

Risk is the chance, high or low, that the investment project could be harmed by a hazard, together with an indication of how serious the harm could be.[6] Risk arises where the future is unclear and where a range of possible future outcomes exist. Sometimes a distinction is made between *risk* and *uncertainty*. Risk is seen as something quantifiable and objective, while uncertainty is unmeasurable and subjective.[7] For investment decisions, this distinction is not particularly useful, as business managers are obviously affected by all kinds of uncertainty whether measurable or not. Thus both words are used interchangeably in this book.

As companies and their shareholders run the danger of losing money due to risk or uncertainty, most business executives focus exclusively on hedging or mitigating risks. And thus assessing risk has become a vital aspect of making the business case. Basically, it allows us to establish whether an investment entails more risk than the organization can reasonably bear.

However, an enterprise's relationship with risk should be far more nuanced than simply trying to avoid all risk. The great companies of this world have not become successful overnight, but have consciously and intelligently sought and exploited risk for business advantage. There is "no free lunch" and those companies that seek greater success will smartly have to expose themselves to uncertainty and control their risk exposure.[8]

Notwithstanding this, successful companies do not necessarily achieve huge success by taking on more and more risk. Sometimes they take the opposite approach, tending to navigate in a conservative, risk-averse approach around four primary risk categories[9]:

- *Death line risk* can kill or severely damage a company.

- *Asymmetric risk* refers to the downside (danger) being much bigger than the potential upside (opportunity).

- *Uncontrollable risk* exposes the firm to forces and events that it has little ability to manage or control.

- *Time-based risk* ties the degree of risk to the pace of events and the speed of action.

High-performing companies typically tend to abhor the death line risk and make fewer decisions involving this boundary; they shun decisions involving asymmetric risk and avoid uncontrollable risk as well. Instead, they spend more time empirically validating decisions before taking them (see Section 6.11), thereby increasing their chance of success. They are vigilant of lurking changes that may signal danger and therefore try to recognize threat early, allowing them in turn to adjust their decision speed to the pace at which events evolve. No matter how fast they need to take decisions, they are always fact-driven and follow a highly disciplined decision-making process. Execution does not compromise on quality, but the intensity of execution is adjusted according to the urgency of implementation.[10]

A complete view of risk and uncertainty thus needs to encompass both sides of risk management: the efforts to manage and reduce risk as well as endeavors to take and exploit risk strategically. The first part of this duality is the central topic of this chapter and the second part will be dealt with in Chapter 7.

6.2 ASSUMPTIONS AND COMPLEXITY

Assumptions as a mirror of risk

To identify the basic input factors for the business case – costs and benefits – it is unavoidable for the business case team to make assumptions. Sometimes it is impossible to wait until every last piece of information becomes available and sometimes there is an unknown quantity left after all the fact-finding which has to be estimated. In this process of fact-finding, most people are only dimly aware of their underlying assumptions, yet they strongly influence feelings and behavior[11], and consequently also the decision-making process.

Business case assumptions are ideas and beliefs which the business case team could not establish as being true, but which are likely to be true. However, such assumptions often turn out to be half-truths at best, and sometimes they even turn out to be wide of the mark. Assumptions can be understood to mirror investment risk and therefore they need to be factored into the business case calculation.

It is essential to document assumptions transparently and carefully; they need to be given a prominent place in the business case presentation (see Section 8.2) so that decision makers are aware of the underlying risk.

If assumptions turn out to be wrong during the implementation of the investment decision, the business case needs to be revisited, adjusted, and recalculated. If the initial risk provision is found to be insufficient, the investment decision needs to be reexamined with a new business case. Depending on the outcome of this new decision-making process, the implementation of the investment may need to be modified, delayed, or even cancelled.

Understanding complexity

Assumptions are grounded in the fundamental belief that a certain level of predictability and order exists in the corporate world; this encourages simplification. As a consequence, organizations trust their approach to decision making on what has worked well in one set of circumstances; business case teams use the tools that business schools have equipped them with. However, all too often they are surprised to see that these methods fail even though logic indicates that they should work; Section 1.2 has shown a number of such corporate blunders.

Many business environments have the characteristics of a complex system.[12] They involve a large number of interacting elements. Interactions are nonlinear and minor changes at one end can produce disproportionate consequences at the other end. The business environment itself is dynamic; solutions emerge from circumstances and cannot be imposed on the system. Its past is integrated with the present, leading to a nonreversible evolution of business history. From the benefit of hindsight, the business environment may even appear to be ordered and predictable; however, hindsight often does not lead to foresight, because external conditions and influencing factors constantly change.

As a result, the success or failure of investment projects is often not only constrained by external factors, but projects constrain each other, especially as time evolves. This means that forecasting, predicting, and establishing assumptions can be close to impossible in real life. To tackle this challenge, business managers first need to diagnose the level of complexity of the situation their organization faces and then select the appropriate methods and tools for supporting the decision-making process; the diagnosis can be accomplished using the nature of the relationship between cause and effect.[13]

Simple contexts show repeating patterns and clear cause-and-effect relationship that are evident to everyone. Once the right investment project is identified, the decision will be undisputed. Exhaustive communication and stakeholder management (see Section 1.10) are usually not required because disagreement about what needs to be done is rare. The business case is the right tool for decision making and its focus is on comparing alternatives to find the best practice. An additional sensitivity analysis (see Section 6.6) of selected factors can help to understand the impact of assumptions. Nevertheless, there can be dangers in simple contexts as well. For one, many top managers constantly ask for condensed information ("the management view") and thereby run the risk of incorrectly classifying a context as simple when it would actually fall into a different category. Second, during the implementation of a project in a simple context, many managers become complacent, resort to micro-management, and do not stay connected with the larger context of the environment. If disruptive changes happen in the environment, the likelihood is high that they will not be spotted; the earlier simple situation begins to collapse and drift into chaos.

Investments in *complicated contexts* may have several good solutions; best practice need not necessarily prevail. The cause-and-effect relationships still exist, but are not immediately evident to everyone; complicated contexts therefore call for expert diagnosis and for real experts to be part of the decision-making team. During the analysis of costs and identification of benefits, different stakeholder groups are likely to provide conflicting advice to the business case team. The business case team should make use of advanced techniques like scenario analysis (see Section 6.7) to overcome the drawback of incomplete data and avoid a state of analysis paralysis, where stakeholders cannot agree on answers because of entrained silo-thinking or inflated egos. In some complicated contexts, real options theory may be useful to evaluate future strategic options and alternatives (see Chapter 7). Making decisions can take a lot of time and there is always a trade-off between finding the right answer and moving ahead by simply taking a decision (see Section 1.2). However, if the right investment decision cannot be taken or the investment decision is based on too many assumptions as a sign of missing data, then the investment situation is probably complex rather than only complicated.

Complex contexts are the realm of the unknown, where even the best analysis cannot ferret out the right decision. This is the domain to which much of today's business world has shifted; some major change like a bad quarter, an unpredicted competitor move, a lawsuit, a merger or acquisition, or a new CEO introduces flux and unpredictability. Patterns, however, can begin to emerge if an investment is not decided and approved right away, but if small experiments are conducted, where the outcome is uncritical, but which allow confirming assumptions. Such empirical experiments reveal the way forward for the investment (see Section 6.11).

If the business case team finds itself in a complex context, it should avoid the temptation to fall back to standard cause-and-effect relationships, it should avoid looking for facts, and it should avoid speeding up the decision-making process. Instead, it needs to allow time for patterns to emerge through empirical experiments (see Section 6.11), which provide the input for a sound business case. Techniques like simulations (see Section 6.8) can help to understand the possible dynamics, but they do not replace the real-life insight generated through empirical validations.

Lastly, in *chaotic contexts*, searching for the right answer is pointless. Even with the most thorough analysis, cause-and-effect relationships cannot be established. In a chaotic context, top management has no time left for thinking and still needs to make many decisions in order to establish order. There is no time left for analysis and asking stakeholders for input. Only through issuing directives and taking action can the situation be moved from chaotic to complex. Once a sense of stability is achieved, the alternatives for further action can be scrutinized by a business case team in a more orderly manner. Mercifully, chaotic contexts are rare. Some leaders in business and politics alike are highly successful in chaotic contexts and even reach a cult-like status, being admired by their supporters. However, this tends to cut them off from accurate information and once the chaotic situation is stabilized, they are not able to switch their decision-making style, losing their glamour and tending to become less successful.

6.3 RISK ASSESSMENT PROCESS

A risk assessment is, simply put, a careful examination of what hazards could cause harm to the investment's success in order to weigh up whether the business case team has taken enough precautions in the form of risk mitigation measures and planned sufficient financial allowance. To start with, the validity of assumptions (see Section 6.2) should be verified. This helps focus on the hazards and risks that really matter. The types of risks that affect assumptions characteristically fall under four different categories:

- *Business risks* impact business processes or structures; it is the risk that the business or technology needs of an organization may not be met. Hence business risks are sometimes also referred to as *impact risks*. Many organizations are completely unaware of their business risks, yet they can quite possibly destroy the entire benefits of an investment project. Examples of business risks are low end-user acceptance or a slower than planned implementation speed.

- *Financial risks* can have consequences for the organization's financial stability. Examples of financial risks are project funding falling through or higher than expected cost of capital.

- *Technical risks* impact the company's technical (or IT) infrastructure. Examples of technical risk are system downtime or interface incompatibility issues.

- *Implementation risk* is the risk that a proposed investment may deviate from the original or expected requirements, resulting in higher costs than expected.

Technical risks are not to be neglected; Case 6.1 showcases how neglecting the technical risks in a software implementation project drove American LaFrance into bankruptcy. Successful companies, on the other hand, consider that hazardous events could turn against them at any moment. In fact, they strongly believe that this could happen without any advance warning at an unpredictable and probably very inconvenient moment in the investment life cycle. They prepare by embracing the myriad of possible dangers and putting themselves in a superior position to overcome this potential danger.[14] Channeling vigilance into preparation and clearheaded action makes companies extremely effective in combating the dangers of risk.

Performing a risk assessment involves going through five steps, as shown in Figure 6.2. This is not the only way to do a risk assessment; there are other methods that work just as well, particularly for very complex risks and circumstances. However, this is a straightforward way that works for most investments: Identify risks associated with the investment or project, assess risk probability and potential impact, plan risk normalization, assess the organizational readiness to deal with the risk, and calculate a risk rating. The first two steps fall under the category of *risk assessment* and the following three under *risk control*. Assessing risk and then sitting around and not doing anything to keep risk under control is not very useful. Companies and their business case teams need to channel the assessment into the risk control process in order to avoid unnecessary risk, which could possibly expose the investment to calamity.

Case 6.1 Failed IT implementation forces American LaFrance into bankruptcy

A failed computer system implementation at *American LaFrance*, one of North America's largest builders of customized firefighting trucks and equipment, is an example where unidentified technical risks led to chaos and finally the filing of Chapter 11 bankruptcy. After a spin-off from Daimler AG's Freightliner in 2005, American LaFrance worked to set up a new ERP (enterprise resource planning) system to integrate accounting, purchasing, inventory, production, payroll, and finance. When the new system was switched on in June 2007, it threw the operations into chaos and crippled production. On top of already shrinking sales and a tense financial situation, this created a liquidity crisis that ultimately forced American LaFrance to file for bankruptcy court protection.[15]

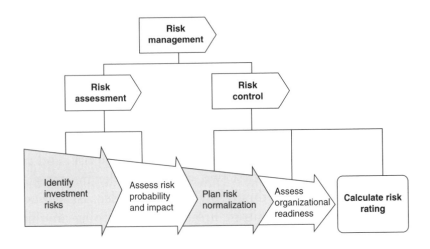

Figure 6.2 *Risk management process*

Risk normalization as a step in the risk management process should directly follow the risk assessment; it involves setting up activities for risk mitigation and contingency planning. Mitigation entails identifying the actions that the corporation can carry out in advance to reduce or eliminate the impact of the risk. Contingency planning is about developing a response plan to deal with risk when the event occurs.

There are two approaches to risk control. The more traditional one tries to identify the key areas within the investment project that are potentially affected by uncertainty. Methods like sensitivity analysis (Section 6.6), scenario analysis (Section 6.7), simulations (Section 6.8), probability trees (Section 6.9), and decision trees (Section 6.10) help to scrutinize the possible outcomes of the investment decision. Although no financial manager will ever be able to look at all possible scenarios, these techniques are still very useful as they provide a broader exposure to risk and an understanding of the dynamics of uncertainty. A more modern approach is discussed in Section 6.12: risk assessment by certainty equivalents varies the discount rate r depending on an assessment of risk. With increasing length of an investment, the range of possible out-comes multiplies, and risk increases. By compound-discounting future cash flows at an adjusted discount rate, the NPV method begins to account for risk contingencies.

The risk management process should be kept simple. In most organizations and for most investment propositions, the risks are well known and the necessary control measures are rela-tively easy to apply.

6.4   RISK PREFERENCES OF DECISION MAKERS

Identifying and managing risks associated with project invest-ments is only one part of the story, the other is about identifying the risk attitude of the business and its decision makers. Risk preference describes what one does when faced with a risky decision and a safer alternative; it is an important predictor of decision-making behavior under risk.[16]

Risk functions

Most companies, investors, and stakeholders are averse to risk; given two investment suggestions with the same expected net present value (ENPV), but with different levels of risk, a risk-averse decision maker will choose the project with a lower level of associated risk. Being averse to risk, however, does not mean being unwilling to take on risky investments; rather, it means that one requires a kind of compensation for taking on risk in the form of higher expected benefits.[17]

In *expected utility theory*, every individual has a utility func-tion between the level of value (sometimes also referred to as satisfaction) received and the amount of benefits achieved through an investment. For risk averseness, the utility function, when shown graphically, will show a downward-sloping curve as in the left-hand diagram of Figure 6.3.

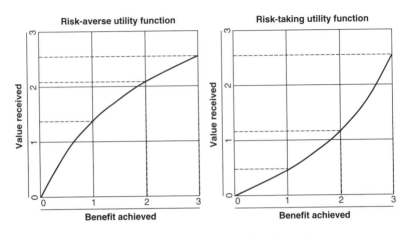

Figure 6.3 *Value functions of expected utility theory*

The utility function has two key properties:

- The *upward slope* implies "more is better." Larger benefits received yield greater utility, and for investments with associated risk, an investment which is first-order stochastically dominant[18] over an alternative bet is chosen; that is, if the probability mass[19] of the second investment alternative is pushed to the right to form the first alternative, then the first alternative is preferred.

- The *concavity* of the utility function implies risk averseness. A sure benefit would always be preferred over a risky investment outcome providing they both have the same ENPV. Moreover, for risky investments, one would prefer a project which is a mean-preserving contraction[20] of an alternative investment, that is, if some of the probability mass of the first alternative is spread out without altering the mean to form the second alternative, then the first alternative is preferred.

For a scenario where the decision makers are indifferent to risk, the marginal utility of benefits will not diminish as described above. Instead, the marginal utility of benefits will remain constant, i.e. the utility function will be a straight line. For risk-seeking investors, the utility function will become convex, meaning that each additional possible benefit provides an increasing amount of utility. The greater the attraction to risk, the more convex the utility function will become.

To prepare a decision justification for a business investment proposition with a business case, assuming a straight linear for the utility function is a reasonable starting point for the following two reasons:

- Each stakeholder is likely to have only a small stake in the investment, i.e. stakeholders are diversified in a sense that the risks being taken in the investment under consideration have only limited impact on the overall position of the stakeholder. Hence the business case is trying to help make the best decision on behalf of diversified stakeholders.

- Second, the uncertainties of the investment are not related to the riskiness of the stakeholder's other interests or the performance of the stock market.

These intuitive reasons are formalized by the *Capital-Asset Pricing Model (CAPM)*, which was independently introduced by Jack Treynor, William Sharpe, John Lintner, and Jan Mossin, building on the earlier work of Harry Markowitz on diversification and modern portfolio theory.[21] It is used to determine a theoretically appropriate required rate of return of an asset if the asset is to be added to an already well-diversified portfolio given a nondiversifiable risk of the asset. The model takes into account the asset's sensitivity to nondiversifiable risk[22], as well as the expected return of the market and the expected return of a theoretical risk-free asset.[23]

Risk aversion differences across subgroups

It may not be unreasonable to handle exposure to risk differently in a company where either the management or the shareholders are either more or less risk adverse.[24] But although expected utility theory provides an understanding of why companies are generally averse to risk and uncertainty, its practical value is pretty limited. It is neither theoretically nor practically possible to combine the utility functions of decision makers and the company's other stakeholders to build a decision-making framework for investment decisions.

Moreover, although a vast amount of research has been conducted on risk preference, little is known about how people predict the preferences of others. Managers typically take decisions based on their own attitudes toward risk and assumptions about the risk preferences of their companies and its stakeholders. However, humans are usually very poor in predicting others' risk preferences and tend to overestimate others' propensity for risk-taking, regardless of whether the choices are between positive outcomes or between negative outcomes. This capability of predicting risk preferences is especially poor when a prediction is made for abstract others, like organizations, where decision makers have no concrete image in mind.[25]

Empirical and experiential studies suggest that risk may be perceived differently by different subgroups of our society. Women in general appear to be more risk averse than men. However, increasing stakes seem to equal out sex differences in risk aversion and men become as risk averse as women when the investment decisions involve higher amounts.[26] Experts appear to be less risk averse than their less experienced colleagues.[27] Older people (above 40) are more risk averse than their younger colleagues (below 30) with the age-related increase in risk aversion being greater among women than with men. Married individuals are also more risk averse than singles.[28]

Differences in risk aversion in national culture have also been extensively researched. In this context, the notion of uncertainty avoidance refers to the extent to which members of collectives seek orderliness, consistency, structure, formalized procedures, and laws to cover situations in their private and professional spheres.[29]

Figure 6.4 provides a summary comparison in terms of typical strong vs. weak uncertainty avoidance orientation based on extreme stereotypes;[30] it is to be noted that no culture will exactly fit into any of these categories.[31]

Figure 6.5 indicates uncertainty avoidance across 25 national cultures worldwide; a higher number denotes a higher degree of uncertainty avoidance on a scale of 0–100.[32] In general, managers from emerging markets are able to maintain a very calm stance when facing risk and are willing to let time pass as long

Low uncertainty avoidance	High uncertainty avoidance
Society	
Uncertainty is a normal "feature" of life.	Uncertainty is considered a threat and needs to be fought continuously.
Low stress and low anxiety; people generally have less worries and feel happier.	High stress and anxiety; people have many worries and feel less happy.
There should be no more rules than absolutely necessary.	Emotional need for rules and regulations to allow predictability of behaviour.
Tolerance for ambiguity and chaos.	Need for precision and formalization.
Show more tolerance for breaking rules.	Show less tolerance for breaking rules.
Organization	
Rely on the word of (trustworthy) others rather than contractual agreements.	Tendency to document everything in carefully crafted contracts.
Be less concerned with maintenance of records and documentation.	Keep meticulous records, document meetings.
Rely on informal interactions.	Rely on formalized policies and procedures; verify communications in writing.
Facilitate initiation phase of a project through high risk taking; minimal planning or controls during implementation.	Facilitate projects through risk aversion and tight controls.
Show less resistance to change.	Show strong resistance to change.
Frequent job changes and shorter durations in one job.	Longer service in one job; frequent job changes are considered as unstable.

Figure 6.4 *Characteristics of uncertainty avoidance*

high	Uncertainty avoidance		low
Band A	Band B	Band C	Band D
Switzerland 100	Netherlands 73	Spain 44	Greece 20
Sweden 98	UK [2] 71	Portugal 41	Russia 0
Singapore 98	France 62	Argentina 31	
Germany [1] 94	Australia 61	Turkey 30	
Finland 86	Hong Kong 58	Colombia 21	
China 83	Ireland 57		
New Zealand 75	Mexico 52		
	India 51		
	USA 51		
	South Africa [3] 49		

[1] former West Germany   [2] England   [3] Sample includes only people of White origin

Figure 6.5 *Uncertainty avoidance practices across cultures*

as the risk profile remains stable.[33] Their upbringing and their cultural environment has taught them that no matter what they do, uncertainty will never fully go away.

By making the business case team aware of this culturally driven risk bias, it becomes possible to predict decision makers' risk preferences and thereby predict investment decisions more accurately. Such a gain in prediction accuracy yields important benefits for presenting the business case (see Chapter 8). Notwithstanding this, in addition to factors like demographics and culture, it is no surprise that an individual's personality adds to differences in risk aversion behaviour.

Asymmetry of choices and preference reversal

Decision makers are not as rational as they would like to think they are. Anomalies and contradictions in human decision-making behaviour were analyzed and formulated as the *prospect theory* by Kahnemann & Tversky (1979), who received the 2002 Nobel Prize in Economics for their findings. Unlike the utility theory described above, which concerns itself with how decisions under uncertainty *should* be made (prescriptive approach), prospect theory deals with how decisions are *actually* made (descriptive approach).

The attitude of the same decision maker toward risk concerning gains can be quite different from the attitude toward
risk concerning losses. Given a choice between two investment
propositions with (A) an NPV of $1 million with certainty or
(B) an NPV of $2.5 million with a 50 per cent chance, a decision
maker may well choose (A), whereas the probability-weighted
NPV of (B) is higher. Although this is a perfectly reasonable attitude of risk aversion, the same decision maker when confronted
with either (C) a certain loss of $1 million or (D) a 50 per cent
chance of no loss or a loss of $2.5 million, often chooses the
riskier alternative (D). Again, this risk-seeking behavior is not
necessarily irrational, but it is important to recognize the asymmetry of human choices. In short, prospect theory predicts that
individuals tend to be risk averse when things are going well and
relatively more risk-seeking in the midst of a crisis.[34] The value

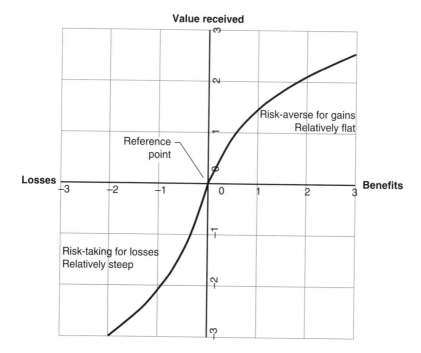

Figure 6.6   *Value function of prospect theory*[35]

function of prospect theory, as shown in Figure 6.6, is defined on variations in changes of benefit from the status quo of an organization (reference point), rather than on the absolute benefit as in expected utility theory. The value function is generally concave (risk averse) for benefits and commonly convex (risk taking) for losses; it is also steeper for losses than for benefits.

Moreover, the shape of value functions is pretty stable across decision makers. As a result, a business case team need not know each and every stakeholder's particular value function; once the domain and environment of the investment proposition is clear, predictions of risk propensity become possible regardless of individual stakeholders.[36]

When risk is involved, something as simple as rewording a question can cause people to change their minds on how they take on risk. *Framing effects* refer to the way in which a decision maker's judgment is affected by the order or manner (positive or negative statement) in which investment propositions or alternatives are presented in the business case. Although most corporate decision makers would argue that a seemingly harmless transformation to a decision paper will not substantively affect their choice, the experiments conducted by Kahneman and Tversky showed the opposite: that rewording can actually lead to *preference reversal*. Decision makers are frequently unaware of such framing effects because they are unable to recognize how framing was initially used for manipulation for two reasons.[37] First, a decision maker will most likely *accept* the structure, construction, and presentation of a reasonable business case and is highly unlikely to reorganize the presentation of alternatives and decisions to be taken. Second, when management takes decisions, it tends to *segregate* factors and focus on those that seem most relevant to the decision. Most decision makers, however, do not adequately account for related factors that may have an impact on the outcome, but which are not directly related to the decision. For instance, the overall probability of how likely it is that a Near-Earth Object will hit our planet (see Case 1.16) may be seemingly irrelevant to the decision about what to do if a meteor arrives. However, the probability is not inconsequential in determining how much should be spent on building related defense mechanisms.

6.5 MEASURING LEVEL OF RISK OF FUTURE ATTRIBUTES

Investors and business managers hate risk and love it at the same time; in their decision-making behavior they show clear signs of both risk aversion and risk seeking. It follows logically that measuring risk is a critical first step toward managing it.[38] This section looks at how the level of risk attached to the attributes of an investment proposition can be described and measured.

Standard deviation as a measure of dispersion risk

The future value of an attribute of a firm, industry, or market can be associated with risk. The greater the potential dispersion of its possible future values, the greater is its riskiness.

For example, assume that the future market space for product A is estimated to be very high with a probability of 5 per cent, high with 20 per cent, moderate with 50 per cent, low with 20 per cent, and very low with 5 per cent. Another product B has a higher dispersion; its possible market space is estimated to be very high with 15 per cent, high with 20 per cent, moderate with 30 per cent, low with 20 per cent, and very low with 15 per cent. As can be seen easily, the dispersion of possible future levels of market space is greater for product B than for product A and thus the level of risk about the future market space is greater for product B.

This dispersion and thus the level of risk can be measured by the standard deviation σ of the probability distribution of the future values:

$$\sigma = \sqrt{\sum_{i=1}^{N} P_i (V_i - \bar{V})^2}$$

		Product A		Product B	
	Value V_i	Probability P_i	$P_i(V_i - \bar{V})^2$	Probability P_i	$P_i(V_i - \bar{V})^2$
very high	7.5	5.00%	0.7605	15.00%	2.2815
high	5	20.00%	0.3920	20.00%	0.3920
moderate	3	50.00%	0.1800	30.00%	0.1080
low	2	20.00%	0.5120	20.00%	0.5120
very low	0.5	5.00%	0.4805	15.00%	1.4415
		Standard deviation (A) =	1.5248	Standard deviation (B) =	2.1760

Probability Distribution Curve for Product A and Product B

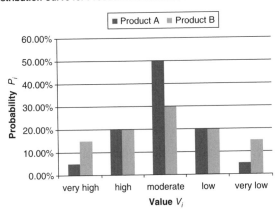

Figure 6.7 *Standard deviation measure of dispersion*

Let there be N possible discrete observations of the market space. Then P_i is the probability of a value V_i (the size of the market space) and $\bar{V}$ is the average of all the possible N values (the average market space value). The standard deviation is a statistic that allows us to make probabilistic statements about sampling averages; it tells how tightly all the various values are clustered around their mean. For the aforementioned example, the standard deviation is calculated in Figure 6.7 for Product A as $\sigma_A = 1.5248$ and for Product B as $\sigma_B = 2.1760$. When the values are quite tightly bunched together (as for Product A) the standard deviation is small and the probability distribution curve is steep. When the values are spread further apart (as for Product B), the standard deviation is bigger and the probability distribution curve is relatively flatter. Decisions made about the future sales of Product B are therefore riskier than about Product A.

Distribution curves as thought models

When thinking of producing and marketing a new product, the fluctuations in the price of a key raw material need to be considered in the business case, as they can affect the NPV bottom-line. From historical data, the distribution of the raw material's market price can be calculated and if such historical data are not available or only sketchy, one of the many different distribution curves available in statistics can help to facilitate discussions and estimate probabilities. This changes the view on distribution curves drastically; in statistics classes distribution curves are used as a description of data, but in the context of business cases they are being viewed as a practical way of visualizing assumptions about input factors.[39]

Assume that raw material prices will range from $70 to $90 with an average of $80. Figure 6.8 shows three simple ways of visualizing the price situation; all three distributions have an area of one. The simplest of them, the *uniform distribution* model, can be rejected quickly; it is highly unlikely that all prices within the range of $70–$90 will be equiprobable. Assuming a *normal distribution* with the typical Gaussian bell shape, the biggest challenge is finding a defensible value for the standard deviation. Sometimes one can draw upon historical data to estimate the standard deviation. However, this is not always possible in real life and one always needs to ask whether past behavior is a good predictor of future behavior. Nonetheless, just like in the aforementioned example, the range of data with its low and high values is usually available. The sample range R is defined as the difference of these two extremes, for example,

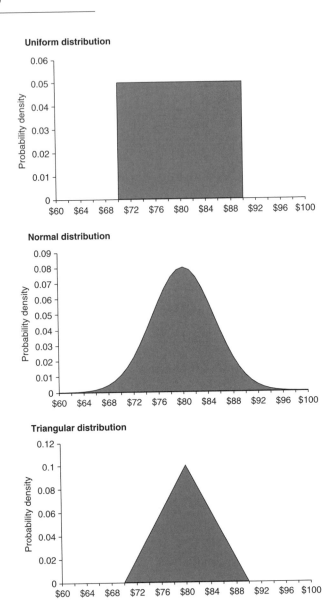

Figure 6.8 *Distribution curves*

$R = \$90 - \$70 = \$20$. As a consultant's rule of thumb, it is then reasonable to set[40]:

$$\sigma \approx \frac{R}{4} = \frac{90 - 70}{4} = 5$$

Hence the situation can be modeled as a *normal distribution* $N(\$80, 5)$, which is a credible model to any business manager. The probability density function in Excel is:

$$f(x) = NORMDIST(x, \mu, \sigma, false) = NORMDIST(x, \$80, 5, false)$$

But although not mentioned in most textbooks, experience suggests that the *triangular distribution* is most intuitive for business managers:

$$T(\text{min, max, mode}) = T(\$70, \$90, \$80)$$

$$\mu = \frac{\text{min} + \text{max} + \text{mode}}{3}$$

$$\text{mode} = 3\mu - \text{min} - \text{max}$$

And its probability density function is:

$$f(x) = \frac{2(x - \text{min})}{(\text{max} - \text{min})(\text{mode} - \text{min})} \, \forall \, \text{min} \leq x \leq \text{mode}$$

$$f(x) = \frac{2(\text{max} - x)}{(\text{max} - \text{min})(\text{max} - \text{mode})} \, \forall \, \text{mode} < x \leq \text{max}$$

The triangular distribution is easy to visualize, flexible, can be skewed, and prevents unlikely extremes[41], in short, it is a very practical distribution curve that is not only understood by statisticians, but also by business practitioners and corporate decision makers.

Sometimes the unawareness about a product, an industry, or a geographic region is so high that it is not possible to specify the future states of all attributes and thus it is not possible to attach probabilities to them. Then, obviously, neither the basic standard deviation formula nor the distribution curves can be applied and one needs to look for more sophisticated risk measurement and management techniques, as described in the following sections.

6.6   SENSITIVITY ANALYSIS

Approach to sensitivity analysis

Sensitivity analysis is a very popular and simple model for assessing risk in a business case calculation; it determines how "sensitive" a business case model is to changes in the value of the parameters of the model and to changes in the structure of the business case model.[42] It does not require the use of probabilities and is therefore often used when there is little information available or when there is no time or money to deploy more sophisticated techniques. Parameter sensitivity analysis is what is usually conducted in business case calculations and it involves identifying the key input variables to the business case calculation, changing their values, and observing how each change affects the NPV calculation. Parameter sensitivity analysis thus attempts to answer a series of simple "what-if" questions, for instance:

- What if the sales volume goes up by 10 per cent?

- What if the machinery can be used for eight instead of five years?

- What if the opportunity cost of capital is six instead of five per cent?

By showing how the business case responds to changes in parameter values, sensitivity analysis is a useful tool in building the business case as well as in evaluating a business case for decision making; looking at the range of NPV outcomes yields a deeper understanding of the dynamics of the proposed investment project and increases the confidence in the business case. Simple spreadsheet NPV calculation models as used in Section 2.2 are especially helpful to run these simulations.

Given an investment project with a positive NPV, it is especially useful to know the most adverse value for any given input that turns the NPV negative. Sensitivity analysis now allows determining what level of accuracy for the estimation of an input variable is necessary to make the business case model sufficiently useful and valid.

For a particular input parameter, the difference between the estimated and the most adverse value is referred to as the parameter's *margin of safety*. By inputting both the estimated and most adverse value into the business calculation, the business case team will gain a good feel for the dynamics of the mathematical model describing the investment suggestion. Highly sensitive variables can be identified and it is a good idea to verify the assumptions for the estimation of these variables once more before proceeding with presenting the business case to top management. Discovering that the business case calculation greatly changes for a certain change in a parameter value can help identify a *leverage point* in the business case model, i.e. a parameter whose specific value significantly influences the performance of the investment proposition.

Sometimes, sensitivity analysis also reveals that the business case calculation is mostly insensitive to a certain input parameter, and then it is possible to use a simple estimate rather than a value with greater precision for this parameter.

Sensitivity analysis in spreadsheets

Sensitivity analysis is at the heart of why spreadsheets like Excel were developed in the first place. Performing sensitivity analysis with inbuilt functions is rather simple, but reading the set of instructions can be rather bewildering, and it pays to think about how one might try to do this analysis without these automated methods – one would have to enter inputs by hand one at a time, keeping manual track of the results or saving the results on separate worksheets.

Excel offers *data tables*, which can track how small changes in inputs affect the results of formulas in the business case calculation that are dependent on those inputs. The advantages of sensitivity analysis automation with data tables are the ability to use an unlimited number of values as inputs to one or more key formulas in the calculation and to see all the outputs in a condensed form, making analysis and comparison pretty easy. However, with data tables it is only possible to identify a maximum of two input variables. Data tables with a single decision input variable (the so-called one-variable data tables) can have an unlimited number of formulae, but data tables with two input variables (the so-called two-variable data tables) are restricted to a single formula. Understanding how to structure data tables and how to respond to the "table dialog prompt" is key to building a successful sensitivity analysis in Excel.

Figure 6.9 shows an example in which a one-variable data table is used to see how different rates of return affect the NPV business case calculation. The list of rates of return is the variable column and entered in cells D23 to D29; the outcome is the NPV and displayed in the adjacent column E23 to E29. To set up this simple sensitivity analysis in Excel, the formula cell for the NPV calculation has to be referenced one row above and one cell to the right of the column of values. In the example shown, the formula is originally contained in cell E16 and referenced in cell E22.[43] Next, the range of cells containing the formulae and values that are to be substituted (D22:E29) must be selected. In the Excel application, on the data tab in the data tools group, the what-if analysis and then data table should be selected. For a column-oriented data table, the input cell has to be captured in the column input cell box; this is the cell that contains the rate of return in the original NPV calculation. Using the example, the input cell is E18. After the data table is created, the result cells can be changed and formatted as currency.[44]

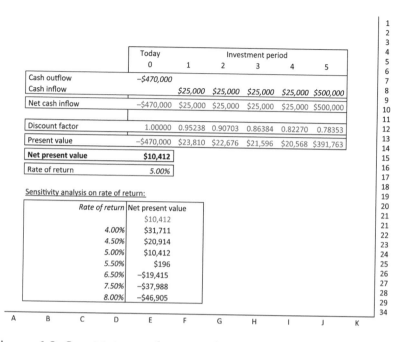

Figure 6.9 *Sensitivity analysis on the discount rate*

The sensitivity analysis for this example shows that the NPV is positive for rates of return lower than 5.5 per cent; should the rate of return be higher than this, the investment should not be approved.

Duration as a measure for sensitivity analysis

An investment's *duration* is defined as its weighted average life, with the weights being calculated as the present value of cash flows received in a period[45]:

$$\text{Duration} = \frac{\sum_{t=1}^{n} \left(t \cdot \dfrac{C_t}{(1+r)^t} \right)}{\sum_{t=1}^{n} \dfrac{C_t}{(1+r)^t}}$$

	Today	Investment period					NPV	Duration
	0	1	2	3	4	5		
Project 1: Net cash flow	−$470,000	$25,000	$45,000	$25,000	$25,000	$470,000	$5,047	4.41
Present value	−$470,000	$23,810	$40,816	$21,596	$20,568	$368,257		
Project 2: Net cash flow	−$470,000	$50,000	$70,000	$50,000	$50,000	$356,860	$5,047	3.93
Present value	−$470,000	$47,619	$63,492	$43,192	$41,135	$279,609		
Project 3: Net cash flow	−$470,000	$13,085	$510,000				$5,047	1.97
Present value	−$470,000	$12,462	$462,585	$0	$0	$0		
Discount factor	1.00000	0.95238	0.90703	0.86384	0.82270	0.78353		
Rate of return	5.00%							

Figure 6.10 *Duration as a sensitivity measure*

Similar to the payback and discounted payback approach, the duration method helps to take a decision between two mutually exclusive investments into the same asset with the same NPV. However, unlike payback and discounted payback, it takes the entire life of the asset into consideration.

Figure 6.10 shows three investment examples with the same initial investment of $470,000 and the same NPV of $5,047, but with very different cash flow streams. The duration of the three examples is calculated as 4.41, 3.93, and 1.97.

If the company thinks that the rate of interest may increase, it might prefer an investment with a shorter duration. Its present value would decline by less as a result of the interest rate increase. Of course, this conclusion is only valid if the interest rates of all periods change by the same amount.

Drawbacks of sensitivity analysis

Although sensitivity analysis has several major strengths, it also comes with two main drawbacks.

First, it is a static analysis in the sense that only one input value can be changed at any point of time and all the other variables are considered to remain constant for each run of the sensitivity analysis. In a complex business scenario, however, it is likely that more than one variable will differ from the estimates. It basically ignores relationships among input parameters.

Second, sensitivity analysis does not come with any clear decision rules. There is no explicit probabilistic measure of risk exposure; sensitivity analysis does not contain an explicit measure of outcome likelihood. There is no "so what" answer to the "what if" analysis and the business case team has to rely on its own judgment to reiterate the results of the analysis into the business case calculation.

6.7 SCENARIO ANALYSIS

To overcome sensitivity analysis's first limitation of only being able to change one variable at a time, *scenario analysis* looks at a number of different variable changes at the same time, each describing a certain view of things: the so-called scenarios. This potentially leads to a more informative way of presenting and assessing risk in a business case. Notwithstanding this added flexibility, scenario analysis does not overcome sensitivity analysis's limitation of not providing a decision rule for accepting or rejecting investment propositions.

History of scenario analysis

The use of scenarios dates back to the development of the atomic bomb at Los Alamos in 1942, when scientists undertook "let's pretend" studies built upon a framework of theory. Following the Second World War, scenarios became popular in military strategy planning in the USA, and in the 1960s they were also applied to public policy decision making. Later they also spread into the area of business management, and by 1980 about 50 per cent of Fortune 1000 companies used scenarios as business forecasting tools.[46] Driven by increased business complexity, uncertainty, and globalization, scenario planning techniques have since then become even more popular. Bigger companies and companies with a long-range planning horizon are generally more likely to have adapted scenario analysis in their strategic planning process.[47]

Approach to scenario analysis

Scenarios can be defined as fundamentally different future states of a business environment considering possible developments of relevant interdependent factors.[48] The aim of scenario analysis is therefore to develop several possible future business pictures (multiple future view) based on a complex network of determining factors. These pictures can then be used to formulate appropriate guiding strategies (see e.g. Section 1.1 for the Rumelt framework of good strategy). The thought and decision-making processes are thus no longer linear, but perceive the company as a networked entity, within itself and with its external environment.[49]

The logic of scenario analysis can best be summarized using the model of a scenario funnel as shown in Figure 6.11. This theoretical model shows that with increasing length of the forecast period, the range of future possibilities opens up. Although the investment path in the medium-term future is still pretty much influenced and restricted by the present, the long term is less influenced by the current framework and uncertainty about its development increases. The set path of an investment can be swayed by an external interference event. The resulting scenarios possible at any point in time are located on the cut surface across the funnel. At the edges are the extreme scenarios, which are described through both optimistic and pessimistic assumptions about the determining factors' development. The spectrum of possible scenarios widens the further one attempts to look into the future; in the very long-term future, nearly everything is possible.[50]

Although an infinite set of scenarios exists based on an infinite set of assumptions, conditions, and combinations of input parameters, popular applications of scenario analysis in business

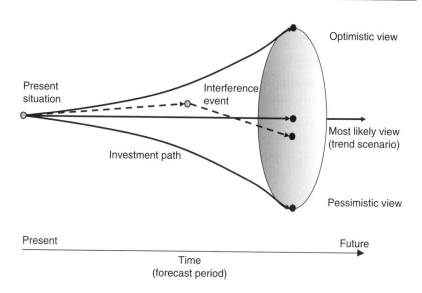

Figure 6.11 *Scenario funnel*

cases often only include three discrete views: the optimistic view, most likely view, and pessimistic view.

The *optimistic view* constructs a *best-case scenario* by using the best possible combination of input values; for each and every parameter, the optimistic values are used. The optimistic view thus answers the question: What is the best possible NPV from the investment proposition? For the *pessimistic view* it is assumed that almost everything goes wrong. By using only the most pessimistic values for each input parameter, a *worst-case scenario* is built. The pessimistic view answers the question: What is the worst possible NPV from the investment proposition? While the optimistic view and pessimistic view emphasize the extremes, the *most likely view* reflects the NPV given the most likely combination of input values according to the business case team's best-guess estimates of what is feasible. The most likely view builds a so-called *trend scenario*, which is the *base case* for the business case.

Practical advantages and disadvantages

Scenario analysis does not look at any in-between constellations, but analyzes only the identified scenarios by varying macroeconomic and investment-specific variables. In contrast to the standard deviation method of dispersion (see Section 6.5), it also does not attach any probabilities to these scenarios and leaves the finance manager with nothing more than a rough feeling of how badly or how well the investment can possibly go; it does not give a direct recommendation for the accept–reject decision. Nevertheless, the outcome of scenario analysis can potentially be very useful information for the business case team.

First, scenario analysis provides decision makers with more in-depth information about the investment proposition. Rather than being presented with a single NPV (most likely view), decision makers now know the probabilities that it will be far less (pessimistic view) or a bit more (optimistic view). By making risk assumptions explicit, dialog about the project's inherent risk is encouraged.[51]

Second, an analysis of the investment's path shows decision makers step by step how internal and external factors could develop the current situation in a logical way into scenarios; the result then looks at the difference between the optimistic and pessimistic views. The pessimistic view can then also serve as a worst-case scenario of what happens when the investment goes completely wrong. It analyzes whether there are any spill-over effects which could drive the organization into default. Scenario analysis can also be understood as a measure of risk, and the optimistic view should be higher for more risky than for conservative investment propositions.

Third, a path analysis also helps to develop strategies for mitigating project risk. For instance, stepwise investment decisions, and more flexibility in a project to scale up in case of success and down in case of failure or to change the focus altogether in case the market potential is found somewhere else, can significantly increase the value of an investment to a company. The creation of such real options is covered in Chapter 7.

Fourth, and last, but not least, scenarios help to get projects approved. Submitting a single NPV is often a poor compromise between just enough realism so that the projected benefits will most likely be reaped and a bit of optimism so that the investment proposition's upside is sufficiently reflected to make the business case attractive. By presenting multiple scenarios, the business case team can show an honest and upright perspective to the decision makers; they can advocate the proposition's full potential as well as disclosing the potential downside risk.

Conducting a scenario analysis

A good and still basic scenario analysis consists of three steps.

As a first step, scenarios need to be constructed by determining the macroeconomic and investment-specific factors that influence the investment. These determining factors can range from the general state of the economy, to a competitor's response, to changes in regulatory or taxation laws, and to acceptance of the product by the market. Choosing and setting up the determining factors is always subjective, but once the key assumptions are established, the comparisons delivered by the scenario analysis are valid.[52] As a general guideline, the business case team should only focus on two or three really relevant factors, as otherwise the scenario analysis will blow up and become too difficult to handle in corporate business case practice.

Second, the number of scenarios to be analyzed for each determining factor needs to be defined. Although more scenarios provide a more realistic view of the investment, it is usually difficult to estimate differences in cash flow forecasts between the scenarios if they are not substantially different. As a rule of thumb, five scenarios per factor are a reasonable compromise between granularity of analysis and feasibility of forecasting.

The third step is the estimation of cash inflows and outflows under each scenario along the investment path. Potential interfering events and decision points, with their consequences as laid out by the factors, are explicitly considered in painting the scenarios. Effectively, a separate monetary business case needs to be constructed around costs and benefits for each combination of factor and scenario.

Forecasting a factor's range of value

A challenge in the above approach is to forecast the range of values that the identified factors can take on. How many customers is the company going to have in three years' time? How is the real estate market developing? What will be the TV of the investment? How high is the inflation going to be? Overly simplistic assumptions, such as taking fixed percentages for the input values above or below the most likely case should be avoided.

A good tool for modeling these factors throughout the forecast period involves drawing a *binomial event tree*.[53] The first step is to establish today's factor values. How many customers does the company have today? What would be the TV of the investment today? What is the inflation rate today? The second step is estimating how much this factor value is likely to move up or down, at most, during the period in question. Assuming that the distribution of possible factor values is fairly normal (see Section 6.5), the multiplier to apply for an up-movement is given by the formula:

$$u = e^{\sigma \sqrt{t}}$$

$e \approx 2.718$ is the base of natural logarithms and σ describes the volatility of the factor; t is the duration of a period measured in years, and in most business cases it will be $t = 1$.

The multiplier for a down-movement is simply the inverse of the up-multiplier, i.e.:

$$d = \frac{1}{u} = e^{-\sigma\sqrt{t}}$$

Other formulae can be used where a normal distribution of the factor cannot be assumed or where the distribution is skewed, i.e. where $d \neq \frac{1}{u}$.

The next challenge is to estimate the σ, which is the factor's volatility. The best option would be to look at the value drivers of the factor, for example, what causes the number of customers to go up? What influences the resale value of real estate? Unfortunately, many times the factor under consideration will already be the factor at the end of a cause-and-effect relationship and further value drivers cannot be identified or (e.g., in the case of inflation) are clearly beyond scope of a business case. Then it is possible to look at historic values and see how the client base has expanded or shrunk, how real estate value has gone up and down, and how the inflation rate has historically changed. The maximum up-movement between two consecutive years over a period of, say, the past five years, would give a good estimate for u and analogous logic would provide a value for d.

For instance, if a company has 1,000 customers today and the volatility of the customer base is established as $\sigma = 18.23\%$, the up and down factors are $u = 1.20$ and $d = 0.833$. Within a year, the customer base will range between 1,200 and 833. If the customer base goes up to 1,200 in the first year, then it will be between 1,440 and 1,000 after another year. If the customer base goes down to 833 in the first year, the year-two span is 1,000–694. Mapped out on the binomial tree in Figure 6.12, these numbers show how many customers the company could have within the investment period.

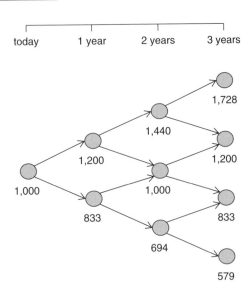

Figure 6.12 *Binomial event tree*

Expected net present value

To overcome the scenario analysis's shortcoming of not working with probabilities, different likelihoods can be attributed to the range of identified scenarios, leading to NPV outcomes with different probabilities. This would be a fourth step in addition to the scenario analysis outlined before.

For example, the corporation can estimate the most likely view at $p_{lv} = 50\%$, the optimistic view at $p_{ov} = 20\%$, and the pessimistic view at $p_{pv} = 30\%$ $p_{lv} = 30\%$. The ENPV of the investment is then the weighted average of the NPV of its scenarios, i.e.:

$$ENPV = p_{lv} \cdot NPV_{lv} + p_{ov} \cdot NPV_{ov} + p_{pv} \cdot NPV_{pv}$$
$$= 0.5 \cdot NPV_{lv} + 0.2 \cdot NPV_{ov} + 0.3 \cdot NPV_{pv}$$

Of course, it is possible to work on more sophisticated scenarios by identifying the key input variables, attaching likelihoods to each of them, and thereby establishing a range of scenarios. Scenarios need to cover the full spectrum of possibilities, i.e. their probabilities need to add up to one so that the ENPV calculation makes sense mathematically.

To get a feeling for risk and uncertainty, many business cases today include an ENPV calculation. However, this is still a static analysis of discrete scenarios and does not take into consideration that any investment project, once started, will be dynamic and allow managers to adjust and fine-tune the course of action. In fact, it takes away the power and usefulness of management. In Section 6.10 a dynamic aspect will be added to business cases; it will outline how decision trees build upon ENPV and thereby help to forecast and manage the dynamic process of alternative implementation routes.

6.8   SIMULATIONS

By taking a more formal and methodical approach to sensitivity analysis, it is possible to establish a set of sometimes complex calculations that mirrors the dynamics of the investment project and simulates the performance of the investment based on this mathematical model.

Simulations use stringent mathematical models for predictions and at the same time take randomness into account; they imitate real life by investigating tens, if not hundreds of thousands, of different scenarios. As a result, simulations furnish decision makers with a full range of possible consequences and their attached probabilities.

Monte Carlo simulation for business case simulations

When calculating the NPV of an investment decision problem with a spreadsheet tool, as introduced in Section 2.2, one can have a certain number of input parameters and a few equations which use these input parameters to calculate the net cash flow and produce the NPV as an output response variable. This is referred to as a *deterministic model*; it is predictable in the sense that it will always give the same result, no matter how often it is calculated. One gets the same NPV every time the deterministic model is run.

A simulation, however, involves using random numbers and probability distributions as inputs, thereby essentially turning the deterministic model into a *stochastic model*, that finds the NPV of the same investment decision problem under conditions of lack of knowledge, estimation error, or random variation. The Monte Carlo method (also known as Monte Carlo simulation) is a sampling method, because the inputs are randomly generated from probability distributions (see Section 6.5) best describing the state of knowledge on an input variable. Because of the randomness in it, the outcome will be different from run to run; one may not get the same NPV every time. The main question and issue is how often it needs to be run on a random sample of all possible values and combinations until one believes the answer. The bigger the sample is, the more reproducible the simulation's result will become.

The difference between a deterministic model and a stochastic Monte Carlo model is summarized in Figure 6.13, and Case 6.2 explains how the Monte Carlo simulation is applied in the pharmaceutical industry to help predict results when several parameters can change at the same time.

Case 6.2 Monte Carlo simulation at Merck

In the pharmaceutical industry, only one in 10,000 explored chemicals becomes a prescription drug, sometimes only after 10 years or more. Business cases using traditional financial valuations accurately appreciate neither the long-term nature of pharmaceutical risks nor the possibility of ultimate rewards.

In 1983, Judith C. Lewent, who later became chief financial officer at Merck (see Case 1.19), turned to the Monte Carlo method in order to be able to predict results based on changes in several parameters at the same time. She developed a model that can project 20 years out, which is critical for the long-term range of pharmaceutical development. The model helps Merck to provide financial information about asset allocations at various junctures of the R&D; investments with marginal returns can thus be eliminated early in the process.[54]

The term "Monte Carlo simulation" dates back to the 1940s when many simulations were performed to estimate the probability that the chain reaction needed for the atom bomb would work successfully. The physicists involved in this research were obviously big fans of gambling, so they gave the simulations the code name Monte Carlo, after the Monaco resort town renowned for its casinos (see Figure 6.14).

The first step in a Monte Carlo business case simulation is to model the investment by identifying its key variables with their interrelationships. They lead to cash benefits via cause-and-effect relationships similar to those discovered in the benefit discovery chart (see Section 4.4), but at a much more granular level. Also, relationships between cash flows occurring in different time periods across the project life span need to be modeled. One can easily see that this leads to a huge number of equations, even for a fairly straightforward investment proposition.

As a second step, the possible value ranges of the input variables with their probability distribution have to be identified. This is again a highly complex task requiring a deep understanding of the market dynamics; refer back to Section 6.5 for probability distributions.

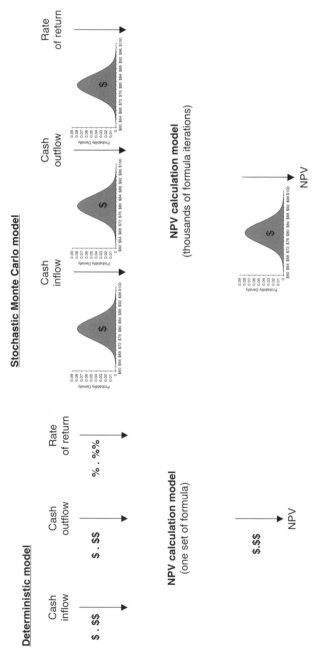

Figure 6.13 *Deterministic and stochastic models for NPV calculation*

Figure 6.14 *Casino at Monte Carlo*[55]

The third step in a Monte Carlo simulation is to run the simulation model by randomly selecting one value for each input variable out of each variable's distribution range. The mathematical model then projects the cash in- and out-flows and thus calculates the NPV of the investment. Then the simulation picks up another trial run with another set of randomly selected values and calculates another NPV. After tens and maybe hundreds of thousands of iterations, a probability distribution of the investment's NPV emerges; it can now help the business case team to assess the riskiness of the project.

Performing simulations in spreadsheets

Unfortunately, spreadsheets like Excel are not optimized for statistics, so complex simulations require special software or at least additions to their calculation software, which not only calculate probabilities, but also permit Monte Carlo simulations to draw repeated samples from a defined probability distribution. It is then possible to study the impact of changes in the input variables on the rest of the calculation. However, it is still possible to use Excel for a simulation on a fairly standard business case.

Going forward, the following scenario will be examined with a Monte Carlo simulation: A company wants to know how profitable it will be to import and market a foreign product over the next three years, realizing there are many uncertainties regarding market size, expenses, revenue, and last but not least, development of the interest rates. This scenario is calculated in Figure 6.15 using the "classic" deterministic NPV model.[56]

The monthly profit is the difference between the income and the expenses. Already income and expenses are uncertain parameters, but stopping here would only scratch the surface. Are both independent variables? Or does income achieved from product sales depend on sales expenses? Do we have a circle here?

To answer this question, both income and expenses need to be further broken down. As the company in this example achieves

	Today	Investment period		
	0	1	2	3
Leads per month (L)		1,000	1,250	1,500
Cost per lead (C)		$0.60	$0.50	$0.40
Conversion rate (R)		3.00%	3.50%	4.00%
Profit per sale (p)		$50.00	$50.00	$50.00
Overhead per month (H)		$1,000.00	$900.00	$800.00
Profit per month		-$100	$663	$1,600
Profit per investment period		-$1,200	$7,950	$19,200
Net cash inflow	$0	-$1,200	$7,950	$19,200
Discount factor	1.00000	0.95238	0.90703	0.86384
Present value	$0	-$1,143	$7,211	$16,586
Net present value	$22,654			
Rate of return	5.00%			

Figure 6.15 *Example of deterministic NPV calculation*

income from pursuing a number of sales leads L, the conversion rate R comes into play. Generating leads is associated with overhead costs H and costs C associated with every lead. Finally, a successful sale generates profits of P. The following equation models this relationship and this is really the simulation's first step:

$$\text{Profit per month} = \text{Income} - \text{Expenses} = L \cdot R \cdot P - (H + L \cdot C)$$

This equation shows that the number of sales leads L affects both income and expenses, proving that income and expenses are not independent. Of course, there are other dependencies involved; for example, the marketing part of the overhead costs H and the sales expenses per lead C may influence the conversion rate R. Further, successful sales in one period will increase the likelihood of even more successful sales in the next period (unless the market is already saturated with the product). For the sake of simplicity, these additional relationships are ignored in this example, but they could be modeled with a few additional simple equations.

One of the key success factors of a Monte Carlo simulation is to generate random and independent inputs; hence it is so important to avoid any correlation between input variables, like income and expenses, which are not independent. Figure 6.16 summarizes the business case team's knowledge about the input variables.

Besides the nominal values, which were also used for the deterministic NPV calculation in Figure 6.15, the min and max values indicate the uncertainty. Another important aspect is the choice of distribution function for the input values (see Section 6.5) as it will influence how random numbers are created. The Excel functions for creating random numbers are:

- *Uniform distribution U[min; max]: min + (max − min) · RAND ()*

Input Values for Period 1

	Nominal	Min	Max
Leads per month (L)	1000	800	1200
Cost per lead (C)	$0.60	$0.20	$0.80
Conversion rate (R)	3.0%	1.0%	5.0%
Profit per sale (p)	$50.00	$47.00	$53.00
Overhead per month (H)	$800.00		
Rate of return (r)	5.0%	4.0%	6.0%

Input Values for Period 2

	Nominal	Min	Max
Leads per month (L)	1250	1000	1500
Cost per lead (C)	$0.50	$0.20	$0.80
Conversion rate (R)	3.5%	1.5%	5.5%
Profit per sale (P)	$50.00	$47.00	$53.00
Overhead per month (H)	$700.00		
Rate of return (r)	5.0%	3.5%	6.5%

Input Values for Period 3

	Nominal	Min	Max
Leads per month (L)	1500	1200	1800
Cost per lead (C)	$0.40	$0.20	$0.80
Conversion rate (R)	4.0%	2.0%	6.0%
Profit per sale (P)	$50.00	$47.00	$53.00
Overhead per month (H)	$650.00		
Rate of return (r)	5.0%	3.0%	7.0%

Figure 6.16 *Knowledge about input values*

- *Normal distribution* $N(\mu, \sigma)$: *NORMINV(RAND(), mean, standard deviation)*

Unfortunately, there is no single-cell Excel function available for the triangular distribution $T(min, max, mode)$, but it can be programmed using two cells and the following short algorithm:

$$temp = RAND\,()$$
$$IF\ (temp \leq (mode - min)/(max - min);$$
$$min + SQRT\,(temp \cdot (mode - min) \cdot (max - min));$$
$$max - SQRT\,((1 - temp) \cdot (max - min) \cdot (max - mode)))$$

Storing the random number in the variable *temp* is important because Excel's random number generator returns a new value each time called; without *temp*, the calculation would use one value for branching and another for calculation.[57]

To run a few thousand evaluations of the model, the data in Excel need to be organized in columns for each variable containing the formula for generating random numbers according to the chosen distribution (see Figure 6.17).

The model's equation is put next to the input columns for each investment period and summed in the right-most column for the NPV. Through dragging down the formula a few thousand cells, Excel can generate the random input and run the simulation. Now the model's output needs to be evaluated, and a good way of getting a first understanding is to create a histogram using a bar chart diagram together with binning technique as in Figure 6.18.

This histogram visually provides the first valuable information. It is based on 5,000 randomly generated input variants and it seems that most of the time the import business is fortunate enough to generate a positive NPV; however, there are also some negative NPVs. The shape of the histogram is quite centered to the middle, but still there is uncertainty attached to the outcome. At least there are no visible outliers.

Statistics provides a set of formulae in order to describe this NPV distribution mathematically; the following formulae have practical relevance and are also calculated in Figure 6.18.

Let the *sample size n* be the number of randomly generated data points for one run of the simulation. The larger the sample size, the smaller the difference will be between repeated simulations; the *standard error StdErr* estimates the standard deviation σ of a repeated run of the simulation[58]:

$$StdErr \approx \frac{\sigma}{\sqrt{n}} = \frac{STDEV(column)}{SQRT(COUNT(column))} \text{ [59]}$$

1 st period						
L (rand)	C (rand)	R (rand)	P (rand)	H (const)	r (rand)	Profit
847	$0.46	3.541%	$51.25	$800.00	5.821%	$3,923.21
1006	$0.34	1.428%	$49.25	$800.00	5.887%	($4,935.45)
969	$0.41	2.069%	$47.90	$800.00	4.938%	($2,748.90)
983	$0.60	3.986%	$49.78	$800.00	4.828%	$6,409.34
1160	$0.42	1.862%	$50.15	$800.00	4.524%	($2,318.99)
1119	$0.35	2.370%	$48.04	$800.00	5.232%	$1,000.42
983	$0.57	3.195%	$52.04	$800.00	4.433%	$3,127.65
1197	$0.62	2.961%	$47.23	$800.00	5.218%	$1,496.25
865	$0.71	1.891%	$50.70	$800.00	4.194%	($6,688.36)
872	$0.32	1.878%	$51.01	$800.00	4.605%	($2,802.98)
935	$0.79	1.298%	$50.99	$800.00	5.485%	($10,413.62)
1046	$0.55	2.459%	$52.71	$800.00	5.484%	($266.08)
908	$0.75	2.946%	$52.86	$800.00	4.748%	($774.79)
863	$0.30	4.134%	$49.92	$800.00	5.060%	$8,209.02
850	$0.54	2.670%	$50.98	$800.00	4.700%	($1,200.18)
1009	$0.38	1.930%	$49.51	$800.00	4.449%	($2,551.37)
843	$0.70	3.374%	$49.46	$800.00	5.608%	$161.78
1063	$0.43	1.280%	$48.77	$800.00	5.816%	($6,750.23)
811	$0.53	1.536%	$52.45	$800.00	5.317%	($6,524.02)
1158	$0.54	2.421%	$52.58	$800.00	5.583%	$591.23
841	$0.29	1.932%	$51.42	$800.00	4.678%	($2,360.39)
911	$0.52	2.803%	$48.15	$800.00	4.319%	($473.80)
1177	$0.76	2.248%	$52.29	$800.00	5.131%	($3,583.29)
941	$0.64	4.846%	$48.67	$800.00	4.840%	$9,379.79
857	$0.77	2.629%	$51.03	$800.00	5.061%	($3,511.57)
1031	$0.76	3.344%	$51.80	$800.00	4.105%	$2,298.35
824	$0.72	4.040%	$49.92	$800.00	4.636%	$3,103.43
1190	$0.38	4.911%	$52.93	$800.00	4.756%	$21,155.65
1049	$0.76	2.910%	$51.35	$800.00	4.170%	($366.70)
919	$0.76	3.239%	$49.71	$800.00	4.564%	($207.48)
912	$0.48	4.242%	$51.19	$800.00	4.042%	$8,615.57
815	$0.77	2.093%	$51.91	$800.00	4.172%	($6,200.89)
1160	$0.76	3.222%	$49.89	$800.00	5.019%	$2,095.34
1041	$0.52	2.826%	$47.44	$800.00	4.558%	$663.83
957	$0.69	3.289%	$48.53	$800.00	5.554%	$819.49
819	$0.76	2.641%	$47.23	$800.00	4.879%	($4,570.61)
989	$0.41	4.401%	$48.85	$800.00	5.292%	$10,510.04
1077	$0.52	2.715%	$51.99	$800.00	4.352%	$1,850.82
1095	$0.75	3.897%	$48.78	$800.00	4.848%	$5,228.59
817	$0.45	1.463%	$47.12	$800.00	5.801%	($6,878.33)
990	$0.78	2.934%	$49.33	$800.00	5.313%	($1,544.86)
977	$0.22	4.042%	$51.28	$800.00	5.995%	$11,454.78
859	$0.63	4.245%	$48.19	$800.00	4.821%	$4,798.27
1044	$0.32	4.309%	$49.11	$800.00	5.480%	$12,223.41
1184	$0.72	2.437%	$50.36	$800.00	4.562%	($2,329.43)
925	$0.21	3.189%	$47.39	$800.00	5.665%	$4,566.65
961	$0.77	4.183%	$48.89	$800.00	5.696%	$4,788.36
955	$0.22	4.657%	$47.65	$800.00	5.224%	$12,700.14
837	$0.35	1.989%	$48.80	$800.00	4.211%	($3,213.28)
1103	$0.76	1.064%	$51.29	$800.00	4.989%	($11,894.35)

2 nd period						
L (rand)	C (rand)	R (rand)	P (rand)	H (const)	r (rand)	Profit
1107	$0.44	3.187%	$51.77	$700.00	3.738%	$7,117.24
1423	$0.39	2.742%	$47.74	$700.00	4.270%	$6,714.48
1377	$0.25	4.817%	$47.35	$700.00	3.714%	$23,325.40
1297	$0.78	5.026%	$48.13	$700.00	6.135%	$15,237.19
1230	$0.75	1.731%	$51.78	$700.00	6.143%	($5,549.17)
1380	$0.40	3.912%	$51.04	$700.00	4.264%	$16,535.95
1251	$0.66	1.920%	$49.65	$700.00	5.501%	($3,526.70)
1397	$0.53	5.499%	$49.64	$700.00	6.454%	$25,177.44
1129	$0.73	2.835%	$49.87	$700.00	4.392%	$825.45
1339	$0.56	2.774%	$52.76	$700.00	4.451%	$5,571.82
1496	$0.71	3.144%	$48.38	$700.00	4.331%	$5,653.97
1352	$0.51	4.993%	$50.62	$700.00	4.201%	$22,467.51
1306	$0.61	2.449%	$51.53	$700.00	5.492%	$1,579.39
1083	$0.21	2.580%	$51.38	$700.00	4.602%	$5,534.95
1442	$0.57	2.247%	$50.63	$700.00	6.435%	$1,314.54
1126	$0.69	5.044%	$50.00	$700.00	5.412%	$14,741.03
1351	$0.70	3.863%	$51.98	$700.00	5.198%	$11,553.31
1152	$0.38	2.009%	$48.30	$700.00	4.154%	($243.71)
1472	$0.60	1.842%	$47.21	$700.00	5.649%	($3,331.23)
1313	$0.71	2.132%	$49.58	$700.00	6.441%	($2,657.16)
1192	$0.46	5.485%	$49.58	$700.00	5.793%	$21,319.95
1210	$0.50	4.843%	$47.37	$700.00	5.835%	$15,813.74
1474	$0.65	4.658%	$50.82	$700.00	4.641%	$20,029.26
1026	$0.73	3.974%	$50.18	$700.00	5.440%	$6,473.75
1069	$0.74	3.771%	$51.42	$700.00	4.362%	$6,366.47
1041	$0.56	2.154%	$51.44	$700.00	4.987%	($1,451.92)
1223	$0.71	5.346%	$51.75	$700.00	5.091%	$19,766.71
1451	$0.71	5.082%	$47.23	$700.00	3.541%	$19,681.41
1365	$0.20	1.575%	$50.69	$700.00	5.501%	$1,216.54
1074	$0.30	1.809%	$51.54	$700.00	4.107%	($214.27)
1054	$0.21	2.014%	$50.53	$700.00	6.404%	$1,557.98
1004	$0.50	3.750%	$49.56	$700.00	5.619%	$7,159.55
1189	$0.57	2.702%	$52.31	$700.00	4.967%	$3,265.99
1471	$0.73	4.776%	$50.47	$700.00	3.945%	$19,748.21
1409	$0.79	1.981%	$50.19	$700.00	6.218%	($4,386.82)
1365	$0.74	2.116%	$47.30	$700.00	3.571%	($3,774.01)
1264	$0.41	4.187%	$51.38	$700.00	4.715%	$16,434.07
1256	$0.35	2.999%	$51.79	$700.00	5.750%	$8,730.74
1123	$0.57	4.458%	$50.74	$700.00	6.412%	$12,711.94
1465	$0.40	2.113%	$52.08	$700.00	4.789%	$3,494.82
1234	$0.44	2.443%	$47.91	$700.00	5.210%	$2,201.33
1186	$0.54	2.359%	$49.64	$700.00	5.597%	$483.14
1173	$0.68	4.884%	$47.86	$700.00	3.683%	$13,850.76
1201	$0.52	4.897%	$51.31	$700.00	6.061%	$18,094.25
1498	$0.43	2.672%	$50.80	$700.00	5.914%	$7,294.89
1274	$0.44	1.890%	$51.60	$700.00	6.201%	($165.88)
1254	$0.26	3.269%	$49.41	$700.00	6.035%	$10,643.20
1053	$0.73	1.586%	$51.13	$700.00	5.616%	($6,589.72)
1461	$0.24	3.043%	$48.36	$700.00	3.646%	$12,221.56
1147	$0.41	3.645%	$51.41	$700.00	3.607%	$10,892.33

3 rd period							
L (rand)	C (rand)	R (rand)	P (rand)	H (const)	r (rand)	Profit	NPV
1343	$0.47	5.930%	$49.84	$650.00	6.369%	$26,861.27	$37,901.72
1388	$0.29	5.114%	$49.13	$650.00	5.888%	$24,614.94	$26,393.97
1685	$0.60	4.648%	$47.21	$650.00	4.782%	$21,310.64	$41,887.13
1792	$0.60	3.123%	$47.41	$650.00	6.271%	$9,345.81	$30,992.34
1697	$0.30	4.336%	$50.71	$650.00	3.966%	$27,532.03	$19,663.87
1596	$0.63	2.796%	$49.74	$650.00	4.850%	$5,912.37	$23,448.74
1311	$0.76	4.166%	$50.72	$650.00	3.945%	$11,947.72	$11,548.67
1511	$0.31	4.991%	$51.33	$650.00	5.536%	$28,102.43	$54,776.12
1272	$0.75	4.709%	$47.90	$650.00	3.932%	$13,588.67	$7,725.75
1669	$0.50	2.599%	$52.49	$650.00	4.982%	$8,284.91	$11,053.76
1311	$0.21	4.118%	$52.56	$650.00	6.750%	$18,895.51	$14,135.86
1251	$0.23	2.591%	$52.55	$650.00	6.063%	$7,655.65	$29,857.08
1682	$0.58	2.860%	$52.11	$650.00	5.333%	$9,125.73	$9,930.34
1747	$0.46	3.918%	$48.42	$650.00	6.932%	$18,306.96	$32,050.93
1509	$0.57	3.067%	$50.84	$650.00	3.899%	$9,032.48	$9,146.84
1352	$0.46	2.950%	$50.45	$650.00	6.816%	$7,317.44	$19,507.10
1348	$0.33	5.826%	$50.64	$650.00	6.776%	$28,347.23	$40,062.32
1293	$0.33	3.278%	$50.99	$650.00	6.919%	$10,585.60	$3,591.66
1441	$0.35	2.137%	$52.91	$650.00	3.879%	$5,039.33	($4,815.93)
1665	$0.79	5.641%	$48.54	$650.00	3.520%	$28,040.32	$25,974.40
1362	$0.34	4.173%	$47.80	$650.00	4.952%	$16,621.13	$35,580.69
1649	$0.35	2.684%	$52.37	$650.00	4.510%	$11,488.96	$26,828.89
1534	$0.63	3.972%	$52.43	$650.00	3.988%	$16,816.50	$33,262.47
1346	$0.58	2.307%	$49.14	$650.00	5.981%	$961.49	$16,815.03
1486	$0.50	4.363%	$51.25	$650.00	6.202%	$19,357.30	$22,212.19
1235	$0.61	5.178%	$50.60	$650.00	5.290%	$18,852.60	$19,699.03
1373	$0.76	2.848%	$48.18	$650.00	5.673%	$1,980.17	$24,850.31
1560	$0.68	4.161%	$51.43	$650.00	4.199%	$17,323.66	$58,160.72
1448	$0.29	5.270%	$47.11	$650.00	6.162%	$25,361.65	$26,211.48
1598	$0.35	4.584%	$47.54	$650.00	4.540%	$23,951.93	$23,530.17
1421	$0.61	3.499%	$50.24	$650.00	3.911%	$10,516.90	$20,690.45
1274	$0.40	5.613%	$52.95	$650.00	4.852%	$27,294.41	$28,253.06
1354	$0.73	3.931%	$51.94	$650.00	5.178%	$11,592.76	$16,954.08
1704	$0.48	2.108%	$50.51	$650.00	4.115%	$3,654.66	$24,066.70
1480	$0.42	4.603%	$49.91	$650.00	4.898%	$22,058.55	$18,491.23
1752	$0.78	2.619%	$47.12	$650.00	6.613%	$1,387.34	($6,957.28)
1263	$0.36	4.971%	$52.50	$650.00	3.507%	$23,699.94	$50,644.05
1250	$0.78	4.725%	$52.46	$650.00	4.692%	$15,451.15	$26,032.71
1481	$0.43	5.227%	$48.08	$650.00	3.176%	$26,539.92	$44,480.45
1342	$0.29	4.690%	$48.91	$650.00	6.371%	$20,380.52	$16,997.01
1385	$0.56	4.471%	$47.26	$650.00	3.606%	$16,265.84	$16,922.31
1268	$0.58	3.445%	$51.11	$650.00	3.816%	$9,111.13	$21,049.05
1724	$0.61	5.520%	$49.77	$650.00	6.718%	$30,027.49	$48,676.53
1736	$0.49	3.855%	$50.14	$650.00	3.263%	$20,267.42	$50,585.08
1503	$0.67	2.439%	$50.81	$650.00	6.091%	$2,122.31	$7,087.77
1685	$0.20	4.869%	$47.52	$650.00	4.598%	$30,496.43	$34,897.19
1363	$0.29	5.115%	$47.69	$650.00	3.304%	$24,761.84	$40,193.40
1261	$0.49	3.272%	$50.03	$650.00	3.489%	$8,627.14	$14,737.56
1362	$0.77	4.073%	$49.87	$650.00	4.673%	$11,120.96	$20,129.24
1660	$0.68	2.512%	$50.61	$650.00	6.711%	$3,343.26	$2,341.23

Figure 6.17 *Random number generation for input variables*

Statistics

Sample Size:	5000
Mean:	$28,070.82
Median:	$27,815.33
Standard deviation:	$14,765.63
Mean Standard Error:	$208.82
Skew:	0.1433
Kurtosis:	−0.2817

Histogramm

95% Confidence interval

95%-ll CoI	$27,661.54
95%-ul CoI	$28,480.09

95% Central interval

95%-ll CeI	$863.58
95%-ul CeI	$57,571.30

Probability NPV>0

Pr(> 0):	98.0%

Figure 6.18 *Histogram and key statistics for the NPV simulation*

The *arithmetic mean* μ is the average of all the *n* NPV outcomes; the *median Med* is the middle value where exactly 50 per cent of the simulation results are less than the median. Both these values describe the central tendency of the distribution. For normal distributions, the arithmetic mean μ will be very close to the median, but for skewed distributions, the median *Med* can be to the left or to the right of the mean:

$$\mu = MEAN(column)$$
$$Med = QUARTILE(column, 2)$$

The *range* is the *maximum value* minus the *minimum value* and as extreme outliers can have an unfiltered effect on the range, a more useful measure is the *interquartile range IQR*, which represents the central 50 per cent of the data:

$$IQR = QUARTILE(column, 3) - QUARTILE(column, 1)$$

The asymmetry of the distribution in comparison to the normal distribution is described by its *skewness* γ_1. A positive skewness indicates a skew toward more positive values, i.e. a longer right-hand tail; a negative skewness indicates a skew toward the negative values, i.e. a longer left-hand tail.

The peakedness of the distribution is described by its *kurtosis* β_2. Positive kurtosis indicates a more sharply peaked curve than the normal distribution; negative kurtosis signifies a flatter curve[60]:

$$\gamma_1 = SKEW(column)$$
$$\beta_2 = KURT(column)$$

Using the simulation model is a bit like trusting in fate that the outcome is not an unusual or freakish example, but that it more or less reflects the true probability. The more simulation runs n are conducted, the more reliable this general assumption will become. At the same time, it is highly unlikely that the simulation model and fate will yield a sample that is going to predict the future with full accuracy. So, how accurate is the NPV estimate as produced by a Monte Carlo simulation? The 95 or 90 per cent *confidence interval* expresses this estimate together with a margin of error; it gives an answer to the question: "Can we be 95 or 90 per cent sure that the true mean of the NPV falls somewhere within this interval?"

Here is the formula for a 95 per cent confidence interval with its lower limit *ll* and upper limit *ul*:

$$^{95\%}_{ll} Col = \mu - CONFIDENCE.NORM(1-0.95, \sigma, n)$$

$$^{95\%}_{ul} Col = \mu + CONFIDENCE.NORM(1-0.95, \sigma, n)$$

However, as a note of warning, in Monte Carlo simulations the importance of the confidence interval is slightly overrated based on the trustworthy name of this statistics measure. Confidence is something that makes managers feel good, but the confidence in the model's output relies largely on the accuracy of modeling and choosing the input variable's distributions. If there is "garbage" as input and if the interrelationships are wrongly understood, the output will also be "garbage," no matter how narrow the confidence interval will be calculated by statistics.[61]

The estimated cumulative distribution function allows us to tell the percentage $P_{[<z]}$ of NPV outputs which are less than a certain value z:

$$P_{[<z]} = PERCENTRANK(column, z)$$

Of greatest interest in business calculations is the probability concerning the percentage of NPV outputs that are greater than zero:

$$P_{[>0]} = 1 - PERCENTRANK(column, 0)$$

It also allows us to describe the spread of data by identifying the 95 per cent *central interval*, which is different from the confidence interval. In contrast to the confidence interval, it estimates what proportion of the data are expected to be within the interval's given limits. The boundaries of this interval are defined based upon the central proportion of the data:

$$^{95\%}_{ll}Cel = PERCENTILE\left(column, \frac{1-0.95}{2}\right)$$

$$^{95\%}_{ul}Cel = PERCENTILE\left(column, 1 - \frac{1-0.95}{2}\right)$$

It is now very interesting to compare the results of the deterministic NPV calculation (Figure 6.15) with the Monte Carlo simulation (Figure 6.18). Obviously, additional knowledge about the distribution of the values with their minimum and maximum values (Figure 6.16) opens a slightly different perspective on the import business case problem. Whether the deterministic or the stochastic answer is more accurate is a very difficult question to answer; the first approach is a deterministic one based on discrete variables implying full knowledge of how sales will proceed during the investment periods. And the other approach is a simulation based on randomness, but taking into account additional insight information on the possible range and distribution of the input variables.

Application of simulations in business case projects

A business case team needs to weigh the additional insights into the project dynamics against the complexity and costs of building and running a simulation. In practice, the task of setting up a simulation is often given to external consultants. First, running a simulation is very time-consuming and second, finance managers rarely have the required knowledge or the tools to build a simulation platform. Unfortunately, by outsourcing business case simulations one of the most important benefits of a simulation, namely, of gaining a deep understanding of the investment's hidden dynamics, is mostly wasted. This comes along with the danger of carrying out simulations in a rather mechanical approach rather than critically evaluating the underlying assumptions and issues.

Because of this complexity and the costs involved in running them, simulations are rarely used by corporations for their standard investment propositions and business cases.

6.9 PROBABILITY TREES

Uncertainty can be frightening to decision makers. But by laying out the set of events that can occur in a systematic way, it is possible to anticipate one's own actions following the resolution of uncertainty. Calculating probabilities can be a hard endeavor, especially in situations where decisions are made sequentially. Sometimes probabilities are added, sometimes they are multiplied – and often it is difficult to figure out what to do. Probability tree diagrams can help to simplify and visualize things.

Whenever countries consider a military solution to a political problem, it is important to lay out all the things that could go right and wrong. In a military engagement, some things will always go wrong, and this risk needs to be anticipated and accepted. By accepting risk, one is better positioned, both mentally and physically, to complete the mission. Former US Marine Corps and Vice Chairman of Joint Chiefs of Staff, General Peter Pace, states that his biggest lesson from Somalia, where he served from 1992 to 1994, was to "never send out armed forces to do something unless we expect them to do it – and are willing to accept the risks and give them the resources."[62]

Probability trees (discussed in this section) and decision trees (discussed in Section 6.10) are techniques to analyze decisions under uncertainty. Uncertain gains and losses can be evaluated with a probability tree, leading to the value of an investment under uncertainty. In addition, decision trees allow modeling a sequence of decisions that a firm undertakes while implementing an investment decision; they are like strategic maps guiding us through the decision-making process.

Decision trees have been in use for approximately 50 or 60 years. One of the first studies using decision trees was conducted by the BBC in 1953 about the effect of television broadcasting.[63] Later, in 1964, the technique was reported in the *Harvard Business Review* as one "which has tremendous potential as a decision-making tool. The decision tree can clarify for management, as can no other analytical tool that I know of, the choices, risks, objectives, monetary gains, and information needs involved in an investment problem. We shall be hearing a great deal about decision trees in the years ahead. Although a novelty to most businessmen today, they will surely be in common management parlance before many more years have passed" (Magee, 1964, pp. 126–7).

Both probability and decision trees require decision problems that have three properties:

- The alternatives or scenarios are well defined;

- The critical uncertainties can be quantified; and

- The objectives are clear.

Although not all complex investment decision problems have all of these three characteristics, probably all of them can be simplified in such a way that these three properties hold.[64]

A probability tree is typically built from left to right showing the various uncertain events diagrammatically in the form of a felled tree. It consists of the following two elements[65]:

- Uncertain events are represented by a circle, also called a *chance node*.

- *Outcomes* are presented by a triangle. The probability tree arrives at an outcome when all uncertainties have been resolved; the outcome shows the payoff that the decision maker will receive from the investment given.

These elements are connected with lines going from left to right, also called *branches*. And while there is no chronology of events in a probability tree, the most important events are usually put more toward the left, and detailed events, or events which do not apply to all branches, can be found toward the right.

Let us look at an example. A fitness center plans to expand into a new city and open a number of new branches. Setting up these fitness centers will cost $300,000, but there is uncertainty about the market demand to justify this large up-front investment. If the market is good, the estimated NPV of cash inflows is $800,000. However, if the market is poor, the NPV of cash inflows will only be $200,000. Should the fitness center make this investment decision?

The decision is difficult because of the uncertainty with respect to market demand. To understand the problem better and to ultimately determine the value of uncertain cash inflows, the fitness center builds a probability tree:

- If the market demand is good, the NPV from the investment will be $500,000, i.e. the revenue of $800,000 minus the initial investment of $300,000.

- If the market demand is poor, the investment means a loss, with the NPV being a negative amount (–$100,000).

Obviously, the fitness center will be more motivated to approve the investment decision the more likely it is for the market to be good. Mathematically, the likelihood of events occurring is expressed by their probability. Hence, the fitness center needs to estimate how likely a good market demand will be; it suggests a probability of $p = .3$ for this scenario. As the sum of probabilities of all possible outcomes needs to be one, and as only two outcomes were identified, the probability of the market demand being poor is consequently $p = .7$. Figure 6.19 shows the resulting probability tree.

The ENPV of this investment opportunity is therefore calculated as the probability-weighted average of the possible outcomes in the probability tree minus the initial investment:

$$ENPV = 0.3 \cdot \$800{,}000 + 0.7 \cdot \$200{,}000 - \$300{,}000$$
$$= \$240{,}000 + \$140{,}000 - \$300{,}000 = \$80{,}000$$

The expansion opportunity of the fitness center has an *expected monetary value* of \$80,000 and it is advisable for the fitness center to invest, as the expected monetary value of investing is higher than of not investing.

More complicated settings can be evaluated by extending the simple probability tree. For example, in a good market environment the competition is rather unlikely to sit still (e.g. $p = 0.2$) and if the competition expands as well (consequently $p = .8$), this will reduce the cash inflows of the fitness center from \$800,000 to \$600,000. However, if the market conditions turn out to be poor, it is rather unlikely that the competition will expand (e.g. $p = 0.1$). But still, this unlikely event would reduce the cash inflow of the fitness center from \$200,000 to \$150,000.

Figure 6.19 *Simple probability tree*

The simple tree of Figure 6.19 can be extended to map the competitor activities and this results in the probability tree shown in Figure 6.20. Just as before, the ENPV of the investment opportunity is calculated as the probability-weighted averages of the possible outcomes, which have extended from two to four. For instance, the probability of the market being good and the competition expanding as well is shown in the topmost branch and calculates to $p = 0.3 \cdot 0.8 = 0.24$. Similarly, the second branch from the top shows the scenario of the market being good and the competitor sitting still with a probability of $p = 0.3 \cdot 0.2 = 0.06$. This calculation can be done for all branches and the sum of the probabilities needs to sum up to $1 = 0.24 + 0.06 + 0.07 + 0.63$.

The ENPV of the investment opportunity can again be calculated by summing the probability-weighted average of each possible outcome, resulting in:

$$
\begin{aligned}
ENPV = {} & 0.24 \cdot \$600{,}000 + 0.06 \cdot \$800{,}000 + 0.07 \cdot \$150{,}000 \\
& + 0.63 \cdot \$200{,}000 - \$300{,}000 \\
= {} & \$144{,}000 + \$48{,}000 + \$10{,}500 \\
& + \$126{,}000 - \$300{,}000 = \$328{,}500 - \$300{,}000 = \$28{,}500
\end{aligned}
$$

Taking the probability of competitor moves into account, the overall monetary value of this investment opportunity has therefore dropped from $80,000 to $28,500. But as it remains positive, the fitness center is advised to go ahead with the expansion plans.

If the fitness center wishes to proactively manage uncertainty and take control of events, it should upgrade its analysis from probability to decision trees. Section 6.10 introduces decision trees, which allow the fitness center to partially control events while uncertainty gets resolved in a chronological sequence of events. Section 6.12 will then show another slightly different way of assessing risk and calculating probability in investment decisions using certainty equivalents.

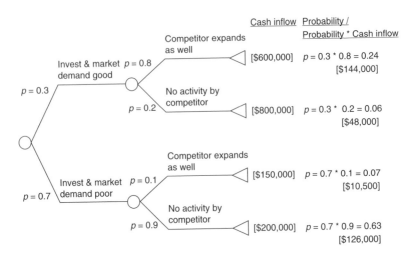

Figure 6.20 *Extended probability tree*

6.10 DECISION TREES

Building upon the concept of probability trees, as introduced in Section 6.9, decision trees support business management in taking dynamic decisions along the implementation of an investment project. A decision problem is not an isolated decision, since today's decision depends on the one that will be made tomorrow; it is also not posed as a sequence of decisions because under uncertainty, decisions taken in the future will be influenced by what has been learned in the meantime. A decision problem is therefore best depicted as a tree of decisions.[66] Peter F. Drucker succinctly expressed the relation between taking decisions in the present and future: "Long-range planning does not deal with future decisions. It deals with the futurity of present decisions."[67] This means that today's decision should be made in light of the anticipated effect it and the outcome of uncertain events will have on future values and decisions. Today's decision sets the stage for tomorrow's decision.[68]

While sensitivity analysis as introduced in Section 6.6 only allows us to change one input value at a time and does not come with any clear decision rules, decision trees help to consider risk in stages. Risk should not only be analyzed once at the deciding point of the investment, but should be followed up in a sequential manner as events occur and time progresses.

To summarize, decision trees serve two primary purposes in business cases[69]:

- Provide advice on which alternatives to choose. They allow managers to decide which decision to take, i.e. to choose between alternatives and devise the right responses to scenarios at each stage of the project.

- Identify the value of having alternatives in the first place, i.e. by how much one alternative is preferred to another.

In addition to the chance nodes and outcomes of the probability tree diagram, decision trees introduce a third important element. *Decision nodes* are represented by squares[70] and refer to a decision to invest (or not to invest), to purchase equipment (or not to purchase it), to invest a certain amount in marketing spent (or invest less or not to invest at all), and so on. The lines that connect the elements of a decision tree are called *branches*, because decisions may lead to other decisions in the future, which again lead to other decisions. The order in which these elements are connected is also important. A square (decision node) followed by a circle (chance node) means that the decision is made before the uncertainty occurs. The other way round, a circle (chance node) followed by a square (decision node) denotes making a decision after uncertainty is resolved.

Revisiting the fitness center example set forth in Section 6.9, the first question was about the market condition. Should the fitness center invest $300,000 not knowing about the market conditions? In good market conditions, the estimated NPV of cash inflows would be $800,000, but in poor conditions, the cash inflows will only be $200,000, leading to a loss for the fitness center on this investment. Conducting market research to resolve uncertainty about the market condition will cost $75,000 – but how can the fitness center decide whether this investment into market research is a good one?

Step 1: Building the decision tree

When examining this investment opportunity with a decision tree, the first decision that the fitness center faces is whether to conduct market research or to skip this step. This decision happens before anything else as the value of market research very obviously lies in helping to make other decisions later down the line. Cash flows such as the decision to spend $75,000 on market research are noted below the branches.

As an outcome of the research, the market opportunities are identified as either good or poor. Obviously, this is out of everyone's control and hence the next node of the decision tree is a circle (chance node). Equipped with the research results, the fitness center can now take the decision to invest or not to invest. This leads to a set of four outcome nodes marked with a triangle. Investing in a good market will lead to cash flows of $800,000 and investing in a poor market to $200,000. In either of the two scenarios of market attractiveness, not investing and abandoning the investment decision will lead to zero cash flows.

The part of the decision tree where the fitness center does not conduct any market research resembles the probability tree of Figure 6.20. The big difference in the upper part of the tree is that the fitness center makes an investment decision before uncertainty about market attractiveness is resolved. Hence the chance node (circle) comes after the decision node (square). The final tree is shown in Figure 6.21 and its decision nodes are marked A, B, C, and D for easier reference.

Step 2: Assigning probabilities to the decision tree

To quantify the uncertainties of the branches leading out of the chance nodes (circles), the fitness center now needs to estimate

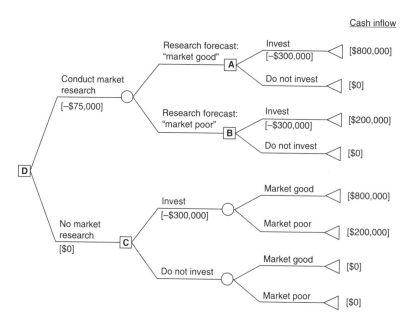

Figure 6.21 *Decision tree*

the probabilities. In the previous example, the market demand was believed to be good with a probability of $p = 0.3$ and poor with $p = 0.7$. These probabilities can be directly assigned to the outcomes of the two chance nodes in the bottom part of the tree.

The top part of the tree also has one chance node, with two outcomes that correspond to these estimated probabilities. Assuming that market research is a 100 per cent reliable predictor of actual market performance, these two probabilities can be assigned to the two branches leading out of the chance node. In a real-life scenario, the predictive quality of market research is also full of uncertainty and in order to reflect this in the decision tree new chance nodes would have to be introduced. The resulting decision tree and its probabilities are shown in Figure 6.22.

At a decision node, a risk-neutral decision maker would always choose the branch with the highest expected monetary value. However, as discussed in Section 6.4, not all decision makers are strictly risk-neutral, deciding based on the expected monetary value of an option. For such cases, a utility function specific to the risk aversion of the decision maker would need to be incorporated into the analysis and the branch would be chosen which maximizes expected utility rather than expected monetary value.[71]

Step 3: Solving the decision tree

The initial decision about implementing an investment is based on which course of action (i.e. which branch of the decision tree) promises the greatest ENPV. Solving a complex problem is best done by breaking it down into a series of smaller problems, which in the case of decision trees are marked by the decision nodes. The fitness center needs to decide what to do at each of the nodes A, B, C, and D in Figure 6.22.

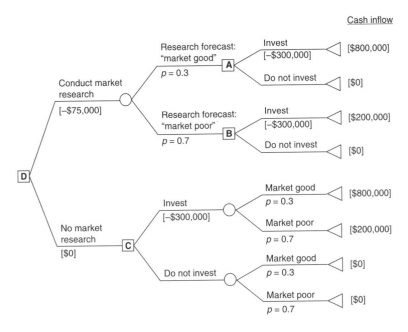

Figure 6.22 *Decision tree with probabilities*

To solve the decision tree, one needs to work backwards from each outcome node (triangle) by folding back the events marked by chance nodes (circles) and decision nodes (squares). It is a bit like solving the question of what to do today by assuming that this very decision is already taken and then considering the next actions.

Decision node A asks the fitness center to imagine that the investment into market research has already been done and that the market was discovered to be favorable. At A, the decision whether to invest or not to invest would have to be taken. Obviously, by knowing that the market is good and that investing $300,000 would yield a positive cash inflow of $800,000 as compared to a zero yield when not investing, the fitness center would choose to invest. Hence the value of being at A is $500,000, i.e. the difference between the inflow of $800,000 and the investment of $300,000.

Applying the same logic to decision node B, the fitness center would choose not to invest in poor market conditions. Investing the $300,000 would only yield a cash inflow of $200,000, resulting in a certain loss of $100,000 and therefore the investment would not be undertaken. Hence, the value of being at B is $0.

At decision node C, the decision is more complicated as the outcome of actions is not known and therefore the expected monetary value of each of the branches of the tree needs to be compared and the best one chosen. The ENPV of investing was calculated in Section 6.9 as $ENPV = 0.3 \cdot \$800,000 + 0.7 \cdot \$200,000 - \$300,000 = \$240,000 + \$140,000 - \$300,000 = \$80,000$. However, the value of not investing is $0.3 \cdot \$0 + 0.7 \cdot \$0 - \$0 = 0$ and hence the fitness center would certainly go for the investment. The value of being at C is the expected monetary value of the best decision $80,000.

Having identified the best decisions at decision nodes A, B, and C allows us to condense the tree into a smaller one as shown in Figure 6.23. In this simplified tree, one can now move further to the left and examine what decision the fitness center should take at D by comparing the first path with the second path.

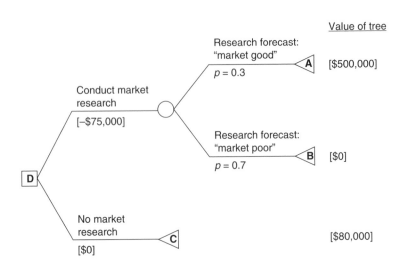

Figure 6.23 *Condensed decision tree*

In the first path, the fitness center has certain costs of $75,000 for the market research and receives $500,000 with a probability of 0.3 and nothing with a probability of 0.7. The expected cash flow is therefore $0.3 \cdot \$500,000 + 0.7 \cdot \$0 - \$75,000 = \$75,000$. In the second path, however, the expected cash flow is $80,000. As the expected cash flow is higher by $5,000 in the second path, the fitness center would be advised not to commission market research, but go into the investment and take a chance on the market conditions.

Step 4: Conducting sensitivity analysis on the decision tree

Before proceeding with the decision to approve the investment without conducting market research, the fitness center will most likely want to run a sensitivity analysis (see Section 6.6) on the decision tree and analyze how the go-forward decision would change given different circumstances, such as:

- The cost of conducting market research is less than $75,000;

- There is an additional market condition labeled mediocre with cash flows of $500,000; or

- The probabilities assigned to the market conditions are different.

To answer such questions, a new decision tree would have to be built and solved for each scenario, looking again at possible actions and at the value of these actions. This can be a huge task.

Usefulness and limitations of decision trees

According to research in cognitive psychology, the working memory[72] of the human brain limits the ability to conceptually understand and manipulate multiple pieces of information. Presentation techniques like decision trees which preserve and aptly translate multidimensional relationships into a more easily comprehensible form are thus at a premium.

Decision trees are useful tools to support a dynamic decision-making process under uncertainty; they are a form of multiple variable, multiple effect analysis allowing us to describe, explain, and predict outcomes. This capability allows decision trees to unveil details in the context of multiple influences.

Decision trees are developed and presented incrementally, i.e. they are built by a collection of one-cause, one-effect relationships dealing quite effectively with the short-term memory limitations of the human brain. In its entirety, this collection of simple relationships explains the combined set of influences on an investment decision.[73] Nonetheless, no decision tree and no sensitivity analysis, however complex, can map every scenario and examine every possible outcome. Even worse, it can lull the decision maker into a false sense of confidence in the "results."[74]

Decision trees are also not useful for projects that require a full commitment right away, since the value of having a choice lies in the ability to spend a little now and decide later whether to forge ahead.

In most services and manufacturing industries as well as for most research-intensive industries, uncertainties related to managing a project are milestone-driven. At such milestones, uncertainties arise as a result of discrete choices presented under a limited number of scenarios; decision trees are very well suited to analyzing, understanding, and managing such uncertainties in multistage projects. In some other areas, however, volatility is high and the future unfolds as an almost infinite number of possible outcomes. Examples are the energy and currency markets.[75] Real options and the Black–Scholes equation, as introduced in Chapter 7, are better suited to dealing with such ongoing uncertainties.

Decision trees for project management

In all kinds of corporations delays in projects are not uncommon. For instance, technology companies and service providers often find that customers do not want to stick to the original and agreed project plan. For them the time of business does not stand still. When they encounter new business challenges, this may lead to new requirements and ultimately a change of the project's scope. The IT provider, often a young company with eager growth targets, will generally try to accommodate the client. But unexpectedly changing course in midstream can be costly and frustrating to both sides; Case 6.3 recounts such a story from the airline industry.

Case 6.3   WestJet changes its booking platform

Changing course in midstream happened to the airline WestJet, the Calgary-based low-cost carrier that began life as a Southwest Airlines clone (Figure 6.24). WestJet believed that future growth in the airline industry would come from carriers seeking more simplicity rather than more complexity. Hence it dropped out of the booking platform Amadeus and instead of building a new reservations platform from scratch, it formed a codevelopment partnership with India-based IBS Software Services, which had achieved some success with other airline applications. The project was delayed several times and yet again, when WestJet changed its business model and was seeking relationships with US carriers to broaden its customer base beyond Canada, it became necessary to interlink and codeshare, which was not part of the planned basic launch version of the new booking system, but only of a later version for the so-called hybrid airlines and full-service carriers. WestJet was unable to go ahead with its plans to link up with other carriers, resulting in lost revenue opportunities. In late 2008, it signed a new support agreement with another provider and suspended its contract with IBS. The airline continued to negotiate an amended contract with IBS for a later version of their booking platform with the desired features, because a dispute resolution process was estimated to potentially result in a write-off of C$30 million.[76]

How can a decision tree help in such scenarios? In general, if companies are faced with a choice of alternatives after the investment decision, which may lead to further alternatives in future years, then these new decisions will have a financial impact on the original choice of the investment. Hence, major alternatives along the implementation of the investment should be included in the initial business case.

This sounds obvious; however, the established business case instruments, such as sensitivity analysis, scenario analysis, and simulation discussed in Sections 6.6–6.8 do not recognize the

Figure 6.24 *WestJet 737 plane approaching Las Vegas*[77]

opportunity to modify projects. They simply assume that a company's management will hold an investment passively and watch the business environment change. Obviously this is not the case and if things go well projects can be expanded; if things don't go as expected, projects can be reduced in size or abandoned. In general, looking at things later on from a different perspective can reveal new areas of opportunity and financial benefits as well as weaknesses and monetary costs. Decision trees help the business case team do exactly this when preparing the investment decision.

6.11   EMPIRICAL VALIDATION

The most successful companies do not have any particular genius for visionary prediction, but they know that they are not smart enough to predict with near certainty what is going to happen. They know that they may bet on the wrong investment or may potentially fail to execute the right one. However, just sitting still and never doing anything new, bold, or daring will quickly result in other companies overtaking them.

A new technology, for example, may sometimes only have value in conjunction with other elements: a good strategy, a responding customer base, or even something as plain and obvious as a good product or service. Teasing out the value that such a technology can deliver to the benefit part of the business case is not easy and is often perceived as hypothetical. Take another example. If a bank makes the monthly printed and posted account statements available electronically, it will help to reduce the bank's printing and distribution costs. But what is the impact on the customer? It may come down to customer retention and attracting new customers, but whether electronic account statements have a positive impact is not clear from the outset. Will customer retention go up or down?

The solution to this dilemma can only be derived empirically and lies in replacing the simplistic formula "innovate or die" with the much more constructive and effective idea of empirical validation: "fire bullets and only then cannonballs."[78]

A bullet is an empirical test aimed at learning and testing the waters. It has low cost relative to the size of the corporation and low risk, but low risk does not necessarily imply a high probability of success either. Low risk just means that the implications of the test bullet not hitting any target or going off beam are limited and do not harm the corporation's financial standing. And though a bullet can be a full-time project for a set of employees, it needs to be low distraction for the overall enterprise.

Adopting this principle requires execution in a disciplined process:

- Develop and fire bullets; then

- Assess the success and terminate unsuccessful bullets early; then

- Extrapolate the effect of firing a bigger cannonball; then

- Concentrate on developing a cannonball; and finally

- Calibrate the cannonball using empirical validation from firing the earlier bullets.

A discerningly calibrated cannonball has a serious impact on the target; Figure 6.25 shows where the metaphor comes from. When the French troops of Gonzalo Fernández de Córdoba besieged Naples in 1503, they fired cannonballs at the bronze doors of Castle Nuovo as they were being shut; one of them is still stuck there today.[79]

The first overarching idea is never to attempt something big without having a solid business case backed up with empirical validation in place. Corporations do not need crystal-ball-reading capabilities to manage uncertainty, but they need capabilities to analyze their way toward the right investment decision. Sensitivity analysis, scenario analysis, simulations, probability trees, and decision trees can help to structure this process, but they need to be backed up with empirical validation to make the analysis and estimation of probabilities realistic and useful. For many investment decisions, companies should run small tests to try out new technologies and

Figure 6.25 *Cannonball stuck in bronze door in Castle Nuovo, Naples*[80]

approaches, or at the very least try to model their impact using simulations. Case 6.4 gives an account of developing innovative store concepts by redesigning, testing, and redesigning all over again in order to get it finally right.

Case 6.4   Apple stores

Even the glamorous Apple stores were not started with a big bang and one worldwide roll-out. Around 2000, Apple was becoming increasingly dependent on mega-retailers, who had little incentive and expertise to position Apple's products as innovative and unique. Apple managed to upend industries from computers to music, but how can a high-tech company leap into retail? It was a standing start and Steve Jobs hired Mickey Drexler, a leading retail executive with Gap, to Apple's board; Ron Johnson, then a merchandising chief at Target, was taken on board to run the retail business. Drexler advised Jobs first to go and rent a warehouse and build a prototype of a store and keep redesigning it until it was right (bullet); only then should Apple roll it out to the world (cannonball). The first iteration did not work. The computer was evolving from a tool to an information and entertainment hub, but their store prototype was laid out by product category according to Apple's internal organization and not matching the customers' evolving interests and needs. So they went on to redesign it until they got it right (bullet), tested the concept once more with two pilot stores in Virginia and Los Angeles (somewhat bigger bullets) and rolled it out to the whole world only once it was working (cannonball).[81]

The second principle is never to stop learning. When a country goes to war, its military strategists, leaders, and soldiers on the ground learn new things every day. As General Peter

Pace, formerly US Marine Corps and Vice Chairman of the Joint Chiefs of Staff, explains about the war in Iraq: "Before we even started operations, our Joint Forces Command put together a *lessons learned* team. Since then, every facet of the operation has provided lessons – targeting and what type of weapon to use on a particular target; the best ways to track friendly forces on the battlefield; how to communicate. Some of these lessons reinforced what we believed going in; some disabused us of what we thought was a good idea, but wasn't. The learning has to be shared person to person, not left in a book on a shelf. It has to stay alive."[82] And what applies to the military world just as well holds true for competition among businesses and corporations.

6.12　RISK ASSESSMENT BY CERTAINTY EQUIVALENTS

Certainty equivalents are yet another way of building risk into the NPV business case process.[83] In financial theory, certainty equivalents are defined as the lower guaranteed return that someone would accept, rather than taking a chance on a higher, but uncertain, return. Investors want to be compensated for choosing an investment alternative where they may not get their money back. However, simply bumping up the discount rate by a few percentage points to reflect a project's uncertainty is a bad idea too, as this section will show.

Time value of money and haircut

Let us go back to the initial investment example of Section 2.2; an investor had the opportunity to purchase land and construct real estate at the price of $470,000 and sell it off again at $C_1 = \$525,000$ a year from now.

Using $r = 5\%$, the investment's NPV was calculated at (see Figure 6.26, step 1):

$$NPV_{risk\ free} = \$525,000 \cdot \frac{1}{1.05} = \$500,000$$

This would mean a profit of $30,000 under certain market conditions (step 2). But how good is the investor's market insight that he can safely calculate with an expected $525,000? As the market insight is uncertain, the investor would, for example, discount with $r_{risky} = 9\%$ instead of $r = 5\%$ in order to adjust for this very uncertainty and thereby be on the "safe side." This gives a NPV of (step 3):

$$NPV_{risky} = \$525,000 \cdot \frac{1}{1.09} = \$481,651$$

Surely, if buyers were to approach the investor and offer to fix the price that they are going to pay a year from today, this would remove a lot of uncertainty from the investor and the investor would certainly be willing to accept a lower price than $525,000. But how much lower? The NPV of the real estate, taking risk into account, is $481,655, as calculated above. So, which amount of certain cash flow (CEQ) is equal to this one being discounted at a risk-free interest rate of $r = 5\%$ (step 4)?

$$NPV_{risky} = CEQ \cdot \frac{1}{1.05} = \$481,651$$

$$CEQ = NPV_{risky} \cdot r = \$481,651 \cdot 1.05 = \$505,733$$

This certain cash flow of $505,733 has the same value to the investor as an expected (but not fully certain) cash flow of $525,000. Hence, $505,733 is called the _certainty equivalent cash flow_ (CEQ) and it consists of two mark-downs from the amount of $525,000:

- First, an amount is taken off to account for the time value of money.

- Second, an additional amount, the so-called _haircut_, is subtracted to compensate for the risk that is attached to an estimate.

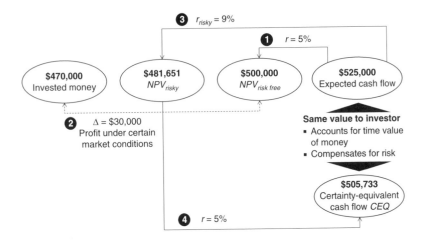

Figure 6.26 *Certainty equivalent method*

The calculations, as summarized in Figure 6.26 lead to two identical expressions:

$$\frac{C_1}{1+r_{risky}} = \frac{CEQ}{1+r}$$

$$CEQ = (1+r) \cdot \frac{C_1}{1+r_{risky}}$$

With the values of the above example:

$$\frac{\$525,000}{1+0.09} = \frac{CEQ}{1+0.05}$$

$$CEQ = (1+0.05) \cdot \frac{\$525,000}{1+0.09} = \$505,733$$

And for cash flows t years away:

$$\frac{C_t}{(1+r_{risky})^t} = \frac{CEQ}{(1+r)^t}$$

$$CEQ = (1+r)^t \cdot \frac{C_t}{(1+r_{risky})^t}$$

Distant cash flows

Ordinarily, a single discount rate r_{risky} is used across all future periods and for all future cash flows, assuming that project risk does not change over time but remains constant. A constant single discount rate r_{risky} already implies a larger deduction for risk from later cash flows as it compensates for the risk borne per period. The more distant the cash flows, the greater the number of periods, and thus the larger the total aggregate risk adjustment.[84] Hence there is no need to discount distant cash flows at a higher rate than earlier cash flows simply because distant cash flows are perceived to be riskier. The certainty equivalent method uses the discount rate to make separate adjustments for time and risk; the aggregate nature of risk discounting automatically takes care of this concern.

Estimating the haircut

Most business cases working with certainty equivalents to assess an investment's risk exaggerate the haircut amount and set it at levels that the underlying risks do not justify, even at a very conservative estimation. Haircuts of three to five per cent above the discount rate prescribed by the time value of money can substantially reduce an investment's NPV, especially if it is a long-running one.

The problem of an exaggerated haircut typically arises when the business case team tries to take shortcuts when estimating an investment's cash in- and out-flow. Most business case teams simply assume that everything will go according to plan, and when the decision makers realize this simplification a haircut amount is added to the discount rate to compensate for the potentially overstated net cash flows.[85]

It is always better to analyze and understand an investment's inherent risk using one of the methods described earlier in this chapter. Nonetheless, if certainty equivalents are used in a business case, the haircut should be calibrated with an estimate of how much net cash flows can possibly fall below the most likely scenario and the probability of this drop occurring. Figure 6.27 shows appropriate haircuts which can be used in real-life business cases. A haircut of 1.5 per cent on top of the discount rate would mean that there is a 50 per cent probability that the net cash flow falls below 40 per cent of its most-likely estimated value, or that there is a 20 per cent probability that the business case will lose all its value. A 6 per cent haircut assumes a 50 per cent probability of the investment not reaping any benefits. Most business case teams, not knowing these guidelines, usually propose haircuts that are much bigger and thereby systematically destroy business case value, ultimately leading to rejection of good investment opportunities.

6.13 GLOBAL INVESTMENTS, COUNTRY RISK, AND INTERNATIONAL CONTRACTS

Many major investment projects include a global component, be it services offshoring to India or selling to a new market in the emerging economies, where inflation, salary hikes, and currency fluctuations can be rampant. Investing in an international company or market is generally perceived to be more risky than investing at home in the domestic market. Investors are typically wary of factors such as political instability, volatile exchange rates, inflation, economic turmoil, adverse repatriation laws, unpredictable fiscal measures, and unpredictable customer behavior.

In the face of globalization, building a business case for any investment proposition requires an understanding of how best to evaluate and convert country risk into appropriate haircuts, which then need to be added to the discount rate (see Section

Haircut increase	Percentage of potential net cash flow reduction				
Probability of lower net cash flow	− 20 %	− 40 %	− 60 %	− 80 %	− 100 %
10 %	+ 0.1 %	+ 0.2 %	+ 0.4 %	+ 0.5 %	+ 0.7 %
20 %	+ 0.2 %	+ 0.5 %	+ 0.8 %	+ 1.1 %	+ 1.5 %
30 %	+ 0.4 %	+ 0.8 %	+ 1.3 %	+ 1.9 %	+ 2.6 %
40 %	+ 0.5 %	+ 1.1 %	+ 1.9 %	+ 2.8 %	+ 4.0 %
50 %	+ 0.7 %	+ 1.5 %	+ 2.6 %	+ 4.0 %	+ 6.0 %

Figure 6.27 *Guideline for estimating the haircut*[86]

6.12). An individual corporation cannot control global market economics and therefore the business case needs to make a provision for adverse macroeconomic effects.

For business cases in multinational corporations (MNCs), which are drawn up to facilitate the decision between investment alternatives, understanding how investment risk varies across countries is central to a fairer and ultimately more profitable allocation of investment capital.

Scenario analysis approach to country risk

A scenario analysis can take into account findings on country risk by examining alternative possibilities for how future net cash flows might develop. At a minimum, two scenarios should be considered. One scenario should assume that cash flows are going to develop according to the business plan (most likely scenario) and the other scenario should reflect how adverse economic conditions might affect the cash flows (pessimistic scenario).

However, it is definitely not recommended to simply reduce net cash flows, by say 75 per cent, and then attach a 20 per cent chance to this pessimistic scenario and a probability of 80 per cent to the most likely scenario. Instead, the underlying macroeconomic factors need to be analyzed and their cause–effect relationship to the cash flows determined. The probability of the adverse scenario will also depend on the nature of the investment and a flat 20 per cent guess should be avoided. Only then will decision makers be able to understand the scenario and believe in a business case that appropriately reflects country risk in the expected value of future cash flows.

Modeling the timing of the onset of the pessimistic scenario can lead to a multitude of subscenarios and complex calculations. Of course, economic distress need not necessarily start in the first investment period, but can occur at any point. For simplicity's sake, business cases should assume for the pessimistic scenario that adverse economic conditions develop in the first period itself.

Haircut approach to country risk

Another possible approach to country risk is to introduce a haircut in addition to the discount rate for an investment (or for a part of the investment) proposition that lies in risky countries. A pessimistic scenario analysis would then not be necessary and certainty equivalents (see Section 6.12) can be calculated on the most likely cash flow projections.

In practice, most business case teams find it hard to estimate a fair country risk haircut and tend to set it too high. Consequently, investment propositions in risky countries are undervalued and run the risk of not being selected by decision makers. What is worse, according to a 2011 study by the International Center for Financial Research at the IESE Business School, more than one in five decision makers worldwide cannot provide a justification for the figure used for country risk; it feels like the haircut amounts are taken out of the blue.[87]

The immediate question is now how best to estimate these haircuts. Unfortunately, there is no systematic methodology in place, but it is pretty clear that historical data cannot be used for two reasons.[88] First, there may simply be no riskless baseline investments available in the past to compare with. Second, countries and their markets change so quickly in all directions that a historical observation is no good basis for predicting a haircut.

One possible and feasible way is to look up a country's local currency sovereign rating on the website of Moody's, the rating agency. The default spread of a rating band can be estimated as traded country bonds over a default free government bond rate (see Figure 6.28). These spreads can directly be used as the country risk haircut (see Figure 6.29).

Rating	Default spread in basis points
Aaa	0
Aa1	25
Aa2	50
Aa3	70
A1	85
A2	100
A3	115
Baa1	150
Baa2	175
Baa3	200
Ba1	240
Ba2	275
Ba3	325
B1	400
B2	500
B3	600
Caa1	700
Caa2	850
Caa3	1,000

Figure 6.28 *Assumption for country default spread in basis points*[90]

Country	Region	Moody's local currency rating	Country risk haircut
Albania	Eastern Europe & Russia	B1	4.00%
Angola	Africa	Ba3	3.25%
Argentina	Central and South America	B3	6.00%
Armenia	Eastern Europe & Russia	Ba2	2.75%
Australia	Australia & New Zealand	Aaa	0.00%
Austria	Australia & New Zealand	Aaa	0.00%
Azerbaijan	Eastern Europe & Russia	Baa3	2.00%
Bahamas	Caribbean	A3	1.15%
Bahrain	Middle East	Baa1	1.50%
Bangladesh	Asia	Ba3	3.25%
Barbados	Caribbean	Baa3	2.00%
Belarus	Eastern Europe & Russia	B3	6.00%
Belgium	Eastern Europe & Russia	Aa3	0.70%
Belize	Central and South America	Ca	2.00%
Bermuda	Caribbean	Aa2	0.50%
Bolivia	Central and South America	Ba3	3.25%
Bosnia and Herzegovina	Eastern Europe & Russia	B3	6.00%
Botswana	Africa	A2	1.00%
Brazil	Central and South America	Baa2	1.75%
Bulgaria	Eastern Europe & Russia	Baa2	1.75%
Cambodia	Asia	B2	5.00%
Canada	North America	Aaa	0.00%
Cayman Islands	Caribbean	Aa3	0.70%
Chile	Central and South America	Aa3	0.70%
China	Asia	Aa3	0.70%
Colombia	Central and South America	Baa3	2.00%
Costa Rica	Central and South America	Baa3	2.00%
Croatia	Eastern Europe & Russia	Baa3	2.00%
Cuba	Caribbean	Caa1	7.00%
Cyprus	Caribbean	Ba3	3.25%
Czech Republic	Eastern Europe & Russia	A1	0.85%
Denmark	Western Europe	Aaa	0.00%
Dominican Republic	Caribbean	B1	4.00%
Ecuador	Central and South America	Caa2	8.50%
Egypt	Africa	B2	5.00%
El Salvador	Central and South America	Ba2	2.75%
Estonia	Eastern Europe & Russia	A1	0.85%
Fiji Islands	Asia	B1	4.00%
Finland	Asia	Aaa	0.00%
France	Western Europe	Aaa	0.00%
Georgia	Eastern Europe & Russia	Ba3	3.25%
Germany	Eastern Europe & Russia	Aaa	0.00%
Greece	Western Europe	Caa1	7.00%
Guatemala	Central and South America	Ba1	2.40%
Honduras	Central and South America	B2	5.00%
Hong Kong	Asia	Aa1	0.25%
Hungary	Eastern Europe & Russia	Ba1	2.40%
Iceland	Western Europe	Baa3	2.00%
India	Asia	Baa3	2.00%
Indonesia	Asia	Baa3	2.00%
Ireland	Asia	Ba1	2.40%
Isle of Man	Financial Center	Aaa	0.00%
Israel	Middle East	A1	0.85%
Italy	Middle East	Baa2	1.75%
Jamaica	Caribbean	B3	6.00%
Japan	Asia	Aa3	0.70%
Jordan	Middle East	Ba2	2.75%
Kazakhstan	Eastern Europe & Russia	Baa2	1.75%
Korea	Asia	Aa3	0.70%
Kuwait	Middle East	Aa2	0.50%
Latvia	Eastern Europe & Russia	Baa3	2.00%
Lebanon	Middle East	B1	4.00%
Lithuania	Eastern Europe & Russia	Baa1	1.50%
Luxembourg	Eastern Europe & Russia	Aaa	0.00%
Macao	Asia	Aa3	0.70%
Malaysia	Asia	A3	1.15%

Figure 6.29 *Look-up table for country risk haircut (September 2012)*[92]

Country	Region	Moody's local currency rating	Country risk haircut
Malta	Asia	A3	1.15%
Mauritius	Africa	Baa1	1.50%
Mexico	Central and South America	Baa1	1.50%
Moldova	Eastern Europe & Russia	B3	6.00%
Mongolia	Asia	B1	4.00%
Montenegro	Eastern Europe & Russia	Ba3	3.25%
Morocco	Africa	Ba1	2.40%
Namibia	Africa	Baa3	2.00%
Netherlands	Africa	Aaa	0.00%
New Zealand	Australia & New Zealand	Aaa	0.00%
Nicaragua	Central and South America	B3	6.00%
Norway	Western Europe	Aaa	0.00%
Oman	Middle East	A1	0.85%
Pakistan	Asia	Caa1	7.00%
Panama	Central and South America	Baa3	2.00%
Papua New Guinea	Asia	B1	4.00%
Paraguay	Central and South America	B1	4.00%
Peru	Central and South America	Baa2	1.75%
Philippines	Asia	Ba2	2.75%
Poland	Eastern Europe & Russia	A2	1.00%
Portugal	Eastern Europe & Russia	Ba3	3.25%
Qatar	Middle East	Aa2	0.50%
Romania	Eastern Europe & Russia	Baa3	2.00%
Russia	Eastern Europe & Russia	Baa1	1.50%
Saudi Arabia	Middle East	Aa3	0.70%
Senegal	Africa	B1	4.00%
Singapore	Asia	Aaa	0.00%
Slovakia	Eastern Europe & Russia	A2	1.00%
Slovenia	Eastern Europe & Russia	Baa2	1.75%
South Africa	Africa	A3	1.15%
Spain	Western Europe	Baa3	2.00%
Sri Lanka	Asia	B1	4.00%
St. Vincent & the Grenadines	Caribbean	B1	4.00%
Suriname	Caribbean	Ba3	3.25%
Sweden	Western Europe	Aaa	0.00%
Switzerland	Western Europe	Aaa	0.00%
Taiwan	Asia	Aa3	0.70%
Thailand	Asia	Baa1	1.50%
Trinidad and Tobago	Caribbean	Baa1	1.50%
Tunisia	Africa	Baa3	2.00%
Turkey	Asia	Ba1	2.40%
Ukraine	Eastern Europe & Russia	B2	5.00%
United Arab Emirates	Middle East	Aa2	0.50%
United Kingdom	Western Europe	Aaa	0.00%
United States of America	North America	Aaa	0.00%
Uruguay	Central and South America	Baa3	2.00%
Venezuela	Central and South America	B2	5.00%
Vietnam	Asia	B1	4.00%

Region	Average of country risk haircut
Africa	3.43%
Asia	3.57%
Australia & New Zealand	0.00%
Caribbean	4.52%
Central and South America	4.85%
Eastern Europe & Russia	3.94%
Financial Center	0.00%
Middle East	2.42%
North America	0.00%
Western Europe	1.81%

Figure 6.29 (*Continued*)

Using the haircut approach for country risk is especially useful when assessing a business case with a relatively short investment period. If country risk has not already materialized, it is unlikely that the business case team would have incorporated risk into the cash flow projections. The longer the investment period is, the more likely it is that the business analysts have already incorporated country risk projections into their own cash flow forecasts;[89] they would have taken a realistic approach on what is possible in this market. Applying an additional haircut might account for the same risk twice, which again drastically reduces the business case value.

Local economic conditions

Every business case should explicitly account for local economic and business conditions, such as inflation, and not hide them in scenarios or haircuts. Section 5.5 provides the mathematical tools to build inflation into the NPV calculation.

As a caveat, it is important to note that the short-term performance of a business case under volatile economic conditions cannot be captured sufficiently with mathematical formulae and figures alone; this is where business intuition and local experience are required to make the right investment decisions.

International risk diversification

Although common sense and the above data table clearly reveal that starting an investment in countries like Greece, India, or Russia is more risky than doing the same in countries like Canada, Switzerland, or the USA, there are two cases where the importance of country risk is reduced.[91]

First, if an investment project is spread across many countries and if there are no spill-over effects from one country to the other, country risk is diversified and will virtually go away in the risk consideration of the business case. This notion of idiosyncratic country risk is built on the presumption that correlations across countries are generally low. Although this may have been true in the 1980s, in today's globalized world and business, correlations across countries have risen,[93] but again this depends on the kind of investment proposition under consideration. Put differently, in today's world country risk is correlated for many investment propositions and thus it is often a good idea to consider different haircut amounts if an investment proposition spans several countries.

Second, if investment alternatives are compared which all have a stake in a sufficiently large global country portfolio, a global haircut can be assumed and used across the countries. However, most companies have a substantial home bias in their investment propositions and at least one investment alternative will prefer the domestic market to an internationally diversified approach. This domestic investment alternative then stands in the way of using the same global haircut across countries and alternatives.

The bottom line is that haircuts vary across countries, with higher haircuts applying to riskier countries. Applying the same global haircut across all countries would lead to an overvalued NPV in business cases that have a high exposure to risky countries.

International sourcing contracts

To forecast and capture provision for the effects of country risk is certainly important, but it is really only one part of the story. Much more importantly, provider managers and deal makers in corporations should confront country risks proactively.

In global procurement, many client companies believe that they have avoided any such risks by contracting in their home currency instead of the "unknown" currency of an emerging country, for example, in the dollar instead of the Indian rupee. Experience shows that Indian offshore providers in particular, when experiencing a revenue crunch due to rising input factor costs or a decreasing revenue stream caused by currency fluctuations, are likely to take steps to regain their financial health at the cost of decreased service delivery. This is when the intention of the contract fires backward.

Most companies hedge currency fluctuations in order to build their business forecasting calculations on a stable basis. However, hedging against the downside risk of currency fluctuations can lock companies into too high service delivery prices when markets move into the opposite direction. The competition might suddenly pay much lower rates, which in turn allows them to sell their end products at better prices to customers, thereby taking over market share. The business case calculation for the company caught in a hedging deal is now at risk from a customer demand side perspective.

Global sourcing clients should employ some tactics together with their providers to help manage currency and inflation risks:

- Define clearly when pricing adjustments should be made and what formula they should follow. Periodic pricing adjustments should follow inflation and cost of living indices for delivery locations.

- Consider paying for offshore services in the provider's local currency, for example, in the Indian rupee. Offshore services costs are mainly made up of labor costs, and paying in the local currency can help to maintain the balance between revenue and service delivered. Further, as emerging market currencies tend to devalue in the medium perspective, corporates are likely to realize additional medium-term cost savings through this approach.

- Leverage flexible global delivery models to counter price increases through rebalancing the global workforce. At the same time, keep the oversight of delivery locations in order to balance cost savings against a possible increase in business continuity risk caused by location risk.

Most provider managers at client firms are relatively inexperienced with the effects of inflation and currency fluctuations in long-running outsourcing or offshoring projects and are advised to seek legal and financial advice to cleverly (and at the same time fairly) structure their sourcing contracts.

6.14 WORKED EXAMPLE CONTINUED: UC REPLACES TELEPHONY SYSTEM

The worked example introduced in Section 5.7 is about UC and collaboration capabilities in a software-based environment, which allows companies to integrate real-time and non-real-time communication services and offer communication solutions to their employees from within their familiar desktop environments. The business case showed a negative NPV but concluded that the investment proposition might still be valuable for the management consultancy as it is an investment in the company's future capabilities. Still, the business case team sees risk for going ahead with the UC solution in the areas of business and implementation risk (see Section 6.3).

The following *business* (or *impact*) *risks* can potentially affect the identified benefits[94]:

- The timing and financial savings from support cost savings of taking the hardware telephone systems out of service in favor of the UC solution may not coincide with the forecasted timelines and the cost-saving estimates.

- User adoption of the new solution over tele- and web conferencing may not meet the forecasts.

- If there are implementation challenges, help desk calls may increase instead of decrease.

- And regarding the nonmonetary benefits, increases in employee productivity and motivation may not be as prompt as expected or may even backfire.

Additionally, the following *implementation risks* can potentially affect the cost side of the analysis:

- There may be cost overruns for rolling out the system affecting the cost for professional services.

- It may take longer for employees to get used to the new functionality; additional training and start-up productivity losses could be expected.

- There is too much load on the servers and the estimated size of the hardware is too small resulting in necessary hardware upgrades.

To analyze and understand the impact of these risks, it is necessary to estimate their effect on the costs and benefits.

A sensitivity analysis would now assume that at any point in time only one of the above business or implementation risks occurs. Nonetheless, it would consider the entire impact of this one risk on all the costs and benefits. It is now possible to observe how each risk affects the NPV calculation. For example, if user adoption of the new solution takes longer than estimated, many of the cost-saving benefit estimates would be postponed to a later period. The costs for teleconferencing may even go up as consultants would find their own external providers who are not part of any agreement with the management consulting company. And looking at another risk, if employees were to take longer to get used to the new system, not only would additional end-user training affect the cost estimates, but a productivity loss coupled with a potential image loss in the market would also add to the costs. Sensitivity analysis typically does not look at cases where combinations of risks happen at the same time; this would be possible but would make the analysis extremely complex.

After a sensitivity analysis has provided an insight into the dynamics of the business case calculation, it is a good idea to take the original estimates as the most likely scenario and then construct a pessimistic scenario (or a number of pessimistic scenarios) describing what would happen to each and every cost or benefit if things were to go wrong, i.e. if the risks were to materialize. The best-case optimistic scenario will most likely coincide with the most likely scenario and therefore does not need to be considered separately. The difference between the most likely and the pessimistic view(s) is a measure of risk, and the higher it is, the more risky the investment proposition has to be judged.

By attributing different likelihoods to the range of identified scenarios, NPV outcomes with different probabilities can be calculated and summed to an ENPV.

Probability and decision trees are most likely not of too much help in analyzing this business case; although scenarios can be defined, it is very difficult to attach discrete probabilities to them.

As the management consultancy is obviously not in a position to predict with near-certainty how the UC system will be accepted by its consultants and how it will shape their work day and their relation to clients, the idea of testing the waters first with empirical validation could come in handy. A disciplined bullet-to-cannonball process needs to be set up comprising the following steps:

- Implement UC for a small business unit or a country (pilot installation); then

- Monitor the acceptance rate and effect on the business; then

- Enter the findings into the business case by extrapolating; subsequently

- Apply what has been learned to fine tune the worldwide roll-out; and finally

- Roll-out UC across the entire management consultancy.

Some of these findings will reinforce what the business case team initially believed what was going to happen; some will contradict the promises and estimates by the vendor of the communication solution. After analyzing the effect of the pilot installation (firing bullets), the management consultancy will get a good idea of whether rolling it out globally (firing cannonballs) would be a good idea, i.e. it will have an increased level of trust in the updated and empirically validated business case. The management consultancy may then find the potential for a compelling business case to justify the investment in UC technology.

7
Factoring Strategic Flexibility

Rapid business changes, risk, and uncertainties produce an increasing need for corporate flexibility, adaptability, and scalability; thus they have traditionally been viewed negatively in a corporate environment. In today's business world, accomplishing an audacious strategic corporate goal can no longer be achieved by protecting the status quo, but only by clear-headed calm execution based on extensive preparation.[1] Flexibility needs to be built into the strategic investment process so that organizations have the capability and preparedness to identify major changes in their external environment to which they can respond with new courses of action by quickly committing resources.[2]

However, strategic investments do not always produce tangible and immediately visible monetary benefits right away. Instead, benefits may only occur later down the timeline, but then the business environment may have already changed. Without the chance to adapt the investment flexibly to external changes while it is being implemented, commissioned, or utilized, the promised benefits will be lost for good. And yet while there are no universally accepted methods of valuing strategic flexibility in investments and making the benefits of flexibility evident in monetary terms for the business case, there are a number of techniques from other disciplines that can be adapted to help put tangible numbers to strategic alternatives.

Section 6.10 introduced decision trees for setting out possible future outcomes and decisions; it also gave several simple examples of dealing with strategic alternatives. However, the analysis method of decision trees does not enable the business case team to put a financial value to the identified options. This will now be the topic of this chapter.

7.1 STRATEGIC REAL OPTION ANALYSIS

Options to modify investment projects are known as *real options*, a term that was coined in 1977 by Stewart C. Myers of the Massachusetts Institute of Technology. And while the earliest application of this new concept was found in the oil, gas, copper, and gold industries, even today the commodity businesses remain some of the biggest users of real options. For instance, Chevron Corp. used real options in forming its (unsuccessful) 1997 bid for Elk Hills Naval Petroleum Reserve, a federal property in California. Anadarko Petroleum Corp. of Houston says real-options analysis gave it the confidence to outbid others for a tract in the Gulf of Mexico called Tanzanite that has proved rich in oil and gas. Anadarko (APC) paid more because Tanzanite's range of possible reserves was so broad. Says Michael D. Cochran, vice-president for worldwide exploration: "Most people looked at it and just saw the minimum case."[3] APC saw the potential and what future options would be opened for the company by having access to this tract.

Case 7.1 shows how the German Department of Transport – probably unknowingly – implemented real options in building a motorway.

Case 7.1 **A strategic real option for autobahn A661 in Frankfurt**

The German autobahn A661 passes the metropolis of Frankfurt am Main on its east. When it was built in 1995, only one carriageway was initially completed. The "Gallery

Seckbacher Road" is a semi-open tunnel serving as a bridge for two roads over the A661 and noise protection for the adjacent residential area (see Figure 7.1). Within the tunnel, ramps for another proposed motorway triangle "F-Seckbach" were prepared, but not yet completed and not yet opened for traffic. It was envisaged that the lanes in this section could later be doubled and two more bridges built. Back in 1995, a simple and less expensive bypass would have most likely been sufficient, but there were plans for extending the motorway network should traffic increase further and should public funds become available again. Hence the Gallery Seckbacher Road was built in a more expensive variant with a real option for doubling the lanes and connecting to another motorway at a later point of time.

This real option was drawn twelve years later when traffic increased to 80,000 vehicles daily. Construction started again on the A661, now aiming to double the lanes and build two more bridges by 2015. The idea of adding the motorway triangle F-Seckbach is not completely shelved either. It is still on the table, but as things stand today, this real option will most likely be drawn in a modified form and at an even later point of time.

Populist German newspapers like *Bild* call it "The slowest autobahn in the world. [...] The 30-million [euro] extension has been going on for years. Everything should be done by 2010. Instead of asphalt, weeds are growing on the new lanes!" (Schlagenhaufer, 2011). Missing approvals certainly contributed to the delay, but the purpose of a real option in motorway construction and government spending is to build upon existing structures if and when the need arises – and public funds become available. As the quote from *Bild* shows, this is not always evident to the public, which may consider a real option to be something that was started and not finished on time.[4]

Figure 7.1 *Motorway extension at Gallery Seckbacher Road*[5]

Most planners and business managers never use the term real option when justifying their investment decisions; they rather list and describe the advantage of flexibility under intangible non-monetary benefits. But as discussed in Section 4.5, non-monetary benefits are rarely taken seriously enough by decision-makers; due to their intangible and evasive nature, they do not find their way into many business case calculations and thus remain unobserved.

When attempting to justify a typical investment idea and valuing it in a business case using the net present value (NPV) method (see Section 2.2 and Chapter 5), one generally considers an initial investment "A" which would produce a return "B" at a later stage. This traditional approach assumes that the firm will hold still during the commissioning and operating phases of a project till "B" is finally reaped – and in the process ignores any real options attached to this investment. One could even say that the NPV approach completely ignores the value of management. It takes flexibility, judgment, and decision-making away from management and downgrades it to a dutiful and obedient execution function.

On looking more closely, however, sometimes an initial investment proposition "A" may offer – in addition to the main return "B" – an arena of further add-on options; let us name them "C," "D," and "E." Thanks to "A" already being implemented, these strategic options "C," "D," and "E" can be undertaken at a cost lower than if considered as standalone new investments of the "A"-type, either individually one after the other, together in one go, or selectively. However, the initial investment may be a little different from "A" and most likely also a bit more expensive; this modified initial investment is therefore referred to as "A*" in Figure 7.2.

Real option analysis maps how to react to new circumstances; for instance, one may invest a little today, see how things develop tomorrow, then either cancel or go full speed ahead the day after with the options. Real options allow a faster reaction at lower cost should the business climate change, for better or worse. In short, the strength of real option analysis is the improved coordination of spending combined with the potential outcomes of active learning.[6]

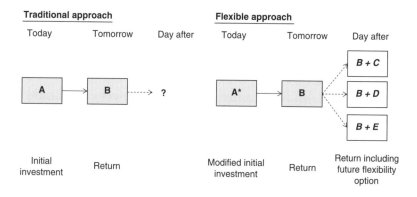

Figure 7.2 *Traditional vs. flexible approach*

Case 7.2   Apple in 1995

Conducting a strict NPV analysis on Apple Computer Inc. in 1995 would have resulted in a recommendation for the company to exit the personal computer business because Apple was not able to earn its opportunity cost of capital. But a real options analysis said that a period of losses could be worthwhile for keeping the company alive because it had some great ideas for earning money in the future. Indeed, some 15 years later nobody doubts any more that Apple is making good money.[7]

Examples of strategic information technology investments with potentially minimal initial returns include moving to a standards based architecture or a de facto industry-standard application suite, upgrading existing applications or providing excess network capacity. Other examples of building strategic platforms with real options to execute at a later point of time can be found across industries. Case 7.2 shows such an example.

Pharmaceutical companies acquire patents which give them the right (but not the obligation) to produce and market a new medicine. An oil company purchases drilling licenses for deep seawater oil fields, which give it the right to exploit the oilfields should there be sufficient oil and should it be sufficiently easily accessible to allow for an attractive margin given tomorrow's oil prices.

The requirement for flexibility is probably well understood in the business world. Investments in strategic options can be beneficial to corporations, allowing a faster reaction at lower cost should the business climate change accordingly. Flexibility can also be viewed as a risk mitigation strategy, which helps the organization to avoid running into deadlocks where it can no longer react to changed market circumstances. However, deciding how much to spend on flexibility options is usually decided by top management via the "rule of thumb"; this kind of capital restriction (see Section 5.4) is obviously very difficult to capture and quantify in a business case.

Real options analysis says that when the future is highly uncertain, it pays to have a broad range of options available. It thus rewards flexibility – and this makes it a superior addition to the standard NPV decision-making tool. While NPV calculates the value of a project by predicting its net cash flows and adjusting them for risk, real options analysis boils down all the possibilities for the future into a single scenario and attaches a monetary value to this strategic flexibility. Today's decision sets the stage for tomorrow's decision and therefore it must balance:

- Economy, i.e. the need to reap profit opportunities; with

- Flexibility, i.e. the capacity to react to future circumstances and needs.[8]

Real options analysis also has its downsides. For one, it is too complex to be worthwhile for minor decisions. Second, it is definitely not useful for projects that require a full investment commitment right at the beginning. The value of a strategic option lies in the ability to spend a little now, establish a strategic platform, and decide later whether to expand based on the earlier investment.

7.2   BLACK–SCHOLES FORMULA

In 1697, a Japanese samurai who wanted to control the rice markets established the Dōjima Rice Exchange in Osaka. Future contracts were written for rice traders and a simple rice futures contract would say that I will agree to buy rice from you in one year's time and all this at a price that we agree right now.[9] By the 20th century, the Chicago Board of Trade (see Figure 7.3) was providing a marketplace for traders to deal not only in futures but in options contracts. A simple options contract would say that we agree that I can buy rice from you at any time over the

Figure 7.3 *Opening of the new Chicago Board of Trade building in 1885*[10]

next year, at a price that we agree right now – but that I do not have to if I do not want to.

The seeds of real options theory were sown in the early 1970s when Myron Scholes, Robert Merton, and the late Fischer Black made a Nobel Prize-winning breakthrough in how to price financial options correctly. They realized that the pivotal factor was volatility. For example, let us consider an option to buy a share at $260 one year ahead when its current price is $230. If volatility is low, there is only a small chance the shares will ever hit the $260 mark and so the option to buy the shares at $260 in a year's time is not worth a lot. But if volatility is high, the chances are good that the share price will cross $260. That makes the option to buy them at $260 much more valuable. Unquestionably, volatile shares can also plummet. But that does not concern the investor, because at any price below $260 the option will simply be allowed to expire.

The *Black–Scholes formula* allows us to calculate the option's value by assuming that the price of the underlying asset follows a lognormal random walk,[11] that investors can adjust their hedge continuously and without expenses, that the opportunity cost of capital (the risk free interest rate) is known, and that the underlying asset does not pay any dividends while waiting to be exercised.

Black–Scholes changed the culture of Wall Street, from a place where people traded based on common sense, experience, and intuition, to a place where the computer said yes or no. On the downside of this development, it has even been argued that the Black–Scholes formula and its descendants helped to start the financial crisis that rocked the world in 2008.[12]

The parallels in financial options and real options in terms of acquiring strategic flexibility have been noted by various researchers, and the Black–Scholes formula can be rewritten for strategic corporate investment scenarios:

$$Value_{opt} = N(d_1) \cdot \frac{PV}{(1+r)^t} - N(d_2) \cdot \frac{C_{opt}}{(1+r)^t}$$

$$d_1 = \frac{ln\left(\dfrac{PV}{C_{opt}}\right)}{\sigma\sqrt{t}} + \frac{\sigma\sqrt{t}}{2}$$

$$d_2 = d_1 - \sigma\sqrt{t}$$

- $N(d)$: cumulative normal probability density function. $N(d)$ is the probability that a normally distributed random variable x will be less than or equal to d standard deviations above the mean.

- C_{opt}: exercise price of the option. Exercising the option usually requires another add-on investment, which turns the option into a tangible asset or benefit for the organization. In the above formula, C_{opt} is automatically discounted at the risk free interest rate r.

- PV: the expected value of the net cash flows generated by the add-on investment discounted to the date when the option is exercised. The formula then automatically discounts PV further down to the present date. The exercise price C_{opt} is not part of this net cash flow calculation.

- t: number of periods to exercise date before the expiration date of the option. For many investments, if the real option is not drawn within a specific number of budget cycles, it becomes unlikely to be ever used again as the organization would have moved forward into another strategic direction. For IT-related investments, t can often be set to two or three years.

- σ: originally the standard deviation per period of continuously compounded rate of return on stock. For real options, σ measures the degree of uncertainty about future business directions. It can be approximated by the volatility of the market in which the organization competes.

- r: opportunity cost of capital, i.e. the risk-free interest rate.

The simplest way to calculate the Black–Scholes formula is to build an Excel spreadsheet. Calculating d_1 and d_2 is only a matter of plugging numbers into a formula; $N(d_1)$ and $N(d_2)$ can best be computed using the Excel formula NORM.S.DIST(d, true).[13] Figure 7.4 shows a simple spreadsheet for the Black–Scholes formula. The figures in italic in the cells [B2] to [B6] are

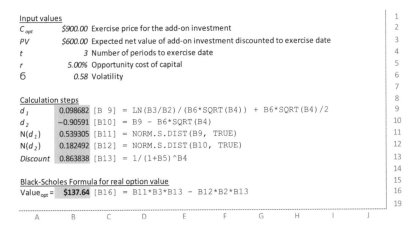

Input values				1
C_{opt}	$900.00	Exercise price for the add-on investment		2
PV	$600.00	Expected net value of add-on investment discounted to exercise date		3
t	3	Number of periods to exercise date		4
r	5.00%	Opportunity cost of capital		5
6	0.58	Volatility		6
				7
Calculation steps				8
d_1	0.098682	[B 9] = LN(B3/B2)/(B6*SQRT(B4)) + B6*SQRT(B4)/2		9
d_2	−0.90591	[B10] = B9 − B6*SQRT(B4)		10
$N(d_1)$	0.539305	[B11] = NORM.S.DIST(B9, TRUE)		11
$N(d_2)$	0.182492	[B12] = NORM.S.DIST(B10, TRUE)		12
Discount	0.863838	[B13] = 1/(1+B5)^B4		13
				14
Black-Scholes Formula for real option value				15
Value$_{opt}$ =	$137.64	[B16] = B11*B3*B13 − B12*B2*B13		16
				19

A   B   C   D   E   F   G   H   I   J

Figure 7.4 *Black–Scholes formula for real options in Excel*

input cells and can be changed; the result of the calculation can be found in cell [B16].

Estimates of market uncertainty can be found by looking at the volatility of stock funds that track a specific industry. These volatility rates are virtually constant over broad time intervals and Figure 7.5 shows these σ for selected verticals.

The financial services (bank $\sigma = 0.47$) and the utilities industry (for instance, electric utility $\sigma = 0.46$; water utility $\sigma = 0.47$) are the most predictable industry sectors. The car industry (automotive $\sigma = 0.93$; auto parts $\sigma = 1.58$) and information technology (computer software services $\sigma = 1.12$; computer hardware $\sigma = 1.31$) sector are at the other end of the spectrum. The industry average is $\sigma = 0.96$. Choosing the right volatility rate is neither easy nor straightforward, yet it can have a significant impact on the estimation of the option's value; Figure 7.6 shows the computation of the value (as per the data in Figure 7.5) in relation to the volatility σ.

Example: Real estate market

Let us look at the example of a real estate developer considering the purchase of a bigger areal. According to current plans, only

Industry vertical	Number of firms	Volatility*	Industry vertical	Number of firms	Volatility*
Advertising	28	1.55	Maritime	53	0.64
Aerospace/Defense	63	1.07	Medical Services	139	0.80
Air Transport	40	0.95	Medical Supplies	231	1.01
Apparel	48	1.32	Metal Fabricating	30	1.44
Auto Parts	47	1.58	Metals & Mining (Div.)	69	1.25
Automotive	19	0.93	Natural Gas (Div.)	32	0.99
Bank	418	0.47	Natural Gas Utility	27	0.45
Bank (Canadian)	7	0.84	Newspaper	13	1.34
Bank (Midwest)	40	0.68	Office Equip/Supplies	24	1.19
Beverage	34	0.86	Oil/Gas Distribution	12	0.61
Biotechnology	120	1.20	Oilfield Svcs/Equip.	95	1.34
Building Materials	47	0.88	Packaging & Container	27	0.85
Cable TV	24	0.97	Paper/Forest Products	37	1.01
Canadian Energy	10	0.94	Petroleum (Integrated)	23	1.12
Chemical (Basic)	17	1.19	Petroleum (Producing)	163	1.17
Chemical (Diversified)	31	1.39	Pharmacy Services	19	0.87
Chemical (Specialty)	83	1.20	Pipeline MLPs	11	0.61
Coal	25	1.45	Power	68	0.78
Computer Software/Svcs	247	1.12	Precious Metals	74	1.15
Computers/Peripherals	101	1.31	Precision Instrument	83	1.31
Diversified Co.	111	0.76	Property Management	27	0.58
Drug	301	1.08	Public/Private Equity	8	1.20
E-Commerce	52	1.19	Publishing	23	0.96
Educational Services	37	0.84	Real-Estate Investment Trust	6	1.07
Electric Util. (Central)	23	0.46	Railroad	14	1.10
Electric Utility (East)	25	0.49	Recreation	52	1.21
Electric Utility (West)	14	0.49	Reinsurance	8	1.09
Electrical Equipment	79	1.29	Restaurant	60	1.21
Electronics	158	1.13	Retail (Special Lines)	143	1.48
Engineering & Const	17	1.85	Retail Automotive	15	1.25
Entertainment	75	1.38	Retail Building Supply	8	0.85
Entertainment Tech	31	1.55	Retail Store	38	1.19
Environmental	69	0.64	Retail/Wholesale Food	29	0.63
Financial Svcs. (Div.)	230	0.75	Securities Brokerage	25	0.75
Food Processing	109	0.74	Semiconductor	115	1.68
Foreign Electronics	9	1.23	Semiconductor Equip	14	1.97
Funeral Services	5	0.94	Shoe	18	1.48
Furn/Home Furnishings	30	1.49	Steel (General)	19	1.43
Healthcare Information	26	0.96	Steel (Integrated)	13	1.43
Heavy Truck/Equip Makers	8	1.55	Telecom. Equipment	104	1.22
Homebuilding	24	1.05	Telecom. Services	85	0.84
Hotel/Gaming	52	1.33	Telecom. Utility	28	0.66
Household Products	22	1.05	Thrift	181	0.74
Human Resources	24	1.57	Tobacco	13	0.66
Industrial Services	137	0.86	Toiletries/Cosmetics	15	1.19
Information Services	26	0.98	Trucking	33	0.97
Insurance (Life)	31	1.44	Utility (Foreign)	5	0.70
Insurance (Prop/Cas.)	67	0.94	Water Utility	12	0.47
Internet	180	1.21	Wireless Networking	48	1.15
Machinery	114	1.05	**Total Market**	**5928**	**0.96**

* The volatility is estimated by regressing weekly returns on stock against a local index, using, if available, up to five years of data. Unlevered by the market value debt to equity ratio for the sector as well as the cash to overall firm value.

Data used as of 01/2011

Figure 7.5 *Volatility rates for selected industry verticals*[14]

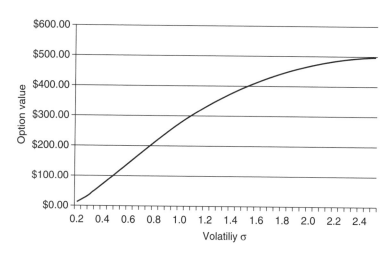

Figure 7.6 *Option value in relation to volatility σ*

a fraction of the areal would be developed immediately and the rest would remain fallow land for some three years. Further developing the rest of the areal would cost $900 million. As the future growth of the real estate market is uncertain, an estimate of the PV three years from now, which the expansion on the fallow land could generate, is a conservative $600 million.

It is a risky project, but it has a lot of upside potential especially looking at the low volatility $\sigma = 0.58$ of the property management industry (see Figure 7.5). According to the Black–Scholes Formula the option is worth $137.64 million today. Of course, the real estate developer would only invest in the expansion of the fallow land if three years from now the NPV calculation were to show a more positive outlook than today's $600 million and at least exceed the add-on investment of $900 million. For any value below $900 million, the net option payoffs would be zero.

Likewise, the real estate market could completely crash and the net option payoff could fall well below today's estimated $600 million. But this is irrelevant, as the developer would only invest the additional $900 million if the expected net value were to more than compensate this amount. If the real estate market were to crash, the developer would let go of the idea of developing the fallow land and the option would remain unused.

Going back to the real estate developer's investment decision to purchase the bigger areal, he would now go for it if and only if the net profit from the scheduled development on the smaller fraction minus the investment into the entire areal would at least generate a certain return in NPV terms of $137.64 million, i.e. at least the value of the option.

Example: Offshoring as a platform

A bank is to consider the offshoring of the application maintenance of its content management system. It plans to team up with a provider and intends to set up an offshore development center (ODC). However, the bank's managers are a little uncertain about the quality and end-user acceptance of the offshore maintenance from India as well as the future development of offshore maintenance cost rates. For this reason, the current plan suggests only to offshore a few selected functional areas and to keep the rest onsite and in-house for the time being. But plans have been made for three years down the line. Further offshoring of the remaining functional areas to the ODC would then cost $900,000 as add-on set-up costs and could generate additional savings estimated as $1,200,000 in PV terms three years from now.

The volatility of the banking industry is $\sigma = 0.47$, but as the offshoring activity relates purely to an information technology application, the higher volatility of the computer software and services industry is chosen with $\sigma = 1.12$. Content management systems are built for the future and are expected to be long-running platforms; hence, the expiry date of this option is set to $t = 3$ years.

After plugging these values into the spreadsheet of Figure 7.4, Black–Scholes says that the option is worth $740,000 today. The bank would only invest in offshoring the remaining functional areas three years from now if a review of the offshoring market and a new NPV calculation were still to show that the savings are around $1,200,000, or at the very least compensate the add-on investment of $900,000. For example, a significant increase in India's rate cards could cause these savings to fall below $900,000, and then the net option payoffs would be negative. Hence, three years from now, the bank would invest the additional $900,000 if and only if the expected net value were to more than compensate this amount. In any other case, the bank would drop the option and refrain from the idea of offshoring any further functional areas.

Looking at the business case from another angle: is it a good idea for the bank to build a more expensive platform today, which enables the easier offshoring of further applications rather than just concentrate on today's limited scope and the applications which should definitely be offshored? The answer can be found in the above calculation: the bank would go for offshoring as a platform if and only if the net profit from the scheduled offshoring program minus the investment into the platform option would at least generate a certain return in NPV terms of $740,000, i.e. the value of the option.

Example: Implementation of a customer relationship management (CRM) system

A travel services provider needs to improve the quality of customer service and considers the implementation of a CRM system. Rather than implementing a simple service center support system, the travel provider thinks about investing in a market-leading suite that would exceed today's functional requirements, but which could be useful in the future once the company decides to move towards direct customer marketing. The travel service provider therefore needs to understand the platform value that this additional functionality could provide versus implementing a straightforward solution.

7.3   SUBJECTIVE REAL OPTION VALUATION

While it is usually possible to value real options in objective monetary terms, a subjective description of the usefulness of real options can help to understand their leverage[15]:

- The lower the exercise price of the real option C_{opt}, the greater is the value of the real option. A lower exercise price suggests a higher probability of the option being exercised; the value created by exercising the option needs to exceed its exercise price.

- The higher the expected value of the net cash flows PV, the greater is the value of the option. These cash flows need to offset the exercise price of the option C_{opt} in order to create value for the organization.

- The longer it is to the expiry date t of the real options, the greater their value. The longer a company has to decide whether to exercise the real option, the more flexibility it retains without having to pay extra.

- The greater the degree of uncertainty σ, the higher the value of the real option. When there are situations where it is not clear which decision to take (high uncertainty), flexibility is often the best strategic choice.

- The higher the opportunity cost of capital (risk-free interest rate) r, the more valuable the option is for the company as compared to making an investment decision without flexibility options. Similarly, if the cost of capital is assumed to go up during the exercise period, the greater the real option's value. It is to be noted, however, that the cost of capital is usually not under the control of the business case team.

A subjective evaluation can be used not only to explain a real option scenario, but also to decide when to enter a detailed mathematical real option analysis and to help pick between different real option investments depending on a company's preferences for either low exercise prices, high expected cash flows, or long expiry cycles.

7.4 REAL OPTION MANAGEMENT

Valuing and calculating real options with a formula such as Black-Scholes is really only one side of the coin. Even more importantly, a company's management needs to adapt its own thinking towards acting under uncertainty and keeping flexibility options open. This creates value for an organization by allowing its managers to take actions later in order to exploit potential upside gains while minimizing downside exposure on investments. Options offer flexibility as compared to investments, which incur financial commitments far into a possible uncertain future. Under conditions of uncertainty, organizations should invest in building a diversified portfolio of projects, a pattern of options. But the purpose and nature of these options are not all the same – and this distinction is seldom made. Rather than making a single bet on a seemingly attractive opportunity, it makes more sense to fund several small investments to capture opportunity in different ways. It is like pursuing an opportunity with different options.[16]

Real options for process and market uncertainty

Real options can be grouped according to process and market uncertainty (Figure 7.7). *Process uncertainty* is the extent to which the process of developing and deploying a new product or service is understood by the organization before it embarks on this path. With low to medium process uncertainty, the type and costs of required resources and skills to develop the product or service are known. High process uncertainty means that the

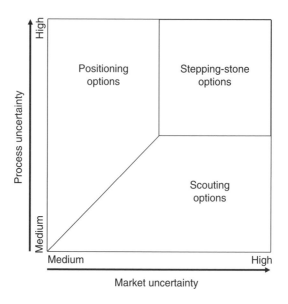

Figure 7.7 *Real option management*

process of developing something new is not yet understood and full of risk. *Market uncertainty* is the extent to which an organization understands how a new product or service will be received by the external market. With low to medium market uncertainty, the business case team knows the best price point, can forecast the number of buyers, and predict the competitive response. High market uncertainty means that the organization has no idea how the market is going to react on the introduction of a new product or service.[17]

Under conditions of both low process and low market uncertainty, new products or services typically build on a company's existing platform of offerings. They will have merit in traditional PV terms, but as flexibility options they add little value. If process and market uncertainty increase slightly, the value associated with flexibility options also increases. Products or services will typically still be related to existing offerings, but, for instance, build upon a new technology platform giving the company the opportunity to introduce additional offerings later.

When process uncertainty is high and market uncertainty is medium, *positioning options* create the right to wait and see. A typical situation is one in which several competing technologies or standards could satisfy high potential market demand, but one does not yet know which technology will make the breakthrough. Future scenarios include a lock-in on one of the standards, a preservation of a multi-standard environment, or even the emergence of another paradigm. An organization should therefore make suitable arrangements through small investments, which buy time and flexibility, but still allow them to be weather-proof should one scenario become prevalent. Committing oneself to one of the scenarios exclusively would be highly risky and not very clever.

When market uncertainty is high, but process uncertainty remains at medium levels, *scouting options* as a form of entrepreneurial experiments can be a prudent way forward. Their intention is to discover or even create new markets for products or services based on existing and probably recently developed capabilities. This allows the exploration of new market segments from an established competency base, gathering new information about the market, and then striking in a big way. In contrast to positioning options, scouting options extend existing capabilities into new areas; they may even break open a market-entry barrier. However, they should always be small, consciously managed as pilots, and meant to predict a market reaction.

When both process uncertainty and market uncertainty are high, but the potential opportunity is irresistibly big, it is advisable to choose *stepping stone options*. These expose the organization to opportunities with high uncertainty about the size and shape of the market as well as high doubtfulness if the company is at the end able to develop the process and technical competencies to provide the products and services to the market. The real option value of stepping stones is thus made up of a staged and sequenced investment along an open-ended trajectory, where it is possible to extend, change direction, or withdraw entirely after carefully monitored decision-making milestones.

Launch options

Launches can be considered to be of two types. *Enhancement launches* go for reconfiguration and re-differentiation opportunities; they build on existing offerings by improving their quality, making them cheaper, or by modifying them in any other way. *Platform launches* intend to create a new business base for a company; they are more risky than enhancement launches and require some market confidence. They frequently take the company into new territory by providing an arena for other investment options.

The challenge of timing the exercise

One of the biggest challenges in reaping the benefits projected by real option management is to exercise them in a timely and rational manner. It is also a challenge that has not been very comprehensively researched. Value is destroyed both when option holders are asleep at the wheel as well as when they are too quick to pull the trigger and cash in on an option which is not yet ripe.[18]

Falling asleep is a particular problem in the industry, as managers may forget about or be unaware of options that have been implemented and paid for in a previous reporting period.

In order to make the most value out of options, companies first need to identify *trigger points* when action can be taken and options are to be exercised. Obviously, triggers should neither be precise dates or numbers, but rather ranges allowing for some flexibility and debate. Second, they should clearly tell managers what to do by setting rules around exercise decisions. Without clear rules, processes, and systems monitoring external conditions relevant to decision-making, decisions do not materialize and action on options does not happen. Monitoring systems are particularly important, as managers' instincts diminish as their decisions grow in scale and impact. Third, companies need to clearly designate who has the final responsibility for exercising the option. After all, it is people who take decisions. And fourth, the responsible people need to be motivated to take the decision to exercise an option. Many of the most valuable exercise options are not glamorous; they are often about shutting down unprofitable business vs. waiting until business recovers, and thus they affect the job security of many employees. Because of this, employees need to be rewarded for taking decisions offering a combination of compensation, promotion, and public acknowledgement.

Having defined trigger points allows to measure the time lag between resolution of uncertainty and taking of appropriate action. Tracking this time lag gives insights into the exercise-decision performance of the company's managers. However, when trigger points are only vaguely defined, this measure ceases to be of value as it would be too easy to reinterpret the triggers in order to favor decisions that have already been made.

When not to use real options

While real options are useful both from the business perspective as well as from a business case point of view, there are situations where an upfront investment and a direct launch of the entire investment program makes more sense.

For instance, companies producing computer chips are well advised to go for an outright launch strategy for every new generation chip. Technical uncertainty as well as demand uncertainty is low as software packages continue to demand more and more powerful processors and consumers want speedy computers to run new programs. Even pharmaceutical companies can usually go with full force into marketing and selling the new product once a drug has received the necessary approvals.[19]

Other good examples are companies like Gillette (Case 7.3). Technology leaders build on their first-mover advantage, claiming

Case 7.3   Gillette's way of developing new products

Gillette operates in five main areas and each one of them has its own brand: Gillette razors and shaving systems, the Right Guard brand of personal products, Duracell batteries and torches, Braun electrical goods, and Oral-B dental care goods. Gillette is the leader in several of its brand categories. Gillette's very first product was the safety razor in 1901, being safer than the "cut-throat" razor then in use and still giving a clean shave (see patent application in Figure 7.8). The key to Gillette's business is to use technology to develop a new product that the customer wants. In order to find out what the customer wants before developing the product, Gillette uses three types of research: qualitative market research involving focus groups or surveys to explore customer choices, quantitative market research to collect data from larger samples, and technological research to find out if it is possible to make the product at a profit. Gillette's success is down to carefully finding out what customers really want and then being the first to give it to them.[20]

and then keeping a big share of the market. If they know what their customers want and if they can deliver the product, they would be ill advised to approach the market tentatively with careful options; instead, a full-scope launch is the preferred alternative for them. Real option management would not capture market value quickly enough; the competition would be likely to imitate, move in, and take over.

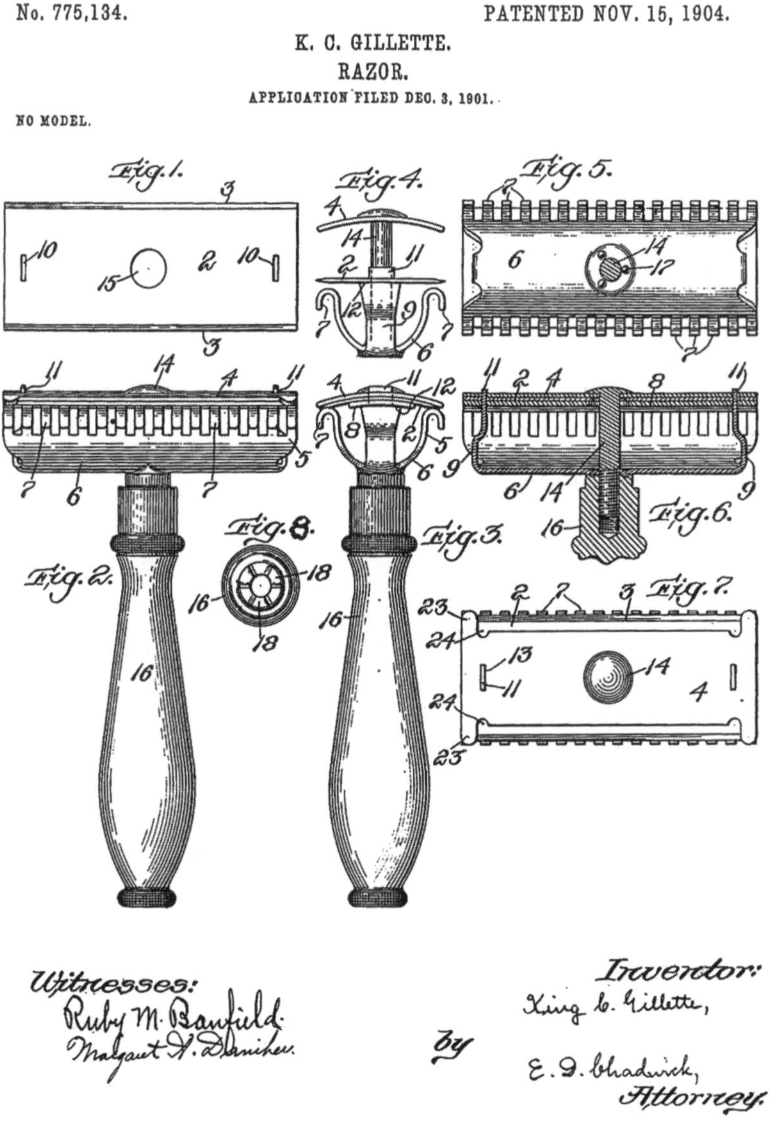

Figure 7.8 *Front page of Gillette's 1901 razor patent*[21]

8
Business Case Presentation

No matter how exhaustive the cost calculation, how compelling the benefit computation, how careful the risk analysis, and how forward thinking the flexibility options, the go ahead for the investment decision does not only depend on how the business case is justified, it largely depends on how it is presented to the decision makers. Someone needs to tell the story, maximize the likelihood of the message being listened to, and most importantly get the story across.

8.1 EXECUTIVE DECISION MAKING

To come to an executive management decision, a consensus of understanding and commitment on the part of the principal stakeholders is very important. This consensus would have been achieved during the business case process through resolving differences and conflicts of interest through research, evaluations, discussions, and reiterations.

Top management and the investment decision governance board typically use no more than four decision criteria for evaluating a business case presentation:

- Business problem and its impact. Do we have a clear understanding of the business opportunity or problem? What impact does the proposed investment project have on the organization?

- Net present value. Does the proposed solution have a compelling NPV argument? Have alternatives been considered?

- Resource capacity and experience. Does the company have the knowledge to deliver a quality business solution?

- How to measure implementation progress. How can the value of the solution be identified? How do you determine when the value is delivered? How do you know when the implementation was a success?

Whenever a business case team prepares for the final presentation, it should review the presentation and the flow of arguments according to these four decision criteria. If any of them is not satisfactorily answered, the likelihood of the business case presentation to fail increases – and this is independent of the merit the business case offers.

8.2 STRUCTURE OF THE BUSINESS CASE REPORT

About two thirds of all organizations have standard business case templates in place, but most of these lack critical components, reducing investment decisions to fuzzy, qualitative, and potentially incorrect guesses.[1] A good business case report with a structure as proposed in Figure 8.1 brings confidence and accountability into the field of making investment decisions; it is therefore made up of a compilation of all the information collected during enterprise analysis and the business case process. Its key purpose is to provide evidence and justification for continuing with the investment proposition.

- **Preface**

- **Table of contents**

- **Executive briefing**
  - Recommendation
  - Summary of results
  - Decision to be taken

- **Introduction**
  - Business drivers
  - Scope
  - Financial metrics

- **Analysis**
  - Assumptions
  - NPV cash flow statement
  - Costs
  - Benefits
  - Risk
  - Strategic options
  - Opportunity costs

- **Conclusion, recommendation, and next steps**

- **Appendix**

Figure 8.1 *Structure of a business case report*

Preface

The preface is a one-sentence summary of the purpose of the business case report. It can be as short as this: "This report presents research, findings, and recommendations to assess the business value of the proposed investment xyz for company XYZ." It is really not necessary to write much more and prefaces which span several pages are nothing more than ego boosters for the business case team; they do not serve the purpose of good decision making.

Table of contents

The table of contents gives details of the structure of the report and the contents of the report's appendix; this section possibly also contains a list of exhibits.

Executive briefing

The executive briefing is written last, but read first. It summarizes all of the findings of the proposal documentation and is presented to top management for a final decision; it should consist of three parts:

- Recommendation. The main story of the business case (see Section 8.3) summarizing the reasons for the proposed alternative or the investment proposition.

- Summary of results. A short and crisp summary of the costs, benefits, risks, and strategic flexibility options.

- Next steps. This is basically a call for action, convincing management that the analysis is thorough and that any further delay in decision making will postpone realization of benefits and thus cost money. The wording should be action-oriented and build a credible threat scenario for decision-making lethargy, for example: "A decision to approve investment decision xyz should be taken within four weeks. A delay in taking this decision in this FY incurs direct costs of x amount of dollars due to postponement of benefit realization."

Some busy stakeholders will only read the executive briefing of the case, so the business case team should ensure that all pertinent information is concisely included in this section. Clarity and brevity are key to a good executive briefing.

Introduction

The introduction sets the scene for the analysis section; most importantly, it gives information on what the document and the business case is about – and what it does not cover:

- Business drivers. Gives background about the industry, company (or business unit), and the business drivers triggering the investment proposition.

- Scope. Explains the purpose of the business case, the options evaluated, the project plan of the business case project, the analysis period and other analysis guidelines provided by management, and the composition of the business case team. Lists the interview partners and the data sources consulted for building the document. Also the boundaries of the business should be specified, i.e. which locations, departments, divisions, technologies, and time frames were not considered.

- Financial metrics. Describes what types of measures (e.g. the NPV method) the business case is based on and why these measures were selected.

Analysis

The analysis is really the core of the business case report providing details and reasoning around the four components of the business case:

- Assumptions. All assumptions (estimates, predictions, averages, non-verified information etc.) for which the business case team cannot take for granted that the audience would automatically make the same assumptions, need to be explicitly highlighted as they are a mirror of risk (see Section 6.2).

- Cash flow statement. The NPV cash flow statement is the pivotal part of the business case calculations; it includes the cash inflows, outflows, and NPV for each scenario. The results need to be summarized and analyzed by highlighting the main points and removing unnecessary details (see Section 2.2 and Chapter 5).

- Costs. Measures costs as cash outflows and gives details about planning, implementation, and maintenance costs over the analysis period as defined in section introduction/scope (see Chapter 3).

- Benefits. Identifies positive business impacts and calculates cash inflows, such as efficiency or revenue gains over the analysis period (see Chapter 4).

- Risk. This section is most welcome by the decision makers and outlines, via sensitivity analysis, scenarios, or simulation, what will happen if the values assumed are different. It tempers the above cost and benefit estimates (see Chapter 6). Some industries have externally mandated requirements for the documentation of risk analysis. For instance, the Basel III requirements in the financial services industry are global regulatory standards on bank capital adequacy, stress testing, and market liquidity risk; the Clinger-Cohen Act (CCA) is a US federal law designed to improve the way in which the US federal government acquires, uses, and disposes of IT. Such requirements to perform risk analysis on mandated systems supersede any form of documentation suggested here.

- Strategic options. Monetizes the value of platform investments and the value of future options created through realizing the investment proposition under consideration of this business case (see Chapter 7).

- Opportunity costs. Costs related to missing other mutually exclusive investment options are not included in the business case cost calculation, but for many investments it makes sense to give information about this cost category as part of the business case report (see Section 3.2).

Conclusion, recommendation, and next steps

Conclusions need to touch on the business drivers, outline the decision criteria applied, and explicitly state the results and findings of the business case. The recommendation is a bit more detailed than in the executive briefing section and the next steps should outline how the business case team thinks the organization should proceed.

8.3 STORYTELLING

Driving home a message to busy senior executives, gaining their attention, and moving them to action is an art; success always relies on two aspects:

- One needs to have a great story.

- One should convey it in a simple and convincing way.

Without a compelling business case, without the homework of cost analysis, benefit identification, contemplation of risk, and consideration of future strategic option, there is no great story and there is no shortcut to building a great story other than following the business case process meticulously, as outlined in Section 1.8.

Having said this, a common mistake in many business case teams is spending too much time on numbers, calculations, and even more calculations; but too little time on explaining the significance of these calculations. Without these explanations, there is no story but only a spreadsheet – and the business case misses the mark. An estimated 20 per cent of business cases fail because of incorrect communication of the business case findings and their rationale.[2]

Storytelling is a narrative process, which gains attention, stimulates retention, and moves to action. Stories work in business just as well as they work for newspapers and magazines, because they connect to deep-felt issues of the listener.[3] Just like best-selling novels usually have a simple plot and a limited set of characters, business case stories also need to be uncomplicated; senior executives overloaded with business information and day-to-day firefighting need to comprehend them at once. There is no second chance for driving home a message.

Building effective stories

An effective business case story needs to mirror the message of the business case and the needs and feelings of the audience:

First and foremost, a story needs to have a goal and it should really only serve *one goal*. Do you use the story to gain attention? Or to overcome a controversial point and get decision-maker buy-in? Second, the story needs to have a *target audience* and it should really only target one (or a group of) stakeholder(s) who needs to be convinced. Third, a superabundance of stories diminishes the effectiveness of each and every story: too much of a good thing can be too much. The business case should have a theme backed up by a very strong and *carefully selected* story and then individual messages of the business case can be supported with separate stories.

Business cases are often delivered as presentations supported by slides and a report. Compelling stories should not only be built into the oral presentation, but also into the headlines and take-away-boxes of slides. They can also be incorporated into reports in the forms of highlighted or framed boxes.

And what is more, good stories can also be placed outside the formal presentation in informal and chance encounters with stakeholders or decision makers; just think about the famous 20 second elevator-talk with the CEO or when meeting a decision maker in the queue for lunch at the office pantry. Stories stick and help to form opinion, but in order to do this, they need to keep to the above three effectiveness criteria: one goal, one target audience, and carefully selected.

Topics that work for business case stories

A memorable business case story is not only attention-getting and colorful, but most importantly it is believable. It needs to enhance the credibility of the business case and reinforce that the business case team has done a thorough research job.

A *factual story* has to be truthful and should not be exaggerated; many decision makers will want to reconfirm stories and do their own background checks with the respective units from where the stories originate. Good factual stories use familiar situations and are about:

- Achieving benefits or cost savings through the proposed investment;

- Avoiding losses through reducing risk; and

- Winning respect, building a brand, and increasing customer satisfaction.

Anything far-fetched, exotic, complicated, or generally unknown does not make a good story, as it does not reach the target audience.

Visionary stories, however, can certainly be about future opportunities and how business can develop as a result of the proposed investment. However, such stories cannot be confirmed by decision makers, and the business case team planting such visionary stories has to be very careful with them, restrict their number, and always be clear that they are about the future and future opportunities.

Verbatim quotes can be used to highlight certain topics and relate the analysis to corporate reality. They are usually collected during the fact-finding process from interview partners, but good quotes also live in coffee rooms, employee newsletters, and intranet forums. Even analyst reports and the external press can be gold mines. Before using quotes, it needs to be verified with the interview partner that the name or department can be used or if the quote should be put up in an anonymous form. Such verbatim quotes can be placed on slides in the form of bubbles and in reports as highlighted quotes.

Writing stories for business case stories

Stories contrast the often dry numbers of a business case. They bring life into the mathematics and can thus afford a more vibrant attention-gaining language. Decision makers read tons of documents every year and most of them are written in similar business-style language. To stand out in the competition for a decision maker's mind share, the language of stories needs to be colorful and to pulsate with relevance.

Figure 8.2 lists some powerful terms that help pump life into stories, but any image-producing text always needs to stay relevant to the central message of the business case. For example, a statement like "This inimitable investment is going to deliver a high-ranking NPV of $25,000" will probably be laughed at

Important	Valuable	Urgent	Unique
• Central	• Eminent	• Burning	• Distinctive
• Chief	• Foremost	• Critical	• Elite
• Critical	• High-ranking	• Crucial	• Exceptional
• Crucial	• Influential	• Exigent	• Exclusive
• Essential	• Notable	• Imperative	• Inimitable
• Focal	• Prominent	• Important	• Irreplaceable
• Imperative	• Worthy	• Pressing	• Matchless
• Key		• Serious	• Only one of its kind
• Main		• Vital	• Rare
• Principal			• Single
• Significant			• Sole
• Vital			
• Weighty			

To win	To avoid something	Problem	
• Accomplish	• Shun	• Catch	• Puzzle
• Achieve	• Skirt	• Challenge	• Quandary
• Acquire	• Steer clear	• Conundrum	• Question
• Attain		• Crisis	• Question
• Collect		• Difficulty	• Riddle
• Come first		• Dilemma	• Setback
• Earn		• Drawback	• Snag
• Gain		• Glitch	• Trouble
• Obtain		• Hindrance	
• Prevail		• Hitch	
• Secure		• Obstacle	
• Succeed		• Obstruction	
• Triumph		• Predicament	

Figure 8.2 *Powerful terms to gain attention*

by decision makers because the attention-gaining terms do not match the amount of NPV promised. If one rephrases and retargets the statement's core message to "This investment is critical to securing our market position within three years; it also delivers a positive NPV of $25,000," credibility is enhanced.

Examples with storytelling language

Figure 8.3 is a slide from the first steering committee meeting of a business case project analyzing the possibilities of improving the customer service center operations of a global travel provider. The slide uses a diagram to explain the different cost drivers to the company's customer service operations on a very objective basis; but it also uses the slide's storyline (top of the slide) and take-away box (bottom of the slide) to highlight the key messages with attention-gaining vocabulary.

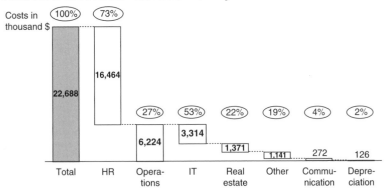

The total costs of customer service is $22.7m p.a.; the highest-ranking component are HR costs with a notable 73 per cent
Total costs of customer service at Tommy Travel Inc.

IT costs are exceptionally high; they cause more than 50 per cent of operating expenses.

Source: Corporate, IT, and HR controlling. Data relates to FY 2011/12.

Figure 8.3 *Example – Business case team presents at steering committee*

Using such powerful words, two messages will stick with the audience:

- If we are serious about reducing costs, we need first and foremost to tackle the costs of human resources and of our IT infrastructure.

- Any other cost-cutting measures (real estate, communication costs) will only have a minor impact.

Expectations have now been set that the business case team is going to propose a project proposing measures to cut HR and IT costs.

In the second steering committee, outsourcing options were examined. Figure 8.4 summarizes the average costs per customer call of the current in-house solution compared with two outsourcing options. As with the previous slide, the main part of the slide is factual and reports objective data: the storyline, the take-away box, and a comment on the right-hand side.

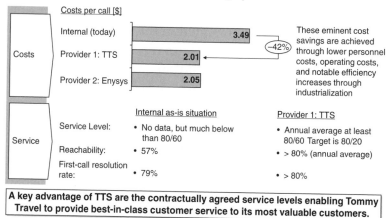

Figure 8.4 *Example – Business case team suggests outsourcing*

However, it also uses powerful words to highlight the potential for 40 per cent cost saving and improving the responsiveness of customer service at the same time. After seeing this slide, two messages will stick with the audience:

- We can reduce our costs by 40 per cent.

- And improve our responsiveness to our clients at the same time.

8.4   DELIVER THE PRESENTATION

Many business case teams are asked to deliver an oral presentation in addition to the slides or the report they have created. As with any presentation, it is important to know who the audience is, what level of familiarity the audience has with the investment proposition, and what the expected duration of the presentation is. Is the purpose of the presentation to provide an introductory overview to the business case material, is it a discussion about the findings, or is it a decision-making meeting about the fate of the investment proposition? The purpose and the scheduled duration really drive the content and format of the presentation.

Charts, diagrams, and visual aids will help to make the presentation look more lively and professional. Most of the key data communicated should be presented in the form of diagrams and graphics; detailed numbers and tables can be put into the appendix or backup slides. Stories should summarize the key findings.

Business case presentations are always controversial; after all, this was the reason why the business case project was commissioned in the first place. Hence during a business case presentation, many challenging questions should be expected. It is therefore not only necessary to reserve about one third of the time for questions and discussions, but also to have a good grasp of even the minutest details of the business case assumptions and its dynamics. Preparation and anticipation of challenging questions are key to meeting the requirements of the audience.

Some members of the audience will be opposed to the investment proposed and will try to find fault in the business case. Such people on the warpath need to be treated with professionalism, and a concise response should be attempted. The purpose of the business case presentation is to explain the investment proposition from a financial and strategic point of view, but not to sell it. However, if the person keeps on asking antagonistic questions, it is best to offer further discussions offline, i.e. separately after the business case presentation. It is a good idea to ensure that this discussion does not take place immediately after the formal presentation, as others might get involved and it may spoil the atmosphere.

A key point to avoid such controversial discussions right from the beginning is to look again at the tools used for discovering benefits: strategic benefit maps (Section 4.2), value panels (Section 4.3), and benefit discovery charts (Section 4.4). The outcome of these tools combines the company's strategic view with the perspective of individual decision makers, who are consciously or unconsciously searching for certain tangible and intangible factors to judge the investment's attractiveness and thereby the quality of the business case from their point of view.

Feedback about the presentation should be collected in two steps. The first round of feedback should be collected immediately after the presentation. Here the feedback question should never be "what was good and bad about this session?," as being given two questions, most people will try (and even feel obliged) to say something positive and negative. A better question would be "what are the key things learned from this presentation?," as it is more likely to result in fact-driven feedback and will not spoil the atmosphere for other participants. The second round of feedback should be collected the following day after the business case presentation; participants should be called individually to provide positive and negative feedback.

This feedback should then be used to further improve the written report and clarify topics.

9
Business Case as Controlling Framework

The business case for the investment proposition may later also be used as a basis for control, i.e. as a framework that helps management to monitor the investment and control if the promised benefits are actually being reaped in. Everybody in an organization is keen to realize benefits, but benefits only come true when management continues to monitor the investment. Otherwise benefits do not make it out of the planning spreadsheet into the organization's balance sheet. Planning and controlling are closely related, and in fact they can be viewed as the blades of a pair of scissors; scissors cannot work unless there are two blades.[1] Without planning, control is not possible, because performance has to be compared against established criteria. And without control, planning remains nothing more than a make-work activity.

The sixth phase of the business case process (see Section 1.8) is about measuring the investment's success in an ongoing management process. For the measurement process to be successful, the organization needs to build its very own benefit realization capability.

9.1 THE CHALLENGE OF BENEFIT REALIZATION

Surveys over the past 30 years show that the returns that organizations derive from their investment projects, especially in information systems and technology-related investments continue to disappoint (see Section 1.2). Benefits that were promised in the business case, never seem to appear – albeit businesses continue to celebrate successful implementations, roll-outs, and other projects. Delivery managers and department heads receive bonuses and promotions after what is declared a successful project delivery.

One possible explanation for this dichotomy may well be due to how success vs. failure is defined and performance is monitored. The project team, as well as the executive management, deems a project to be successful if the commissioned piece of work is delivered on time, on budget, and according to the initial specification. And if the affected end users are happy, the project is considered to be a great success. But making monetary benefits happen as identified in the business case through improved working practices, organizational change, or marketing spend is by no means a straightforward endeavor. It is no secret that realizing monetary business benefits is a tough job. And when managers do not know how to deliver this tough job, the same kind of reasoning is given over and over again[2]:

- The business case was built by consultants; managers operate in the real world.

- The business case team never talked to the business people; and the implementation team never talked to either of them.

- The business case was then; the world keeps changing. There is no formal process to keep up with this change.

- Benefits are not managed and shortfalls are never discovered; once the project is funded, no one cares to monitor benefit realization.

An organization needs two things. For one, it needs to get the right people involved and apply the right frameworks for building the business case; Chapters 1–8 have dealt with this task. Second, it needs to set up benefit realization as a management process with the only objective of ensuring that the projected business benefits expected to happen from an investment on paper do in fact occur in the real world as well.

Business studies knows the *resource-based view* (RBV) of an organization, which provides a starting point for building the conceptual framework of a benefit realization process. RBV emerged toward the end of the 20th century and postulates that organizations should invest in those assets and resources that they believe will best assist them in successfully gaining a sustainable competitive advantage.[3] Organizations cannot achieve sustainable competitive advantage just by selecting the right combination of products and services, and positioning them to appeal to attractive target market segments. Although these decisions may lead to desirable economies of scale and scope, they are too easy for competitors to notice and copy.[4] Instead, an organization's primary competitive advantage comes from resources that are simultaneously valuable, rare, inimitable (or imperfectly imitable), and nonsubstitutable.[5] Subsequent developments around RBV focused on the importance of tacit knowledge, i.e. the things that an organization has learnt to do, but about which its members are rather unconscious or unaware. Because such tacit knowledge is not explicit – it is not codified or written down in procedures and manuals – it is almost impossible for competitors to identify, acquire, and replicate it.[6] Today, there is a growing recognition that resources *per se* do not create value; rather it is the ability of an organization to utilize these resources adequately through the application of capabilities and competencies.

The difference between a competency and a capability is a subtle one:

- *Competencies* are routines that have potential to be used in many places in an organization; they are the attributes of a team, function, or even the entire organization. Each competency is underpinned by the behavior, skills, knowledge, and experience of people resources, which are deployed in combination with other specific organizational processes and resources.[7]

- *Capabilities*, on the other hand, are a higher level of construct and enacted through the application of competencies in order to perform a set of tasks utilizing organizational resources in order to achieve an end result. An organization's capabilities are therefore being noticed by customers and stakeholders when dealing with the organization.[8]

Benefits realization can therefore be conceptualized as an organizational capability, which ensures that investments generate value through the enactment of competencies.[9] Unfortunately, little is known of how knowledge resources that underpin competencies should be coordinated and integrated; they have even been referred to as a "huge can of worms" (Wernerfelt, 1984, p. 180). So, how does one best develop benefits realization competencies for project management?

9.2   OPERATIONALIZING COMPETENCIES WITH PRACTICES

Granularity and thereby practical applicability can be added to the concept of capabilities and competencies by decomposing competencies into a number of fundamental *practices*, which describe what people do, in a specific domain, to achieve a defined and measurable outcome. They are not a predefined mechanical reaction to a given situation, but a regulated improvisation that allows an appropriate response given the circumstances. The concept of practices has recently emerged from organizational sciences.[10]

Figure 9.1 shows the relationship between benefits realization capabilities, competencies, and practices. It becomes clear from

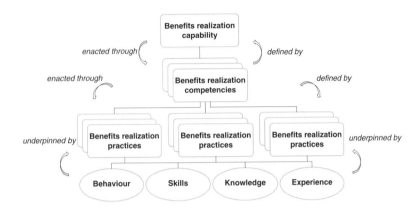

Figure 9.1 *Relationship between capabilities, competencies, and practices*[11]

this relationship that the capability of realizing the business case benefits of an investment will need to be enacted through a coherent set of benefit realization competencies in an organization. Each competency is underpinned by a set of benefits realization practices; in their totality they will help to define the competency.[12]

9.3   BENEFITS REALIZATION COMPETENCIES FRAMEWORK

Following the benefits *identification* competency (see Chapter 4), three more competencies can be identified leading finally to a quantifiable realization of benefits[13]:

- Benefits *delivery* competency,

- Benefits *review* competency, and

- Benefits *exploitation* competency.

The relationship between these competencies can be understood in a number of ways. An obvious relationship is a seamless linear process moving from the identification of benefits to their delivery, followed by a major review, and finally by the ongoing benefit exploitation once the investment is fully operational. The second and maybe more realistic view puts the review competency in the center while leaving the basic linear relationship intact. It interprets benefits review as an ongoing activity, which reviews and adjusts the benefits, reviews and modifies the delivered benefits, and also examines the ongoing exploitation.

The above three competencies can be decomposed into clearcut practices focusing on stakeholder involvement, project outcomes, and organizational change; Figure 9.2 provides a definition of each suggested practice and lists its outputs.

Benefits delivery competency

Benefits typically arise from organizational change that surrounds an investment, but not from the investment itself.[14] Consequently, organizations need to develop a benefits delivery competency accompanying the investment's entire life cycle from the point that the business is approved all the way through to its deployment and further beyond into the utilization phase.

Although many projects today certainly adopt an agile approach in order to be adaptive to an ever-changing business environment, the main focus is on deployment of features and functions (but not on organizational change), realization of quick wins and win–wins (but not looking at the big picture), and cutting short-term costs during the implementation (but not on long-term strategic flexibility options).

Benefits review competency

Ultimately, benefits will only be realized if they are being measured, monitored, and managed in a systematic and ongoing way. At the core of the benefits review competency are therefore

Benefits delivery			
1	Establish an adaptive project life-cycle	Establish a project life-cycle enabling change during a project broken down into incremental delivery steps which are controlled by a small number of milestones. Be able to respond to learning as uncertainty gets resolved	Project plan, including definition of phases, deliverables, and milestones
2	Actively lead the business change	Design, build, and lead the project team with a focus on realizing benefits. Define who is responsible for benefit delivery for the various stakeholder groups	Role descriptions
3	Ensure continuing active involvement of stakeholders	Ensure there is communication and involvement with all stakeholders as per stakeholder analysis to gain support for change	Participation and communication plan
4	Specify changes to work and organizational design	Consider business processes, working practices, structures, roles, management framework, performance measures, corporate culture, etc.	Change request to business solution design
5	Make benefits-driven trade-offs	Decide on trade-offs (features, schedule, costs, risk, strategic flexibility options) from a benefits perspective	Change log, decision log
6	Ensure benefits-driven risk management	Take a proactive approach to risk modified by change	Updated risk assessment and risk control
7	Ensure benefits-driven strategic flexibility management	Take a proactive approach to flexibility options modified by change	Updated real option valuation
8	Implement changes	Implement changes as per [4] and [5]. Note: This activity needs to be monitored to ensure that planned changes are implemented	Changes implemented
9	Communicate, educate, and train	Ensure all communication, education, and training are focused on the realization of benefits	Stakeholders trained
Benefits review			
1	Establish evaluation metrics	Establish project evaluation framework consisting of metrics related to realization of business benefits	Evaluation framework
2	Appraise project	Use evaluation framework to systematically assess the status of benefit realization	Benefits appraisal report
3	Identify actions	Establish an action plan for areas where planned benefits have not been achieved	Action plan
4	Facilitate lessons learned reviews	Carry out lessons learned reviews at key stages in the project, including project completion	Lessons learned report and action plan
5	Complete strategic facility options review	On completion of the project, carry out a review to consider the contribution to the organization's overall strategic flexibility	Updated strategic flexibility options list
Benefits exploitation			
1	Ensure ownership of continued benefits exploitation	Establish a clear business role with ownership for ongoing realization of benefits	Active benefits owner
2	Communicate, educate, and train	Maintain all communication, education, and training	Communication, education, and training resources updated. On-going provision of training to stakeholders
3	Evolve working practices	Continue to evolve working practices post deployment to maximize realization of benefits	Revised working practices

Figure 9.2 *Framework of project management practices*[15]

capabilities that help the organization to assess the success of a project in terms of the benefits promised in the business case. It answers questions about what benefits have already been delivered and to what extent, as well as what needs to be done to realize further benefits.

Ideally, the review should be done on a forward-looking basis so that deviations may be detected in advance of their occurrence and avoided by appropriate actions. Historical data, such as those received from accounting reports, are always unsatisfactory and inadequate. At best, it tells the management in financial year x that the organization did not meet its targets in year $x-1$ because of something that was done in year $x-2$. Coming this late, information only becomes an interesting, if not distressing, historical postmortem as no one has yet found a way to change the past. Companies need a future-directed evaluation framework, and one common way of doing this is through repeated use of forecasts based on the latest available information. By comparing what benefits were identified with the forecasts, managers can appraise an investment and identify actions that will make the forecasts more promising.[16]

Notwithstanding the need for future-directed control, reference to historical data is still better than no control at all – on the problematic and doubtful hypothesis that what is past is the opening to the future.

Benefits exploitation competency

The mission to leverage benefits from an investment should not be stopped as soon as the implementation project is completed. On the contrary, many benefits from an investment project will only materialize after the investment has become fully operational, integrated into the organization, and the stakeholders have become sufficiently acquainted and trained with its use. But project teams, especially the ones consisting of external consultants, tend to be disbanded very soon after the go-live date. Frequently the operational transfer from the project or the service provider to the line organization does not take place.

But the line organization with its focus on the ongoing management of people, processes, and technology is indeed in an ideal position to leverage the investment for the full exploitation of its benefits. Consequently, the benefits exploitation practices help an organization to realize benefits over the entire operational life of an investment all the way until its decommissioning.

10
Influencing Decisions in Sales

To most clients' purchasing officers and vendors' account managers, the dance around the sales and evaluation process is frustrating, especially because both of them need to answer the same ultimate question: Do the business benefits offered by the vendor at a certain cost match the client's need for business value?

10.1 TURNING SELLING AROUND

Traditionally, the buyer's evaluation starts with a request for information (RfI) and is then followed by a request for proposal (RfP). The client (buyer) company puts together a team of people who are reasonably familiar with the service or the product to be purchased.

Because of this team's familiarity with the features to be expected and hoped for, many evaluations degenerate into a discussion about features and functions, rather than concentrating on a business value conversation. In the area of IT evaluations, it is estimated that up to fifty times more effort is spent on feature–function discussions than on the value analysis.[1]

In addition, vendors contribute to the neglect of a substantiated business value discussion by writing proposals in jargon-infested language, which are difficult to understand, but where the real content remains hidden in sales terminology; they describe intangible benefits in glamorous words but omit to substantiate their claims in monetary terms; and finally, they rely on their own size, power, and importance to intimidate the client (Figure 10.1). Often, the client does not quite know what kind of features or functions are really necessary, the requirements are not clear, and there are also many stakeholders sometimes with hidden agendas involved. Combined with the vendor's behavior, this leads to excessive evaluations and longer-than-necessary buying cycles. And at the end of it, there is an unfortunate likelihood that despite all the effort spent, the wrong decision will be taken. Owing to the confusion and neglect of value, more often than not the vendor offering the best value for money is rejected.

10.2 BUSINESS CASE SELLING

Providing customer value – the true meaning of marketing

The legendary management pioneer Peter F. Drucker observed in the late 1970s that in many companies, "marketing still means no more than systematic selling. [But] the true meaning of

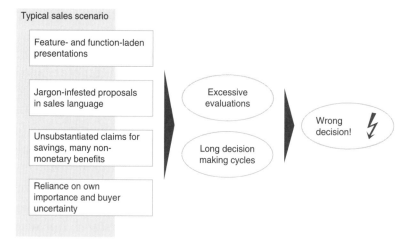

Figure 10.1 *The challenge of typical sales and buying scenarios*

marketing [is]: knowing what is value for the customer" (Drucker, 2010, p. 41).

The provider shapes the value it can offer to its customers through its value proposition. However, every customer assesses this value proposition differently, and this leads to the business value that the client receives from a provider's offering. The world-renowned business advisor and author Ram Charan says "The heart of the new approach to selling is an intense focus on the prosperity of your customers. This is a radical departure from what most salespeople and selling organizations do. The entire psychological orientation is shifted 180 degrees. No longer do you measure your own success first. Instead, you measure success by how well your customers are doing with your help. You're not focussed on selling a specific product or service; you're focused on how your company can help the customer succeed in all the ways that are important to that customer. [...] This ability to create value for customers will differentiate you in a crowded marketplace, and you will be paid a fair price for it – one that is commensurate with the value customers perceive they are getting and the value you do in fact provide. I call this new approach *value creation selling*" (Charan, 2007, pp. 5–6). In this book we refer to it as business case selling.

Responding to clients' value needs

As more and more companies want to see proof of the value promise before buying, providers are responding. Unfortunately, many are trying their luck through shortcuts; ROI calculators and TCO quick scans may look impressive at first sight, but the processes and the calculations that produce these estimations are based on some industry best practices and mostly do not hold up to due diligence. Here is one example of such a promise: "The TM [Transportation Management] Quick Scan can help identify opportunities for improvement and build the business case for change along with the necessary action plans.

The power of this tool is in its repository, which contains our transportation industry business models. These models, in turn, are tied to best practices, key metrics, potential business benefits, and representative application architectures. Our TM Quick Scan will help ensure that technology and business processes are aligned to support a company as it competes in an ever-changing business environment" (Bootsma & Tiels, 2011, p. 3). And another one: "The Total Cost of Ownership Estimator is a complimentary tool that enables aggregation of all cost and risk factors into one cost for simpler, more objective decision making. From companies currently or considering offshoring and local suppliers competing with offshore sources to salesmen or economic development groups advising on the benefits of reshoring, [... it] allows users to determine which sources best meet their company's profitability and strategic objectives" (Moser, 2013).[2] If only a few spreadsheet formulae could perform the magic of a good strategy, a business case, and IS/IT alignment at the same time, the industry would not see the huge number of project failure rates (see Section 1.2) and this book would not be needed.

Providers are not necessarily deceptive in their sales approach; however, many do not deem it to be necessary to invest effort in researching the cost and benefit drivers and putting them together in a consistent, professional, and (most importantly) believable manner. Such criticism apart, a good number of providers are getting serious about proving the value of their services and products to their clients; they are incorporating the idea of business case selling in their pitches. From such value-motivated providers, clients typically expect support on:

- Business case content to quantify the dimensions of costs and benefits in monetary terms, and

- Tools and consultancy to build the client- and situation-specific business case.

Business case selling is much more than attaching a spreadsheet with some cost and benefit calculations to an email. It is in fact an active business strategy with the aim of establishing value as the key decision criteria for purchasing. And it is sweepingly different from today's systematic selling in the following four ways.

First, vendors need to devote time and energy to learn about their customers' businesses in greater detail. Only after understanding their clients' important financial measures, market value creation processes, product differentiation factors, and needs can they start to look for ways to help their prospects and clients.

Second, short-term gains and quarterly reporting of sales figures become less important for the vendor in comparison with medium- and long-term opportunities. It is now about working together with the client to understand where value can be provided to the client to help leverage the client's business. In the end this will result in mutually beneficial sales. However, the top management in vendor organizations needs to completely overhaul and reengineer its recognition and reward systems to make sure that the focus is not only on the quarterly sales funnel.

Third, selling today is based on much more than free-flowing information. Vendors need to build social networks, from their client to their sales team and directly into the vendor's departments, and especially from the sales team to the vendor's various in-house departments.

Fourth, business case selling requires patience as well as determination to build the necessary degree of competency and trust with the client. But once it is going, it helps to reduce the length and cost of the sales cycle while simultaneously giving access to bigger deals. Vendors are being viewed as valued business advisors; they get access to their clients' most senior decision makers; and they are able to deal with price competition much more effectively. What more does a vendor need to move quickly up the value chain?

Introducing business case selling

Successfully introducing the spirit of business case selling into a vendor organization requires more than just building business cases for specific sales opportunities; it necessitates the implementation of a strategy encompassing content development, tool design, training, alignment and integration, promotion, and maintenance. These six components are detailed in Figure 10.2.[3]

Business case selling entails profound changes in the sales force and the account managers themselves. They are no longer "solo operators," but rather orchestrators, organizing input from diverse areas in the vendor organization. And various functions need to learn to take sales leaders seriously, reply to their requests for information, and in general synchronize their own activities with execution of the business case selling strategy.[4]

Salespeople need to master a new body of knowledge, mathematical skills, and analytical tools in order to succeed. They need consulting skills to research and understand the customer's business, its needs, and how it engages with the customer's customers and thereby makes money, today and in the future.

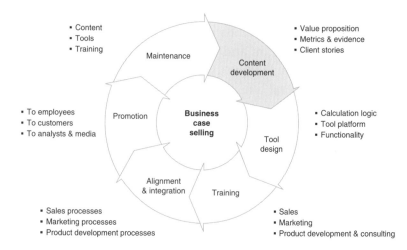

Figure 10.2 *Six components of a business case selling strategy*

Clients, investors, and business managers are generally risk averse, but some are more so than others, and some may even be risk neutral or risk loving. And as outlined in Section 6.4, some of these differences can be attributed to certain demographic or cultural factors. But many observed differences are not consistent with the rational utilizer theory of economics. Many times the prospect of gains vs. losses and the framing of choices affect the risk-taking willingness of decision makers. Consequently, the way the new account managers propose business cases needs to take into account these behavioral inclinations.

After the deal is closed

Business case selling is an ongoing process; it does not end once the deal is closed. It is critical that the interaction between client and vendor continues on a sustainable and long-term basis, not only for building lasting relationships between clients and vendors, but especially for ensuring successful value delivery.

In Section 1.8, this was referred to as the bottom-up business case. Whether it is external selling or taking an internal investment decision, the business case as a project management tool and controlling framework needs to ensure that the value is not only promised but also being brought home.

Business case selling does not just benefit both buyers and sellers by saving time and expenses during the sales cycle; it especially provides the path for higher value sales, transforming the account manager from a salesperson to a general manager who takes P&L responsibility for each and every customer deal, both internally in the vendor organization, as well as externally in the client organization.

10.3 AVOIDING WEAK BUSINESS CASES

If a business case drawn up by an end-user organization is considered to be of poor quality by the senior decision makers, the reasons are typically to be found in a lack of credibility or in overcomplicated calculations. Section 1.5 has dealt with how to avoid the two most frequent killer phrases of business cases:

- "I don't believe it," and

- "I don't understand it, it's too complicated."

Missing buy-in of customer stakeholders or insufficient validation of data presented in the business case can easily make a customer stand up and shout "I don't believe it" – and the sales pitch has come to a sudden and unexpected end. So if a business case is used by account managers as a sales support tool, the very same guidelines need to be followed as if an investment business case were to be drawn up and presented. In addition, some quite different challenges and problems can make a potentially strong business case weak in the eyes of the client (see Figure 10.3).

First and foremost, the entire setup may be wrong and the baseline of the business case too optimistic. Maybe not all cost areas are included or the development of existing costs in future periods was judged too pessimistically. This immediately leads

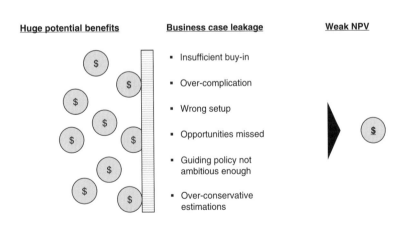

Figure 10.3 *Problems weakening a potentially strong business case*

to a gap between the baseline and what the sales proposition can deliver. The business case's NPV becomes weak.

The sales team may have spent too little time on identifying benefit areas and may thus have missed a lot of cost-saving or revenue-generating opportunities (see Chapter 4 for benefit identification techniques). As a result, the list of benefits is too short to attractively offset the costs associated with the investment proposition.

The goals set by the sales team may not have been ambitious enough, and the entire sales pitch may not simply have been designed as an action to support a strong enough guiding policy (see Section 1.1). Again, as a result, the business case will show a weak NPV.

Last but not the least, the sales team may have agreed too quickly with the client on overconservative estimations in order not to lose client buy-in for the end result. Although it is certainly wrong to try to persuade, entice, or even lure the client to be more optimistic, the right approach would be to find the reasons behind such modest behavior. If the reason is to be found in risk and uncertainty, then the sales team should try to identify measures to manage the risk and build the costs for them right into the business case. This is a slightly different approach from the factoring of risk and uncertainty as proposed in Chapter 6; it assumes that risk will entirely go away with proper risk management measures. But then, even if this approach to selling uses a business case, the business case remains a sales tool with the main idea of closing a deal. The way in which uncertainty and risk are dealt with is probably the key difference between selling using a business case and deciding on an investment proposition backed by a compelling business case.

Glossary

80/20 rule *See* Pareto law.

Accounting rate of return *See* return on investment (ROI).

Assumption Something that is accepted as true or as certain to happen, but without proof. Assumptions in a business case mirror investment risk; they are ideas and beliefs, which the business case team could not establish to being true, but which are likely to be true.

Average return on book value *See* return on investment (ROI).

Balance sheet A financial statement that is a snapshot of a company's assets and the sources of money used to procure these assets.

Benefit Relates to the business outcome.

Benefit cost ratio (BCR) Ratio between the present value and the upfront investment.

Benefit discovery chart Framework for benefit identification. Helps to understand the objectives of stakeholders and the underlying decision-making criteria.

Benefit realization A management process to ensure that the projected benefits of the business case (which may be on paper or in a spreadsheet) are being reaped in the real world as well.

Benefits Cash inflows in the business case calculation.

Black–Scholes formula The Nobel Prize-winning breakthrough Black–Scholes formula is one of the most important concepts in modern financial theory; it is regarded as one of the best ways of determining fair prices of options. It was developed in 1973 by Fisher Black, Robert Merton, and Myron Scholes. Noting the parallels in financial options and real options, the Black–Scholes formula can be rewritten to attach a monetary value for strategic flexibility options in business cases.

Business architecture The first step of enterprise analysis. It helps to understand the current state of the organization and its plans for the future.

Business case An analysis supporting the decision-making process on investment options; it provides a top–down justification for a rational decision and helps to build consensus among stakeholders. As such, a business case has two perspectives: as a tool and as a process.

Business case selling An approach to using the business case methodology for showing clients proof of value in a sales situation.

Capital rationing Constraint on the amount of new investment projects undertaken by an organization.

Cash flow Net value of the cash inflows and outflows for each period of a business case analysis.

Cash flow statement A financial statement, which records cash inflows and outflows, thereby helping to assess and maintain an adequate liquidity level. It is mainly used internally in an organization.

Certainty equivalent In financial theory, it denominates the lower guaranteed return that someone would accept, rather than taking a chance on a higher, but uncertain, return.

Cohort A group which has shared a particular event together.

Commissioning costs Span all costs incurred from the time the investment is decided until it is handed over to operations.

Compound interest Arises when interest is added to the principal amount, so that it will also earn interest from that moment on.

Contingent investment An investment that is complementary to another investment.

Costs Cash outflows in the business case calculation.

Cost-saving investment An investment in something new, changing technology, or adapting processes, which promises future cost savings.

Country risk A collection of risks associated with investing in a foreign country that adversely affects the net present value of an investment.

Decision The process of reaching a conclusion by passing judgment on a number of propositions and choosing the right one.

Decision tree An approach to analyzing decisions under uncertainty and supporting management in taking dynamic decisions along the implementation of an investment project. Uses a tree-like graph with chance nodes, decision nodes, and outcomes. *See* probability tree.

Decommissioning costs Capture every activity and expenditure to ramp-down an investment at the end of its life.

Deflation Decrease in the average price level. Opposite to inflation.

Discount rate *See* rate of return.

Discounted payback method A specific method of calculating a business case, a variant of the payback method. It answers the question of how many periods an investment has to last in order to make sense in net present value terms.

Diversification investment An investment in new product lines, services, or hitherto not served markets. Often used as a strategic entry point into new markets.

Economies of scale Increase in efficiency as numbers increase. Costs per unit typically decrease until an optimal volume is reached, after which diseconomies of scale cause the unit costs to increase again.

Effectiveness The degree to which the objectives are achieved ("doing the right thing"). In contrast to efficiency.

Efficiency Extent to which time or effort is well used for the intended task or purpose ("doing the thing right"). In contrast to effectiveness.

Empirical validation Validating a hypothesis based on practical experience gained by experimenting, but not theory.

Enterprise analysis Identifies areas where investment decisions make sense by creating the business architecture, conducting feasibility studies, and scoping business opportunities.

Expansion investment An investment in existing or very similar product lines, services, or geographies; often with the aim of increasing sales or gaining market share.

Expected utility theory A tool to help make decisions among various possible choices by way of balancing risk vs. reward in a mathematical function.

Feature Represents an element of functionality.

Financial management A company's financial management operates between strategy and operations (what the business does) and the financial markets (where the business gets its money from). It takes decisions about where a company should invest its money and how it should pay for these investments in a cyclical way.

Financial ratio A relative figure of two values taken from a company's financial statements.

Future value The value of an asset (or cash) at a specified date in the future being equivalent in value to a specified sum today.

Hard costs Costs that can be extracted from an accounting system and which are not really up for debate.

Hidden costs Come up after the investment is approved and which have not been thought of.

Hurdle rate *See* rate of return.

Independent investment An investment that can be considered independent of other investments.

Inflation Rise in the average price level. Opposite to deflation.

Intangible benefits *See* nonmonetary benefit.

Internal rate of return (IRR) A specific method of calculating a business case. It is defined as the rate of return that makes the net present value (NPV) zero, i.e. the rate of return that makes equivalent the cash inflows and the cash outflows.

Investment cycle The process of identifying an investment opportunity, developing a supporting business case, taking the investment decision, implementing the project, and reporting back on the success of the investment.

Investment A commitment of resources made with the prospect of realizing benefits in the future.

Knock-on costs Changes in one part of the organization are the reason for costs incurred in another part of the organization.

Leasing Process by which someone (the lessee) obtains the use of assets from someone else (the lessor) under a lease contract for a predefined period of time.

Legal investment An investment mandated by the regulator or by law. Also called must-do or nondiscretionary investment.

Monetary benefit Advantages that reduce costs or increase revenues.

Must-do investment *See* legal investment.

Mutually exclusive investment An investment that involves an either-or decision with respect to another investment.

Net present value (NPV) A specific method of calculating a business case. The net present value is defined as the sum of all present values of all future cash flows, at a given rate of return, minus the initial investment.

Nondiscretionary investment *See* legal investment.

Nonmonetary benefit Of intangible nature and cannot be directly captured in financial terms. Also called soft benefits or intangible benefits.

Operating costs Incurred after the investment is handed over to production.

Opportunity cost of capital *See* rate of return.

Opportunity costs Missed economic benefits from other mutually investment options.

Overhead costs Ongoing expenses of operating a business not directly related to the manufacturing of a product or to the delivery of a service.

Pareto law A rule of thumb of marketing management. It states that 80 per cent of the total profit of a business is generated by just 20 per cent of its customers and that 80 per cent of all the customer servicing costs are incurred by only 20 per cent of its customers; but in most cases those two 20 per cents won't be the same 20 per cent. Also called 80/20 rule.

Payback method A specific method of calculating a business case focused on calculating how rapidly they can recover the cash outflow caused by the investment.

Payback period The time it takes to recover an initial investment.

POLDAT framework A framework used to create a business architecture. It proposes six different categories (data, technology, organization, process, application, and location) from which the business situation is viewed.

Prebusiness case costs Sunk costs that are incurred before the business case is initiated.

Precommissioning costs Occur between initiation of the business case and before the go/no-go decision is taken.

Present value The current worth of a future sum of money (or stream of cash flows) given a specified rate of return.

Probability tree An approach for analyzing decisions under uncertainty. Allows modeling of a sequence of decisions that a company undertakes while implementing investment decisions. Uses a tree-like graph with chance nodes and outcomes. Evaluating uncertain gains and losses leads to the value of an investment proposition under uncertainty. *See* decision tree.

Profit and loss account (P&L) A financial statement that measures a company's sales and expenses over a specified period of time and thus shows how much profit or loss a business is making.

Profitability index (PI) Ratio between an investment's net present value and the upfront investment. Used to rank projects when there are limitations on the investment program.

Prospect theory A framework to analyze and explain anomalies and contradictions in human decision-making behavior. Formulated by Kahnemann & Tversky (1979).

R&D investment An investment into the future of the business that aims to produce an economically viable investment proposal through research and development efforts. Also called seed corn investment.

Rate of return The interest rate that investors demand for accepting delayed payment. In a net present value calculation, it is the percentage by which the value of a future cash flow is reduced for each time period by which it is removed from the present. Also called discount rate, hurdle rate, or opportunity cost of capital.

Real option An option to modify an investment project.

Response option An investment taken to mitigate negative effects of a trigger event before the impact is felt.

Return on capital employed *See* return on investment (ROI).

Return on investment (ROI) A catchword that is often confused with a specific method of calculating a business case. In its broadest sense, ROI attempts to measure the profitability of an investment through dividing the benefit of an investment by the cost of it. However, there is no commonly agreed formula for doing this. Also known by average return on book value, return on capital employed, and accounting rate of return.

Risk Quantifiable chance, high or low, that a chosen investment project can be harmed. It also includes an objective indication of how serious the harm could be. *See* uncertainty.

Rumelt framework of good strategy Rumelt (2011) suggests that good strategy is a mixture of thought and action with a basic underlying structure, which he refers to as the kernel of strategy. This kernel contains three elements: diagnosis, guiding policy, and coherent actions.

Scenario analysis An approach for assessing risk in a business case calculation. The process of estimating the net present value of an investment after a given period of time, assuming specific changes in the variables or key factors that would affect the cash flows. Scenario analysis commonly focuses on estimating what an investment's value would decrease to if an unfavorable set of variables (the "worst-case scenario") was realized.

Seed corn investment *See* R&D investment.

Sensitivity analysis An approach for assessing risk in a business case calculation. It determines how sensitive a business case model is to changes in the value of the parameters of the model and to changes in the structure of the business case model.

Simulation An approach for assessing risk in a business case calculation. The imitation of the performance of an investment project is based on a stringent mathematical model. To build this model, key characteristics and behaviors of the investment need to be selected and simplifying approximations and assumptions used. Randomness comes into play to investigate thousands of possible scenarios.

Soft benefit *See* nonmonetary benefit.

Soft costs In contrast to hard costs, soft costs (such as productivity decreases) cannot be measured easily and are often difficult to justify.

Stakeholder A person (or a group of persons) who has (or have) a vested interest in the impact of a proposed investment.

Standard deviation A measure of the dispersion of a set of data from its mean. The more spread apart the data, the higher the deviation and thus the higher the level of risk attached to future values.

Storytelling A narrative process that gains attention, stimulates retention, and moves to action. Business case stories need to mirror the message of the business case and at the same time the needs and feelings of the audience.

Strategic flexibility Organizational capability and preparedness to identify major changes in the external environment and respond with new courses of action by quickly committing resources. This also includes reversing strategic decisions that have turned out to be ineffective.

Strategy map A framework used to create a business architecture; also a framework for benefit identification. It has evolved from the four-perspective model of the balanced scorecard and serves as a communication tool to describe and document strategic goals.

Sunk costs Have irreversibly occurred.

Taxes Financial charge opposed upon a taxpaying entity by a legislative authority. It can come under the name of toll, tribute, tollage, impost, duty, custom, excise, subsidy, aid, supply, etc.

Terminal value Residual value of an investment at the end of its economic life; can be positive or negative.

Time horizon The time period over which an investment is made before it is assumed to end.

Uncertainty Unmeasurable chance that a chosen investment project can be harmed. An objective indication of how serious the harm could be is difficult. *See* risk.

Unified communication (UC) Integration of communication services by synchronizing all technologies into a seamless, unified communications platform. UC weaves communications capabilities directly into the way business operates.

Value panel Framework for benefit identification. It combines the strategic view with the perspective of individual decision makers.

Zachman framework A framework used to create a business architecture. It is essentially a six by five matrix with the rows representing different perspectives of the enterprise and the columns representing the questions that have to be answered to design a business entity.

Notes

1 DECIDING ON CORPORATE INVESTMENTS

1. Cf. Denning (2013), Gulati (2009, p. 3), and Martin (2011, p. 37).
2. As cited in Rehak (2002).
3. Cf. Rehak (2002).
4. Cf. Kistinger, n.n.
5. Cf. Useem (2005).
6. In an interview and cited in Nichols (1994).
7. This view of strategy very closely follows Rumelt (2011, pp. 9–10, 58–9, 77–9).
8. The concept is based on Rumelt (2011, pp. 77–94).
9. Cf. Kwak & Yoffie (2001) and Montgomery (2012).
10. Cf. Dayananda *et al.* (2002, p. 3).
11. Balance sheet for Procter & Gamble, FY 2010/11; data from P&G Investor Relations (2012).
12. Industry vertical is the industry sector (such as engineering, hospitality industry, financial services). It's an expression frequently used in the consulting business.
13. Cf. Brealey *et al.* (2007, p. 791).
14. Profit and loss account for Procter & Gamble, FY 2010/11; data from P&G Investor Relations (2012).
15. Cash flow statement for Procter & Gamble; data from P&G Investor Relations (2012).
16. Financial ratios for Procter & Gamble, October 2012; data from P&G Investor Relations (2012).
17. Cf. Standish Group (1995); the 2009 results are quoted in Brady (2009) and Levinson (2009).
18. Eason (1988) suggested that in the late 1970s only 20 per cent of projects "achieved something like their intended benefits" and

Hochstrasser & Griffiths (1991) estimated that by the late 1980s up to 70 per cent of IS projects failed. Clegg *et al.* (1997) reported that "up to 90% of all IT projects fail to meet their goals" and British Computer Society (2004) reported that "only around 16 per cent of IT projects can be considered truly successful". See Ashurst, Doherty, & Peppard (2008) and (Doherty, Ashurst, & Peppard (2012).

19. Cf. Ganapati (2010).
20. Cf. Zeman (2010).
21. Cf. Ziegler (2010).
22. Source: IconShock, http://findicons.com/icon/457538/microsoft_kin (accessed: 29 June 2012), classified as freeware.
23. For example, Clarke (2009).
24. Quoted by Raghavendra (2006).
25. Cf. Messner (2010, p. 94) and Mitchell (2006).
26. Cf. Hanssens, Thorpe, & Finkbeiner (2008, p. 93).
27. Cf. Hanssens, Thorpe, & Finkbeiner (2008, p. 93) quoting research led by Leonard M. Lodish; see for example, Hu, Lodish, & Krieger (2007) and Lodish *et al.* (1995).
28. Cf. Lodish *et al.* (1995, p. 139).
29. The presidential helicopter fleet included 11 VH-3D helicopters that achieved initial operational capability (IOC) in 1975 and 8 VH-60N helicopters with IOC in 1989. The upgrade plan can be traced back to the late 1990s and a fleet operational needs document dated March 1998; a mission needs statement (MNS) was formally approved in September 1999.
30. Cf. Cole (2009) and O'Rourke (2009).
31. The transcript of the Q&A session is available at The White House, Office of the Press Secretary (2009).
32. Cf. Useem (2005).
33. A US joint services honour guard stands by next to the presidential helicopter *Marine One*, a Sikorsky VH-3D *Sea King* operated by Marine helicopter squadron HMX-1, prior to its departure from the Mall, Washington, DC (USA), on 1 April 1985. Source: US DefenseImagery.Mil, photo by Maurice G. Fitzgerald, VIRIN DF-ST-86-11982, http://www.defenseimagery.mil/imageDownload.action?guid=0bc366ba598bd627214f86754c1013afd49c3716#, photo in public domain.

34. Paul Rinaldi was interviewed by Barney Gimbel (Useem, 2006).
35. Simon Yates was interviewed by Barney Gimbel (Useem, 2006).
36. Marine Corps Base Hawaii (7 July 2004). US Navy air traffic controllers monitor and direct the launch and recovery of all aircraft at Marine Corps Base Hawaii during exercise Rim of the Pacific (RIMPAC) 2004. Source: US Navy, photo by Mate 2nd Class Richard J. Brunson, ID 040707-N-6932B-042, http://www.navy.mil/view_single.asp?id=15902, photo in public domain.
37. Cf. General Peter Pace in an interview by Jerry Useem (Useem, 2006).
38. See Section 1.1 and Rumelt (2011).
39. 2nd Lt. Samuel Campbell, 15th Sustainment Brigade Personal Security Detachment platoon leader gives orders to his soldiers while under a simulated attack during training. Source: US Army, photo by Sgt. Matthew C. Cooley, 15th Sustainment Brigade Public Affairs, http://usarmy.vo.llnwd.net/e2/-images/2009/09/30/51957/ (accessed: 30 April 2013), photo in public domain.
40. Cf. (Collins & Hansen (2011, pp. 110–11).
41. Cf. McGee (2004, pp. 8–14).
42. A similar sentence is proposed by Forrester Research, cf. Gliedman (2010, p. 11).
43. Cf. Gliedman (2013).
44. Cf. BBC News (1998).
45. Data from 2011, cf. Mayo Clinic (2013).
46. Cf. Jacobsen (2013).
47. As quoted by Blackden (2001).
48. Cf. Blackden (2001), Ebrahimmi (2011), Nestlé Health Science S.A. (2011), and Riley (2011).
49. Cf. OECD/The World Economic Forum (2011, pp. 149–57).
50. Source: CIA Central Intelligence Agency, World Factbook, https://www.cia.gov/library/publications/the-world-factbook/geos/kz.html (accessed: 30 April 2013).
51. Cf. Sulphur Daily News (2013).
52. Cf. Procter & Gamble (2008).
53. Quoted in Procter & Gamble (2008).
54. Cf. McGee (2004, p. 29).
55. Cf. Alauddin, *et al.* (2002).

56. The approach to this case study and the data presented are adapted from Ross, Sicking, & Zimmer (1993), Khasnabis, Mishra, & Safi (2012), and Mishra & Khasnabis (2012).

57. Cf. Ross & Beath (2002) who have described these dimensions and the following four types for IT investments; expanded by the author to cover all types of infrastructure investments.

58. Based on the framework for IT investments proposed by Ross & Beath (2002, p. 53).

59. In a standard ERP environment, data automatically flows between integrated applications. A publish-and-subscribe environment is an alternative in which middleware links independent applications.

60. Cf. Corcoran (2000), Ross (2001), and Ross & Beath (2002).

61. Cf. Knowledge@Wharton (2006); citation attributed to Judith C. Lewent as per source.

62. Component business model (CBM) is a technique originally developed by IBM; cf. Pohle, Korsten, & Ramamurthy (2005) and van Diessen, Sierman, & Lee (2008).

63. Various methods and techniques are available for business process modelling, cf. Böhm & Fuchs (2002, p. 109) and Österle & Winter (2000).

64. Cf. Jacobson *et al.* (1992).

65. Cf. TOGAF Open Group (2013).

66. Cf. Drucker (1988).

67. Cf. Sessions (2008, p. 3).

68. There are several versions of the Zachman framework in various publications and Internet sources, cf. Zachman & Locke (2008) and Sessions (2008, p. 15).

69. POLDAT is an acronym for process, organization, location, data, applications, and technology. In strict terms, it is not a framework in its own right, but it is at the core of CSC's catalyst methodology; cf. CSC (2011).

70. For the balanced scorecard concept see Kaplan & Norton (1996).

71. Cf. Kaplan & Norton (2004).

72. For example, cf. Messner (2010).

73. The PSIA study is documented in Holland (2007, pp. 38, 86–93, 161–6) and Jorgensen & Loudjeva (2005).

2 KEY FINANCIAL CONCEPTS

1. Data from Global-Rates.com (2013). Euribor is short for Euro Interbank Offered Rate and is the rate at which European banks borrow funds from one another. There are 15 different Euribor rates with maturities ranging from 1 week to 12 months. The rates are determined by supply and demand in the first place; some external factors such as economic growth and inflation also influence the level of the rates.
2. Cf. Dayananda *et al.* (2002, p. 3).
3. Typical cut-off dates are around four years after the investment is initialized with the first initial cash outflow.
4. Cf. Brealey, Myers, Allen, & Mohanty (2007, p. 95).

3 FUNDAMENTALS I: COSTS

1. Cf. U.S. Department of Justice (2011).
2. The Organisation for Economic Co-operation and Development (OECD) is an international economic organization of 34 countries with the aim of stimulating economic progress and world trade.
3. Cf. Löscher (2012).
4. Operating costs in this case study from BigBelly Solar (2009).
5. Quoted in ICIS Heren (2008).
6. Quote from EDF Energy (2012).
7. Cf. Ballance (2004), ICIS Heren (2008), IET (2008), and *The Times* (2012).
8. Image Copyright Lynne Kirton. This work is licensed under the Creative Commons Attribution-Share alike 2.0 Generic Licence. Source: http://www.geograph.org.uk/photo/438750 (accessed: 31 July 2012).
9. Cf. Kahneman & Tversky (1979).
10. Cf. Arkes & Blumer (1985).
11. Cf. Oxford University (2012); cost data is adjusted for inflation and currency exchange rates.
12. Quoted in Oxford University (2012).
13. Figure from Oxford University (2012); other reports quote an even lower figure, for example, BBC News (2007).
14. Cf. Oxford University (2012).
15. Figures compiled from DCMS (2012, pp. 14, 17, 21).

16. The problem of the traditional RfI/RfP process is described in Messner (2010, pp. 102–28), where one can also find a practical five-step S-LEAN RfP™ process for selecting outsourcing/offshoring providers and negotiating the contract.
17. Cf. Gropper (1995, p. 184).
18. Cf. JVI (nn) and Wilson (1981).
19. This can be seen directly from the diagram, or by differentiating the LRAC function with respect to x, setting it equal to zero, and solving it for x.
20. Cf. Kamarkhar (2004) and Thun (2008).
21. Both management and other overhead costs need to be directly related and attributable to the investment in order to count for the business case.
22. Cf. Cyr (2007) and Stewart, Wyskida, & Johannes (1995, pp. 179–80).

4   FUNDAMENTALS II: BENEFITS

1. Cf. Österle & Winter (2000).
2. For strategy maps cf. Kaplan & Norton (2004). For the purpose of benefit identification, the concept of strategy maps is slightly adapted and the focus is really put on how investment components drive value and finally deliver monetary benefits. The author names this adapted framework a strategic benefit map.
3. Cf. Kumar (2008).
4. Cf. Bharti Airtel (2012).
5. Cf. Thakkar (2012).
6. Cf. Kumar (2008).
7. Cf. Slater (1997) and Woodruff (1997).
8. For an overview of the cost/sacrifice value literature see Smith & Colgate (2007).
9. Cf. Woodall (2003).
10. This perspective is based on work by Woodall (2003, p. 10) and further developed by the author.
11. Cf. Messner (2004) and Smith & Colgate (2007, p. 8).
12. A brown paper is a visual wall display created on brown wrapping paper and utilizing post-it notes to capture key information.

A key objective of this technique is that the team together explores a task.

13. The benefit discovery chart method builds upon the concept of benefit logic as proposed by Capgemini for business cases; for a publicly available description of the benefit logic see David, Skjotskift, & Ostmoe (2008, p. 5) and Local e-gov CRM (2004, p. 6).

14. EPA is the United States Environmental Protection Agency.

15. Cf. Knowledge@Wharton (2007).

16. Adapted from Keen & Digrius (2003, pp. 116–19).

17. Cf. Christopher, Payne, & Ballantyne (2002, p. 40).

18. Cf. Link & Hildebrand (1997, p. 163) and Schirmeister & Kreuz (2001, p. 295).

19. The 80/20 rule was created by Joseph M. Juran (1904–2008); the Pareto principle is named after the Italian economist Vilfredo Pareto (1848–1923); cf. Bunkley (2008).

20. This model for calculating the value of the customer base was first proposed by Gupta, Lehmann, & Stuart (2004) and then further developed and at the same time simplified for practical calculations by Messner (2004) and Messner (2005, pp. 38–40, 322–4).

5 MAKING INVESTMENT DECISIONS WITH NPV

1. In financial terms, *perpetuities* are securities issued by the government, which offer a fixed income for each year in perpetuity. The government, however, is not obliged to repay the principal amount.

2. If the cash flow growth is not significantly less than the discount rate, the terminal value of the investment can exceed the value placed on earlier cash flows during the investment period, which is highly unlikely.

3. Consider the infinite geometric series in the main brackets. Let $a = \dfrac{C}{1+r}$ and $x = \dfrac{1+g}{1+r}$. Then $TV = a(1 + x + x^2 + x^3 + \ldots)$ (1), multiplying both sides by x yields $TV \times x = a(x + x^2 + x^3 + x^4 + \ldots)$ (2). Subtracting the second formula from the first one (1)−(2) results

in $TV(1-x)=a$. Substituting a and x back into the formula and multiplying both sides by $(1+r)$ results in $TV = \dfrac{C}{r-g}$ after a few rearrangements (q.e.d).

4. In financial terms, an *annuity* is an asset that pays a fixed sum each year for a specified number of years.

5. This method is adapted from the approach for calculating the terminal value as an annuity as outlined in Moran (2000, pp. 221–2).

6. This method is adapted from the annuity valuation approach as outlined in Brealey *et al.* (2007, pp. 41–2).

7. Cf. Scott (2003) and Morris and Morris (2007).

8. This case was originally reported in Coy (1999) and is adapted here.

9. See the suggestion by blogger "Armchair General" to use a free wiki platform added to the report on SCOPE in Young (2009).

10. This follows the convention introduced in Biermann and Smidt (2007, p. 335).

11. Cf. Biermann and Smidt (2007, pp. 335–6).

12. The word "scenario" is consciously avoided as it might be confused with the "scenario planning" technique: see Section 6.7.

13. This scenario builds upon realistic information, data and assumptions provided by Microsoft on Lync2010 Server; see http://lync. microsoft.com/en-us/launch/Pages/customer-testimonials.aspx (accessed: 19 July 2011) and especially North (2010).

14. The source of these statements is the Microsoft case study on Lync 2010 for A.T. Kearney, cf. Microsoft (2010).

15. Not all productivity savings will be realized by the consulting company, i.e. not all saved time will be converted into productivity.

16. Calculation based on 48 working weeks per year:
$$1h * 50\% * \frac{\$50}{h} * 48 * 5.000 = \$6m \cdot$$

6 FACTORING RISK AND UNCERTAINTY

1. Cf. Kretschmer (1927).

2. Reverse of a Roman coin, dated AD 220–221 with Fortuna standing left holding cornucopia and rudder on globe. Photo courtesy of Classical Numismatic Group, Inc. http://www.cngcoins.com.

3. Cf. Useem (2005).

4. Until recently most texts have regarded emotion – whether hot or cold – as an impediment to constructive decision making and reaching agreements in negotiations. But passions matter and one needs to understand, channel, and learn from emotions; cf. Leary, Pillemer, & Wheeler (2013).

5. Cf. Herodotus, de Sélincourt, & Marincola (403 BC/2003, p. 62).

6. Regarding the definition of hazard and risk, cf. HSE (2011).

7. Cf. Knight (1921).

8. Many people believe that the Chinese Mandarin word for risk and crisis (wēi jī) is made up of two characters meaning danger and opportunity; see for example, Damodaran (2007, p. 6) and Ehrenfeld (2009). Although this would be a good sounding moment and take-away for corporate strategy planning and business cases alike, it unfortunately remains an old saw. While it is true that the first syllable wēi actually means danger, the second one jī does not stand for opportunity. Instead, the second syllable only gets its meaning of quick-wittedness, resourcefulness, machine, and device in connection with multisyllabic terms into which it enters. For example, when jī is added to the word occasion (hua), it creates the word for opportunity; cf. Mair (2009).

9. Cf. Collins & Hansen (2011, pp. 107–13, 234–6).

10. For the cultural aspects of dealing with time-based risk, see Section 6.4.

11. Cf. Leary, Pillemer, & Wheeler (2013).

12. Cf. Snowden & Boone (2007, p. 41).

13. The following builds upon the Cynefin Framework for determining the prevailing context, as suggested by Snowden & Boone (2007).

14. Cf. Collins & Hansen (2011, pp. 27–30).

15. Cf. Kelleher (2008).

16. Cf. Hsee & Weber (1997, p. 45).

17. Risk preference is understood as a continuum, i.e. the term "more risk averse" subsumes both "more risk averse" and "less risk-seeking" in their strict sense.

18. Gamble *A* is said to have *first-order stochastic dominance* over gamble *B* if for any outcome *x*, *A* gives at least as high a

probability of receiving at least x as does B, and for some x, A gives a higher probability of receiving at least x. In notation form, $P[A \geq x] \geq P[B \geq x]$ for all x, and for at least some x, $P[A \geq x] > P[B \geq x]$.

19. A *probability mass function* is a function that gives the probability that a discrete random variable is exactly equal to some value. Such functions exist for either scalar or multivariate random variables with a discrete distribution. A probability mass function differs from a probability density function in that the values of a density function are defined only for continuous random variables and are not probabilities as such. Instead, the integral of a probability density function over a range of possible values $(a, b]$ gives the probability of the random variable falling within that range.

20. A *mean-preserving spread* is a change from one probability distribution A to another probability distribution B, where B is formed by spreading out one or more portions of A's probability density function while leaving the mean (the expected value) unchanged. As such, the concept of mean-preserving spreads provides a stochastic ordering of equal-mean gambles (probability distributions) according to their degree of risk; this ordering is partial, meaning that of two equal-mean gambles, it is not necessarily true that either is a mean-preserving spread of the other. By definition, if B is a mean-preserving spread of A, then A is said to be a mean-preserving contraction of B. Ranking gambles by mean-preserving spreads is a special case of ranking gambles by second-order stochastic dominance; namely, the special case of equal means: If B is a mean-preserving spread of A, then A is second-order stochastically dominant over B; and the opposite holds if A and B have equal means.

21. Cf. French (2003), Merton (1990), Reilly (1994), and Sharpe & Alexander (1978).

22. The sensitivity to nondiversifiable risk of an asset is also known as systematic risk or market risk and often represented by the quantity beta (β) in the financial industry.

23. Cf. Atrill, 2003 (pp. 236–40) and French, The Treynor Capital Asset Pricing Model (2003).

24. Cf. Damodaran (2007, p. 43).

25. Cf. Hsee & Weber (1997, pp. 45, 52).
26. Cf. Byrnes, Miller, & Schafer (1999) and Holt & Laury (2002).
27. Cf. Dyer, Kagel, & Levin (1989).
28. Cf. Harrison, Lau, & Rutström (2004).
29. Cf. DeLuque & Javidan (2004).
30. Cf. Messner & Schäfer (2012, p. 34).
31. Cf. DeLuque & Javidan (2004, p. 618).
32. In the years 2004–2007, the worldwide GLOBE study of Global Leadership and Organizational Behaviour Effectiveness surveyed more than 17,000 middle managers from 950 organizations worldwide. One of the attributes of culture found to have an effect on the functioning of societies, groups, businesses, and individuals is uncertainty avoidance (House *et al.*, 2004). The values reported by DeLuque & Javidan (2004, p. 622) for uncertainty avoidance are normalized between 0 and 100, signifying the worldwide minimum and maximum (Messner & Schäfer, 2012, p. 29).
33. Cf. Collins & Hansen (2011, p. 113).
34. Cf. McDermott (2001, p. 18).
35. Based on Kahnemann & Tversky (1979, p. 279).
36. Cf. McDermott (2001, p. 20).
37. Cf. McDermott (2001, p. 23).
38. Cf. Damodaran (2007, p. 65).
39. Cf. Doane (2004).
40. This is based on the fact that $\mu \pm 2\sigma$ covers the central 95.4% of the normal distribution; cf. Browne, 2002 (p. 293).
41. Cf. Doane (2004).
42. Cf. Breierova, Choudhari, & Forrester (1996, p. 47)
43. Data tables can also be row-oriented, i.e. the variable values are in a row instead of a column. Then the formula needs to be captured in the cell one column to the left of the first value and one cell below the row of values.
44. A more detailed description of one- and two-variable data tables is available in Ecklund (2001).
45. Cf. Biermann & Smidt (2007, pp. 102–3). This form of duration is also referred to as *Macaulay duration*, named after Frederick Macaulay, who defined duration as the weighted average maturity of cash flows in 1938, cf. Coleman (2011).

46. Cf. Linneman & Klein (1983).
47. Cf. Meyer-Schönherr (1992); quoted in Link, Gerth, & Voßbeck (2000, p. 93).
48. Cf. Brauers & Weber (1988) and Markham & Palocsay (2006).
49. Cf. Link, Gerth, & Voßbeck (2000, p. 89).
50. Cf. Link, Gerth, & Voßbeck (2000, p. 90).
51. Cf. Davies, Goedhart, & Koller (2012, p. 3).
52. Cf. Goedhardt & Haden (2003).
53. The following builds upon an idea suggested by Copeland & Tufano (2004, pp. 93–4) in a different context.
54. Cf. Knowledge@Wharton (2006); citation attributed to Judith C. Lewent as per source.
55. Source: Photo by Wikimedia user Berthold Werner, http://commons.wikimedia.org/wiki/File:Casino_2005.jpg (accessed: 29 March 2013), picture in public domain.
56. The basic idea of this example is adapted from Wittwer (2004) and expanded to a multi-period NPV calculation.
57. Cf. Brighton Webs Ltd (2008).
58. For the following formula, assume that the NPV output can be found in column [Y] of the spreadsheet, then in Excel notation, *column* should be replaced with the array [Y:Y].
59. *n* has to be sufficiently large for the approximation to yield a reasonable result.
60. Kurtosis is also referred to as the *coefficient of excess*.
61. Cf. Wittwer (2004).
62. General Peter Pace was interviewed by Useem (2006), where the quote is taken from.
63. See Belson (1956).
64. Cf. Greenwood & White (2006, pp. 1–2).
65. The notation used goes back to Magee (1964, p. 128).
66. Cf. Massé (1962, p. 250).
67. Drucker (1959, p. 239).
68. Cf. Magee (1964, p. 134).
69. Cf. Greenwood & White (2006, p. 5).
70. The notation used goes back to Magee (1964, p. 128).
71. Cf. Greenwood & White (2006, pp. 9–10).
72. *Short-term memory* is the capacity for holding small amount of information in mind in an active, readily available state. Short-term

memory should be distinguished from *working memory*, which refers to structures and processes used for temporarily storing and manipulating information; cf. Becker & Morris (1999).

73. Cf. de Ville (2006, pp. 8–9).

74. Cf. Moran (2000, p. 131).

75. Cf. D'Souza (2002).

76. Cf. McDonald (2007).

77. Source: Photo by Frank Kovalchek, 13 April 2008; http://commons.wikimedia.org/wiki/File:Westjet_737_approaching_Las_Vegas_(2412776016).jpg (accessed: 2 October 2012); licensed under Creative Commons Attribution-Share Alike 2.0 Generic; permission granted by photographer on http://www.flickr.com/people/72213316@N00.

78. The mantra 'fire bullets, then fire cannonballs' was proposed by Collins & Hansen (2011, pp. 69–89) based on empirical research of high-performing companies called 10Xers.

79. Another story says that the cannonball dates from a sea battle off Genoa in 1495, when the door was being shipped to France as part of a war booty, which as later returned.

80. Source: Photo by Marie-Lan Nguyen; Wikimedia Commons, http://commons.wikimedia.org/wiki/File:Bronze_door_cannonball_Castel_Nuovo.jpg (accessed: 29 March 2012); licensed under Creative Commons Attribution 2.5 Generic CC-BY 2.5; permission granted by photographer on http://commons.wikimedia.org/wiki/User:Jastrow/Reuse. Castle Nuovo in Naples is also none as Maschio Angioino.

81. Cf. Collins & Hansen (2011) and Useem (2007).

82. General Peter Pace was interviewed by Useem (2006) from where the quote is taken.

83. Cf. Brealey *et al.* (2007, pp. 228–33).

84. Cf. Brealey *et al.* (2007, p. 231).

85. Cf. Davies, Goedhart, & Koller (2012, p. 2).

86. Adapted from Davies, Goedhart, & Koller (2012, p. 3).

87. Cf. the study by Fernández, Aguirreamalloa, & Corres (2011, p. 7).

88. Suggestion for the default spreads taken from Damodaran (2012), based on June 2012 data.

89. Cf. Goedhardt & Haden (2003).

90. Cf. Damodaran (2012) and http://www.stern.nyu.edu/~adamodar/pc/datasets/ctrypremJune2012.xls (accessed: 13 September 2012); permission granted.
91. Cf. Damodaran (2012).
92. Based on rating data from Moody's, 6 September 2012.
93. Cf. Jacob & Rasiel (2011) and Damodaran (2012). Other authors, such as Goedhardt & Haden (2003), hold the belief that there remains a low correlation of country risk.
94. Adapted from North (2010, pp. 28–9).

7 FACTORING STRATEGIC FLEXIBILITY

1. Cf. Collins & Hansen (2011, p. 30).
2. Cf. Shimizu & Hitt (2004, p. 44).
3. As quoted in Coy (1999).
4. Further details about this motorway project are available at Amt für Straßen- und Verkehrswesen Frankfurt (2006), Riebsamen (2007), and Günther (2011).
5. Source: Photo by Wikimedia user Dontworry, March 2008 http://commons.wikimedia.org/wiki/File:A661-seckbacher-ffm008.jpg (accessed: 14 September 2012); photo modified; licenced under Creative Commons Attribution-Share Alike 3.0.
6. Cf. D'Souza (2002).
7. Cf. Coy (1999).
8. Cf. Magee (1964, p. 134).
9. The Dôjima Rice Exchange was dissolved only in 1939 and absorbed by the Government Rice Agency.
10. Source: http://commons.wikimedia.org/wiki/File:Chicago_Board_of_Trade_Opening_Invitation.jpg (accessed: 19 April 2013); the image is believed to be in public domain worldwide as it is more than 70 years old.
11. The *lognormal random walk model* for the behavior of the price of a stock is an industry-standard model, also known as *geometric Brownian motion with drift*; it has been found to work well in practice. A random walk process is one in which the change in value over any time interval is independent of any changes that have occurred in preceding time intervals; the size and direction

of the changes in value are in some sense random. It is applicable to stock prices assuming that the stock market is efficient. Changes in the natural logarithm of the stock price are assumed to be normally distributed (lognormal distribution). In addition, there is a systematic component to the stock market as well due to the fact that stock prices tend to increase over time, and this is reflected by the drift representing deviations up and down from that trend; cf. Mulholland (2005, pp. 1–2).

12. Cf. Harford (2012).
13. Excel versions 2007 and earlier use the function NORMSDIST(d).
14. Extracted from an industry volatility listing of 5,928 companies; maintained by Damodaran Industry Betas (2011); permission granted. Note that this listing has a US-centric view.
15. Cf. Barney (2007, pp. 263–5).
16. Cf. McGrath & Macmillan (2000, pp. 166, 171).
17. The following nomenclature is adapted from McGrath & Macmillan (2000, pp. 167–9, 179); cf. also Barney (2007, p. 266).
18. Cf. Copeland & Tufano (2004, pp. 96–8) from where the metaphor is borrowed.
19. Cf. McGrath & Macmillan (2000, p. 172).
20. Cf. *The Times* (2011).
21. Source: United States Patent and Trademark Office, patent number 775,134; http://patimg1.uspto.gov/.piw?Docid=77513 4&idkey=NONE and http://commons.wikimedia.org/wiki/File: Gillette_razor_patent.png (accessed: 15 March 2013); the image is believed to be in public domain worldwide as it is more than 70 years old.

8 BUSINESS CASE PRESENTATION

1. Cf. the May 2007 Global IT Governance and Steering Committee Online Survey by Forrester Research, as quoted in Gliedman, The Total Economic Impact (TM) Methodology: A Foundation for Sound Technology Investments (2008, pp. 2–3).
2. Cf. Keen & Digrius (2003, pp. 90–1).
3. Cf. Keen & Digrius (2003, pp. 131–2).

9 BUSINESS CASE AS CONTROLLING FRAMEWORK

1. Cf. Koontz & Weihrich (1998, p. 393).
2. Adapted from Keen & Digrius (2003, p. 160).
3. Cf. Barney (1991), Penrose (1995), and Wernerfelt (1984).
4. Cf. Haberberg & Rieple (2008, p. 284).
5. These so-called VRIN criteria were first laid down by Barney (1991).
6. Cf. Nelson & Winter (1982), Amit & Schoemaker (1993), and Peteraf (1993).
7. Cf. Amit & Schoemaker (1993, p. 35), Ashurst, Doherty, & Peppard (2008, p. 354), Haberberg & Rieple (2008, p. 296), and McGrath, MacMillan, & Venkatraman (1995).
8. Cf. Ashurst, Doherty, & Peppard (2008, p. 354), Haberberg & Rieple (2008, p. 296), Helfat & Peteraf (2003, p. 1000), and Teece, Pisano, & Shuen (1997).
9. Cf. Ashurst, Doherty, & Peppard (2008, p. 354).
10. This definition is adapted from Ashurst, Doherty, & Peppard (2008, p. 355). See also Schultze & Boland (2000) and Wenger & McDermott (2002).
11. Adapted from Ashurst, Doherty, & Peppard (2008, p. 355).
12. Cf. Ashurst, Doherty, & Peppard (2008, pp. 355–6).
13. Cf. Ashurst, Doherty, & Peppard (2008, p. 356).
14. Cf. Hughes & Scott Morton (2006) and Peppard & Ward (2005).
15. Modified and adapted from Ashurst, Doherty, & Peppard (2008, pp. 358–60).
16. Cf. Koontz & Weihrich (1998, pp. 394–5; 400–6).

10 INFLUENCING DECISIONS IN SALES

1. Cf. Keen & Digrius (2003, pp. 168–9).
2. Cf. Stackpole (2011).
3. The six components are based on the work of Keen & Digrius (2003, p. 179) and further developed by the author.
4. Cf. Charan (2007, pp. 9–12).

Bibliography

Accenture. (2013). *Accenture Helps Meetic Build a Culture of Analytics to Drive Significant Year-on-Year Growth.* Retrieved July 7, 2013, from Accenture: http://www.accenture.com/us-en/Pages/success-meetic-build-culture-analytics-year-growth.aspx.

Alauddin, M. F., Alhade, A., Barton, A., Dhedah, K., Edweeb, O., & Ismail, S. H., et al. (2002). *Charting Response Options for Threatening Near Earth Objects.* International Space University, Strasbourg.

Amit, R. & Schoemaker, P. J. (1993). Strategic Assets and Organizational Rent. *Strategic Management Journal, 14,* 33–46.

Amt für Straßen- und Verkehrswesen Frankfurt. (2006). *A 66, Frankfurt am Main – Fulda.* Wiesbaden: Land Hessen. Retrieved July 7, 2013, http://www.riederwaldtunnel.de/riederwaldtunnel_data/riederwaldtunnel.pdf.

Arkes, H. R. & Blumer, C. (1985). The Psychology of Sunk Cost. *Organizational Behavior and Human Decision Processes, 35*(1), 124–140.

Ashurst, C., Doherty, N. F., & Peppard, J. (2008). Improving the Impact of IT Development Projects: The Benefits Realization Capability. *European Journal of Information Systems, 17,* 352–370.

Atrill, P. (2003). *Financial Management for Non-Specialists* (3rd ed.). Harlow: Financial Times Prentice Hall.

Bach, D. (2005). *The Automatic Millionaire.* London: Penguin.

Ballance, C. (2004). *They Work for You. Keeping Tabs on the UK's Parliament & Assemblies.* Retrieved July 31, 2012, from Gretna-Lockerbie-Annan Economic Regeneration Prospectus: http://www.theyworkforyou.com/sp/?gid=2004-11-04.11659.0.

Barney, J. (1991). Firm Resources and Sustained Competitive Advantage. *Journal of Management, 17*, 99–121.

Barney, J. B. (2007). *Gaining and Sustaining Competitive Advantage* (3rd ed.). Upper Saddle River, NJ: Pearson Education.

BBC News. (1998, December 22). *BBC Online Network*. Retrieved July 10, 2012, from Euro Case Study: Siemens: http://news.bbc.co.uk/1/hi/events/the_launch_of_emu/inside_emu/221149.stm.

BBC News. (2007). *BBC News*. Retrieved August 07, 2012, from Experts Debate Games Bid Benefits: http://news.bbc.co.uk/1/hi/scotland/glasgow_and_west/6422367.stm.

Becker, J. T. & Morris, R. G. (1999). Working Memory(s). *Brain and Cognition, 41*(1), 1–8.

Belson, W. A. (1956). A Technique for Studying the Effects of a Television Broadcast. *Journal of the Royal Statistical Society. Series C (Applied Statistics), 5*(3), 195–202.

Bharti Airtel. (2012). *About Bharti Airtel*. Retrieved October 05, 2012, from Airtel: http://www.airtel.in/wps/wcm/connect/about+bharti+airtel/bharti+airtel/about+bharti+airtel/.

Biermann, H. & Smidt, S. (2007). *The Capital Budgeting Decision. Economic Analysis of Investment Projects* (9th ed.). Oxon, UK: Routledge.

BigBelly Solar. (2009). *Cost-Savings from Solar-Powered Compactors for Trash and Recycling*. Newton, MA: BigBelly Solar.

Blackden, R. (2001, March 24). Nestlé Expands Health Business with $1bn Purchase of Diagnostics Company. *The Telegraph*.

Böhm, R. & Fuchs, E. (2002). *System-Entwicklung in der Wirtschaftsinformatik* (5th ed.). Vdf Hochschulverlag Ag.

Bootsma, E. & Tiels, E. (2011). *Accelerated Transportation Management. A State-of-the Art, Preconfigured Solution Based on SAP Transportation Management*. Paris: Capgemini.

Brady, K. (2009, June 29). *Project and Programme Failure Rates*. Retrieved January 14, 011, from Clarety: http://www.claretyconsulting.com/it/comments/project-and-programme-failure-rates/2009-06-27/.

Brady, S. D. (2011, October 17). *Risk Taking and Preference Reversal*. Retrieved October 8, 2012, from Science in Our World: Certainty & Controversy: http://www.personal.psu.edu/afr3/blogs/SIOW/2011/10/risk-taking-and-preference-reversal.html.

Brauers, J. & Weber, M. (1988). A New Method of Scenario Analysis for Strategic Planning. *Journal of Forecasting, 7,* 31–47.

Brealey, R. A., Myers, S. C., Allen, F., & Mohanty, P. (2007). *Principles of Corporate Finance* (8th ed.). New Delhi: Tata McGraw-Hill.

Breierova, L., Choudhari, M., & Forrester, J. W. (1996). *An Introduction to Sensitivity Analysis.* Massachusetts: Massachusetts Institute of Technology.

Brighton Webs Ltd. (2008). *Triangular Distribution.* Retrieved July 28, 2011, from Data & Analysis Services for Industry & Education: http://www.brighton-webs.co.uk/distributions/triangular.asp.

British Computer Society. (2004). *The Challenge of Complex IT Projects.* London: BCS.

Browne, R. H. (2002). Using the Sample Range as a Basis for Calculating Sample Size Power Calculations. *The American Statistician, 55*(4), 293–298.

Bunkley, N. (2008, March 3). Joseph Juran, 103, Pioneer in Quality Control, Dies. Retrieved March 20, 2011, from *The New York Times*: http://www.nytimes.com/2008/03/03/business/03juran.html?_r=1.

Byrnes, J. P., Miller, D. C., & Schafer, W. D. (1999). Gender Differences in Risk Taking. A Meta-Analysis. *Psychological Bulletin, 125,* 367–383.

Charan, R. (2007). *What the Customer Wants You to Know.* London: Penguin.

Christopher, M., Payne, A., & Ballantyne, D. (2002). *Relationship Marketing. Creating Stakeholder Value.* Oxford, UK: Elsevier Butterworth-Heinemann.

Clarke, T. (2009). *Auditor-General Not Happy with Victorian Smart Meter Rollout. Investigation Calls for Re-evaluation of Economic Case.* Retrieved March 03, 2011, from Computerworld Australia: Investigation calls for re-evaluation of economic case.

Clegg, C., Axtell, C., Damodaran, L., Farbey, B., Hull, R., Lloyd-Jones, R., et al. (1997). Information Technology: A Study of Performance and the Role of Human and Organizational Factors. *Ergonomics, 40*(9), 851–871.

Cole, A. (2009). *Pentagon Cancels Work on Marine One Helicopter Project.* Retrieved March 08, 2011, from The Wall Street Journal, Politics & Policy: http://online.wsj.com/article/SB124242919729925469.html.

Coleman, T. S. (2011). *A Guide to Duration, DV01, and Yield Curve Risk Transformations.* University of Chicago, Becker Friedman Institute for Research in Economics. Chicago, IL: SSRN.

Collins, J. & Hansen, M. T. (2011). *Great by Choice.* New York, NY: Harper Business.

Copeland, T. & Tufano, P. (2004). A Real-World Way to Manage Real Options. *Harvard Business Review, March,* 90–99.

Corcoran, E. (2000). The E-Gang. *Forbes,* July 24, pp. 145–172.

Coy, P. (1999). *Exploiting Uncertainty. The "Real-Options" Revolution in Decision-Making.* Retrieved March 25, 2011, from Bloomberg Businessweek: http://www.businessweek.com/1999/99_23/b3632141.htm.

CSC. (2011). *Catalyst Concepts.* Retrieved March 21, 2011, from CSC: http://www.csc.com/delivery_excellence/ds/11388/13193-catalyst_concepts.

Cyr, K. (2007). *Cost Estimating Web Site – Learning Curve Calculator.* Retrieved May 19, 2011, from National Aeronautics and Space Administration: http://cost.jsc.nasa.gov/learn.html.

Damodaran, A. (2007). *Strategic Risk Taking. A Framework for Risk Management.* New Delhi: Dorling Kindersley publishing as Pearson Power.

Damodaran, A. (2011). *Industry Betas.* Retrieved March 28, 2011, from Stern School of NYU: http://pages.stern.nyu.edu/~adamodar/New_Home_Page/datafile/Betas.html.

Damodaran, A. (2012). *Musing on Markets.* Retrieved September 13, 2012, from Equity Risk Premiums: Globalization and Country Risk: http://aswathdamodaran.blogspot.co.uk/2012/07/equity-risk-premiums-globalization-and.html.

David, P., Skjotskift, T., & Ostmoe, M. (2008). *The Capgemini Smart Meter Valuation Model.* Retrieved March 20, 2011, from Capgemini Austria: http://www.at.capgemini.com/services/themen/smart-energy-services/publikationen/the-capgemini-smart-meter-valuation-model/.

Davies, R., Goedhart, M., & Koller, T. (2012). Avoiding a Risk Premium that Unnecessarily Kills Your Project. *McKinsey Quarterly*, August.

Dayananda, D., Irons, R., Harrison, S., Herbohn, J., & Rowland, P. (2002). *Capital Budgeting. Financial Appraisal of Investment Projects*. Cambridge: Cambridge University Press.

DCMS. (2012). *Department for Culture, Media, and Sport*. Retrieved August 7, 2012, from London 2012 Olympic and Paralympic Games Quarterly Report June 2012: http://www.culture.gov.uk/images/publications/DCMS_GOE_QR_JUNE-2012.pdf.

DeLuque, M. S. & Javidan, M. (2004). Uncertainty Avoidance. In R. J. House, P. J. Hanges, M. Javidan, P. W. Dorfman, & V. Gupta (eds), *Culture, Leadership, and Organizations. The GLOBE Study of 62 Societies*. Thousand Oaks, CA: Sage Publications.

Denning, S. (2013). The Surprising Reason Why America Lost Its Ability to Compete. *Forbes*.

de Ville, B. (2006). *Decision Trees for Business Intelligence and Data Mining: Using SAS Enterprise Miner*. Cary, NC: SAS Publishing.

Doane, D. P. (2004). Using Simulation to Teach Distributions. *Journal of Statistics Education, 12*(1). Retrieved July 7, 2013, www.amstat.org/publications/jse/v12n1/doane.html.

Doherty, N. F., Ashurst, C., & Peppard, J. (2012). Factors Affecting the Successful Realisation of Benefits from Systems Development Projects: Findings from Three Case Studies. *Journal of Information Technology, 27*, 1–16.

Drucker, P. F. (1954). *The Practice of Management*. New York, NY: Harper Business.

Drucker, P. F. (1959). Long-Range Planning. *Management Science*, April.

Drucker, P. F. (1988). The Coming of the New Organization. *Harvard Business Review*, January–February.

Drucker, P. F. (2010). *The Changing World of the Executive*. Boston, MA: Harvard Business Press.

D'Souza, F. (2002). Putting Real Options to Work to Improve Project Planning. *Harvard Management Update*, August.

Dyer, D., Kagel, J. H., & Levin, D. (1989). A Comparison of Naive and Experienced Bidders in Common Value Offer Auctions: A

Laboratory Analysis. *Economic Journal,* *99*(394 (March)), 108–115.

Eason, K. (1988). *Information Technology and Organizational Change.* London: Taylor & Francis.

Ebrahimmi, H. (2011, May 25). The Smarties Money Is on Healthcare. *The Telegraph.*

Ecklund, P. (2001). *Tools for Excel Modelling. Introduction to Data Tables and Data Table Exercises.* Retrieved July 25, 2011, from Duke – The Fuqua School of Business: http://www2.gsu.edu/~dscaas/pptdsc/ExcelDataTables.pdf.

EDF Energy. (2012). *EDF Energy.* Retrieved July 31, 2012, from Nuclear Waste. Decomissioning and Waste: http://www.edfenergy.com/about-us/energy-generation/nuclear-generation/nuclear-waste/decommissioning-and-waste.shtml.

Ehrenfeld, J. (2009). *Sustainability by Design.* Retrieved September 12, 2012, from Crisis = Danger + Opportunity: http://www.johnehrenfeld.com/2009/02/reading-ben-barbers-piece-in.html.

Fernández, P., Aguirreamalloa, J., & Corres, L. (2011). *Market Risk Premium Used in 56 Countries in 2011: A Survey with 6,015 Answers.* IESE Business School – University of Navarra. CIIF.

Ford Motor Corporation. (1958). *Edsel.* Retrieved June 28, 2012, from Kistinger: http://www.edsel.kistinger.com/ad_58_2.jpg.

French, C. W. (2003). The Treynor Capital Asset Pricing Model. *Journal of Investment Management, 1*(2), 60–72.

Ganapati, P. (2010). *Wired.com Gadget Lab.* Retrieved August 21, 2012, from Hands-On: Can KIN Phones Make Microsoft Cool again?: http://www.wired.com/gadgetlab/2010/04/microsoft-kin-phone-first-look/?utm_source=feedburner&utm_medium=feed&utm_campaign=Feed:+wired/index+(Wired:+Index+3+(Top+Stories+2)).

Gliedman, C. (2008). *The Total Economic Impact(TM) Methodology: A Foundation for Sound Technology Investments.* Forrester Research.

Gliedman, C. (2010). Total Economic Impact™ (TEI): Justify Business-Critical IT Investments. *ITF EMEA* (p. 308C). Lisbon: Forrester Research.

Gliedman, C. (2013). *Do Business Cases for "Must Do's"? – Absolutely!* Retrieved February 07, 2013, from Forrester – Chip Gliedman's

Blog: http://blogs.forrester.com/chip_gliedman/12-06-15-do_
business_cases_for_must_dos_absolutely.

Global-Rates.com. (2013). *12 Month Euribor Interest Rate*. Retrieved
February 22, 2013, from global-rates.com: http://www.global-
rates.com/interest-rates/euribor/euribor-interest-12-months.aspx.

Goedhardt, M. & Haden, P. (2003, December). Emerging Markets
Aren't as Risky as You Think. *McKinsey Quarterly*.

Greenwood, R. & White, L. (2006). *Decision Trees*. Boston, MA:
Harvard Business School.

Gropper, D. M. (1995). Product-Line Deregulation and the Cost
Structure of US Savings and Loan Associations. *Applied
Economics, 27,* 183–191.

Gulati, R. (2009). *Reorganize for Resilience. Putting Customers at
the Center of Your Business*. Boston, MA: Harvard Business
Press.

Günther, B. (2011, October 26). Flüsterasphalt soll Lärm der A661
mindern. *Frankfurter Allgemeine Rhein-Main*.

Gupta, S., Lehmann, D., & Stuart, J. (2004). Valuing Customers.
Journal of Marketing Research, XLI, February, 7–18.

Haberberg, A. & Rieple, A. (2008). *Strategic Management. Theory
and Application*. New York, NY: Oxford University Press.

Hanssens, D. M., Thorpe, D., & Finkbeiner, C. (2008). Marketing
When Customer Equity Matters. *Harvard Business Review*,
May, 93–99.

Harford, T. (2012). *Black–Scholes: The Maths Formula Linked to
the Financial Crash*. Retrieved April 13, 2013, from BBC News
Magazine: http://www.bbc.co.uk/news/magazine-17866646.

Harrison, G. W., Lau, M. I., & Rutström, E. E. (2004). *Estimating Risk
Attitudes in Denmark: A Field Experiment*. Retrieved February
28, 2012, from http://karlan.yale.edu/fieldexperiments/pdf/
Harrison,%20Lau%20and%20Rutstrom_Estimating%20Risk%
20Attitudes%20in%20Denmark%20A%20Field%20Experime
nt.pdf.

Helfat, C. E. & Peteraf, M. A. (2003). The Dynamic Resource-Based
View: Capability Lifecycles. *Strategic Management Journal,
24*(10), 997–1010.

Herodotus, de Sélincourt, A., & Marincola, J. (403 B.C./2003). *The
Histories*. London: Penguin Classics.

Hochstrasser, B. & Griffiths, C. (1991). *Controlling IT Investment.* London: Chapman Hall.

Holland, J. (2007). *Tools for Institutional, Political, and Social Analysis of Policy Reforms: A Sourcebook for Development Practitioners.* Washington, DC: The International Bank for Reconstruction and Development/The World Bank.

Holt, C. A. & Laury, S. K. (2002). Risk Aversion and Incentive Effects. *The American Economic Review, 92*(5), 1644–1655.

Hölzle, U. (2010, August 04). *Update on Google Wave.* Retrieved March 04, 2011, from The Official Google Blog: http://google blog.blogspot.com/2010/08/update-on-google-wave.html.

Hornby, L. & Chiang, L. (2012). *Reuters.* Retrieved July 03, 2012, from China Economy Shows Unexpected Signs of Weakness: http://www.reuters.com/article/2012/05/11/us-china-economy-idUSBRE84A08Z20120511.

House, R. J., Hanges, P. J., Javidan, M., Dorfman, P. W., & Gupta, V. (2004). *Culture, Leadership, and Organizations. The GLOBE Study of 62 Societies.* Thousand Oaks, CA: Sage Publications.

HSE. (2011). *Five Steps to Risk Assessment.* Health and Safety Executive. Bootle: HSE.

Hsee, C. K. & Weber, E. U. (1997). A Fundamental Prediction Error: Self-Others Discrepancies in Risk Preference. *Journal of Experimental Psychology, 126*(1), 45–53.

Hu, Y., Lodish, L. M., & Krieger, A. M. (2007, September). An Analysis of Real World TV Advertising Tests: A 15-Year Update. *Journal of Advertising Research, 47*(3), 341–353.

Hughes, A. & Scott Morton, M. S. (2006). The Transforming Power of Complementary Assets. *MIT Sloan Management Review, 47*(4), 50–58.

ICIS Heren. (2008). *ICIS Heren.* Retrieved July 31, 2012, from Rising Decommissioning Costs will not Hamper New Nuclear Build: http://www.icis.com/heren/articles/2008/01/30/9302005/rising-decommissioning-costs-will-not-hamper-new-nuclear-build.html.

IET. (2008). *Nuclear Decommissioning.* Stevenage: The Institution of Engineering and Technology.

Jacob, J. & Rasiel, E. (2011). *Country and Sector Contagion in Emerging Markets.* Sydney: Lazard Asset Management.

Jacobsen, K. (2013). *$5b Mayo Clinic Expansion Investment.* Retrieved February 07, 2013, from Northland's Newscenter: http://www.northlandsnewscenter.com/news/video/5B-Mayo-Clinic-Expansion-Investment-189135471.html.

Jacobson, I., Christerson, M., Jonsson, P., & Övergaard, G. (1992). *Object-Oriented Software Engineering. A Use-Case Driven Approach.* Reading: Addison-Wesley.

Jorgensen, S. L. & Loudjeva, Z. (2005). *A Poverty and Social Impact Analysis of Three Reforms in Zambia: Land, Fertilizer, and Infrastructure.* Washington, DC: World Bank.

JVI. (nn). *JVI Alumni Community.* Retrieved July 31, 2012, from A Cost Function for the Savings and Loan Industry: www.jvifamily.info/files/micro_cases_en.pdf.

Kahneman, D. & Tversky, A. (1979). Prospect Theory: An Analysis of Decision under Risk. *Econometrica, 47*(2), March, 263–291.

Kahnemann, D. & Tversky, A. (1979). Prospect Theory: An Analysis of Decision under Risk. *Econometrica, 17*(2), 263–292.

Kamarkhar, U. (2004). Will You Survive the Services Revolution. *Harvard Business Review* (June), 100–107.

Kaplan, R. S. & Norton, D. P. (1996). *The Balanced Scorecard. Translating Strategy into Action.* Boston, MA: Harvard Business School Press.

Kaplan, R. S. & Norton, D. P. (2004). *Strategy Maps. Converting Intangible Assets into Tangible Outcomes.* Boston, MA: Harvard Business School Publishing.

Keen, J. M. & Digrius, B. (2003). *Making Technology Investments Profitable. ROI Road Map to Better Business Cases.* Hoboken, NJ: John Wiley & Sons.

Kelleher, J. B. (2008). *Firetruck Maker Files for Bankruptcy, Blames IBM.* Retrieved March 08, 2011, from Reuters: http://www.reuters.com/article/2008/01/28/us-americanlafrance-bankruptcy-idUSN2848407720080128.

Khasnabis, S., Mishra, S., & Safi, C. (2012). *An Evaluation Procedure for Mutually Exclusive Highway Safety Alternatives under Different Policy Objectives.* College Park, MD: National Center for Smart Growth Research & Education.

Kistinger, M. (n.n.). *Edsel*. Retrieved June 28, 2012, from http://www. edsel.kistinger.com/EFrame_01.htm.

Knight, F. H. (1921). *Uncertainty and Profit*. New York, NY: Hart, Schaffner, and Marx.

Knowledge@Wharton. (2006). *Merck's Judy Lewent: Once Again, 'Talking about the Future'*. Retrieved October 02, 2012, from Knowledge@Wharton: http://knowledge.wharton.upenn.edu/ article.cfm?articleid=1591.

Knowledge@Wharton. (2007). *Back to the Basics: Accounting for IT in Business Performance*. Retrieved October 05, 2012, from Knowledge@Wharton Microsoft: http://knowledge.wharton. upenn.edu/microsoft/070302.html.

Koontz, H. & Weihrich, H. (1998). *Essentials of Management* (8th ed.). New Delhi: Tata McGraw-Hill.

Kretschmer, M. (1927). Atrox Fortuna. *The Classical Journal, 22*(4), 267–275.

Kumar, P. (2008). Distance from the CORE. *CFO Connect*, October, pp. 12–14.

Kwak, M. & Yoffie, D. B. (2001). *Gucci Group N.V. (A)*. Boston, MA: Harvard Business School.

Leary, K., Pillemer, J., & Wheeler, M. (2013). Negotiating with Emotion. *Harvard Business Review*, January–February.

Levinson, M. (2009). *Recession Causes Rising IT Project Failure Rates*. Retrieved January 14, 2011, from CIO: http://www. cio.com/article/495306/Recession_Causes_Rising_IT_Project_ Failure_Rates_.

Link, J. & Hildebrand, V. (1997). Ausgewählte Konzepte der Kundenbewertung im Rahmen des Database Marketing. In J. Link, D. Brändli, C. Schleuning, & R. Kehl (eds), *Handbuch Database Marketing* (2nd ed.). Ettlingen: IM Fachverlag Marketing-Forum.

Link, J., Gerth, N., & Voßbeck, E. (2000). *Marketing Controlling*. Munich: Vahlen.

Linneman, R. E. & Klein, H. E. (1983). The Use of Multiple Scenarios by U.S. Industrial Companies: A Comparison Study, 1977–1981. *Long Range Planning, 16*, 94–101.

Local e-gov CRM. (2004). *The Benefits of CRM. National Projects at the Heart of Excellent Services*. Retrieved March 20, 2011, from JISC

Cetis. Supporting Innovation and Interoperability in Educational Technology: http://jisc.cetis.ac.uk/crm-tools/documents/benefits-of-crm.pdf.

Lodish, L. M., Abraham, M. A., Livelsberger, J., Lubetkin, B., Richardson, B., & Stevens, M. E. (1995). A Summary of Fifty-Five In-Market Experimental Estimates of the Long-Term Effect of TV Advertising. *Marketing Science, 14*(3), 133–140.

Löscher, P. (2012). How I Did It … The CEO of Siemens on Using a Scandal to Drive Change. *Harvard Business Review*, November.

Magee, J. F. (1964). Decision Trees for Decision Making. *Harvard Business Review*, July–August, 126–137.

Mair, V. H. (2009). *Pinyin.info*. Retrieved September 12, 2012, from Danger + Opportunity <> Crisis. How a Misunderstanding about Chinese Characters Has Led Many Astray: http://www.pinyin.info/chinese/crisis.html.

Markham, I. S. & Palocsay, S. W. (2006). Scenario Analysis in Spreadsheets with Excel's Scenario Tool. *INFORMS Transactions on Education, 6*(2), January, 23–31.

Martin, R. L. (2011). Fixing the Game. Bubbles, Crashes, and What Capitalism Can Learn from the NFL. *Harvard Business Review Press*.

Massé, P. (1962). *Optimal Investment Decisions: Rules for Action and Criteria for Choice*. Englewood Cliffs, NJ: Prentice-Hall Inc.

Mayo Clinic. (2013). *Mayo Clinic in Rochester, Minnesota*. Retrieved February 07, 2013, from Mayo Foundation for Medical Education and Research: http://www.mayoclinic.org/rochester/.

McDermott, R. (2001). *Risk-Taking in International Politics: Prospect Theory in American Foreign Policy*. Ann Arbor, MI: The University of Michigan Press.

McDonald, M. (2007). *Without Reservations*. Retrieved March 08, 2011, from ATW Air Transport World: http://atwonline.com/it-distribution/article/without-reservations-0309.

McGeee, K. G. (2004). *Heads Up. How to Anticipate Business Surprises and Seize Opportunities First*. Boston, MA: Harvard Business School Press.

McGrath, R. G. & MacMillan, I. C. (2000). *The Entrepreneurial Mindset. Strategies for Continuously Creating Opportunity in an Age of Uncertainty.* Boston, MA: Harvard Business School Press.

McGrath, R. G., MacMillan, I. C., & Venkatraman, S. (1995). Defining and Developing Competence: A Strategic Process Paradigm. *Strategic Managmeent Journal, 16,* 251–275.

Merton, R. C. (1990). *Continuous-Time Finance.* Cambridge: Blackwell.

Messner, W. (2004, December). Ein Modell zur Steuerung des Wertbeitrags von Kundensegmenten. *BIT Banking and Information Technology* (4), 45–52.

Messner, W. (2005). *CRM bei Banken. Ein Vorgehensmodell zur Erarbeitung einer Strategie, Prozess- und Systemarchitektur.* Norderstedt (D): BoD GmbH.

Messner, W. (2010). *Intelligent IT Offshoring to India. Roadmaps for Emerging Business Landscapes.* Houndmills: Palgrave Macmillan.

Messner, W. & Schäfer, N. (2012). *The ICCA™ Facilitator's Manual. Intercultural Communication and Collaboration Appraisal.* London: Createspace.

Meyer-Schönherr, M. (1992). *Szenario-Technik als Instrument der strategischen Planung.* Ludwigsburg: Wissenschaft & Praxis.

Microsoft. (2010, November 17). *A.T. Kearney: Consulting Firm Upgrades Communications Solution to Further Boost Productivity.* Retrieved July 04, 2011, from Microsoft Case Studies: http://www.microsoft.com/casestudies/Case_Study_Detail.aspx?CaseStudyID=4000008683.

Mishra, S. & Khasnabis, S. (2012, May). Optimization Model for Allocating Resources for Highway Safety Improvement at Urban Intersections. *Journal of Transportation Engineering, 138*(5), 535–547.

Mitchell, A. (2006). *Apple Downscales in India – Raising Doubts about Offshoring.* Retrieved July 03, 2009, from CRMBuyer: http://www.crmbuyer.com/story/50931.html.

Montgomery, C. A. (2012). How Strategists Lead. *McKinsey Quarterly,* July.

Moran, K. (2000). *Investment Appraisal for Non-Financial Managers. A Step-by-Step Guide to Making Profitable Decisions.* Harlow: Pearson Education.

Morris, V. B. & Morris, K. M. (2007). *Dictionary of Financial Terms*. New York, NY: Lightbulb Press.

Moser, H. (2013). *Reshoring Initiative. Bringing Manufacturing Back Home*. Retrieved March 11, 2013, from Total Cost of Ownership Estimator™: http://www.reshorenow.org/TCO_Estimator.cfm.

Mulholland, M. (2005). *Lognormal Random Walk Model for Stock Prices*. Retrieved July 11, 2011, from Networthstrategies: http://www.networthstrategies.com/Support/Files/Lognormal%20Random%20Walk%20-%20Part%20I%202-22-05.pdf.

Murphy, P. (2008). *Intelligence and Security Committee Annual Report 2006–2007*. Retrieved March 08, 2011, from Official-Documents: http://www.official-documents.gov.uk/document/cm72/7299/7299.pdf.

Nelson, R. S. & Winter, S. (1982). *An Evolutionary Theory of Economic Change*. Cambridge, MA: Harvard University Press.

Nestlé Health Science S.A. (2011). *Nestlé Health Science*. Retrieved July 06, 2012, from http://www.nestlehealthscience.com.

Nichols, N. A. (1994). Scientific Management at Merck: An Interview with CFO Judy Lewent. *Harvard Business Review*, January–February.

North, J. (2010). *The Total Economic Impact of Microsoft Lync Server 2010*. (Forrester Consulting) Retrieved June 29, 2011, from Microsoft Lync Benefits – Forrester Total Economic Impact Whitepaper: http://go.microsoft.com/?linkid=9751775.

OECD/The World Economic Forum. (2011). *Competitiveness and Private Sector Development: Central Asia 2011: Competitiveness Outlook*. Paris, France: OECD Publishing.

O'Rourke, R. (2009). *VH-71 Presidential Helicopter Program: Background and Issues for Congress*. Congressional Research Service.

Österle, H. & Winter, R. (2000). *Business Engineering. Auf dem Weg zum Unternehmen des Informationszeitalters*. Heidelberg: Springer.

Oxford University. (2012). *University of Oxford*. Retrieved August 07, 2012, from London Olympics on Track to be "Most Costly Games Ever": http://www.ox.ac.uk/media/news_stories/2012/120625.html.

P&G Investor Relations. (2012). *Procter & Gamble Financial Reporting*. Retrieved October 02, 2012, from Fundamentals – Annual Balance Sheet: http://www.pginvestor.com/phoenix. zhtml?c=104574&p=irol-fundBalanceA.

Pearson, D. D. (2009). *Towards a "Smart Grid" – the Roll-Out of Advanced Metering Infrastructure.* Retrieved March 04, 2011, from VAGO Victorian Auditor-General's Office: http://download.audit.vic.gov.au/files/111109_AMI_Full_Report.pdf.

Penrose, E. (1995). *The Theory of the Growth of the Firm* (2nd ed.). Oxford: Oxford University Press.

Peppard, J. & Ward, J. (2005). Unlocking Sustained Business Value from IT Investments. *California Management Review, 48*(1), 52–69.

Peteraf, M. A. (1993). The Cornerstones of Competitive Advantage: A Resource-Based View. *Strategic Management Journal, 14*, 179–191.

Pohle, G., Korsten, P., & Ramamurthy, S. (2005). *Component Business Models. Making Specialization Real.* Somers, NY: IBM Global Services.

Popick, S. & Roth, J. D. (2001). *Get Rich Slowly.* Retrieved July 30, 2012, from The Time Value of Money (or Why 25 Years of Cable TV doesn't Cost as much as you Think): http://www.getrichslowly. org/blog/2011/02/15/the-time-value-of-money-or-why-25-years-of-cable-tv-doesnt-cost-as-much-as-you-think/.

Procter & Gamble. (2008). *2008 Annual Report.* Retrieved July 05, 2012, from Designed to Innovate: http://www.pg.com/annual report2008/investing.shtml#/investing/.

Raghavendra, R. (2006). Apple Software Logs Out of India. *The Times of India*, June 03.

Rehak, J. (2002). Tylenol Made a Hero of Johnson & Johnson: The Recall that Started Them All. *The New York Times*, March 23.

Reilly, F. K. (1994). *Investment Analysis and Portfolio Management* (4th ed.). Fort Worth: Dryden.

Remenyi, D. & Remenyi, B. (2009). *How to Prepare Business Cases. A Practical Guide for Accountants.* Oxford: CIMA Publishing/ Elsevier.

Riebsamen, H. (2007). Ausbau der Frankfurter Ostumgehung bis 2010. *Frankfurter Allgemeine Rhein-Main*, November 22.

Riley, J. (2011). *Nestle and Diversification – Investing in Healthcare.* Retrieved July 06, 2012, from Business Studies Blog: http://tutor2u.net/blog/index.php/business-studies/comments/nestle-and-diversification-investing-in-healthcare/.

Ross, J. (2001). *E-Business at Delta Air Lines: Extracting Value from a Multi-Faceted Approach.* MIT Sloan School of Management. Cambridge, MA: Center for Information Systems Research.

Ross, J. W. & Beath, C. M. (2002). Beyond the Business Case: New Approaches to IT Investment. *MIT Sloan Management Review*, *43*(Winter), 51–59.

Ross, H. E., Sicking, D. L., & Zimmer, R. A. (1993). *Recommended Procedures for the Safety Performance Evaluation of Highway Features.* National Research Council, Transportation Research Board. Washington, DC: National Academy Press.

Rumelt, R. (2011). *Good Strategy. Bad Strategy. The Difference and Why It Matters.* London: Profile Books.

Schirmeister, R. & Kreuz, C. (2001). Der investitionsrechnerische Kundenwert. In B. Günter, & S. Helm (eds), *Kundenwert. Grundlagen, innovative Konzepte, praktische Umsetzungen.* Wiesbaden (D): Gabler Verlag.

Schlagenhaufer, S. (2011). Die langsamste Autobahn der Welt. *Bild*, August 24.

Schultze, U. & Boland, R. (2000). Knowledge Management Technology and the Reproduction of Knowledge Work Practices. *Journal of Strategic Information Systems, 9*(2–3), 193–212.

Scott, D. L. (2003). *Wall Street Words. An A to Z Guide to Investment Terms for Today's Investor.* Boston, MA: Houghton Mifflin Harcourt.

Sessions, R. (2008). *Simple Architectures for Complex Enterprises.* Redmond, WA: Microsoft Press.

Sharpe, W. F. & Alexander, G. J. (1978). *Investments.* Englewood Cliffs: Prentice-Hall.

Shimizu, K. & Hitt, M. A. (2004). Strategic Flexibility: Organizational Preparedness to Reverse Ineffective Strategic Decisions. *The Academy of Management Executive, 18*(4), 44–59.

Slater, S. (1997). Developing a Customer Value-Based Theory of the Firm. *Journal of the Academy of Marketing Science, 25*(2), 162–167.

Smith, J. B. & Colgate, M. (2007). Customer Value Creation: A Practical Framework. *Journal of Marketing Theory and Practice, 15*(1), 7–23.

Snowden, D. J. & Boone, M. E. (2007). A Leader's Framework for Decision Making. *Harvard Business Review*, November, 39–46.

Stackpole, B. (2011). *DesignNews*. Retrieved March 11, 2013, from DFMA Practices Can Play a Role in Manufacturing Reshoring: http://www.designnews.com/document.asp?doc_id=230726.

Standish Group. (1995). *The Standish Group Report Chaos*. Retrieved January 14, 2011, from Project Smart: http://www.projectsmart.co.uk/docs/chaos-report.pdf.

Stewart, R., Wyskida, R., & Johannes, J. D. (1995). *Cost Estimator's Reference Manual* (2nd ed.). New York, NY: John Wiley & Sons.

Sulphur Daily News. (2013, January 24). *$13.4m Expansion Investment in Lake Charles Announced*. Retrieved February 07, 2013, from Sulphur Daily News: http://www.sulphurdailynews.com/article/20130124/NEWS/130129816.

Teece, D. J., Pisano, G., & Shuen, A. (1997). Dynamic Capabilities and Strategic Management. *Strategic Management Journal, 18*, 509–533.

Thakkar, P. (2012). *Telecom Industry – India's Success Story*. Retrieved October 05, 2012, from *Business Review* India: http://www.businessreviewindia.in/technology/software/-telecom-industry--indias-success-story.

The Times. (2011). *Gillette: Developing New Products*. Retrieved July 11, 2011, from The Times 100: http://www.thetimes100.co.uk/download-brief--Z2lsbGV0dGUvZ2lsbGV0dGVfMTBfYnJpZWYucGRmXVtESVJFQ1Q1Q=.

The Times. (2012). *The Times 100 Business Case Studies*. Retrieved July 31, 2012, from The Business of Nuclear Decommissioning. A Nuclear Decommissioning Authority Case Study: http://business

casestudies.co.uk/nda/the-business-of-nuclear-decommissioning/introduction.html.

The White House. Office of the Press Secretary. (2009). *The White House President Barack Obama*. Retrieved July 02, 2012, from Briefing Room. Speeches & Remarks: http://www.whitehouse.gov/the_press_office/Remarks-by-the-President-in-question-and-answer-session-at-the-closing-of-the-Fisc/.

Thun, F. (2008). Industrialization of Application Implementations. In A. Hendel, W. Messner, & F. Thun (eds), *Rightshore! Successfully Industrialize SAP Projects Offshore* (pp. 45–62). Heidelberg: Springer.

TOGAF Open Group. (2013). *Business Scenarios*. Retrieved February 08, 2013, from TOGAF 8.1.1 Online, Part IV Resource Base: http://pubs.opengroup.org/architecture/togaf8-doc/arch/chap34.html.

U.S. Department of Justice. (2011). *2011 Financial Guide*. Retrieved February 28, 2013, from Office of Justice Programs: http://www.ojp.usdoj.gov/financialguide/PostawardRequirements/chapter16page7.htm.

U.S. House of Representatives. (2002). *Permanent Select Committee on Intelligence*. Retrieved July 03, 2012, from Findings of the Final Report of the Joint Inquiry Into the Terrorist Attacks of September 11, 2001: http://www.au.af.mil/au/awc/awcgate/congress/911_final_findings_part1.htm.

Useem, J. (2005). Decisions, Decisions. Second in a Series of Anniversary Specials. *Fortune*, June 27.

Useem, J. (2006). How I Make Decisions. *Fortune*, May 31.

Useem, J. (2007). Apple: America's Best Retailer. *Fortune*, March 8.

van Diessen, R. J., Sierman, B., & Lee, C. A. (2008). Component Business Model for Digital Repositories: A Framework for Analysis. *Proceedings of the Fifth International Conference on Digital Preservation (iPRES)*. London.

Wenger, W. & McDermott, R. S. (2002). *Cultivating Communities of Practice*. Boston, MA: Harvard Business School Press.

Wernerfelt, B. (1984). A Resourced-Based View of the Firm. *Strategic Management Journal, 5*, 171–180.

Wilson, J. H. (1981). A Note on Scale Economies in the Savings and Loan Industry. *Business Economics*, January, 45–49.

Wittwer, J. W. (2004). *Monte Carlo Simulation Example: Sales Forecast.* Retrieved July 26, 2011, from Vertex42.com: http://www.vertex42.com/ExcelArticles/mc/SalesForecast.html.

Woodall, T. (2003). Conceptualising "Value for the Customer": An Attributional, Structural and Dispositional Analysis. *Academy of Marketing Science Review,* (12), 1–41.

Woodruff, R. (1997). Customer Value: The Next Source for Competitive Advantage. *Journal of the Academy of Marketing Science, 25*(2), 139–153.

Young, T. (2009). *Whitehall Intelligence Sharing System Scrapped.* Retrieved March 08, 2011, from Computing.co.uk: http://www.computing.co.uk/ctg/news/1844868/whitehall-intelligence-sharing-scrapped.

Zachman, J. A. & Locke, S. (2008). *The Concise Definition.* Retrieved March 20, 2011, from Zachman Framework Associates: http://www.zachmanframeworkassociates.com/index.php/the-zachman-framework.

Zeman, E. (2010). *Does It Matter How Many Kins Microsoft Sold?* Retrieved March 03, 2011, from Information Week: http://www.informationweek.com/news/mobility/smart_phones/showArticle.jhtml?articleID=225702679.

Ziegler, C. (2010). *Life and Death of Microsoft Kin: The Inside Story.* Retrieved March 03, 2011, from Engadget: http://www.engadget.com/2010/07/02/life-and-death-of-microsoft-kin-the-inside-story/.

Index

Printed and bound in Great Britain by
CPI Group (UK) Ltd, Croydon, CR0 4YY